THERAPEUTIC RECREATION
FOR EXCEPTIONAL CHILDREN

Second Edition

THERAPEUTIC RECREATION FOR EXCEPTIONAL CHILDREN

Let Me In, I Want to Play

Edited by

AUBREY H. FINE, ED.D., F.A.A.M.R.

Licensed Psychologist
Professor
School of Education and Integrated Studies
Director, Center for Special Populations
California State Polytechnic University, Pomona

NYA M. FINE, M.ED.

Consultant

With a Foreword by
Chester L. Land, M.Ed., R.T.R., C.T.R.S.

CHARLES C THOMAS · PUBLISHER, LTD.
Springfield · Illinois · U.S.A.

Published and Distributed Throughout the World by

CHARLES C THOMAS • PUBLISHER, LTD.
2600 South First Street
Springfield, Illinois 62794-9265

© *1996 by* CHARLES C THOMAS • PUBLISHER, LTD.
ISBN 0-398-06661-2   (cloth)
ISBN 0-398-06662-0   (paper)

Library of Congress Catalog Card Number: 96-8263

Printed in the United States of America
SC-R-3

Library of Congress Cataloging-in-Publication Data

Therapeutic recreation for exceptional children : let me in, I want to
   play / edited by Aubrey H. Fine ; Nya M. Fine, consultant ; with a
   foreword by Chester L. Land. — 2nd ed.
      p.   cm.
   Earlier edition's m.e. under Fine.
   Includes bibliographical references and index.
   ISBN 0-398-06661-2. — ISBN 0-398-06662-0 (pbk.)
   1. Recreational therapy for children.   2. Handicapped children—
Recreation.   3. Play therapy.   I. Fine, Aubrey H.   II. Fine, Nya M.
RJ53.R43F56   1996   96-8263
616.8'5153'083—dc20   CIP

CONTRIBUTORS

MEG CLARK, Ph.D.
Associate Professor
California State Polytechnic University, Pomona

ROBYN COFFMAN
Recreational Therapist
Casa Colina Hospital

JESSE DIXON, Ph.D.
Professor/Associate Dean
San Diego State University

FRANK GIBBONS, Ph.D.
Professor
California State Polytechnic University, Pomona

KATHLEEN HENDERSON, B.S., CTRS
VA Hospital—Dallas, Texas

SHERRY KIRWIN, M.S.
Director, Hope Therapy Program
Moody Gardens, Galveston, Texas

JULIE LEE, B.A.
Research Assistant
University of California, Los Angeles
National Research Center on Asian American Mental Health

LONNIE NOLTA, M.A.
Consultant
Developmental Disabilities

SUSAN NAKAYAMA SIAW, Ph.D.
Professor
California State Polytechnic University, Pomona

v

ROBERT L. SCHALOCK, Ph.D.
Chair, Department of Psychology
Hastings College

SUSAN A. ZAPF, M.O.T. OTR, B.S., CTRS
President
Texas Delta Society Affiliate

FOREWORD

When my friend and colleague, Dr. Aubrey Fine, asked that I write this foreword, I was honored and pleased for several reasons. First of all, ever since my first meeting with him at a conference in Fresno, California, he has impressed me with his unique orientation to life and exceptional contributions to the field of therapeutic recreation, especially as it relates to children with special needs. My admiration for him has not waned since that day. Secondly, the opportunity allows me to introduce the second edition of this excellent book, *Therapeutic Recreation For Exceptional Children.* As in the case of the first edition, this is one of the few works that deals exclusively with "recreative" needs of the exceptional child.

Therapeutic recreation as a profession has grown considerably over the last ten years. During that time, many texts have been published that have increased the knowledge base of the field. This newly revised text not only has accomplished that task but has given the field of therapeutic recreation a unique and in-depth look at the needs of the exceptional child. The information within the text allows the reader to learn and understand that the basic goal of this population group "is to have fun." It provides a look into the theoretical and practical aspects of play and development in essence, the how and why children play.

In addition to the updated, revised, and well written chapters of the first edition, Dr. Fine has added new chapters. Specifically, the chapter on laws to assist people with disabilities provides a comprehensive overview of various statues and public laws that pertain to children with disabilities. Furthermore, within the chapter, attention is also given on how to become an effective advocate for change. The book also has an excellent new chapter on understanding quality of life in children. This information is extremely important, in my perception, in understanding one of the major benefits of leisure and play. Finally, the book has an expanded look at animal-assisted and horticultural therapy, both excellent options for children with special needs.

I am certain that parents, students, and professionals alike will benefit from and be inspired by this well written and totally enjoyable book. I am certain that the message sent by this work will be that exceptional children are worthy of and deserve the best there is in their quest for leisure opportunities.

CHESTER L. LAND, M.ED.
Chief of Recreation Therapy
West Los Angeles Veterans Administration Medical Center
Past President, National Therapeutic Recreation Society

PREFACE

It has almost been a decade when both Nya and I sat down to write the first edition of *Therapeutic Recreation for Exceptional Children.* Our conviction that leisure experiences enhance quality of life have not changed at all. In fact, our beliefs have been amplified. With the advent of recent legislation recognizing the rights of all citizens (e.g., A.D.A.), it is apparent that the leisure contributes to an overall quality of life.

When we first sat down to write the book, we were not only impressed with the importance of recreational involvement but in addition the variety of skills that could be taught through leisure activities. Skills that relate to cognition, language, social and motor skills can be directly impacted by involvement. It is our intention throughout this book to demonstrate that leisure in and of itself is critical. However, we will also illustrate how a recreational therapist can utilize the medium of recreation to enhance developmental processes.

The purpose of **Therapeutic Recreation for Exceptional Children: Let Me In, I Want to Play,** is to sensitize the readers to the rationale of play and leisure experiences for children with various disabilities and to illustrate how they and others can learn from their experiences. One of the major purposes of the book is to answer some of the basic concerns that recreators, educators, child life specialists, social workers, and parents have when providing or attempting to locate recreation services for children with disabilities.

A decade ago, it was common to observe numerous segregated recreational activities. This is no longer considered the norm and the professional community is encouraged to review new ways that promote integrated activities within the community as well as at home. The new edition of this book reviews this position and demonstrates to practitioners and parents how they can take a more active role in strengthening the opportunities. The reader will find the chapters organized in a logical fashion and that the new addition has integrated various pieces of information which were not given as detailed attention in the previous edition (e.g., quality of life of children, law and persons with disabilities, the scope of leisure within the home and the community, unique contributions of play facilitated approaches such as animal assisted therapy and horticulture therapy).

It is hoped that this book will continue to offer encouragement to parents and professionals who are involved with exceptional children to continue searching and expanding their own ways to working with children. We owe it to our future generation to preserve their opportunities not only for their therapeutic value but in addition to the quality they contribute. A life full of rewarding leisure and recreational experiences will tremendously impact a child's life. Too many children have been neglected in the past and have not had the opportunities to develop through their leisure time experiences. This book is intended to not only offer some solutions but also to be a source of inspiration to both present-day and future recreation service providers. Winston Churchill elegantly once said, "Never, Never Give Up." We owe it to ourselves to advocate for the field's contribution to the welfare of a child's life, and to urge others to understand that no child should experience a void when it comes to his/her leisure/social experiences.

AHF
NMF

CONTENTS

THERAPEUTIC RECREATION
FOR EXCEPTIONAL CHILDREN

Chapter 1

INTRODUCTION:
LET ME IN, I WANT TO PLAY

Aubrey H. Fine

The child is there...
Beyond the hurt and handicap...
Beyond the difference...
Beyond the problem and probing...
How can we reach him? How can we
set him free?...
Buck, 1950

EXCEPTIONAL CHILDREN: WHO ARE THEY?

Working with exceptional children can be extremely exciting and fascinating. However, to provide unique and challenging experiences, one must be cognizant of their needs. Haring (1982), as the word implies, defines that "exceptional individuals are those who differ in some way from what society regards as normal" (p. 1). They are children whose performance deviates markedly from the norm, either with higher or lower than average performance or ability in the areas of cognition, emotion and physical abilities.

There are several terms utilized by professionals in the field to categorically classify exceptional individuals. The words **handicapped, impaired, disabled** or **disordered** are at times selected to describe special populations. Disabled persons, as Dunham and Dunham (1978) describe, are individuals who are structurally, physiologically or psychologically different from the normal person because of an accident, disease or developmental problem. At times, the term **disabled** is more commonly applied as a descriptor of physical problems. The term **impaired**, on the other hand, is frequently utilized to characterize sensory deficits such as hearing or sight.

Heward and Orlansky (1988) point out that the term **handicap** refers

3

to the problems or difficulties a person encounters because he or she is different. Their deviations may at times inhibit or for that matter prevent achievement or acceptance. A person who is handicapped may feel less adequate than others (Dunham and Dunham, 1978). One must understand that not all disabled people have to feel handicapped, for example, an individual who is blind can modify his home to compensate for his disability. This individual may not feel disadvantaged in that specific environment. He knows where everything is and therefore can readily adapt. However, place the same man in a new setting and he may feel handicapped until he is more acquainted and comfortable.

In regards to special populations, the term **handicapped** is more restrictive than exceptional. The term **exceptional** has a broader concentration and includes the gifted, i.e. individuals whose skills and performance can be considered above the norm. In general, exceptional children can be classified into one or more of the following categories:

1. visually impaired
2. hearing impaired
3. mentally retarded
4. learning disabled (learning disabilities which are not caused by any visual, hearing or motor handicaps as well as mental retardation or emotional problems)
5. communication disorders (speech and language problems)
6. physical handicaps and other health impairments (including neurological, orthopedic, and birth defects such as cerebral palsy and spina bifida, as well as diseases such as leukemia and kidney disorders)
7. behavior disorders (emotionally disturbed)
8. multiply handicapped (for example, cerebral palsy and mental retardation)
9. gifted and talented

In reference to the special populations focused within the text, a general concentration will be given to the first eight categories noted. Attention will not be given to the gifted and talented, because their programming concerns normally do not fall under the domain of therapeutic recreation.

Many of you may be curious in knowing how many exceptional children live in the United States. Stating precisely how many would be extremely difficult, because accurate data at the present time does not exist. The United States office of Special Education and Rehabilitation believes that 11 percent of all school-age children may be classified as handicapped. However, the present findings are much lower. Data collected indicates that approximately 4,300,000 children receive special education services. Furthermore, it was estimated by the National Center for Health Statistics (1975) that there are approximately 25,868,000 persons within this country (at all ages) who may be considered disabled to some degree.

The Office of Special Education and Rehabilitation, Department of Education has projected figures representing by category of exceptionality the number of nationwide children who received special education within the 1984–1985 academic year. Table 1 displays the recent government estimate. This data was compiled from the **Eighth Annual Report to Congress** which was prepared by the Office of Special Education in 1986. For the interest of the reader, the table also incorporates the number of children with disabling conditions who received special education services in 1976–1977. This will allow the reader the ability for comparison.

Table 1. Handicapped Children by Exceptionality.

Type of disability	Estimate number of children age 3–21	
	76–77	84–85
Mentally retarded	969,547	717,785
Behaviorally disordered	283,072	373,207
Visually impaired	38,247	30,375
Learning disabled	797,213	1,839,292
Physically handicapped	87,008	58,835
Multihandicapped	50,722	71,780
Speech impaired	1,302,666	1,129,417
Hearing impaired	89,743	71,230
Deaf-blind	2,330	1,992
	3,620,548	4,293,913

Adapted from the Eighth Annual Report to Congress on the Implementation of the Education of the Handicapped Act (p. 4), 1986, U.S. Department of Education.

SOCIETY'S RESPONSE TO EXCEPTIONALITY

People who are disabled may encounter a wide variety of prejudicial experiences. Heward and Orlansky (1988) point out that society has responded towards the exceptional in virtually every human emotion and reaction—from extermination and ridicule to respecting them as human beings first and handicapped persons second.

Gleidman and Roth (1981) state that "to grow up handicapped in America is to grow up in a society that, because of its misreading of the significance of disability, is never entirely human in the way it treats the person within" (p. 301).

Society establishes the means of categorizing persons. People who fall short of our expectations (those exhibiting a stigma) constitute a special discrepancy between virtual and actual social identity. In his classic book, Goffman (1974) classifies three characteristics of stigma: stigma developed due to (1) physical deformities, (2) blemishes in character, and finally (3) stigma of race, nation and religion. Although each of these variables differ, the end result is similar. Society appears to construct a stigma theory to explain inferiority. The stigma in itself causes a variety of discriminatory acts. Unfortunately, persons with disabilities are frequently confronted with many of these deplorable instances.

Handicapism is a term utilized frequently to refer "to the prejudice, stereotyping and discrimination against the handicapped" (Kelly and Vergason, 1978 p. 65). In fact, Biklen and Bogden (1976) prepared an extremely interesting and relevant article on this topic, entitled "Handicapism in America." They defined handicapism as a set of practices that promote unequal and unjust treatment of people because of an apparent or assumed disability. They noted that many individuals in the general public are often uncomfortable in relating with handicapped persons. They listed several of the following common reactions:

1. Presume sadness on the person who is disabled.
2. Pity the individual.
3. At times focus so strongly on the disability that it is sometimes difficult to remember that disabled individuals are **people** first.
4. Disabled adults are often treated as children and are not given mutual respect.
5. People are uncomfortable being around disabled individuals and therefore avoid an interaction. They conclude by noting that if

you are labeled "handicapped," handicapism is your greatest disadvantage. You are not treated as an ordinary person.

Many of these reactions are personally echoed in the collection of articles in Brightman's (1984) **Ordinary Moments.** Within this book, unique accounts of the everyday experiences associated with being disabled are openly discussed. **Ordinary Moments** explores with readers how individuals make it in a society which has difficulty accepting them. What makes the book so unique are all of the personal accounts incorporated. For example, an interesting title for one of the articles incorporated was "If I Were a Car, I'd Be a Lemon."

There are many other books that have been written over the years that sensitively portray what it is like to grow up being disabled or, for that matter, parenting a child who happens to be handicapped. Greenfield's books about bringing up a son with autism (Noah) demonstrates vividly the love and frustration a parent may encounter (Greenfield, 1970, 1978). Other books such as Brown's (1976) **Yesterday's Child,** Crews's (1979) **A Childhood: The Biography of a Place,** and Jones's (1977) **The Acorn People,** all have sensitive and critical statements to share. The following are a couple of quotes from the books noted:

> Right there, as a child I got to the bottom of what it means to be lost, what it means to be rejected by everybody. . . . But if I was never able to accept my affliction, I was able to bear it and finally accept the good natured brutality and savagery in the eyes of those who came to wish me well. (Crews, pp. 171–172)

> You might say she was captured by good intentions. Kids would huddle around her proposing things to do. It was as if she possessed some kind of magic. Well, maybe she did. After all, she stripped those labels off all of us. She gave us back the chance to be children. To dream and play. (Jones, p. 54)

Forms of Discrimination and Public Understanding of Disabilities

A person with a disability may become the recipient of numerous forms of discrimination. Some of the individuals may be intentionally excluded from activities and/or services. Furthermore, the discrimination may be experiences via overprotective rules and policies. With the advent of ADA, it is evident that we will see less discriminatory outcomes, especially in the areas of transportation, architectural and communication barriers. ADA is a comprehensive law for people with disabilities, enacted in 1990. ADA appears to be sweeping national policy protecting the rights of people with disabilities in all aspects of life. It seems, however, that economic and attitudinal barriers still continue to be the greatest obstacles to full integration. Although there have been numerous strides in the area of public acceptance, discrimination still continues.

In 1991, the National Organization of Disability (NOD) commissioned a survey by the Louis Harris organization to study the attitudes of the American Public in regard to citizens with disabilities. The survey was designed to explore public views, beliefs and attitudes towards persons with disabilities. The survey revealed numerous crucial issues. The following represents a synthesis of the data generated.

The data seemed to indicate that younger and more educated Americans know more about the disability movement and seem much more supportive. It seems that embarrassment and pity continue to be the most common public views of disabilities.

The data also generated a perceived substantial difference in the public's comfort with persons with various disabilities. The data from the poll suggested that mental illness causes the greatest unease, followed by facial disfigurement, senility, and mental retardation. In general, physical disabilities engender less feelings of discomfort.

An important finding within the poll is the fact that 85 percent of those polled believed that there is less discrimination against people with disabilities than there was a decade ago.

Labeling

It is apparent today that labels are utilized to classify the special needs of an exceptional individual. In the past, derogatory terms, such as moron, idiot as well as imbecile, were clinically utilized to classify individuals with specific levels of mental retardation. At times, these labels prevented individuals from specific privileges that were given to the non-handicapped population. To assist in your understanding of this point of view, I would like to share a simulated experience that I encountered several years ago. I had the fortune or for that matter the misfortune to play a nonpublished table game which revolved around this topic: labeling.

The game was similar to any general table game. The major objective was to travel around the board without receiving a label and experiencing any devastating life experiences. The winner would be the individual who moved around the board and who would not deviate from the mainstream path. In the simulated experience, the winner was the participant who was the successful person: one with a good academic background, an important occupation and was happy with life's fortunes. In essence, the game simulated life experiences. It began at birth and progressed into middle adulthood.

The game began by dicing on the board to be conceived. A majority of the game players were born as normal, healthy infants. However, there were some who were less fortunate. For example, some were born with serious birth defects and found themselves severely disabled. For those individuals, the game was extremely boring and frustrating. While everyone else was moving around the main parameters of the table game, these individuals followed a very small circular path. They were not able to compete because they were classified as severely handicapped. Throughout the game, other factors were presented which impeded the performance of some. For example, while entering the school-age era in the game of life, some participants were assessed as being learning disabled. It was found that this classification influenced some of the players' opportunities for the rest of the game. They were segregated and could never get back on the mainstream track. However, some were fortunate enough to overcome their disadvantage and continued playing competitively. Other obstacles such as accidents or diseases were scattered throughout the game to further complicate attaining the final goal: successful living.

While playing the game, those who experienced the handicapping conditions felt many of the frustrations and prejudices that an exceptional individual may encounter. However, because this was just a game, the players could return to their regular lives when it was all over.

Does labeling have any advantages? There are several arguments that have been made for and against the classification and labeling of exceptional individuals. Heward and Orlansky (1988) and MacMillian (1982) have cited several benefits and disadvantages. The highlights are as follows:

Benefits

1. Categories and labels can assist in the diagnosis and specific treatment of individuals.
2. Labels can allow special-interest groups to promote specialized programs.

3. Labeling can assist professionals in communicating and clarifying specific research findings on specific special groups.

Disadvantages

1. Labels can conceptually cause others to think about the disabled child only in terms of inadequacies or deficits.
2. Labels may cause many to develop certain expectations in reference to the child being categorized. These expectations may actually hinder the potential progress of the individual.
3. Labels may lead to reflection of the labeled child and may cause that specific child to feel inferior.
4. Labels may lead peers to reject or ridicule the labeled child.
5. After being labeled, a child may have difficulty ever again achieving the status of being a regular child.

As can be seen, there are both positive and negative sides to this issue. Labels have disadvantages only because we cause their development. Classification systems are theoretically established to assist in treatment. They allow for more systematic intervention. You must understand that, as potential service providers, it is your responsibility to not misuse labels; furthermore, we need to be more familiar of the potential misuse. If we can treat exceptional persons as individuals first and be cognizant of their differences second, we may find ourselves being more effective practitioners.

Conclusions

Changes in our attitudes and acceptance of children with disabilities has been altered dramatically over the past two decades. Some of these changes have been brought about due to the legislation pertaining to disability. This legislation is based on familiar civil rights such as equal opportunity, non-discrimination, integration and free choice. The apparent thread linking all of these principles is the concept of access: access to education as well as other resources needed to support citizens with disabilities.

Biklen (1985) suggests that we are at a crossroads in regards to integration and a person with a disability. In his article, entitled "Integration in School and Society," he explores five principles that he believes could help shape fuller integration of the child with a disability in society. Briefly, a synthesis of the principles are as follows:

1. Equity requires support of all of us.
2. Activism and rights, not pity, compassion, and benevolence, will foster the development of integration.
3. Normalization (the treatment of the person with a disability as being as normal as possible) must be accepted as the most optimal format to follow.
4. The success of our ability to promote integration will be determined by our commitment to it.

Now that these issues have been briefly discussed, the role that recreation can provide these individuals will be explored. Understanding who exceptional children are should dramatically assist in your understanding and application of the materials being disseminated.

A DEFINITION OF TERMS

Fine (in press) reviewed the literature in an attempt to synthesize a more concrete definition of leisure. The following represents a synthesis of the impressions found. The concept of leisure is intimately related to the cultural context which it is used. Leisure came to use through the Latin word *licere* which means to be permitted (Rybczynski, 1991). The French refined the term and developed the word *loisir*, which means free time. This eventually evolved into another English word, that of license. The word leisure literally means *exception* or *permission* as applied to an opportunity. According to Rybczynski (1991), leisure was the opportunity to do nothing. The action of doing nothing was not describing an emptiness but rather an occasion for self-reflection.

Many scholars, including this writer, believe that leisure is much more than occupying oneself in free time. Productive leisure time experiences definitely will become critical dimensions of an individual's lifestyle. Kando (1980) suggests that leisure is not a definite category of social behavior. Leisure should be inferred as a style of behavior, which may occur in any activity. This may mean that whether an activity is leisure or not is subjective to the meaning attached to it.

It seems to be the consensus of many researchers that recreation and leisure fill a significant need in the lives of many. Iso-Ahola (1980) points out that within the literature there is a significant body of research which suggests that leisure satisfaction is a principle source of perceived quality of life. Iso-Ahola's (1980) perceptions also highlight that meaningful leisure can be tremendously helpful in reducing feelings of helplessness. The author strongly agrees with this perception and also recognizes that positive recreational experiences can contribute to a person's sense of self-efficacy as well as empowerment. It would not be difficult to recite the numerous incidences where productive leisure opportunities have enhanced the quality of life for children and really made a difference, for instance, the child who joins a team, and is made to feel like an important link in the team. This experience could have a monumental impact on the child. The sense of belonging and feeling wanted could enhance the way the child views himself. Another example could be a child who is involved in any martial arts program. The outcome of the experience has been noted by many as an avenue to enhance self-discipline and self-concept.

Iso-Ahola (1980) also suggests that the most important dimension within the leisure experience is that of perceived freedom. It appears that an individual must feel that he/she has choices to choose before participating.

Furthering this perception, Austin and Crawford (1991) suggest that leisure would seem to offer one of the best opportunities for people to experience a sense of self-determination because it really does offer a chance for an individual to be in control. Leisure participation also offers an individual occasions where he/she can demonstrate mastery and competence over activities. In addition, Iso Ahola (1984) points out that leisure provides an escape from everyday personal and interpersonal environments. Leisure can be utilized as an opportunity to set aside issues and difficulties and engage in activities which are enjoyable and personally satisfying.

QUALITY OF LIFE, LEISURE, AND ITS BENEFITS

Fine (1991), Datillo and Schleien (1994) strongly suggest that recreation opportunities and leisure experiences have been given low priority in the education and preparation of citizens with disabilities. Today, its worth is viewed entirely differently. The community as a whole seems to appreciate that there has to be quality in life, if people are to lead satisfying and enriched existences (Fine, 1994). Furthermore, how can one judge life satisfaction without addressing the critical elements which assist in instilling joy and satisfaction.

As can be illustrated by the previous cited information, a concise definition of leisure appears difficult to ascertain. However, there has been tremendous agreement on the benefits of leisure. A number of authors agree with the writer that leisure can be utilized as a catalyst for psychological and emotional change. For example, Tinsley and Johnson (1984) identified seven psychological benefits of leisure. They are as follows: intellectual stimulation, catharsis, hedonistic companionship, secure solitude, moderate security, and expressive aestheticism. Kabanoff (1982) offered a different perspective when he identified eleven needs commonly met through leisure. The following briefly articulates his position. The needs cited in his article were autonomy, relaxation, family activity, interaction with others, stimulation, skill development and utilization, challenge/competition, leadership/social power, and health.

Research points out that the role of leisure in enhancing quality of life has become increasingly more well known and widespread during the last twenty years. Flanagan (1978) found that active involvement in recreation was one of the six areas showing the largest correlation coefficients with overall quality of life.

Fine (in press) points out that there is more to leisure than just participating and having fun. Fine (in press) agrees with Gold (1989) who emphasizes that leisure should not be construed only with recreation programming and involvement. Leisure is about life. Leisure has to do with choices, interactions, and freedom. Ferrel (1989) in her poignant article on community recreation states that recreation "enables us to function differently in a world that demands conformity" (p. 6). Recreation opportunities can be a major means of introducing people into the communities they live. Furthermore, Ferrel (1989) reports very sensitively that recreation can also help people learn to relax and to cope with many stressors in life.

She also points out that many persons with disabilities, including children, have numerous voids in the area of social opportunities. She insinuates in her article that many persons with disabilities are unfortunately taught to follow very rigid domestic routines so they can learn to live independently. She begins to question that a majority of the professional community appears to be more concerned about task mastery than human relationships. Could some of the voids in community living for adults be avoided if efforts early in life attempted to train and develop more self-initiated leisure choices? The author forcefully believes that some of the pitfalls could be avoided. To strengthen this position, the author turns to the research of Marinoble and Hegenauer (1988) who reported the growing need to examine the key variables which will assist in the transition planning for young people with disabilities. Students judged the importance of the training they received in school and which elements appeared to be the most helpful to them in secure quality living. They rated social skills and independent living training along with the use of leisure time as far more valuable to them than traditional academic training. Unfortunately, the problems in the social realm are still significant for many citizens with disabilities. Social isolation and lack of community networks remain a constant problem for many adults and children with disabilities.

Fine (in press) forcefully questions if there really can be quality in life when there may be a tremendous void in expressing leisure/social activities? The author feels compelled to explicitly suggest that it is his belief that life satisfaction cannot be celebrated in its entirety without an awareness of what successful avocational opportunities can contribute. Healthy lifestyles usually incorporate stability and foster well-being in the individual. Optimal life satisfaction cannot be achieved if there is a void in one of the major life settings (e.g., home, community, and work). It is evident that satisfying and appreciated leisure involvement can enhance the quality of one's life as it is celebrated in both the community and the home.

THE RATIONALE OF RECREATION
FOR ALL CHILDREN

In today's fast-moving world, many individuals are faced with an enormous amount of free time. Now more than ever, recreation and leisure activities are being used as outlets for engaging free time in a positive fashion.

It's the same for many children. The time spent outside of school is freely utilized in unorganized or structured-play activities. Children may find themselves participating in a variety of activities. There is athletics, hobbies, reading, informal play or simply watching television. The possibilities are endless. Whatever mode is chosen, a major need is being met by these children. They are attempting to use play as a constructive activity and an outlet for excess energy.

As we begin to explore the complexity of childhood play, we will start to see the importance of these play experiences. Leisure outlets are critical facets in a child's being. Children find themselves pursuing resources which can help them use their free time appropriately. Ellis (1973) pointed out that the time spent playing by a child fulfills a very large element in the child's profile of daily activities. Additionally, he stresses that this outlet "represents a major opportunity for influencing the development of the child" (pp. 3–4).

As we unfold our thoughts within this book, we will all explore with you the importance of recreational experiences for children. Additionally, we will point out that the experiences gained are not merely affective and enjoyable but contribute to the stability and growth of a child. Kraus (1966) stresses that play is an important laboratory for growing up in the lives of various children. Some of the benefits which are consequences of a child's involvement will be explored in greater detail in an upcoming section in this chapter. Nevertheless, it seems important to elaborate that intuitively many people feel that through these encounters with their environment and peers, children explore their own capabilities as well as preparing for leisure pursuits at an older age (Kraus, 1966).

However, let us now focus more specifically on exceptional children. The daily challenges and obstacles presented to them by their various handicapping conditions can, at times, prevent them from fulfilling their leisure desires. The outcome of this situation can be extremely frustrating to a child whose basic needs are no different than others in the pursuit of recreation and leisure (Wehman, 1979). In fact, their involvement in these activities may be of greater importance to them, since along the pathway to play many secondary benefits can occur simply due to their involvement. The areas of socialization, communication, and motor development are just a few end products that could be enhanced.

As stated earlier, there are a variety of reasons why some handicapped children are not given enough opportunities to engage socially with others. This may be due in part to the lack of resources in a community, public attitudes towards the disabled, or, perhaps, just living in a region where there are not many children. The child's possible rejection by his mainstream peers may cause other problems. All of this leads to the exceptional child's failure to realize the potential opportunities existing for him/her. Being handicapped does not include the word **never** when it comes to play. Indeed, how many sports include the word **handicap?**

Just like anyone learning a new skill, the child with a disability will also have to be taught.

All of the above-noted problems are distinct and can be handled in different fashions. Attention will be given to these problems in upcoming chapters. Nevertheless, the problems do exist, and frustration can develop both in the parents and in the child. These frustrations are realistic and must be examined more carefully.

In addition to these frustrations, individuals with exceptionalities experience a sense of loss when faced with leisure time. For example, we find many handicapped young adults not properly prepared to deal with their leisure and this causes them a great deal of anguish. Therefore, not only are we attempting to answer concerns for youth, but, by attempting to involve children in play and recreational experiences at a young age, we are also teaching them to utilize leisure skills which can offset future problems as an adult.

One of the major purposes of this book is to eliminate situations where this type of problem occurs, or at least to offset some. The following is an example of a situation that can occur and, if handled differently, could completely change the outcome.

For eight-year-old Billy, that afternoon was like all the other afternoons. He had returned home after attending a specialized school for the physically handicapped and fixed himself a snack. His attention then turned to the television. This time, however, his concentration was distracted. Billy could hear the sounds of shouting and laughing coming from the street. Hands clutched to the tires of his wheelchair, he steered himself to the window to see what was happening. A wave of frustration and sorrow washed over him, for outside was a group of neighborhood children playing catch. Three years Billy had lived in the neighborhood and the closest he had been to interacting with his peers was an occasional hello. Billy lifted his hands. He could play catch, he could laugh, and shout. What was wrong?

Billy has spina bifida; he has been bound to his wheelchair since birth. Because of his birth defect he leads an extremely restricted life, and for Billy, this has sharply restricted his social interaction with his peers.

This example of a child only describes one individual's misfortune. Billy, at this young age, rarely gets the social opportunities that other young boys enjoy. Though it is realized that he has had some very difficult years medically and educationally, his lack of social interaction is crucial.

When looking at a spectrum of activities in which a child should be engaged, the social area seems, in most cases, to receive the least attention. It is not surprising that parents are so concerned with the health and well-being of their exceptional child. Living with a child who is prone to illness can cause a great deal of stress within the family. Without possible realization, parents at times place so much emphasis on the medical area that they do not even realize that they fail to direct some of their energy into other important areas. Thus, no one should be alarmed to find that the area of affective development does not seem to be a priority in many homes.

Many of us overlook this area until the child is much older. If we would try to attend to the child's early life and his/her affective experiences, not only would we be allowing the child to gain useful social and enriching experiences, but we would significantly enhance his/her later development.

For children, play has a variety of purposes. At first glance, play seems to be merely an opportunity to engage in leisure. Actually, play is a mysterious and complex set of interacting behaviors that fulfills a definitive need for most children. Play may be considered intrinsically motivating to the child, a need to be occupied: being with others and, most important, having fun (Fine, 1978; Fine, 1982).

In Billy's case he has not had enough chances to socially interrelate with children his own age. This handicap is not the only barrier that separates Billy from his peers. For many children, play experiences are not recognized as having a very important part in their lives. Some handicapped individuals live very secluded lives and special attention is not given to recreational outlets. The fact that these valuable play experiences are not comprehended completely by those who should understand is unfortunate.

We want children to have the best life possible. So much of our efforts are placed on preserving their health and attempting to develop sound educational experiences. For too long now, we have ignored the right of all children to have access to their leisure. The pity is that it is the child who loses from our shortsightedness. Our efforts to place emphasis on all other areas, while neglecting to ensure that appropriate play experiences are provided, deprives the exceptional child of an alternate route from which to develop. Advocates of play for the handicapped would argue that this is caused by our own upbringing and that we were taught these manners and methods of placing values. Too often, recreation and informal play are viewed superficially. We overlook the therapeutic value and basic importance of play to children. If the non-handicapped (the mainstreamed) can be given these dynamic opportunities, so should all children.

Therapeutic Recreation for Exceptional Children will attempt to emphasize the importance of leisure exploration in the growing child. Hopefully, this will develop a more positive attitude towards the area of leisure. We believe very strongly in the medium of play, not only for its enjoyment value, but as a unique and dynamic rehabilitative force. We also feel that a child must not be deprived of his/her **fun time** and that every effort must be enforced to secure it. Iso-Ahola (1980) contends that play cannot be underestimated in its ability to prepare a child for practical life. Learning that one has self-worth and feeling better about oneself are two qualities which can be enhanced by play. A child who does not play with others may eventually question his/her existence. The child may also become dependent on others to find things for him/her to do.

Another problem occurs when youngsters have the misfortune of being excluded from activities. In most cases, these children are chastised by others and are never really given a chance to engage effectively. For example, there were numerous occasions when Susan, an amputee, was left on the sidelines by her classmates when they went out to play during their recess. Although she wanted to be involved, her handicap caused some segregation.

A poem has been written specifically for this book by Charles Kraus, an individual who has been afflicted with cerebral palsy. We believed that, although this short verse is slightly dramatized, it shares the loneliness that some children encounter when being left out by others. "The child waited at the playground fence today wanting to be let in to play. After the attendant came quite near, upon the child's cheek was revealed a tear. Unable to speak; longing looks did say. Please accept me . . . I want to play."

In just a few words this poem describes what many individuals go through on a daily basis. Feeling left out cannot be described vividly. Perhaps only looking at a child's face and attempting to understand his/her feelings can partially explain this dilemma.

Throughout the book, we will address these problems and answers will be formulated. The authors feel that children must not be deprived of their **free time** and that every effort must be made to allow for their participation.

In the upcoming sections of this chapter, basic needs and benefits from play experiences will be described. The purpose is to ensure that play should be considered important to all individuals. Furthermore, restrictions placed on exceptional children can pose serious threats to their development.

Before moving on to other related topics, it is imperative that we once again reinforce the primary theme of the text. We believe that no child should be disqualified from involvement in leisure activities. We would like to portray, initially, the importance of recreational experiences in the lives of children. After completing this orientation, the focus will be geared to developing unique experiences for exceptional children in formal and informal settings. If people can begin to develop this sense of understanding, we honestly feel that more will be done to ensure the play rights of the child who is disabled.

NEEDS OF ALL CHILDREN
TO EXPLORE THEIR LEISURE

Now let us focus our attention to the general needs of all children to explore their leisure. As we look at this area, we may find ourselves pointing out distinctive differences between various age groups, the exceptional population, and the mainstream. Granted, there are differences and special problems that are unique to the various populations of children (i.e., various age ranges, handicapped children, etc.), but that is not to say that similarities do not exist. Too often, many individuals have the tendency to continually point out the obvious differences between the norm and the disabled. Although there are some significant differences between the handicapped and nonhandicapped, it must be stressed once again that the disabled must be viewed as individuals first and disabled second. Furthermore, even within the mainstream, all children have their own individual makeups. In effect, everyone is different.

In play experiences, all children have certain needs. The first priority of any child is to have fun. The activities of various children may differ, but the goals are universal. We must assume that the intrinsic drive to amuse oneself is a critical variable in one's pursuit of leisure-time activities. Furthermore, the satisfaction that is gained from playing appears to reinforce a child's involvement. Nevertheless, there are many children who are not exposed to these opportunities and at times their leisure needs are not fulfilled.

Hutchinson (1949) stated that "recreation is a worthwhile, socially accepted leisure experience that provides immediate and inherent satisfaction to the individual who voluntarily participates in an activity" (p. 2). Furthermore, he states that motivation of an individual to take part in the activity could stem from a short-lived or profound interest which defines the motivational desire as one of the most important characteristics of a true recreational experience.

In a similar point of view, Pomeroy (1964) discusses the fact that certain fundamental human desires such as the need to be wanted and understood are important to all individuals and can be satisfied through participation in recreation activities.

Some of the needs Pomeroy discusses are that recreation programs fulfill the human need for: joy of creation, adventure, a sense of achievement, physical well-being, a sense of relaxation, and plain enjoyment. In addition to the qualities noted by Pomeroy (1964), I would like to expand the list and incorporate some of my perceptions. The following represents some additional points of view:

- the needs of belonging to a group
- the sense of personal understanding
- the need to pursue interests that will stimulate enjoyment during leisure time
- the need to develop a sense of responsibility and independence.

Before continuing to discuss these needs, the writer needs to point out that the role that play fulfills in the child's world may be comparable to the work life of an adult. Play is the child's career and has as much effect on his or her life as any adult's career. Therefore, recreation for all individuals really does, in some way or another, attempt to fulfill all the basic needs and desires required for total human existence.

The Sense of Belonging

The example of Billy discussed earlier in this chapter described a child who is in desperate need of acceptance and friendship. He is lonely and lacking companionship. In addition, Billy is not unique. There are many children like him, both handicapped and non-handicapped, who find themselves without frequent social contact. The reasons for this may be limitless; the response to it is not. A sense of worthlessness can develop when it appears that no one cares. Furthermore, being isolated may instill a sense of boredom.

Recreation activities can be one solution to this dilemma. Through recreation, children can be given the opportunity to meet new individuals and make new friendships. They can be given the chance to socialize and thus develop the feeling of belonging. Knowing that you are an integral part of a group and that you are **wanted** is important to everybody.

The Opportunity to Be Creative

Children enjoy the chance to be creative. Most children are inquisitive and enjoy an opportunity to put their mind to work. Although one might find that exceptional children occasionally lack the acquired abilities to complete fine artwork, play and recreational experiences can help all individuals find ways for creative self-expression no matter how small the achievement. During these moments, children may also begin to realize that there is a wealth of activities in which they can learn to be both creative and successful.

Self-Satisfaction and Achievement

The need for self-satisfaction and achievement is prevalent in all children. Have you ever attempted to recall situations in which your own child or another child displayed exuberant pride because he/she has completed a task? Some children are frequently denied these opportunities and become easily frustrated with themselves, thereby developing poor self-images. For example, Danny, a child who was classified as mildly mentally retarded, never really felt good about his accomplishments. He was involved for several years in recreational programs that were integrated. Many of the tasks presented to Danny were too demanding and complicated. To be noticed by others and to be given recognition for personal gain is pleasurable to every child.

In organized recreation programs the area of recognition is continually being addressed, either by the child's own accomplishments or by his/her group's progression. In play situations, where children tend to be less inhibited than in the classroom, a child may begin to attain a degree of success. This usually occurs when activities are organized in advance and a child can successfully compete. Organizing activities that take into account the skill levels of the participants usually enhances the probability of successful involvement. They allow the child to participate in activities that are the most appropriate. It is also important to realize that being able to use their leisure time competently will also bring a sense of achievement to a child. Knowing that one can amuse oneself without the aid of others is an achievement in itself.

When discussing the area of achievement, the relationship between the internal and external feelings should not be underscored. For many children the recognition they receive from others is crucial to their well-being. They are dependent on the thoughts of their peers for motivation. Nevertheless, there is also the intrinsic sense of achievement when individuals feel good about themselves for a specific reason. It would be difficult to ascertain which is more important to children. Yet, the need to obtain a sense of satisfaction is probably one of the most important basic needs for all children as they explore their leisure time.

The Need for Enjoyment and Relaxation

Just because a child is sitting in a wheelchair does not mean the child is always relaxed. For these individuals, wheelchairs are an integral part of their existence, their means of mobility. There is no reason for them to be deprived of the opportunity of reducing stress through play. Leisure is a time for an individual to relax and enjoy. It is an opportunity for all children to smile, laugh, and have fun. That is the reason they are playing!

Many decades ago handicapped individuals had to seek emotional satisfaction as passive observers rather than active participants (Pomeroy, 1964). As times have changed, one can begin to see a general transition where activities have been adapted to allow the exceptional child the chance to be involved. Both organized and unstructured play provides children with unique opportunities.

Too often, we find children who are unaware of the various leisure resources which are available to them. Due to this lack of knowledge or companionships, various children are denied an opportunity. As a consequence of their lack of awareness, numerous youngsters rely on adults to provide them with the experiences and structure needed to acquire and meet their needs. Furthermore, some parents find it necessary to help their child meet these goals, because when a child's needs are being thwarted, resulting frustration may be redirected towards the family.

As adults, our responsibilities should not be merely to provide answers for children so that they can engage in relaxing and enjoyable experiences. We must invest our time profitably by teaching them to discover the resources to develop the skills necessary to participate and function. Depending on the severity of the handicap, this will be accomplished to a greater or a lesser degree. At this point, we develop the child's sense of independence. When children are alerted to the activities that are available to them, they may acquire new skills and thus have more appropriate use of their leisure time.

This whole idea is reminiscent of an old proverb. If we simply feed an individual for life, we develop a sense of dependency. However, if we teach an individual to fish on his/her own (in this case teach them to be responsible for locating one's own leisure pursuits), we permit and reinforce growth and learning.

Responsibility and Independence

A child who learns such responsibility will be less apt to depend on others for entertainment. Most children do enjoy being as independent as possible. This need to be more responsible for one's actions and to become independent is an area of adaptive behavior strongly valued by our society. Children are being taught at early ages the primary steps to obtain goals. Through play/recreational experiences, all children can begin to excel in this area. For example, if a child is going to play later in the day, at that time for play, one has a responsibility to be there at the expected time. Children will learn that if they do not want to disappoint others, they will fulfill their obligations. If they are continually irresponsible, they will not find themselves invited back.

Part of the parent's responsibility to the child is to allow the child opportunities to face these problems. We find ourselves in a peculiar position, because normally we do not want to see our child fail. If we continually pamper our children, they may never learn to stand on their own. The need to have some responsibility and independence appears to be strong in all individuals.

In the chapters that follow, this area will be addressed again from the perspective of how these affective concerns can be enhanced through the utilization of recreation.

Physical and Mental Well-Being

Physical and mental well-being are two general areas which are basic needs of all children. These needs can be fulfilled, in part, by participation in play.

Play experiences are satisfying outlets for physical energy. All children need these opportunities whether they are handicapped or not. They allow a child an appropriate outlet to release excess tension and energy.

The area of mental well-being appears to encompass a majority of the areas previously discussed. Briefly, all children have the need to use their mental capacities. Throughout their leisure time, many hours can be spent pursuing interesting hobbies such as reading, writing, music and art (Pomeroy, 1964). Some children may find these activities mentally challenging and enjoyable.

Areas such as enjoyment, achievement, relaxation, responsibility and independence are greatly important to most children. Through play experiences, these areas can be enhanced (Fine, Lehrer, and Feldis, 1982; Hayes, 1977; CEC and AAPHER, 1966; Shivers and Fait, 1975, 1985).

Benefits from Participation

The premise that this book will continually explore is the importance of play involvement for exceptional children. In the previous section, general needs that can be facilitated through recreation have been discussed. Yet, children not only learn to enjoy their leisure time, but they also gain a great deal from their involvement.

For too long now, recreation has been deprived of its recognition as a general therapeutic tool. Many are unaware that along with sheer pleasure, a child attains many learning skills (CEC and AAPHER, 1966; Tizard and Harvey, 1977; Wehman, 1979).

Information will be shared later in the book not only to strengthen this conviction but also to provide plausible approaches to enhance the experiences. In the upcoming section, goals of play will be discussed. As the reader will soon realize, the goals that will be listed may also be interpreted as the benefits that can be gained by involvement. It is also important to note that all of these goals may, to some degree, be enhanced through recreational involvement. Nevertheless, it is also the role of the recreation leader to implement experiences utilizing activities that concentrate on these goals, which is a skill that will be thoroughly described in upcoming chapters.

Reading the following sections will be helpful in understanding the importance of play experiences for the handicapped. Furthermore, this information will bring into focus one of the primary functions of the book: To highlight the importance of play experiences for the special child and the challenges that are ahead for all of us in providing these services.

GOALS OF PLAY

Just as all of us have both personal and professional goals, goals should also be developed for activity programs. Many of these goals will be similar in nature to those specific goals of children previously discussed. For a child, the primary goal when playing is to have fun. Recreational activities, however, not only provide this outlet but many by-products as well. Among the areas that will be discussed are the enjoyment of play for its intrinsic pleasure and the use of recreation to enhance social adjustment, social development, physical health, language, and cognitive development. Evidence of the benefits that recreation and play experiences can provide seem to encourage many professionals to establish programs that can enable handicapped individuals to participate in recreation (Pomeroy, 1964).

It is important to also realize that the activities selected should reflect the goals chosen. Frequently, one must ask, "Why am I leading this activity?" or "What goals does this activity address?" These questions should be asked periodically to assess the programs implemented and to determine if these programs actually address the needs of the children involved. Activities should also be selected on the basis of a child's development preparation for an activity. A great deal of research has been done by Arnold Gessell and his associates in developing developmental norms for specific age groups (Muro and Dinkmeyer, 1977). These norms provide guidelines that suggest what accomplishments should be expected. Furthermore, the norms also provide guidelines to professionals on what type of activities should be implemented.

The Joy of Playing

As stated earlier, the joy of playing should be the primary aim of any activity. To get children to want to be involved, it must first be determined that they enjoy themselves. From a child's point of view, knowledge of the underlying benefits is unnecessary. They want to enjoy their free time either by playing games, being involved in activities with peers, or completing tasks individually. That is why play can become such a dynamic vehicle to induce change when working with youngsters. If one can provide experiences where enjoyment is not the sole benefit, then the opportunity can become therapeutic as well as fun.

We establish this goal initially because we genuinely believe that fun must come first. Some handicapped and non-handicapped individuals have not had enough opportunities to enjoy themselves due to an unexplained number of misfortunes. We must not destroy this primary intrinsic need to play in order to attempt to teach a variety of secondary skills. This would definitely alter the primary purpose for the interaction; that is, to have fun. All children deserve the right to enjoy their leisure time, and this must be primary on everyone's list if we are to truly classify the activities as play or recreation.

The other goals are generally what one may consider secondary benefits to the child's enjoyment. They are a result of providing useful activities, formulated in advance, which are not only fun but also encompass basic development needs.

Social Adjustment and Social Development

It has been mentioned that recreation can allow a child the opportunity to grow up and learn effective traits to interact. For many special children, there lacks the daily opportunities for realizing personal achievement and to interact positively with other young people their own age. For some, their only group experience with children may be in an academic setting where there is a deficit in the optimum amount of chances to develop self-confidence with others.

One goal of recreation is to provide these youngsters with this basic need: a chance for them to develop skills in interacting more comfortably with others. This point brings out two basic issues. At first, we recognize the need for learning; we recognize how to adjust to group norms and the behavior that is needed to fit in. Throughout a child's experience with others, he or she will begin to realize what behavior is or is not acceptable. He/she will learn this through experience or by people informing him/her. These experiences are of the utmost importance to most children.

The fact that all children have a wealth of leisure hours makes it equally important for them to acquire the necessary skills to afford them adequate use of their time. As a consequence, some of the play skills that are being taught could be implemented during their free time. This could also be helpful in eliminating the feeling of loneliness, boredom, and anger. I recall an experience with a child that dramatically explores this area.

When I first encountered Bob, he found it very difficult to interact with group members. In addition to having a learning disability, he also had a severe speech impediment. He was a sensitive person who wanted to fit in but had a difficult time using the appropriate interpersonal skills. Initially, the group members picked on him by laughing at his speech and not allowing him the opportunity to play freely. After working with him, a strong relationship was developed. With some coaching and guidance, he started to feel more comfortable with the group. He attempted to learn from his mistakes. With this new dimension to his personality, he would confidently perform social encounters correctly when confronted with new situations. For Bob, the turnaround was tremendous. One could begin to see the change in him. Not only was he learning to play more effectively with his peers, he was also beginning to feel better about himself.

Learning to feel better about one's self, learning skills to relate with others, developing a sense of responsibility and independence, and becoming aware of feelings of others, should all be goals of a recreation program. All of these areas, to some degree, are encountered when children are playing, and they can be enhanced and taught through their experiences.

An area that was briefly examined earlier was the feeling of being a part of a group. An important aspect of a play experience is a child's willingness to be with others and to become part of the group. It is also imperative to realize that when interacting with others, a group must function as a whole to be effective.

An example comes to mind to illustrate this point of view. Several years ago I had the opportunity to work with a group of boys in a camp setting. The boys had emotional problems and were constantly fighting with each other. Surprised by this behavior, I responded in the following manner. Immediately I shouted, "Everyone look at your hands." The group members were surprised into silence by this seemingly insane request. Now, I had to quickly think of something to say before I lost their attention. "If I cut away your palms," I continued, "what would you do with your fingers?" Various youngsters remarked that nothing could be done with their fingers, since their palms keeps the fingers together and makes them work. Slowly, the boys then began to discuss how fortunate they were that all of their bodily functions were in order. Some of them related stories about individuals who were disabled and how difficult they thought it was for them.

Eventually, we arrived to the desired point. A group, like the palms of our hands, is what keeps individuals working together. A disjointed group whose members continually fight with each other is one that is ineffective. It also would be an unpleasurable experience. Just as a palm gets the fingers to work in unison, so does a group with its members. After discussing these issues, it was pointed out that if they could not work together, they would probably spend more time doing nothing than having fun. The end result was positive and the boys attempted to work hard on relating to each other.

One goal of play, then, is not only to work on individual social adjustment but also to allow children to become more comfortable in working and playing with each other. Group recreational experiences represent prime opportunities to work on these skills and definitely merit our attention.

Physical Well-Being

Participation in a variety of recreational experiences can contribute to healthier physical and motor development. For some exceptional children, there may not be ample opportunities to release this physical energy. Since a goal of play is to expend excess energy in a constructive fashion, handicapped individuals also need this outlet.

Activities can be adapted to provide physical enjoyment. In the chapters that will follow, effective ways to adapt activities will be discussed in more detail. Furthermore, play experiences can also enhance motor development (sensory motor and gross motor skills). Since a variety of activities involve both fine motor and gross motor skills, recreators can try to enhance these areas by providing activities that are suitable for the child. Activities can also have several purposes for specific children. For example, an activity can be used to develop social skills along with motor skills.

Additionally, certain youngsters may not enjoy certain activities. Perhaps it is not the task that is upsetting them but, rather, they lack prerequisite skills necessary to complete the activity. That is the reason why they are frustrated! For example, in the making of a puppet, a child with poor fine motor skills may find it extremely difficult to manipulate the scissors or to place buttons as eyes on the puppet. If we are able to realize this in advance and select an activity that is more suitable, then the frustration will be diminished. Provisions then can be implemented not only to make a child's experience more satisfying but also effective in enhancing physical and motor abilities.

Language and Cognitive Skills

An important area that we continually face when developing programs for special children is the improvement of language and cognitive skills. Though enjoyment is the primary goal of play, there are many underlying traits that can be incorporated. While a child is playing, he/she is usually in a situation where communication is necessary. If it is determined that communication skills should be developed with a specific child, there are ways to implement an approach that would strengthen this area. At times, activities may pose challenges to the child where he/she will find himself/herself in a problem-solving situation. In addition, many activities also make use of the child's memory. Card games such as Concentration are good examples. With games, a child may incorporate visual and auditory discrimination skills. Therefore, although the child is on the surface simply playing, all of these skills are being used and hopefully stimulated.

It is imperative, then, to realize that a host of skills are being used in a child's world of play. They should be considered goals that recreators can focus upon when working with children. In the following chapters, sections will be presented illustrating recent findings on how play can be used as a dynamic facilitator of these basic skills.

SUMMARY

The literature reviewed in this chapter points favorably towards the critical importance of recreational experiences for the exceptional child. Indeed, it can be seen that all children seem to have the same basic needs and drives so important for their development. The exceptional child has in the past been deprived of his academic and social rights. We must realize that these children deserve a chance to explore their leisure. Furthermore, the writers believe that not only will the child gain satisfaction with himself/herself due to his/her involvement, but the experiences gained may be helpful in improving the developmental skills of the handicapped child.

The critical importance of recreational involvement for all people has been emphasized. With increased knowledge of the effectiveness of this resource, we may begin to appreciate it more fully and tap into it more carefully. We may also begin to carefully examine the provisions made for our children and place play experiences as one of our priorities.

REFERENCES

Austin, D. & Crawford, M. (1991). *Therapeutic recreation.* Englewood Cliffs, NJ: Prentice-Hall.

Biklen, D. & Bogden, R. (1977). Handicapism in America. In B. Burton, D. Biklen and R. Bogden (Eds.), *An Alternative textbook in special education.* Denver: Love.

Biklen, D. (1985). Integration in school and society. In D. Biklen (Ed.), *Achieving the complete school.* New York: Teachers College Press.

Brightman, A. (Ed.). (1984). *Ordinary moments.* Baltimore: University Park Press.

Council for Exceptional Children, American Association for Health, Physical Education, and Recreation. (1966). Recreation and physical activity for the mentally retarded. Washington, American Association for Health, Physical Education, and Recreation.

Crews, H. (1979). *A childhood: The biography of a place.* Boston: G.K. Hall.

Datillo, J. & Schleien, S. (1994). Understanding leisure services for individuals with mental retardation. *Mental Retardation, 32,* 53–59.

Dunham, J. & Dunham, C. (1978). Psychosocial aspects of disability. In R. Goldensen (Eds.), *Disability and rehabilitation handbook.* New York: McGraw-Hill.

Ellis, M. (1973). *Why people play.* Englewood Cliffs: Prentice-Hall.

Ferrel, M. (1989). Community recreation. *Entourage, 4(1),* 1–7.

Fine, A. (in press). Leisure, Living and Quality of Life. In Rebecca Renwick, Ivan Brown and Mark Nagler (Eds.), *Quality of life in Health Promotion and Rehabilitation: Conceptual Approaches, Issues and Applications.* Beverly Hills, CA: Sage.

Fine, A. (1994). Life, Liberty and Choices: A commentary of leisure's values in life. *Journal of Developmental Disabilities, 3,* 16–28.

Fine, A. (1982). Therapeutic recreation: An aspect of rehabilitation for exceptional children. *The Lively Arts, 4.*

Fine, A. (1978). Therapeutic recreation: The new boy on the block. *Alabama Inserve Project Newsletter, 1,* 4, 3.

Fine, A.H. (1991). *Recreation: Community integration and quality of life.* Paper presented at the 114th Annual Meeting of the America Association on Mental Retardation, Atlanta, Georgia, May 27–31.

Fine, A., Lehrer, B., and Feldis, D. (1982). Therapeutic recreation programming for autistic children. *Therapeutic Recreation Journal, 16,* 6–11.

Flanagan, J. (1978). A research approach to improving our quality of life. *American Psychologist, 33,* 138–147.

Gliedman, J. & Roth, W. (1980). *The unexpected minority: Handicapped children in America.* New York: Harcourt Brace Jovanovich.

Goffman, E. (1974). *Stigma.* Englewood Cliffs, NJ: Prentice-Hall.

Gold, D. (1989). Putting leisure into life. *Entourage, 4(1),* 10–11.

Greenfield, J. (1970). *A child called Noah.* New York: Holt Rinehart and Winston.

Greenfield, J. (1978). *A place for Noah.* New York: Holt Rinehart and Winston.

Haring, H. (1982). *Exceptional children and youth.* Columbus: Charles Merrill.

Hayes, G. (1977). Recreation and the mentally retarded. In T. Stein and Sessoms (Eds.), *Recreation and special populations.* Boston: Holbrook Press.

Heward, W. & Orlansky, M. (1988). *Exceptional children.* Columbus: Charles E. Merrill.

Hutchinson, J. (1951). *Principles of recreation.* New York: A.S. Barnes.

Iso-Ahola, S. (1980). *The social psychology of leisure and recreation.* Dubuque, IA: William C. Brown.

Iso-Ahola, S. (1980). *The psychology of leisure and recreation.* Dubuque, IA: William C. Brown.

Iso-Ahola, S. (1984). Social Psychological foundations of leisure and resultant implications for leisure counseling. In E.T. Dowd (Ed.), *Leisure counseling: Concepts and applications.* Springfield, IL: Charles C. Thomas.

Jones, R. (1977). *The acorn people.* New York: Butan Books.

Kabanoff, B. (1982). Occupational and sex differences in leisure needs and leisure satisfaction. *Journal of Occupational Behavior, 3,* 233–245.

Kando, T. (1980). *Leisure and popular culture in transition.* St. Louis: C.V. Mosby.

Kelly, L. & Vergason, G. (1978). *Dictionary of special education and rehabilitation.* Denver: Love.

Kraus, R. (1966). *Recreation today: Program planning and leadership.* New York: Appleton-Century-Crofts.

MacMillian, D. (1982). *Mental retardation in school and society.* Boston: Little Brown.

Marinoble, R. & Hegnauer, J. (1988). *Quality of life for individuals with disabilities: A conceptual framework.* Curriculum and training unit program. Sacramento, CA: State Department of Education.

Muro, J. & Dinkmeyer, D. (1977). *Counseling in the elementary and middle schools.* Dubuque, IA: William C. Brown.

Pomeroy, J. (1964). *Recreation for the physically handicapped.* New York: Macmillan.

Rybczynski, W. (1991). *Waiting for the weekend.* New York: Penguin Books.

Shivers, J. & Fait, H. (1975). *Therapeutic and adapted recreational services.* Philadelphia: Lea and Febiger.

Shivers, J. & Fait, H. (1985). *Special recreational services: Therapeutic and adapted.* Philadelphia: Lea and Febiger.

Tinsley, H., & Johnson, T. (1984). A preliminary taxonomy of leisure activities. *Journal of Leisure Research, 16,* 234–244.

Tizard, B. & Harvey, D. (1977). *Biology of play.* Philadelphia: Lippincott.

Wehman, P. (1979). *Recreation programming for developmentally disabled persons.* Baltimore: University Park Press.

Chapter 2

PRACTICAL APPLICATIONS OF THEORIES OF PLAY

SUSAN NAKAYAMA SIAW, MEG CLARK, AND AUBREY H. FINE

OVERVIEW

Imagine four distinguished scientists observing a child cranking the handle on a musical jack-in-the-box. Each observer, having been trained in a different school of thought, interprets the child's play from a unique perspective. When asked, "Why is the child doing that?" the first observer, a staunch Piagetian, replies, "The child is trying out his cranking scheme, and he is gaining logicomathematical experience regarding the cause-effect relationship between cranking and the clown popping out of the box. He is asking himself, "What happens if I crank fast? Slow? At an irregular pace? Will the clown still pop out?" The second observer, a learning theorist, is particularly attentive to the child's behavior. He suggests that "The child is merely repeating a response that previously led to an interesting and rewarding consequence; that is, turning the handle leads to the reinforcement of having a clown pop out of the box. So, of course, he is going to repeat this response." The third observer, trained in the psychoanalytic school, is obviously uncomfortable with the two previously offered explanations. "I disagree! You two are merely focusing on the cognitive and behavioral aspects of this situation. It is clear to me that the child's actions reflect his need to protect his emotional well-being. Given his age, the child is dependent upon his parents. Thus, he has a need to show mastery and independence without losing the emotional connection with his parents. He is obviously enjoying this activity because he is running the show. He is in control of the cranking and the clown popping out of the box." The fourth observer, entertained but not convinced by these previous interpretations, fidgets in his seat and complains that his three companions are thinking too deeply about the purpose of the child's activities. He responds, "It is highly likely that the child is alleviating boredom.

33

The child's interaction with the jack-in-the-box is merely a means of arousal."

A fifth scientist, observing the other four through a one-way mirror, is excited by all four explanations. Although she sees weaknesses in each of the explanations, she also realizes that each is worth consideration. The scientist is reminded of the old parable about the blind men who are individually exploring a magnificent elephant. One is at the trunk, another is at an ear, a third is stationed at its side, and the last is at its tail. Each man exclaims that he has discovered what the elephant is. The first exclaims that elephants are round and firm like telephone poles; the second disagrees and says that elephants are pliable and soft like cloth; the third is certain that elephants are flat and round like rugs; and the fourth, exasperated that the other three are so far off, asserts that elephants are obviously like long thin ropes! The point is, of course, that no man is absolutely wrong and no man is absolutely right. The fifth scholar, in fact, concludes that a child may play for a variety of reasons and feels comfortable accepting an eclectic viewpoint.

Following a brief overview of four classical or historical interpretations of the purpose of play, basic concepts from four major contemporary theories—Piagetian theory, learning theory, psychoanalytic theory, and stimulus-arousal theory—will be presented. As suggested in the above fictional scenario, each theory "examines the elephant" from a different vantage point. Discussions will include contributions and limitations of each theory in explaining play and implications for special populations according to each theory. The chapter will focus on how play promotes cognitive, social, and emotional development and will conclude with a consideration of how the context or setting a child finds herself in affects play.

HISTORICAL PERSPECTIVES: FOUR CLASSICAL THEORIES OF PLAY

There were four major explanations of play proposed by early theorists. The first was the surplus energy theory of play, which originated in the writings of eighteenth century philosopher Friedrich von Schiller (1954) and psychologist H. Spencer (1873). According to this theory, humans have a reservoir of energy that is utilized to satisfy primary needs such as the need for food. After primary needs are met, leftover energy in this reservoir is spent on play. Play is motivated by an inborn drive to use up energy within this reservoir. Once depleted, the reservoir is revitalized and the cycle repeats. A major criticism aimed at the surplus energy theory of play is that it is not consistent with predictions of evolutionary theory. For example, if play involves the expenditure of superfluous energy, play should be eliminated through natural selection. But analysis indicates that as one moves up the phylogenetic scale, less time and energy are necessary to satisfy primary needs and more time and energy are available for play. A second major criticism is that there is no physiological evidence that unused energy "backs up and creates a pressure, demanding release" (Beach, 1945, p. 528).

A second classical theory is the relaxation and recreation theory of play, which was proposed by philosophers Lazarus (1883) and Patrick (1916). In contrast to the surplus energy theory, the relaxation and recreation theory characterized play as the result of an energy deficit. After engaging in physically and mentally exhausting work, the body needs to sleep. However, in order to achieve full restoration, the body first needs to engage in play activities that help the person escape from the reality-based pressures of work. Patrick (1916) also proposed that play is motivated by race memories, which are traces from human evolutionary past. Thus, for example, children enjoy reading books about animals and playing with teddy bears, because primitive ancestors depended on wildlife for sustenance. One of the major criticisms of this theory is that children do not engage in work to the same extent that adults do, although children do engage in more play than adults do. A second criticism is that there is no evidence to support the existence of race memories.

A third classical theory is the practice or pre-exercise theory of play, which was presented by Groos (1898, 1901). Groos, a neo-Darwinian, believed that play is driven by instinct and has been acquired by natural selection. The purpose of play, according to this theory, is to practice skills necessary for adulthood. Thus, in species higher on the phylogenetic scale that use complex skills during adulthood, there has been a selection for an extended childhood period. The longer childhood period was believed to be necessary to prepare the individual for the complexities of adulthood via play. A major criticism of this theory is that it is difficult to predict which play activities will serve as preparation for the tasks of adulthood. Indeed, in the age of *Future Shock* (Toeffler, 1970) and *Escape From Freedom* (Fromm, 1941) in which changes are inevitable and unpredictable, it would seem increasingly difficult to predict the skills which should be practiced in anticipation of the future. For example, in the 1960s, high school students struggled to master the slide rule for algebra and chemistry classes, while in the early 1970s, pocket calculators were available, although initially too expensive for all students' pocketbooks. In the present computer age, even a preschooler may be exposed to a family's personal computer while the slide rule joins the abacus in the attic. The rapid technological changes in contemporary society hit home when the university graduate who majored in computer sciences learns that her recent training is rapidly outdated once she reaches the workforce. What does all this mean in regard to play? It suggests that play can in no way anticipate or prepare the person for every technological skill that will be required in the future.

The last major classical theory is the recapitulation theory of play, which was presented in the writings of G. Stanley Hall (1920) and Luther Gulick (1898). The recapitulation theory is based on the principle that ontogyny recapitulates phylogeny (i.e., developmental changes during childhood reenact the evolutionary progression of humans). For example, embryonic development appears to mirror evolutionary development from the protozoan to Homo sapiens. Hall and Gulick interpreted play as a vestige of human evolutionary past, suggesting that the hard running, the aiming toward a target when throwing, and the use of a bat in baseball are contemporary versions of the hunting activities characteristic of early humans. There are numerous criticisms of the recapitulation theory. One criticism is that the assumption that play must follow a certain developmental course reflecting human ancestral past has not been supported by empirical evidence. Many evolutionary changes are not represented in the development of play. Moreover, the theory cannot account for the fact that regressions may occur in play. For instance, Sutton-Smith (1969) suggests that adult play is often similar to children's play, an interpretation that contradicts the forward-moving direction predicted by evolutionary theory.

The importance of these classical theories is that they drew the attention of scholars to play, and they influenced the formulations of contemporary theories of play (see Rubin, Fein, & Vandenberg, 1983, for further discussion of the roots of contemporary theories). These early theories form the background for the development of four contemporary theories of play: the Piagetian, learning, psychoanalytic, and arousal theories.

PIAGETIAN THEORY

Piaget focused on cognitive development, interpreting play in terms of its relation to the development of knowledge. According to Piaget, the person's way of thinking about the world is organized into a framework for thinking which he called **cognitive structures.** Cognitive structures reflect the individual's way of viewing the world; this way of viewing changes **qualitatively** with development. Table 2 presents basic Piagetian concepts and terminology.

Table 2. Basic Piagetian Concepts and Terminology.

1. **Schemes** — Organized patterns of behavior.
2. **Operations** — The mental equivalents of schemes. They do not appear until age six or seven years.
3. **Assimilation** — The imposition of an existing cognitive structure or framework for thinking on the world. Assimilation involves taking content from the world and molding or bending that content to fit a current cognitive structure.
4. **Accommodation** — The alteration of a cognitive structure in order to adjust to information from the outside world that does not fit with a current framework for thinking. Assimilation and accommodation are complementary processes; neither occurs without the other.

FOUR MAJOR STAGES OF DEVELOPMENT

1. **Sensorimotor Stage** (birth to two years of age) — During this stage, infants exercise their schemes and discover properties about objects around them. A major accomplishment of this stage is the acquisition of object permanence, which is the discovery that objects exist independently of oneself.
2. **Preoperational Stage** (approximately ages two to seven) — Thinking in this stage is intuitive and illogical. The child focuses on salient perceptual features of the world and often ignores other relevant information.
3. **Concrete Operational Stage** (the middle childhood years of seven to twelve) — This stage marks the advent of operational thinking. A major accomplishment of this stage is the ability to conserve. A limitation is that thinking is primarily at a concrete level.
4. **Formal Operational Stage** (12 years and above) — An individual in this stage can think abstractly and hypothetically.

Piaget and Play

Piaget recorded his ideas about play in his book, *Play, Dreams, and Imitation in Childhood* (1962). He defined play as pure assimilation. Thus, playing involves the child imposing his way of thinking upon the world. But, as defined above, assimilation and accommodation are complementary processes; play is a state in which assimilation predominates over accommodation. A child at play is exercising his schemes and operations just for the sheer joy of exercising them. He might try out a banging scheme on everything encountered, e.g., banging the table, banging the crib, or banging toys.

Qualitatively different types of play are engaged in at different developmental stages, and these are divided into three broad categories of play. The first category, **practice play,** occurs during the sensorimotor stage. During this stage, when schemes are especially evident, the infant can be seen displaying **circular reactions,** which involve practicing schemes. Around one to four months of age, babies engage in primary circular reactions in which schemes are exercised just for the sheer joy of it. Babies' first schemes are basic reflexes and are centered on the babies' own bodies, i.e., they involve interesting things that babies can do with their own bodies and involve no interaction with outside stimuli. At ages four to eight months, Piaget noticed that babies repeat interesting actions that involve outside stimuli. For example, a baby may accidentally kick the side of his crib, which causes the mobile above it to jangle. These are secondary circular reactions. At eight to twelve months, the baby's knowledge about cause-effect relationships between her own actions upon outside stimuli emerges, e.g., the baby deliberately kicks in order to see the mobile jangle. Finally, around 12 to 18 months of age, the infant engages in tertiary circular reactions. By this time, the baby has a better understanding of cause-effect relationships and will deliberately try out schemes with a "let-me-see-what-will-happen-if-I-do-it-this-way" attitude. For example, a baby might continually knock her bottle off of her high chair, much to her parents' exasperation. She will knock it hard one time, harder another time, a slight tap a third time, and so forth. She is using trial and error by experimenting with her schemes to find out more about the world.

As the child enters the preoperational stage, the predominant category of play is **symbolic play.** Make-believe play is symbolic, because it involves having one thing represent something else. For example, when five-year-old Timmy pretends that he is riding a horse as he straddles a broom, he is assimilating by making that broom fit his structure of what a horse is. During this period, play is engaged in for the sheer joy of it, and the child progresses from solitary play, in which schemes are tried out on one's own to parallel play and cooperative play. **Parallel play** is demonstrated by young preschoolers who, while playing with the same toys (e.g., blocks) sitting side-by-side, are not interacting in any way. Finally, during the later preschool years or so, cooperative play emerges. In this type of play, children interact together during play, simultaneously and cooperatively engaging in an identical activity. This type of play is probably related to the greater language abilities of these older children since communication facilitates interaction with others. Piaget suggests that during this period, children are very egocentric. They are not cognitively capable of taking someone else's perspective. As a result, parents may often encounter instances where children are not able to share. This is not a matter of the child being selfish; rather, the child cannot take the other's perspective and does not fully grasp how the other child feels when he will not share.

With increasing age, play becomes more competitive and abstract. The third category of play, involving playing games with rules, emerges during middle and later childhood. During this period, playing is not always for the sheer joy of playing; playing is to win. Even in situations such as playing computer games in which children have an opportunity to play without peers, the goal is still to win. Piaget's examination of moral development, however, indicates that children initially have an inaccurate understanding of rules and how games should be played. At first, in a stage called **moral realism,** children believe that rules are fixed and that the way games are played today is the same way their grandparents played them and the same way their own children will play them. Children are very inflexible and do not realize that rules can be changed by mutual agreement of all players. By early adolescence, children enter a second stage called **moral autonomy.** By this time, the child has a basic understanding of democracy and understands that rules are not fixed. Piaget would suggest that being able to play games as the child grows up provides opportunities to accommodate to the fact that rules are changeable. Moreover, the ability to take another's perspective, coupled with the ability to think hypothetically and abstractly during the adolescent period, enables the adolescent to play more complex strategic games such as chess.

Limitations of Piagetian Theory

Sutton-Smith (1966), a well known authority in the field of play, provided two major criticisms of Piaget's ideas about play. First, if play is primarily assimilation, and if by definition assimilation does not involve any changes in the child's cognitive structures, then play is not an important factor in development. However, because assimilation plays the role of exercising schemes and operations so that they do not atrophy with disuse, and because assimilation does not occur without accommodation, play does in fact play a role in intellectual development.

A second criticism of Piaget's theory of play advanced by Sutton-Smith is that adults engage in play that resembles the play of children. If Piaget's ideas about developmental changes in cognitive structures are correct, then it should be impossible for adults to regress to play that is qualitatively at a child's level. Sutton-Smith's concern about the quality of play in adulthood is restated in a different way by Flavell, Miller, and Miller (1993). They believe that a major problem with Piaget's theory is his characterization of development as an invariant sequence of stages in which there is no turning back. They cite evidence indicating that although the basic sequence of development through the stages is correct, the stages are not as discrete as originally suggested. That is, at any given time an individual may perform at levels reflecting thinking at different stages; performance may vary with factors such as fatigue, task requirements, and content. An individual does not think exclusively at a given level.

Bee (1986) presents a further limitation of Piaget's theory. Piaget formulated his theory with the goal of describing general developmental trends. As such, its explanation of individual or group variability in development (e.g., special populations) is limited. However, while Piaget focused on development in normal populations, others such as his close colleague, Barbel Inhelder (1968), have tested his ideas with developmentally disabled samples. Generally, it is believed by some scholars that youngsters with developmental disabilities progress through Piaget's stages in the same sequence but at a slower rate than children who are not similarly challenged.

Implications of Piagetian Theory for Children with Disabilities

Piaget believed that there are three influences on development. The first is maturation, the second is physical and logicomathematical experience, and the third is social environment. Maturation is genetically-programmed change, and aside from modifications made via genetic engineering, there is not much that can be done to affect this influence.

The second influence is physical and logicomathematical experience. Physical experience is the type of experience in which the child learns about the physical properties of objects, e.g., rocks are hard, cotton is soft, and ice cream is cold. Logicomathematical experience is the type of experience gained from seeing what can be done with things in the environment, e.g., realizing that five rocks lined up in a row equals five rocks, and that five rocks in a pile still add up to five rocks, and realizing that five is five in these configurations regardless of whether one is counting rocks or shells or candy or whatever. Learning that a Transformer can be a robot or a vehicle, but that it is always the same toy, is another example of logicomathematical experience.

Some exceptional children may be limited in physical and logicomathematical experience. If the child is physically disabled, he may not have the types and ranges of experience anticipated by Piaget. For example, a child who is blind does not get visual feedback concerning how objects appear from different perspectives. Sandler and Wills (1965) observed the play of infants with a form of congenital blindness and found that these children displayed delays in early play experiences, which included delays in exploring the environment.

In order to gain physical and logicomathematical experience, a child must be a participant in development. Indeed, Piaget characterized the child as taking an active role in development. The child who exercises her schemes and operations can be likened to a scientist performing mini-experiments upon the world to discover what the world is all about. Observations of children with mental retardation indicate that these special children do not interact with toys in the same way as children who are not cognitively challenged do. Their play seems to be less spontaneous. It seems that this special population does not take as active a part in performing mini-experiments upon the world as other youngsters do. Thus, their understanding of the world is limited and does not develop as rapidly. Furthermore, Barnett and Kane (1985) suggest that the most frequently investigated feature in the play of the child with mental retardation pertains to the apparent absence of symbolic play forms. Several studies have documented that symbolic fantasy play has been severely hampered (Cooper, Moodley & Reynell, 1978; Hill & McCune-Nicolich, 1981). A similar finding has also been noted with children with infantile autism (Fine, Lehrer, & Feldis, 1982; Rutter, 1978).

The third influence fostering development is social environment.

Piaget suggested that one way to advance through the cognitive stages is for the child to interact with people who think at a slightly higher stage than herself. The probability of accommodating to another's way of thinking is greatest if the other's thinking is only slightly ahead of one's own. This is an advantage of being in a setting with slightly older children. One implication is that some exceptional children, e.g., those with mental retardation, should be provided with opportunities to interact with peers who are more cognitively advanced. Exposure to ways of thinking that are slightly higher than the child's own may encourage accommodation, thus providing the means for cognitive development. This position has been an important reason why many professionals and parents have advocated more integrated programming in all aspects of a child's life.

LEARNING THEORY

Learning theory is concerned with the acquisition, alteration, maintenance, and extinction of observable behaviors. Learning approaches particularly stress the effects of environment and experience on behavior. Relying on the principles of classical conditioning, operant conditioning, and social learning (see Table 3), learning theorists describe the child's development in terms of an enlarging behavioral repertoire allowing for adaptation to the environment.

Table 3. Basic Learning Theory Concepts and Terminology.

1. **Classical Conditioning** — The process by which automatic, reflexive (or unconditioned) responses to specific environmental stimuli can, through repeated pairings, come to be elicited (as conditioned responses) by previously neutral stimuli. This is Pavlov's theory of stimulus substitution.
2. **Operant Conditioning** — The process by which new behaviors emerge as a result of environmental consequences to emitted acts. According to Skinner, behaviors followed by reinforcement tend to be repeated; those followed by undesirable punishment are not likely to be repeated.
3. **Social Learning Theory** — The process of acquiring behaviors through the use of observation and modeling in a process of vicarious learning. Bandura identifies both social and cognitive processes as important elements in this mode of learning.

Learning Theory and Play

Learning theorists view play as behavior that is learned in the same manner as any other behavior; it is influenced by reinforcement, punishment, and modeling. Thus, reinforcement influences play when spontaneously emitted behaviors are repeated by the child following desirable environmental consequences. For example, an infant in her crib who continuously flails her arms in her line of vision, continuously kicks the side of her crib, or repeatedly knocks her bottle off of her high chair tray, is presumed to be repeating a response that led to a pleasant consequence in the past.

Punishment, or unpleasant consequences following an action, is also thought to affect play. In a series of studies, Lamb and his colleagues (Lamb & Roopnarine, 1979; Lamb, Easterbrooks, & Holden, 1980) found that punishment by peers may contribute to playing with sex-appropriate toys. When three-year-olds encountered a peer playing with a sex-inappropriate toy (e.g., a boy playing with a doll), they ceased playing with the child. This behavioral outcome also occurred with five-year-old children, but only after a series of other strategies were attempted (e.g., such as demanding that the child stop playing with the sex-inappropriate toy or manually trying to take the toy away). In most instances, the child playing with the sex-inappropriate toy stopped playing with that object. Reinforcement and punishment could also explain the relationship between activities children seem to enjoy and level of accomplishment. The example presented in Chapter 1 of the youngster who ceased participating in art activities after his father crumpled his one attempt at artwork and threw it to the ground (defined by learning theorists as a punishment) illustrates this point.

Finally, modeling has an effect on play. The premise of social learning theory is that play affords the child an opportunity to learn a variety of play activities through observation and subsequent imitation; vicarious experiences of reinforcement and punishment help shape the child's behavior. For instance, a child who is presented with a toy such as a Bo-Bo doll may not initially know how to play with such a toy, but he is readily able to learn to punch and kick the doll after watching a model do so, particularly if the model is rewarded for this aggressive behavior (e.g., Bandura, 1973; 1983). Similarly, researchers have found a positive correlation between amount of aggression viewed on television and aggressive play behavior (Eron & Huesmann, 1984, 1986; Huesmann & Miller, 1994).

Limitations of Learning Theory

First, learning theory is not and was not intended to be a developmental theory. Therefore, no specific developmental trajectory is proposed; rather, development is seen as more effectively adapting to the environment. Thus, the theory provides no timeframe identifying when specific types of play behaviors might appear in the behavioral repertoire of the child. In fact, in some of the earlier and more extreme versions of this theory, it would have been assumed that any child could acquire any play behavior, no matter how complex, were all of the underlying prerequisite skills identified and acquired.

A second limitation of learning theory is that it is reductionistic; it directs attention to small units of behavior, assuming an additive model in which the whole is nothing more than the sum of its parts. However, play among children may be more than a simple collection of behaviors. Examinations of and interventions in the play experiences of children may need to incorporate a comprehensive and holistic perspective to insure understanding for theorists and optimal play experiences for children.

Third, and finally, the focus on behavior may obscure the impact of biological factors. Liebert & Spiegler (1994) suggest that the biological endowment of the individual can impact the learning process in three ways: by affecting the ability to learn, by limiting the capacity to perform requisite behaviors, and by influencing the perception and processing of environmental cues. This limitation may be of critical concern in dealing with the play needs of exceptional children.

Implications of Learning Theory
for Children with Disabilities

According to learning theory, the child's play behavior is learned behavior that is based on experience. The assumption that play is a learned behavior has three implications for children whose behaviors are limited by disabilities. The first implication concerns the enhancement of instructions related to play for children who are disabled. Play must be broken down into smaller, more manageable units so that children can exhibit mastery in a hierarchical manner. What does this mean? For example, a child who is limited in his play (e.g., a child with mental retardation who does not play spontaneously in the manner that a nonretarded child does) can be taught how to play via shaping. Shaping is defined as the rewarding of successive approximations of a desired response. This is a technique that is used when the target response is initially too complex to perform. The play response may be broken down into a hierarchy of smaller, prerequisite responses, and then the child may be rewarded for accomplishing each successive step in the response hierarchy. In contrast to Piaget who depicted development as a series of qualitatively different stages, learning theorists view development quantitatively as a series of small, incremental, and cumulative steps. Every time the child learns something new, more behaviors are added to the child's cumulative repertoire.

A second implication of learning theory for play among children with disabilities is that since imitation appears to be an expedient way to learn new responses, it is important to provide opportunities for special children to play with peers who are not disabled. In providing such opportunities, attention must be given not only to enhancing the skills of exceptional children but also to increasing nondisabled children's knowledge about their special friends. Playing with nondisabled peers would affect not only play behavior per se but also would affect social interaction skills for both children with and children without disabilities.

Third, and finally, learning theory suggests that a child who does not engage in what is deemed appropriate play behavior may not do so because such play is not reinforcing. A child who fails at a given play activity will not continue to engage in that play activity because failure can be likened to punishment, and punished behavior is not repeated. Iso-Ahola (1980) suggests that helplessness limits a person's ability to believe he can perform a task successfully. Most children engage in activities that they are skilled at. Activities that children feel inadequate at are usually avoided. The learning theory interpretation of this outcome may help explain why exceptional children avoid certain play situations. For example, Sarah had many negative experiences with other children. Thus, when she had developed the basic skills of bowling and her mother attempted to enroll her in a bowling league, she adamantly refused to participate. Learning theory would argue that her previous experiences with other children discouraged her involvement in bowling.

This suggests that play and its related variable must be made into a reinforcing activity for the child.

The roles of reinforcement and punishment in encouraging or discouraging play behaviors suggest that motivation may influence a child's desire to participate in play activities. Three theoretical orientations related to the phenomenon of motivation are (a) attribution theory, (b) locus of control, and (c) the theory of flow. **Attribution** refers to inferences made by an individual concerning the causes of behaviors or events, particularly concerning success or failure in those circumstances. Success or failure can be attributed to one of four causal factors: (1) ability, (2) effort, (3) task, and (4) luck (Dixon, 1979). Bernard Weiner (1985), a primary contributor to this theory, suggests that there are a number of causes that are used to explain success or failure in achievement-related contexts. He points out that causes are inferred on the basis of several factors, including specific informational cues (e.g., past history of success and social norms), causal preferences, reinforcement history, and communication from others. Attribution theory is an excellent alternative for explaining why children prefer specific play activities. The theory implies that these children appear to select behaviors during which they feel competent and able to display mastery behavior.

Locus of control pertains to the belief held by an individual that his responses will or will not influence the attainment of reinforcements. Weiner (1985) suggests that locus of control is considered as a problem-solving generalized expectancy, addressing whether behaviors are perceived as instrumental to goal attainment, regardless of the specific reinforcer. Attributing success or failure to internal factors such as ability or effort is characteristic of internal locus of control, where the individual feels the results obtained were a direct outcome of actions for which he was responsible. Conversely, external locus of control describes the child who perceives his actions as irrelevant to the outcome. Dudley-Marling, Snider, and Tarver (1982) suggest that efforts should focus on enhancing the internal locus of control of persons with disabilities, since many activities are avoided by persons with disabilities (including poorly executed leisure time) due to their external locus of control.

Finally, **flow theory** emerged from Czikszentmihalyi's (1974) observation that individuals involved in play sometimes experience a cohesion of their self-awareness. He classified this as flow, an interactive concept. While observing people in various work and play situations, Czikszentmihalyi discovered that some people become so involved in the activity that they lose a sense of reality, and they experience what has been described as an ecstatic flow. Flow does not just occur due to the child's skills and challenges. These elements (skills and challenges) have to be matched with the situation so that skills have appropriately and objectively matched the challenge, which is an outcome that does not always occur in every play situation. It may well be that flow is a **level of consciousness** that many children would aspire to reach, because it represents being in total control. Scholars have also tried to correlate flow theory to the potential delays displayed by persons with developmental disabilities. Wade and Hoover (1985) hypothesized a negative correlation between low intelligence and the ability to experience flow by suggesting that persons with mental retardation may be less able to enjoy traditional flow producing activities. Many activities which demand the use of strategy may be aversive and frustrating. Note that a more complete elaboration of the implications of attribution, locus of control, and flow theory will appear in Chapter 10.

PSYCHOANALYTIC THEORY

Psychoanalytic theory, pioneered by Freud and extended by Erikson to include social influences, focuses on the emotional, intrapsychic development of the child. Two tenets central to this approach are the assertion of psychic determinism (all mental events are interrelated) and the notion of unconscious influences on everyday life. Freud is particularly noted for his tripartite description of the mind and for his articulation of the psychosexual stages of development (see Table 4). In the psychoanalytic view, childhood experience is profoundly related to adult personality and pathology.

While holding to Freud's basic notions about the mind and developmental stages, Erikson (1950) emphasized the ego and expanded the stage theory to encompass social and cultural influences on development. Erikson asserted that development proceeds according to an innate, sequential genetic plan which has its counterpart in social and cultural expectations. For example, biological development dictates the age at which the child can reasonably be toilet trained; members of society, especially parents, expect the child to conform. The process of development is seen by Erikson as a series of eight **normative crises,** each representing a dichotomy. During each crisis, the individual is vulnerable to a particular challenge; optimal resolution of these challenges is

Table 4. Basic Freudian Concepts and Terminology.

Structural Elements of the Mind

1. **Id** — The structural component of the mind composed of innate, instinctual drives. The id is irrational and functions according to the pleasure principle. It constitutes the whole of the infant's mind at birth, is completely unconscious, and seeks immediate gratification.
2. **Ego** — The rational, administrative component of the mind. The ego emerges during the anal period to help the id in meeting its needs by dealing with reality; ego helps id delay gratification.
3. **Superego** — The conscience or moral arbiter. Emerging during the phallic stage, the superego is a demanding and inflexible enforcer of parental injunctions and societal norms. The superego operates at both the unconscious and conscious levels and strives for the ideal.

Psychosexual Stages of Development

1. **Oral stage** (birth to 18 months) — Needs and gratifications are oral. The issues of pleasure and dependency are confronted by the infant in the process of weaning.
2. **Anal Stage** (18 months to 36 months) — Pleasure and energy are centered in one's anal area. With increased physical development, the child confronts, in the conflict of toilet training, societal demands for delay of pleasure.
3. **Phallic stage** (3 to 6 years) — Energy is centered in genital area. A pivotal issue of this stage is the Oedipal conflict, in which the child first desires and then relinquishes the opposite sex parent, developing instead an identification with (a willingness or drive to become like) the same sex parent in the interest of self protection. The development of a sexual identity, acquisition of socially validated sex roles, and emergence of the superego occur during this time.
4. **Latency stage** (6 years to pubertal onset) — Consolidation and recuperation following the Oedipal conflict. The child gives attention to the acquisition of skills and development of peer relations.
5. **Genital stage** (age 12 through adulthood) — Energy is in the genital area. Freud believes issues of earlier stages manifest themselves as fixations as the adult seeks to effectively love and work.

toward the positive pole of the dichotomy (see Table 5 for a description of Erikson's crises).

Psychoanalytic Theory and Play

Psychoanalytic theorists suggest that play serves three major purposes for the child. Reflecting the tenet of psychic determinism, they argue that play allows the child to reduce anxiety and enhance ego-strength by fulfilling undesirable or impossible wishes, by gaining control over threatening or traumatic events, and by expressing otherwise unacceptable feelings. Children are confronted with many situations in which what they wish to do is not allowed. For example, in the effort to identify with

Table 5. Basic Eriksonian Concepts and Terminology.

Psychosocial Stages

1. **Trust vs. Mistrust** (birth to 18 months)—Developing a basic sense that needs will be met and that both the world and the self can be trusted. The risk is that the child will come to have a basic and pervasive sense of insecurity about the self, others, and the world.

2. **Autonomy vs. Shame and Doubt** (18 months to 36 months)—Increasing physical development offers the opportunity to exert control over the body and in the world. The risk is that parental expectations will be so demanding that failures on the part of the child will lead to shame.

3. **Initiative vs. Guilt** (3 to 6 years)—Opportunities to take initiative in the world conflict with the need to avoid violating norms and experiencing guilt. Corresponding to Freud's phallic stage, this crisis contains similar issues of sex-role and moral development.

4. **Industry vs. Inferiority** (6 to 12 years)—Development of skill in using tools and in personally relating to peers poses the risk of feeling inferior. Optimally the child comes to feel competent.

5. **Identity vs. Identity Diffusion** (adolescent years)—Struggle to know the self and become prepared to make occupational and value commitments. The risk is that the accumulated knowledge about the self, the proliferation of options, and the demands of significant others will make it impossible for the individual to develop a unique identity.

6. **Intimacy vs. Isolation** (early adulthood)—Involves being able to share the self in relationships.

7. **Generativity vs. Stagnation** (adulthood)—Involves taking responsibility for future generations.

8. **Ego integrity vs. Despair** (old age)—Being able, or not able, to accept life as it has been lived.

the same-sex parent (important to the child in the phallic stage), the child may wish to engage in developmentally inappropriate behaviors. In play, unlike life, the child can fulfill the wish to be the parent, acting the role of disciplinarian or rule setter. Conversely, the child faced with many environmental demands to mature may, in play, take the opportunity to regress to an earlier state, pretending to be a baby or an animal (Peller, 1952). Sometimes the child's wish is for greater attention or care from parents. Bettelheim (1987) suggests that doll play may reflect a child's efforts to compensate for parental deficiencies. In these instances, play provides the child an acceptable (therefore ego-mediated) avenue for acting out otherwise disallowed behaviors.

As a result of their physical and psychological immaturity, children are faced with many circumstances in which they lack control. Play affords them the opportunity to acquire a sense of control over traumatic or threatening events. Freud identified the repetition compulsion, in which the individual reenacts traumatic events numerous times in order to come to terms with them. Terr (1985) provides an example of this type of play. A school bus full of children in Chowchilla, California, was hijacked, and the kidnappers imprisoned the children in an underground vault. Fortunately, the children were able to escape from the vault to safety. For some time after this event, one of the involved children repeatedly played a game she called "bus" in which she took an active role while commanding her sister and her dolls to play passive roles as her passengers. Psychoanalytic theorists suggest that with each repetition of this game, a larger and larger portion of the trauma of being kidnapped was mastered. The reason why play is more frequent in childhood than in later life may be that the child, who is more likely to be a passive recipient of events, has a greater need to act out the part of the active participant.

Finally, play allows a child an arena for open expression of feelings with fewer restraints than in other areas of life. For example, adults who might otherwise correct a child will allow anger, aggression, and messiness in play. Children whose parents frown on overt sibling rivalry can have dolls or trucks "playfully" attack each other. This presumed free expression of feeling in play is one reason play has become a significant therapeutic technique for dealing with children who have emotional conflicts. (A thorough explanation of play therapy is provided in Chapter 8.)

Limitations of Psychoanalytic Theory

Psychoanalytic theory has been criticized for its subjectivity and lack of scientific rigor; psychoanalytic interpretations of play are no exception to these criticisms. For example, in *Why People Play,* Ellis (1973), asserts that psychoanalytic theory is poorly structured and lacking in testable hypotheses. Even Erikson has suggested that there are times when play is just play, without meaning beyond itself. These criticisms, while valid, have not diminished the attraction of the theory.

Barnett-Morris (personal communication, July 28, 1987) and her colleagues provide examples of the continuing challenges to and attractions of psychoanalytic theory as it applies to play. Initially seeking to discredit the theory, Barnett-Morris found that preschool children used play to work through confusing and upsetting events. In one instance, children facing the potentially difficult experience of their first day at preschool and its attendant separation from their mothers were studied. Children who were disturbed by the novel situation were identified, and physiological and psychological assessments were made. The children were given a choice between being read a story by themselves or in a small group, or being allowed to play with carefully selected toys which presence of others. The children who chose play often enacted scenes involving the imminent arrival of their mothers, and these children showed lower levels of anxiety than those who were read a story. Barnett-Morris suggests that these findings support the psychoanalytic notion that free play helps children work through unpleasantness.

In summary, even though many question the contribution of psychoanalytic theory to the understanding of play, it is felt that this theory makes an important contribution by focusing attention on the role that play serves in the child's emotional development. Piaget's theory and learning theory have not paid much attention to this aspect of play. Moreover, play therapy, which is partially based on psychoanalytic theory, has become nearly standard clinical practice. Play is a widely accepted tool for the assessment of children's emotional states (Goodman & Sours, 1967).

Implications of Psychoanalytic Theory
for Children with Disabilities

Issues of wishes, need for control, and desire to express feelings are as likely to occur among children with disabilities as among children without disabilities. For example, exceptional children may experience numerous situations in which they do not feel in control. This may be particularly true with respect to the frequency of medical treatment. A wealth of material suggests that play, or acting out elements of the experience, allows the child to regain a feeling of control. Many preparation programs urge giving hospitalized children an opportunity to play with hospital related toys or equipment in order to master the trauma of the treatment. The children are encouraged to play out the role of administering the treatment rather than being the recipient of the treatment (Azarnoff & Woody, 1981; Elkins & Roberts, 1983).

Issues of control may also arise among children from special populations, as they are more likely to experience the benevolent overreaction syndrome (Boone & Hartman, 1972). This syndrome describes parents and others who overprotect the child because of her special problems. One result of this overprotection is that the child is not given an opportunity to master situations that she has the capacity to master, because others do things for her. For example, in a midwestern state, children with cancer are invited to attend a special summer camp. One of the 12-year-old campers, whose cancer had been in remission for years, came to camp and was not able to tie his own shoes. His mother had always tied his shoes for him because of her benevolent overreaction to his cancer. Play opportunities may allow exceptional children to feel in control and enable them to demonstrate the range of abilities they have for mastering a situation.

Finally, both Freud and Erikson postulate that development is driven by biological processes. In their theories, children are presumed to be dealing with a series of maturationally induced, age-specific psychological crises or issues. As both devised their theories based on studies of children without disabilities, it is not known how differences in physical and cognitive development may impact the developmental trajectory. Just as theorists suggest that children with disabilities progress through the same sequence of cognitive stages but more slowly than children without disabilities, so children facing physical and cognitive challenges may move through the sequence of emotional crises (in Erikson's terminology) at a slower rate than less challenged children. Thus, parents, peers, and others may need to carefully assess the maturational readiness for normative behaviors in children with disabilities. In some instances, a two-year-old child may not have the physical capabilities for the autonomy crisis; in other instances, the two-year-old may exhibit autonomy issues in ways reflective of his disability. Further, it is not unreasonable to hypothesize that children from special populations face distinct, possibly greater, challenges in resolving the normative crises, placing them at greater risk for a negative outcome. For example, issues of control might continue longer and be exacerbated by benevolent overreaction, thus impairing the child's acquisition of a sense of autonomy. Issues of competency in acquiring skills characteristic of the work requirements of the culture or in relating to peers, which are pivotal to the industry versus inferiority stage, may present more demands to the special child, impinging on later identity development.

AROUSAL THEORY

Arousal theory focuses attention on biological factors, in particular the activities of the central nervous system in keeping the person at an appropriate level of arousal. According to arousal theory, there is an optimal level of arousal that the person seeks to maintain in the reticular activating system. Schultz (1965) called this **sensoristasis** (analogous to the biological concept of homeostasis). When the person is bombarded with stimulation and is overaroused, he seeks to reduce the stimulation. Likewise, if underaroused, the person seeks to increase stimulation. The habituation response and the needs of the reticular activating system (see Table 6) are basic to this theory.

Table 6. Basic Arousal Theory Concepts and Terminology.

1. **Habituation** — This is a loss of interest in a stimulus following repeated presentations. This is a decline of a reflexive response and is the simplest type of learning.
2. **Orienting response** — This is attention directed at a novel stimulus. This response facilitates responding to stimuli and includes physiological changes such as alteration in heart rate and use of visual and auditory systems to incorporate the stimulus.
3. **Reticular activating system** — Located in the lower portion of the brain, this system plays a key role in consciousness, serving as a filter of sensory input. It is a mediating center between incoming sensory stimulation and higher cortical areas.

Arousal Theory and Play

Several versions of the arousal theory of play have been offered: (1) Berlyne (1960, 1966, 1969), (2) Ellis (1973), and (3) Fein (1981). The basic difference between these versions lies in their characterizations of the desired level of arousal and of the influence of play on the direction of arousal (low, moderate, high). A detailed discussion of the distinctions between the three versions is beyond the scope of this chapter; the present elaboration of arousal theory most closely reflects the views of Ellis (1973). (See Rubin, Fein, & Vandenberg (1983) for further discussion.)

"Play is that behavior that is motivated by the need to elevate the level of arousal toward the optimal" (Ellis, 1973, p. 110). According to Ellis (1973), play occurs in situations where the child is underaroused. It is stimulus seeking behavior. Play provides stimulation because it is concerned with characteristics that are associated with stimulation, namely novelty, uncertainty, or complexity. Not just any stimulus will do. The person seeks stimuli that are moderately stimulating, because stimuli that are too novel, too unpredictable, or too complex cause discomfort and neophobia (avoidance of anything unknown), and stimuli that are not novel, not unpredictable, or too simplistic are not arousing.

Limitations of Arousal Theory

White (1959) suggested that arousal theory cannot account for repetitious behavior. In other words, the assertion that novelty, uncertainty, and complexity are necessary for arousal is inconsistent with the observation that perseverative behavior that presumably becomes old, certain, and no longer complex still continues. When discussing repetitious behavior, White implies that each instance of a repetitious behavior is an identical copy of the previous instances of that behavior. Thus, White proposed a variation of the arousal model which he referred to as the Competence/Effectance Model. Basically, this model echoes psychoanalytic theory in proposing that the person engages in repetitious behavior in order to demonstrate control and mastery over the environment. White argues that the urge to control and master the environment explains why an organism would engage in repetitious behavior.

Most scientific research now converges on the view that intrinsic motivation is based on the organismic needs to be competent and self-determining. White (1959) referred to effectence motivation as the innate drive to use playful exploration, learning, and adaptation to develop competency within the environment.

Self-determination refers to the ability of the particular individual to choose an action. To be truly intrinsically motivated, a person must be free of controls, rewards, or contingencies. Research confirms that the opportunity to be self-determining greatly increases intrinsic motivation, while thwarting that behavior certainly undermines intrinsic motivation (Deci & Ryan, 1985). As the development of intrinsic motivation within exceptional children is desired, optimal play activities are those helping to effect this goal. This suggests that not only should play activities incorporate this emphasis, but other alternatives will have to also be considered (e.g., working with families so they will encourage the transfer and maintenance of this behavior in other aspects of the child's life). The data on the impact of locus of control on leisure participation are, at best, unclear. On the one hand are findings similar to those of Pittman, Emery and Boggiano (1985), which suggest that those who are highly intrinsically motivated place a high value on leisure time, in comparison to those who are extrinsically driven who appear to have opposite conceptions. However, the work of Kleiber (1979) and Kleiber and Crandall (1981) suggests that persons motivated internally are less, rather than more, likely to have a significant commitment to recreation participation. The interpretation given is due in part to the fact that recreation involvement may inconsistently uphold the traditional values of a Puritan work ideology.

Implications of Arousal Theory for Children with Disabilities

Goldstein and Lancy (1985) proposed a cognitive deficit hypothesis that complements the stimulus arousal theory of play. According to the cognitive deficit hypothesis, one of the problems that may dramatically influence some children with disabilities is their faulty reticular activating system. For example, autistic children who engage in perseverative behaviors, such as spinning a top for hours, may do so because their filtering system allows too much stimulation in. These children are overwhelmed by all of the stimuli coming through their faulty filtering system, and their way of coping is to structure and order incoming stimuli by engaging in perseverative behavior. Note, however, that while this is an intriguing hypothesis, it is not widely accepted. Ellis (1973) points out that institutionalized individuals with mental retardation also emit stereotyped, perseverative behavior but for a different reason. He hypothesized that persons with mental retardation emit stereotyped responses, not because there are not enough complex stimuli in their environments, but because they are incapable of systematizing and manipulating the cognitive or symbolic elements that they represent.

SUMMARY AND THE ROLE OF CONTEXT

Historically, four classical theories were proposed to explain the nature of play. Each of these received little empirical support; all were refuted on philosophical grounds. Contemporary theories, whose formulations were probably influenced by classical theories, each have unique contributions to an understanding of play. Piaget's theory addressed the role of play in cognitive development. An important implication of Piaget's ideas is that if children with and without disabilities play together, intellectual development will be enhanced for both groups of children. Specifically, children without disabilities may exhibit slightly more mature levels of thinking to the children with disabilities, which may cause the children with disabilities to accommodate to these slightly higher levels of thinking. The children without disabilities also benefit cognitively by being in a teaching role. Also, Piaget's theory draws attention to the importance of providing physical and logicomathematical experience for children with special needs, either in areas in which they may have a deficit due to their disability or in areas that may compensate for their disability.

Learning theorists characterize play as one among many types of actions making up the child's behavioral repertoire. Play serves as a means for learning about the social world. For example, play provides opportunities for acquiring sex-role and aggressive or nonaggressive behaviors. Learning principles can also be used to shape the play behavior of children who do not play appropriately. This may require breaking down the goal behavior into smaller, manageable parts and teaching each of these prerequisite behaviors.

The focus of psychoanalytic theory is on the role of play in the child's emotional development. A major contribution of this theory is its highlight on the importance of permitting special children to express mastery through play and to come to terms with things that bother them through this medium. As such, the psychodynamic implementation of play and art therapy are excellent resources for aiding children in self-expression and discovery.

Arousal theory focuses attention on biological factors in play. Its major contributions are the hypothesized role of the reticular activating system in mediating arousal and the influence of overarousal and underarousal on play. This theory provides a starting point for thinking about how to provide optimally arousing play activities for children with special needs.

At the beginning of this chapter, it was suggested that the adoption of an eclectic perspective about play may be useful. As can be seen from the above review of the major theories of play, each has its strengths and limitations. It was also pointed out that these theories tend to focus on different aspects of development. It is crucial to be concerned with the whole child, i.e., with the cognitive, social, emotional, and physical aspects of a child, and thus it is valuable to consider the contributions of all theories.

The chapter also opened with a fictional scenario involving four theorists behind a one-way mirror who were analyzing a child who was playing with a jack-in-the-box. **Ecological systems** theorists (e.g., Belsky, 1980; Bronfenbrenner, 1979, 1993) have noted the importance of considering how a child's unique characteristics interact with his surroundings, or context. There are three implications of this theory.

First, since all individuals live within a context, assumptions about children according to any of the theories discussed in this chapter (i.e., Piagetian, Learning, Psychoanalytic, Arousal) must be made within the umbrella of the child's context. In other words, context envelopes ideas presented by any of these theories. Second, assessments of a child playing in a laboratory setting may present a distorted picture of how a child typically plays in a more naturalistic setting. Thus, it is recommended that children with special needs be assessed in a naturalistic rather than solely in a laboratory or clinical setting. A second implication of the ecological systems perspective has to do with the idea that the child and his context continually influence each other in a bidirectional or transactional manner. As one example of this bidirectionality, consider timidity and context and how they affect each other. Kagan and his associates (Kagan, Snidman, & Arcus, 1992) find evidence that timidity is a temperamental trait that is relatively consistent over childhood and has a biological basis. Parents of a timid child with disabilities may react to him by overprotecting him, e.g., by limiting his social interactions and limiting his responsibilities. Andy, a 10-year-old in a wheelchair, is articulate and composed when speaking with his parents. However, because of his timid nature around nonfamily members, his parents always answer for him when others ask him questions as simple as "How old are you?" Andy has had fewer opportunities to communicate with others outside his family and is relatively immature and dependent upon his family. Thus, his timidity affects how his parents and others interact with him and how social situations and experiences in turn affect him.

In planning any type of program to enhance play experiences for exceptional children, it is important to heed the thoughts expressed by psychologist David Elkind (1981) in *The Hurried Child.* He suggests that children are not allowed to play anymore because play is poorly understood in today's society. Children are often robbed of their childhood; rather than having opportunities to play at their own pace, children are enrolled in structured activities to fill up their play time, such as ballet lessons, organized team sports (where the goal may be winning, not just having fun), and computer camp. The traditional rites of passage come too early for most children. They are constantly confronted with the fear of failure and of living up to someone else's expectations. Unfortunately, the children of the nineties are forced to achieve more as well as earlier than those of any other generation. With this orientation, children are cheated out of having fun and exploring. Being a dreamer has become a taboo for these children. Along the same line, Brian Sutton-Smith (1985) writes that contemporary technology may be robbing children of important developmental opportunities. The wide availability of expensive, attractive toys may promote increased isolated play, limiting the child's opportunity to engage in the rich social exchanges afforded by group play. An important avenue for future study is to explore whether the complexity and sophisticated nature of contemporary toys, from computer simulations to dolls that can become instantly pregnant by donning a special smock, will ultimately enrich or rob children of developmental opportunities. An important implication is the need to promote and enhance play for special children without hurrying them through childhood.

The theories overviewed in this chapter have focused on cognitive, social, emotional, and biological aspects of play. Considered together, the chapter highlights the major strands of development (Santrock, 1986) associated with play.

REFERENCES

Azarnoff, P. & Woody, P.D. (1981). Preparation of children for hospitalization in acute care hospitals in the U.S. *Pediatrics, 68,* 361–367.

Bandura, A. (1973). *Aggression: A social learning analysis.* Englewood Cliffs, NJ: Prentice-Hall.

Bandura, A. (1983). Psychological mechanisms of aggression. In R.G. Geen & E.I. Donnerstein (Eds.), *Aggression: Theoretical and empirical reviews* (Vol. 1). New York: Academic Press.

Barnett, L. & Kane, M. (1985). Individual constraints on children's play. In M.G. Wade (Ed.), *Constraints on leisure* (pp. 43–81). Springfield, IL: Charles C Thomas.

Beach, F.A. (1945). Current concepts of play in animals. *American Naturalist, 79,* 523–541.

Bee, H. (1986). *The developing child* (4th ed.). New York: Harper and Row.

Belsky, J. (1980). Child maltreatment: An ecological integration. *American Psychologist, 35,* 320–335.

Berlyne, D.E. (1960). *Conflict, arousal, and curiosity.* New York: McGraw-Hill.

Berlyne, D.E. (1966). Curiosity and exploration. *Science, 153,* 25–33.

Berlyne, D.E. (1969). Laughter, humor, and play. In G.L. Lindzey & E. Eronson (Eds.), *Handbook of social psychology* pp. 795–853). New York: Addison-Wesley.

Bettelheim, B. (1987). *A good enough parent.* New York: Alfred A. Knopf.

Bronfenbrenner, U. (1979). *The ecology of human development: Experiments by nature and design.* Cambridge, MA: Harvard University Press.

Bronfenbrenner, U. (1993). The ecology of cognitive development: Research models and fugitive finds. In R.H. Wozniak & K.W. Fischer (Eds.), *Development in context: Acting and thinking in specific environments.* Hillsdall, NJ: Erlbaum.

Boone, D.R. & Hartman, B.H. (1972). The benevolent over-reaction. *Clinical Pediatrics, 11,* 268–271.

Cooper, J., Moodley, M., & Reynell, J. (1978). *Helping language development.* Bath, England: Arnold.

Czikszentmihalyi, M. (1974). *Flow: Studies of enjoyment.* Chicago, IL: University of Chicago Press.

Deci, E. & Ryan, R. (1985). *Intrinsic motivation and self-determination in human behavior.* New York: Plenum.

Dixon, J. (1979). The implications of attribution theory for therapeutic recreation service. *Therapeutic Recreation Journal, 8*(1), 3–11.

Dudley-Marling, C., Snider, V., & Tarver, S. (1982). Locus of control and learning disabilities: A review and discussion. *Perceptual and Motor Skills, 54*(4), 503–514.

Elkind, D. (1981). *The hurried child: Growing up too fast too soon.* Reading, MA: Addison-Wesley.

Elkins, P.D. & Roberts, M.C. (1983). Psychological preparation for pediatric hospitalization. *Clinical Psychology Review, 3,* 275–295.

Ellis, M. (1973). *Why people play.* Englewood Cliffs, NJ: Prentice-Hall.

Erikson, E. (1950). *Childhood and society.* New York: Norton.

Eron, L.D. & Huesmann, L.R. (1984). Television violence and aggressive behavior. In B.B. Lahey & A.E. Kazdin (Eds.), *Advances in clinical child psychology* (Vol. 7). New York: Plenum.

Eron, L.D. & Huesmann, L.R. (1986). The role of television in the development of prosocial and antisocial behavior. In D. Olweus, J. Block, & M. Radke-Yarrow (Eds.), *Development of antisocial and prosocial behavior.* Orlando, FL: Academic Press.

Fine, A., Lehrer, B., & Feldis, D. (1982). Therapeutic recreation programming for autistic children. *Therapeutic Recreation Journal, 15,* 6–11.

Fein, G.G. (1981). Pretend play: An integrative review. *Child Development, 52,* 1095–1118.

Flavell, J.H., Miller, P.H., & Miller, S.A. (1993). *Cognitive development* (3rd ed.). Englewood Cliffs, NJ: Prentice-Hall.

Fromm, E. (1941). *Escape from freedom.* New York: Rinehart.

Goldstein, G.I. & Lancy, D.F. (1985). Cognitive development in autistic children. In L.S. Siegel & F.J. Morrison (Eds.), *Cognitive development in atypical children.* New York: Springer-Verlag.

Goodman, J.D. & Sours, J.A. (1987). *The child mental status exam.* New York: Basic Books.

Groos, K. (1898). *The play of animals.* New York: Appleton.

Groos, K. (1901). *The play of man.* New York: Appleton.

Gulick, L. (1898). Some psychical aspects of physical exercise. *Popular Science Monthly, 58,* 793–805.

Hall, G.S. (1920). *Youth.* New York: Appleton.

Hill, P. & McCune-Nicolich, L. (1981). Pretend play and patterns of cognition in Down's syndrome children. *Child Development, 52,* 611–617.

Huesmann, L.R. & Miller, L.S. (1994). Long-term effects of repeated exposure to media violence in childhood. In L.R. Huesmann (Ed.), *Aggressive behavior: Current perspectives.* New York: Plenum.

Inhelder, B. (1968). *The diagnosis of reasoning in the mentally retarded.* New York: John Day.

Iso-Ahola, S. (1980). *The social psychology of leisure and recreation.* Dubuque, IA: William C. Brown.

Kagan, J., Snidman, N., & Arcus, D.M. (1992). Initial reactions to unfamiliarity. *Current Directions in Psychological Science, 1,* 171–174.

Kleiber, D. (1979). Fate control and leisure attitudes. *Leisure Sciences, 2,* 239–248.

Kleiber, D. & Crandall, R. (1981). Leisure and work ethics and locus of control. *Leisure Sciences, 4,* 477–485.

Lamb, M.E., Easterbrooks, M.S., & Holden, G.W. (1980). Reinforcement and punishment among preschoolers: Characteristics, effects, and correlates. *Child Development, 51,* 1230–1236.

Lamb, M.E. & Roopnarine, J.L. (1979). Peer influences on sex-role development in preschoolers. *Child Development, 50,* 1219–1222.

Lazarus, M. (1883). *Die reize des spiels.* Berlin: Ferd, Dummlers Verlagsbuchhandlung.

Liebert, R.M. & Spiegler, M.D. (1994). *Personality strategies and issues* (7th ed.). Pacific Grove, CA: Brooks-Cole.

Patrick, G.T.W. (1916). *The psychology of relaxation.* Boston: Houghton-Mifflin.

Peller, L.E. (1952). Models of children's play. *Mental Hygiene, 36,* 66–83.

Piaget, J. (1962). *Play, dreams, and imitation in childhood* (G. Gattegno & F.M. Hodgson, Trans.). New York: Norton.

Pittman, T., Emery, J., & Boggiano, A. (1985). Intrinsic and extrinsic motivational orientations: Reward induced changes in preference for complexity. *Journal of Personality and Social Psychology, 42*(5), 789–797.

Rubin, K.H., Fein, G.G., & Vandenberg, B. (1983). Play. In P.H. Mussen (Ed.), *Handbook of child psychology* pp. 693–774. New York: Wiley.

Rutter, M. (1978). Diagnosis and definition. In M. Rutter & E. Schopler (Eds.), *Autism: A reappraisal of concepts and treatment.* New York: Plenum.

Sandler, A. & Wills, D. (1965). Preliminary notes on play and mastery in the blind child. *Journal of Child Psychotherapy, 1,* 7.

Schiller, F. (1954). *On the aesthetic education of man.* New Haven, CT: Yale University Press.

Schultz, D.D. (1965). *Sensory restriction: Effects on behavior.* New York: Academic Press.

Spencer, H. (1873). *Principles of psychology* (Vol. 2, 3rd ed.). New York: Appleton.

Sutton-Smith, B. (1966). Piaget on play: A critique. *Psychological Review, 73,* 104–110.

Sutton-Smith, B. (1985, October). The child at play. *Psychology Today, 19.*

Terr, L.C. (1985). Psychic trauma in children and adolescents. *Psychiatric Clinics of North America, 8,* 815–836.

Toeffler, A. (1971). *Future shock.* New York: Random House.

Wade, M. & Hoover, J. (1985). Mental retardation as a constraint on leisure. In M. Wade (ed.), *Constraints on leisure.* Springfield, IL: Charles C Thomas.

Weiner, B. (1985). *Human motivation.* New York: Springer.

White, R.W. (1959). Motivation reconsidered: The concept of competence. *Psychological Review, 66,* 297–323.

Chapter 3

THERAPEUTIC RECREATION— WHAT IS IT ALL ABOUT?

Nya Fine, Robyn Coffman and Aubrey Fine

Let me be the best I can. . . . Let me be me. . . . Let me in,
I want to play . . .

INTRODUCTION

Therapeutic recreation (TR), a viable avenue for providing leisure involvement for individuals with limitations, has grown tremendously over the last thirty years. Consequently, the outcome of these services has helped children, their parents, and other professionals recognize that recreation is a basic human need that must be met.

The purpose, practices, and the impact of therapeutic recreation will be discussed as well as its complimentary occupations known as the allied health professions. The following questions will be answered.

1. Therapeutic recreation—What is it all about? Why did it evolve?
2. What is the philosophical orientation of therapeutic recreation and how did it originate? What are the significant implications of the proposed philosophy on services for children?
3. How has recreation and persons with disabilities been viewed through various stages of history?
4. Where does one find therapeutic recreation programs today? How has the community's perception been effected due to integration?
5. What is the allied health profession? What allied health services compliment therapeutic recreation?

THERAPEUTIC RECREATION—
ITS CONTENT AND EVOLUTION

Back in the late 1950s, recreation theorists warned that due to reduced working hours, people would have to learn how to spend their time in a wholesome manner (Rathborne and Lucas, 1970). As a result, recreation developed into a distinct discipline. Play, recreation, and leisure have been recognized by many as valuable elements for the development of many skills in people. All people—young, old, able, or disabled—have the same basic needs for physical release, creative self-expression, social interaction, and the desire to have fun. Thus, individuals with disabilities should have equal opportunity to experience recreation and receive its benefits even though this is often denied to them.

Therapeutic recreation seeks to serve, not ignore, the needs of people of all ages particularly those who may be developmentally disabled, physically disabled, mentally ill, socially deviant, aged, or have a traumatic brain injury. Populations in need of therapeutic recreation have not greatly shifted over the course of time. However, a new population has emerged in the 1980s and 1990s that many times silently cries out for such a service. They are commonly referred as "at-risk youth." They consist of street kids, early teens in schools, gangs, and the like who are easily tempted or prone to a life of crime, violence, or indifference which is often used as a mechanism to seek attention, resolve boredom, or release anger and energy (Wooden, 1995).

Throughout the development of therapeutic recreation services, there existed a particular need to have a philosophical frame of reference. The term **therapeutic recreation** created many questions that needed to be answered. As a result, many individual definitions, philosophies, and concepts were formulated based on one's own view of recreation, education, and experience. Is the philosophy of therapeutic recreation any different than the philosophy of recreation? Is not all recreation therapeutic in nature? Yes. However, the application and the utilization of recreation activities are the key ingredients in the development and delivery of therapeutic recreation services.

Therapeutic recreation harnesses a powerful source (recreation) and channels the energies, benefits, and results within the delivery of services. In turn, it opens the door for leisure involvement for individuals who have limitations.

The conception of therapeutic recreation at its most earliest known definition is dated back to 1936.

Recreational therapy may be defined as any free, voluntary and expressive activity; motor, sensory or mental, vitalized by the expressive play spirit, sustained by deep-rooted pleasurable attitudes and evoked by wholesome emotional release. (Davis, 1936, p. xi)

However, it was believed the term therapeutic recreation was first applied in 1938 by the Work Progress Administration to describe all recreational activities intended to serve the disabled, maladjusted or other institutionalized persons. With the growth of recreation programs in hospitals and institutions, recreation activities often were (and continue to be) prescribed by the medical personnel. "Therapeutic recreation became a term applied to programs of prescribed recreation activities as well as to those programs in which persons with illnesses or disabilities participated" (Shivers and Fait, 1985, p. 7). Hospital recreation, medical recreation, recreation for the ill and handicapped, and recreation for special populations were terms utilized in the developmental stages of the profession.

Doctor William C. Menninger (1948) is one of the earliest professionals who made a statement in reference to the value of recreation with special populations:

It has been the privilege of many practicing medicine in psychiatry to have some very rewarding experiences in the use of recreation as an adjunctive method of treatment. Along with direct psychological help, hydrotherapy, shock, and insulin therapy, many of us have for years used various forms of education, recreation, and occupation in the treatment of our patients. Recreation has not only played an important part in the treatment program of many illnesses, but it has been a considerable factor in enabling former patients to remain well. (p. 304)

Virginia Frye (1969) provided another perspective on therapeutic recreation's impact.

Therapeutic pertains to the art and science of healing. Recreation can be said to be therapeutic only to the extent that specific beneficial efforts of a recreative experience can be identified and predicted. It is in relation to the specific medical treatment that therapeutic recreation becomes a specialized area within the total recreation profession. (p. 12)

Since Doctor Menninger's thoughts on the value of recreation for the mentally ill and Frye's point of view, many different perspectives have developed. Although diverse, these perspectives contained similar ideas that incorporated both the value of recreation for fun and the purposes of rehabilitation. Many professionals have spent countless hours searching, discussing, and developing a conclusive philosophical statement that the entire profession could utilize. In order to produce a quality definition of therapeutic recreation, it must employ the following components: acknowledgement of the purpose of therapeutic recreation, recognition of the populations needing to be served, identification of the focus areas given the population that must be addressed, and incorporation of therapeutic perspectives and values along with the true essence of recreation, i.e. enjoyment. Simply, it focuses on two themes: "(1) the purposeful nature of the use of recreation/leisure as an intervention, and (2) the personal enhancement of the client as a result of the intervention" (Austin and Crawford, 1991).

In May 1982, a statement was adopted by the Board of Directors of the National Therapeutic Recreation Society (NTRS), a branch of the National Recreation and Parks Association. NTRS is one of the professional organizations that fosters the development and advancement of therapeutic recreation. The lengthy philosophy states:

> Leisure, including recreation and play are inherent aspects of the human experience. The importance of appropriate leisure involvement has been documented throughout history. More recently, research has addressed the value of leisure involvement in human development, in social and family relationships, and in general as an important aspect of the quality of life. Some human beings have disabilities, illnesses or social conditions which limit their full participation in the normative social structure of society. These individuals with limitations have the same human rights and needs for leisure involvement.
>
> The purpose of therapeutic recreation is to facilitate the development, maintenance and expression of an appropriate leisure life-style for individuals with physical, mental, emotional or social limitations. This purpose is accomplished through the provision of professional programs and services which assist the individual in eliminating barriers to leisure, developing leisure skills and attitudes, and optimizing leisure involvement. (NTRS, 1982)
>
> > Therapeutic recreation utilizes three areas of service: therapy, leisure education, and recreation participation. When and where each of these services is provided depends on the assessment of client's needs. A client may need programs from all three areas of services, while another client may need assistance in one area.
> >
> > The **therapy** service focuses on the improvement of functional behaviors that limit or inhibit leisure involvement. The therapeutic recreation professional determines what individuals require to enable them to be involved in meaningful leisure experiences. In this role, the therapeutic recreator is an integral member of the interdisciplinary treatment team, and with the development of

the treatment goals, leisure-related functional behaviors and leisure ability are incorporated.

The **leisure education** service provides individuals with the opportunity to acquire and develop leisure skills and behaviors. This service area is very important, since a majority of individuals with limitations lack the skills necessary to engage in leisure experiences.

The third service area is **recreation participation.** All individuals are entitled to recreation opportunities. The therapeutic recreator provides opportunities which allow voluntary involvement in recreation skills and activities.

The philosophy adopted by NTRS supported that recreation is an important aspect in everyone's lifestyle. Therapeutic recreation provides opportunity for individuals with disabilities to express themselves via the use of recreation. However, the position statement differs from previous definitions in that the statement incorporates how therapeutic recreation services can be utilized. Assessment of the individual's needs provides for the development of the program plan. The planned application of recreation is vital to the delivery of the services. The process, a planned recreation intervention, should also be fun, thus basing the activities on the individual being served.

It has been noted by the National Therapeutic Recreation Society that therapeutic recreation serves to "improve physical abilities, build confidence, promote greater self-reliance, ease fear, anger, and despair, strengthen interpersonal skills, manage stress, and enrich the quality of life" (NTRS, 1986). By doing so, the participant acquires or enhances invaluable personal qualities. Recipients of therapeutic recreation may begin to find more effective and/or appropriate ways to "accept responsibility, learn by doing, set goals, act assertively, express feelings, learn new skills, develop new interests, and use leisure well" (NTRS, 1986). By incorporating these goals of therapeutic recreation into the lives of exceptional children, integration and participation from childhood through adulthood with mainstream society becomes a challenge that is promising and worthwhile!

The philosophical base of the profession is and will continue to evolve, resulting in a better understanding which will increase the identity of therapeutic recreation and have greater effects on the population it serves.

PHILOSOPHY OF THERAPEUTIC RECREATION AS IT RELATES TO CHILDREN

The philosophical statement has definite implications to all disabled individuals, including children. However, one must realize that although the philosophy differentiates between the various areas of services (therapy, leisure education, recreation participation), it does not focus on the process (techniques) utilized in working with children. Such processes will be lightly addressed momentarily.

Throughout the book it has been discussed that it is important for a child to be involved in fun, productive, free time. Professionally, we feel strongly that play can contribute to the well-being (physical, mental, social, emotional). We must also recognize that a major contribution of therapeutic recreation is that it allows a child to be involved in a fun activity which may enhance learning. Dixon (Chap. 4) suggests that recreation can serve as an important resource for a child by providing accessibility information to leisure opportunities.

What exactly can therapeutic recreation offer an exceptional child? It simply helps to facilitate healthy relationships in so doing, allowing children the opportunity to "let off steam" and gain insight into their behavior and that of others which serves as a basis for reality testing and developing of socially appropriate behavior. In essence, it satisfies their social hunger or deprivation, enhances maturity, diminishes fears, identifies roles with society, and when designed for success, it may relieve feelings of failure and unacceptance.

All the services of therapeutic recreation are valuable, but the main goal for a child should focus on the awareness and acquisition of skills that would enable a child to participate in self-selected activities throughout life. Therefore, it is imperative that this goal not be overlooked but be incorporated into all programs when working with children.

HISTORY OF RECREATION AND THE TREATMENT OF PERSONS WITH DISABILITIES

Throughout history, it has been documented that even the earliest society had some form of recreation. Dance, music, arts, and games were important aspects of the primitive cultures. These forms of recreation and others are now considered part of an allied health profession, offering an accredited degree and certification to become a dance, music, or art therapist. More information about these professions will be given later in this chapter. From a historical perspective, let us look at how recreation and the attitudes toward the disabled were viewed.

In the primitive ages man lived in an environment that placed a high priority on survival skills. Recreation was utilized as a means of obtaining and improving those survival skills through games. Since survival skills were the utmost importance, those who did not possess these skills had no support.

In ancient civilization it was believed that the use of recreational activities was a form of therapy. Music, reading poems, and walks in the gardens were planned or prescribed activities by the medicine men, priests, and healers. In early societies of Egypt, Greece, Rome, and China, they had well-organized systems of care and treatment for afflicted people (Shivers and Fait, 1985). As time progressed so did the belief that disabilities were caused by evil spirits. Consequently, it became an accepted fact by many that the only way to destroy the spirit was to kill the individual (Beyer, 1979).

The Greek civilization was concerned with the treatment of the whole person. Music, exercise, and other activities were used to relax the mind and body. Hippocrates was the first to endeavor in understanding disabilities. He taught that illnesses and disabilities were not a form of punishment from God. However, the emphasis remained on treating the well person to being more healthy rather than addressing the needs of the disabled.

The philosophy of taking care of the sick evolved in the Roman era. A hospital was established to take care and provide assistance to the injured while incorporating various activities as a form of treatment. However, at the same time, the Romans did not accept disabled individuals. They frequently placed defective children in baskets which were then thrown into the river or abandoned on a public street. It was quite common for someone to come along and take a child and raise the child as a slave (Beyer, 1979).

A change occurred during the fourteenth and fifteenth centuries. Leisure and play were being viewed as evil and were not to be partaken. The attitudes toward the disabled person fluctuated between acceptance and rejection. The church provided custodial care in the monasteries, but there was an inherent attitude problem. Through various teachings, the birth of a handicapped child was accepted proof that the parents were involved in witchcraft. Consequently, the deformed or abnormal child was regarded with great fear as if a family was being punished by God. It was also during this time when a large number of men and women who were handicapped were burned as witches.

As the Renaissance era began, social events and village activities made a significant contribution to the people of the villages. There were great advances in scientific thinking in which doctors discovered some of the causes and symptoms of physical disabilities. Thus, fewer people believed that the disabled were possessed by evil spirits. Custodial support was to be found which brought an end to confinement for the physically disabled and the mentally retarded. However, the disabled population still remained the outcasts of society. During this time many of the disabled were in constant demand to be court jesters or village fools. In fact, today's view of one who exhibits deviant behavior as either a public nuisance or a subhuman object stemmed from this era (Carter, Van Andel, and Robb, 1985).

During the seventeenth century the highlights of leisure activities consisted of adults and children partaking in festivals and games. Involvement in play promoted an understanding for children in learning their roles in society, while adults used leisure outlets for relaxation and diversion from work (Butler, Gotts, and Quisenberry, 1978).

When the English settlers began their way to the New World, the disabled settlers were prohibited from the journey. Life in the New World for disabled citizens consisted primarily of being farmed out for assistance or for basic board care. The young government did accept its responsibility for the welfare of the soldiers and civilians who were permanently injured during the Revolutionary War. These individuals were accepted as dependent on the government or the members of the community. It appears that a definite difference existed between the war heroes and the general disabled population.

The negative attitudes and barriers of the disabled also existed in the early days of this nation. However, there were some prominent individuals who did not let their physical disabilities stop their great contributions to society. Peter Stuyvesant had lost a leg during the war and wore a peg leg. He was a successful leader and became the first governor of the Dutch colony of Amsterdam (New York). Stephen Hopkins, an individual afflicted with cerebral palsy, was one of the signing members of the Declaration of Independence.

The Americans and the British began treating the disabled with more consideration in the eighteenth century. This was due to the influence of the Protestant attitude. This attitude reflected that each individual must strive for perfection and acceptance of all. Consequently, this led to a change towards helping the ill and the disabled.

During the eighteenth and nineteenth centuries the focus began to change from primarily custodial care to attempts of basic rehabilitation. Jean Itard, a French physician, initiated the first documented scientific attempt at habilitating a mentally retarded child. The now famous story of the Boy of Averon was initiated through Itard's efforts. Although his efforts did not demonstrate significant growth in the child's cognitive and language abilities, the boy displayed significant growth in his adaptive behavior. In 1773, an asylum for the mentally ill was established, and a private school for the deaf in the early 1800s. Between 1829–1832, schools were founded in New York, Pennsylvania, and Massachusetts.

Samuel Howe organized the first school for the blind, later called the Perkins Institute. Thomas Hopkins Gallaudet was one of the first involved in working with the deaf. He became involved with a neighbor's child who became deaf at the age of four. Through his efforts he taught her how to be independent and self-sufficient. In 1817, he founded the Hartford School for the Deaf, and in 1864 his brother, Edward Gallaudet, opened a college in Washington, D.C. for the deaf. Although services began to develop for persons who were blind and deaf, people with other disabilities still did not have the same opportunities. These individuals remained the responsibility of their family.

Various physicians utilized planned activities such as gardening, reading, and music as a form of treatment for their patients. Florence Nightingale introduced recreational opportunities for hospitalized soldiers. She utilized music and pets as a form of treatment. Before World War I, structured recreation programs were virtually nonexistent. Institutions in the early 1900s organized programs directed at alleviating overcrowding and to provide human care and resident services. Activities were planned and implemented to consume time, prevent boredom, and prevent the occurrence of behavior problems (Wehman, 1979).

Various charitable organizations were evolving to assist the disabled. President Hoover in his first year of presidency was involved with the development of a conference for the protection of children. In this conference, national goals for children were established. One of these goals stated that

> every child who is blind, deaf, crippled, or otherwise physically or mentally handicapped, that such measures as early diagnosis, care, treatment, and the

training of the child will be evaluated. Through the training the individual may become a asset to society rather than a liability. Expenses of these services should be met publicly when they cannot be met privately (Dean, 1972).

The American Red Cross headed one of the major thrusts in providing recreation for the disabled in the armed forces. The position relating to leisure services stated that

> recreation is helpful in sustaining and cultivating morale favorable to treatment and in developing human capacities. We do not consider that recreation is therapy. We do consider that it should be an added constructive force in the recovery of the patient. Perhaps that is what other people call therapeutic, but that it should be part of the medical treatment is not one of the basic fundamental principles of the American Red Cross (Rathborne and Lucas, 1979, p. 11).

When World War I began, the American Red Cross established the Division of Recreation. Along with the initiation of these services in the armed forces, recreation programs began to appear in state hospitals. It was at this time that recreation really began to be acknowledged for its therapeutic benefits. As a consequence of World War II, there was an apparent attitude change toward all disabled individuals. This was due to the many new disabled veterans about to reenter the country.

In 1945, the Veterans Administration established services as part of their programs. Hospitals provided appropriate recreation activities that enabled patients with physical or mental limitations to participate. Recreators modified the activities to meet the special needs (Shivers and Fait, 1985). Doctor John Davis also built into the care system his ideas of sports, prescribed exercises, and graduated activities.

Another historical milestone was the emergence of organizations promoting the development and growth of the therapeutic recreation profession. During the late 1940s and early 1950s three important organizations were formally established: the American Recreation Society (ARS, 1949), the Recreation Therapy Section of the American Association for Health, Physical Education, and Recreation (RTS–AAHPER, 1952), and the National Association for Recreation Therapists, Inc. (NART, 1953) (O'Morrow, 1986). These organizations merged to form form the National Recreation and Park Association (NRPA). This change unified the park, recreation, and leisure service movement. In October 1966, the National Therapeutic Recreation Society became a part of the National Recreation and Parks Association. This created a major evolution for the profession. The future direction of the field continued to develop. The American Therapeutic Recreation Association (ATRA, 1985) is the most recent established professional organization concerned with the development and the growth of therapeutic recreation.

All of these societies represent the hearts and souls of the field. Consequently, attempts to ensure the quality as well as to voice the concerns of the field as a whole has been a major goal. The bottom line is that they provide the professionals with the unity and dedication it takes to transform a young, powerful, and ever-growing profession. This will guarantee the evolution of a valuable and prominent profession that will enhance the lives of many.

THERAPEUTIC RECREATION — WHERE DOES ONE FIND THESE PROGRAMS?

Most therapeutic recreation programs do not function independently but operate within a system that provides a specific type of care or service (O'Morrow, 1980). These services are often found in clinical or community-based settings. It is imperative that parent and other professionals become aware of these services in order to tap into all possible resources for direction and assistance.

Clinical Settings

Therapeutic recreation services may be found in the following clinical settings: general hospitals, physical rehabilitation centers, extended and long-term health care facilities, private and public psychiatric facilities, residential or school centers, and community health centers.

In the clinical settings, the therapeutic recreation specialist looks at the behavioral and functional skills for the individual and how they affect their leisure. Carl Rogers, who developed the client-centered therapy, believed that the helping professional should be supportive, empathetic, and genuine. Through this mode the therapist allows the client to feel secure and to grow at his/her own pace. The client-oriented approach is often applied to therapeutic recreation.

The medical-clinical model, a widely accepted approach, is "characterized by a doctor-centered, illness-oriented approach to patient care and treatment. Treatment is directed at rehabilitating the disease alone rather than the whole person" (O'Morrow, 1980, p. 169). In this type of setting the doctor is the one who prescribes the treatment and how it will be done. The professional staff is involved only in the delivery of the services as ordered by the physician.

This model is still adhered to in some settings, but many are incorporating an interdisciplinary approach to treatment. In this approach the entire staff of professionals are involved with the formation of goals and treatment plan for the client. An interdisciplinary team will consist of doctors, nurses, psychologists, therapeutic recreation specialists (may be referred to as recreation therapist, activity therapist), physical therapists, occupation therapists, social workers, and other individuals who are involved with the treatment of the individual.

Each discipline contributes to the various goals that are formulated for the client. The therapeutic recreation specialist is responsible for incorporating the importance of leisure in the context of the total treatment plan (Peterson and Gunn, 1984).

Several institutions in the United States have demonstrated the utilization of therapeutic recreation services as a key ingredient in the multidisciplinary setting. Casa Colina Centers for Rehabilitation located in southern California has a national reputation not only for its institution but also for their therapeutic recreation programs. Therapeutic recreation programs play an integral part in the overall rehabilitation process.

Community Recreation

Leisure and recreational activities play a major role in the lives of most community residents, and a large number of these residents are disabled. Through history it is evident that society's perception of people with disabilities has been damaging to the awareness and acceptance of their right to a quality lifestyle. Segregation, until the last twenty-five years, had been the chosen way to deal with and treat the disabled population. Deinstitutionalization began in the sixties and led to the flight of normalization and integration as an effort to acknowledge the disabled population's rights, needs, and dignity. The normalization principle, a process to make mainstream society's patterns and norms available to persons with mental retardation, was introduced into society by Bengt Nirje (1969). Although it was geared directly towards those who were mentally retarded, it has had a rippling effect on the disabled population as a whole by emphasizing the quality of life which every person deserves. "When people are grouped together and then separated from others, for whatever reason, the differences between the groups, rather than the similarities, appear to become the focus of attention" (Austin and Crawford, 1991). Integration has served to break the traditional mold of stereotyping groups and classes judged on differences and reinforce the commonalities, the need for socialization into mainstream, and the rights of those segregated to participate normatively as possible. However, one's physical presence does not constitute integration. Integration is only meaningful when it involves social integration and acceptance (Wolfensberger, 1972). Not only is integration effective for people with disabilities, it has made an impact on mainstream society as well by promoting an accurate awareness of the often stereotyped population. With the movement of deinstitutionalization and integration, there is a greater need for the expansion of community-based programs. Participation in recreational activities may well be one of the easiest ways a person with a disability can become active in the community.

It is the responsibility of the public, private, and voluntary sectors to provide recreation programs for all persons, including the disabled. Active participation in planned recreation activities in the community can have positive results. These programs should and must be provided. The responsibility is no longer just a moral issue but, in many ways, a legal obligation. In 1990, an incredible advancement regarding equal opportunities took place. President Bush signed into law the Americans with Disabilities Act (ADA) which ensures equal opportunity for individuals with disabilities in both public and private sectors so that there is no discrimination based on one's disability regarding every aspect of living (Premo, 1994).

For the exceptional child it is important to be involved in recreation and leisure experiences at an early age. The results from participating in these experiences can foster growth in the physical, cognitive, emotional, and social areas of the child (Piaget, 1962). One of the main goals for a child involved in recreation is to have fun, but the benefits from participating in these activities are limitless. Recreation can provide the child with the opportunity to acquire leisure and developmental skills and to function in an integrated setting. The greatest gift we as parents and professionals can give a child is the ability to function as independently as possible. There exists a need for a variety of programs for the disabled population, but the ultimate goal of any program should be that of preparing a person for independent and normative functioning (Wolfensberger, 1972).

The community-based programs must also be based on the individual's needs and must provide opportunities to participate in self-selected activities. When an individual demonstrates the abilities to participate with his/her mainstream peers, services are essential. However, for those who need more structure and assistance and/or are not yet capable of being integrated for whatever reason, special recreation programs should still be provided.

Programs have to exist before the disabled population can participate. During the last twenty years there have been many local level recreation programs initiated and expanded, but there exists a continual need in providing community leisure services for the disabled. There are many reasons for this dilemma: funding, lack of accessible facilities, and the lack of transportation. However, the biggest factor appears to be the lack of awareness concerning the needs of the disabled members in the community.

Humphrey (1979) sees the role of a community therapeutic recreation specialist as a catalytic resource leader. The therapeutic recreation specialist may have many roles to fulfill in the community. She/he may function as a consultant, an advocate, an educator-teacher, but the most important role is to provide appropriate recreation programs for the disabled. Understanding the capabilities, determining the activities, and the leadership modifications necessary for participation creates the need for a therapeutic recreation specialist within the community sector. A close working relationship between the community recreator and the therapeutic recreation specialist will create quality and diverse programming for the community members and must be cherished.

What programs exist in the community? Primary sources should be found in public recreation and parks departments or voluntary agencies. Voluntary agencies such as the Association for Retarded Citizens, Special Olympics, Young Men's and Women's Christian Associations, and Easter Seals Societies sponsor recreation programs specifically designed for disabled children. Furthermore, community colleges and universities provide various types of programs ranging from motor development services to special recreation programs for numerous disabling conditions.

One should check into the community for additional services offered by religious agencies. One of the services offered by the Jewish community center in Mobile, Alabama, was a social recreation program for children with learning disabilities. In another community a local group of dedicated college and high school students organized a social recreation group for a wide range of disabled children. The purpose primarily being for fun. In addition to the inherent value gained by the children through these experiences, the community was exposed to these children and gained a deeper understanding which increased their sensitivity and awareness.

Another resource may be found in hospitals or special group organizations. For example, a summer recreation program for children with myelomeningocele (spina bifida) was offered to the clients of the Myelomeningocele Clinic at the University Affiliated Cincinnati Center for Developmental Disorders (CCDD). The program provided experiences in many activities that the children had never participated in. Thus, through these experiences the children gained the ability to carry out a leisure lifestyle more independently.

There remains a void in the provision of recreation programs for the disabled members in the community. Parents, professionals, and the disabled members of the community must voice their needs. It is the community's responsibility to be aware and provide these needed services.

THE ALLIED HEALTH PROFESSIONS: A COMPLEMENTARY COUNTERPART

Therapeutic recreation is complimented often by the allied health professions for its similar goals and effective benefits. Through the use of targeted arts as a means to gain therapeutic value, professions have been able to achieve greater progress in their treatment programs. Pediatric occupational therapy, outdoor adventure programs, wheel chair sport, summer camps, and child-life specialists are a few that fall under the umbrella of the allied health profession. Not until recently has the medical field caught on and acknowledged the benefits of these specific trades. Each of the mentioned therapy programs will be explained briefly.

Other terms under which one may find allied health profession categorized include activity therapy, adjunctive therapy or rehabilitation therapy services which are known as action-oriented therapies (Austin and Crawford, 1991).

Pediatric Occupational Therapy

A valued asset to the allied health profession regarding treatment for exceptional children is the field of pediatric occupational therapy. Approximately fifteen percent of all occupational therapists in practice work within pediatrics (Clark and Allen, 1985). This form of therapy offers treatment to infants and children of all ages in a number of different settings. It is most often found in general (neonatal and/or pediatric units) and children's hospitals, preschool centers such as Headstart, public and private schools, home health agencies, community and county health centers, rehabilitation centers, and in some day care programs (Clark and Allen, 1985).

The treatment provided may focus on a variety of issues depending on the needs of the child.

> Promoting oral-motor development, instructing caregivers about development, play or physical handling of the infant . . . preventing deformity, facilitating normal development and play behavior, improving motor development, self-concept and emotional maturation, promoting age appropriate independence in daily living skills, designing, fabricating and applying assistive technology devices and services, adapting the environment to allow increased independence, and providing sensory stimulation as well as consultation are all specialties of a pediatric occupational therapist (AOTA).

As one can see, for example, the use of play therapy can often have recreation value as well as occupational and other disciplinary benefits. Pediatric occupational therapy has similar goals as recreation therapy, thus providing a cohesive treatment plan.

Outdoor Adventure Programs

Outdoor adventure programs emphasize the right to risk for individuals with disabilities. These programs require the participant to trust in risk-taking environments, practice teamwork, cooperation, goal setting, problem solving, processing and communicating. The overall desired result from participating in such adventures is to experience personal growth and confidence, fulfillment, empowerment, and expanded leisure experiences (McAvoy, 1989). An evergrowing outdoor program directed and facilitated by Anne Morash Johnson from Casa Colina Centers for Rehabilitation offers a variety of therapeutic adventures suitable for youth and serves as motivating examples of how the outdoors can be utilized for therapeutic gains with children. Sailing, rock climbing, snow and water skiing, and deep sea fishing are a few to choose from. In fact, River Rampage is offered just for teens. This outfit, generated from the Phoenix Special Populations Office, offers high adventure rafting and wilderness programs incorporating both able and disabled youth. Spots are earned for the trip by contributing volunteer service hours which in turn, makes the expedition all the more meaningful (Crase, May/June 1995).

Ropes courses are another challenge used with youth with various disabilities which has proven effective on a participant's self-concept. Even therapeutic recreation practitioners become "true believers" of the effectiveness that ropes courses instill in their clients after such an experience. It has positive results in the areas of emotional, behavioral, physical, and social efficacy (Johnson, 3rd Quarter 1992).

Caregiver's lack of trust or overprotectiveness of their children, an often neglected issue, can be reformulated using these adventures as tools toward acceptance of their child's right to risk and growth toward independence (Fields, July/August 1991). Of course, quality outdoor adventure programs also must include key instruction in wilderness training, emergency procedures, and risk management.

Wheelchair Sports

At one time, wheelchair sports referred to participants who were significantly and permanently impaired in the lower extremity which restrained them from the ability to participate in able-bodied sports. Now the term designates persons with paresis, paralysis, or amputation and even quadrapalygics are eligible to participate in the National Wheelchair Athletic Association (NWAA). However, those with locomotor disabilities would not fall into this category (Sherrill, 1986).

Children and adolescents have a wide variety of wheelchair sports to choose from, and the list continues to grow. Wheelchair basketball and wheelchair tennis are the two most popular sports for juniors. Quad rugby, road-racing, water and snow skiing, hand-cycling, track and field events, swimming, wheelchair softball, raquetball and table tennis are a few other available options (Maddox, 1993). Sports N' Spokes, one of the most popular magazines dedicated to report on the latest developments of wheelchair sports and recreation, includes a section for juniors and acts as a great resource for those interested in further information on featured wheelchair sports.

Whereas schools have often segregated physical education from special education, today's trend prefers to mainstream (to a degree) all children into adaptive physical education classes. Adaptive sports are offered as long as equal distribution of abilities are ensured. Such a mixture opens the participant's eyes to see that he/she is more similar than different from each other regardless of ability levels. (Crase, May/June 1995). Incorporating disabled and able bodies helps to break down barriers, educate, and create respect for one another.

Summer Camps

Camping options for children with disabilities has grown tremendously. Specifically, Easter Seals Society of North Carolina has played a revolutionary part in changing summer camp philosophies by expanding the leisure and camping experiences. The latest alternative camping styles fall under the term "progressive mainstreaming model" which opens the once segregated camp sites into three options: segregated, modified mainstream, and mainstream, allowing each child the most least restrictive environment possible (Bullock, Mahon and Welch, 4th Quarter 1992).

The benefits of integrated day camps, sport camps, and summer camps continue to surface. A new appreciation, insight, and positive attitude develops as children with varying degrees of abilities spend the days and nights together participating in the routine schedule (Sable, 3rd Quarter 1992). Even initial hostile social interactions tend to decrease as more time is spent together in an integrated environment (Edwards and Smith, 3rd Quarter 1989).

Although the push is toward integrated camp settings for children, there exists a wide variety of camps to meet children's particular interests and needs. "The American Camping Association (ACA), which accredits camps nationwide, devotes a section in its directory to camps for kids with disabilities ranging from relatively mild to severe" (Crase, May/June 1995). In fact, there are free camps offered for kids which include day clinics with a daily focus on different wheelchair sports. University of Hartford, Connecticut, as well as the Easter Seal's Action Days clinic, have designed summer day clinics like this (Crase, July/August 1991 & July/August 1995).

Overall, the future for camps which specialize in serving children with disabilities will continue their vision toward normalization or mainstreaming to one degree or another. The options for youth are limitless with the growth of such innovative programs!

Exceptional children have had no greater opportunity than now to be exposed to, participate in, and learn from therapeutic recreation and its supporting professions. The enthusiasm and growth for this area of therapy, whether in a clinical or community setting, will ensure its successfulness and effectiveness for the future.

Child Life Specialists

A most needed and well-received facet of the allied health profession is the role of child life specialists (mostly located in the hospital setting). The Association for the Care of Children in Hospitals (ACCH), located in Washington, D.C., was established as a means to better serve children. By addressing their rights and needs as pediatric patients through the utilization of child life services, a child life staff is generated. The staff may consist of a child life administrator, specialist or assistant. Titles are contingent upon amount of education and experience as well as ability to perform tasks at varying levels of expertise. Child life specialists are most commonly found in hospital settings. They require a bachelor's degree level of education along with supervised practical experience.

ACCH defines the purpose of the child life staff as that which provides opportunities for gaining a sense of mastery, for play, for learning, for self-expression, for family involvement, and for peer interaction (ACCH, 1979). For an infant, child, or adolescent, one's first hospital experience, extended hospital stay, or even unfamiliar procedures can create a significant amount of anxiety coupled with fear, intimidation as well as stress and possible pain that is already associated with the illness. Because of this, the role of a child life specialist was created.

The Association for the Care of Children in Hospitals outlines three essential goals for the staff to pursue within their child life programs. ACCH states the goals as follows: (1) Minimizing stress and anxiety for the child and adolescent, (2) Provision of essential life experiences, and (3) Providing opportunities to retain self-esteem and appropriate independence (ACCH, 1979). A thorough child life specialist will address issues in all three of these areas using treatment aids such as play, orientation visits, in-hospital family visits, home-like assimilated activities and atmosphere (i.e. outdoor play, eating in groups), in-hospital community and school programs and activities, and appropriate equipment. In so doing, the child's anxiety level will decrease as he/she realizes that the child life specialist is aware of his/her need to be respectful, warm, encouraging, empathetic, understanding, and focused on treating each child as a unique and competent person. In order to ensure quality treatment, the child life specialist-to-child ratio should be no more than one to ten, seven days a week (ACCH, 1979). A child life specialist's job description does not translate into being merely a "play partner" for the child during his/her hospitalization (although this is a very effective way to reach out and comfort children). The child life specialist is directly involved with the medical team regarding treatment planning and recommendations, is an advocate for the child within the medical delivery system and provides the families with education and resources on various related subjects and procedures which their child might experience.

For more information about the role and effects of child life specialists, one may refer to the *Journal of the Association for the Care of Children's Health.*

REFERENCES

American Occupational Therapy Association (AOTA). *Occupational therapy services for infants and children.* Pamphlet put out by the association. Rockville, MD: AOTA.

Association for the Care of Children in Hospitals (ACCH), (1979). *Child life activity study section position paper.* Pamphlet put out by the association. Washington, D.C.: ACCH.

Austin, D. & Crawford, M. (1991). *Therapeutic recreation, an introduction.* Englewood Cliffs, NJ: Prentice-Hall, 3, 19, 173.

Beyer, G. (1979). *Physical disabilities.* New York: Franklin Watts.

Bullock, C.C., Mahon, M.J. & Welch, L.K. (1992). Easter seal's progressive mainstreaming model: options and choices in camping and leisure services for children and adults with disabilities. *Therapeutic Recreation Journal, 26(4),* 61–70.

Burgdorf, R. (1980). *The legal rights of handicapped persons: Cases, materials and text.* Baltimore: Paul H. Brookes.

Burgdorf, R. Jr. & Spicer, P. (1983 supplement). *The legal rights of handicapped persons: Cases, materials, text.* Baltimore: Paul H. Brookes.

Butler, A., Gotts, E., & Quisenberry, N. (1978). *Play as development.* Columbus: Charles E. Merrill.

Carter, M., Andel, G., & Robb, G. (1985). *Therapeutic recreation: A practical approach.* St. Louis: Times Mirror/Mosby.

Clark, P.M. & Allen, A.S. (1985). The role of occupational therapy in pediatrics. *Occupational Therapy for Children*. St. Louis: C.V. Mosby.

Coyne, P. (1981). The status of recreation as a related service in PL 94-142. *Therapeutic Recreation Journal, 15*, 3, 5.

Crase, C. (1985). Just for juniors. *Sports 'N Spokes, 21(3)*, 73.

Crase, C. (1985). Just for juniors. *Sports 'N Spokes, 21(4)*, 29.

Crase, C. (1985). Just for juniors. *Sports 'N Spokes, 17(2)*, 43.

Davis, J.E. (1936). *Principles and practices of recreation therapy.* New York: A.S. Barnes.

Dean, R. (1972). *New life for millions: Rehabilitation for Americans disabled.* New York: Hastings House.

De Loach, C. & Greer, B. (1981). *Adjustment to severe physical disability.* New York: McGraw-Hill.

Edwards, D. & Smith, R. (1989). Social interaction in an integrated day camp setting. *Therapeutic Recreation Journal, 23(3)*, 71–78.

Fields, C.D. (1991). Exercising the right to risk. *Team Rehab Report, 2(4)*, 16–18.

Fine, A. (1982). Therapeutic recreation: An aspect of rehabilitation for exceptional children. *The lively arts,* 4.

Frakt, A. & Rankin, J. (1982). *The law of parks, recreation, resources, and leisure services.* Salt Lake City, UT: Brighton.

Frye, V. (1969). A philosophical statement on therapeutic recreation services. *Therapeutic Recreation Journal, 3*, 11–14.

Heward, W. & Orlansky, M. (1988). *Exceptional children.* Columbus: Charles E. Merrill.

Humphrey, E. (1970). Therapeutic recreation and the 1970's. *Therapeutic Recreation Annual, 7*, 8–13.

Johnson, J.A. (1992). Adventure therapy: the ropes wilderness connection. *Therapeutic Recreation Journal, 26(3)*, 17–26.

Knapczyk, D.R., & Yoppi, J.O. (1975).

Kraus, R. (1983). *Therapeutic recreation services, principles and practices.* Philadelphia: W.B. Saunders.

Maddox, S. (1993). *Spinal Network.* Boulder, CO: Spinal Network & Sam Maddox.

McAvoy, L.H., Schatz, E.C., Stutz, M.E., Schleien, S.J. & Lais, G. (1989). Integrated wilderness adventure: effects on personal lifestyle traits of persons with and without disabilities. *Therapeutic Recreation Journal, 23(3)*, 50–64.

Menninger, W. (1948). Recreation and mental health, 340.

National Therapeutic Recreation Society (NTRS). (1986). *About therapeutic recreation.* Pamphlet by the society (1993 edition). Arlington, VA: National Recreation and Park Association.

Nirje, B. (1969). The normalization principle and its human management implications. In R. Kugel & W. Wolfensberger (Eds.), *Changing patterns of residential services for the mentally retarded.* Washington DC: President's Committee on Mental Retardation.

O'Morrow, G. (1980). *Therapeutic recreation: A helping profession.* Reston: Reston.

Peterson, C. & Gunn, S. (1978). *Therapeutic recreation program design: Principles and procedures.* Englewood Cliffs, NJ: Prentice-Hall.

Philosophical position statement of the National Therapeutic Recreation Society (1982). Arlington, VA: *National Therapeutic Recreation Society.*

Piaget, J. (1962). *Play, dreams, and imitation in childhood.* London: Heinemann.

Premo, B. (1994). *Americans with disabilities act, a comprehensive overview.* Sacramento, CA: Department of Rehabilitation.

Protection Advocacy (1986).

Rathborne, J. & Lucas, C. (1970). *Recreation and total rehabilitation.* Springfield, IL: Charles C Thomas.

Reynolds, R. & O'Morrow, G. (1985). *Problems, issues, and concepts in therapeutic recreation.* Englewood Cliffs, NJ: Prentice-Hall.

Sable, J. (1992). Collaborating to create an integrated camping program: design and evaluation. *Therapeutic Recreation Journal, 26(3),* 38–48.

Sherrill, C. (1986). *Adapted Physical Education and Recreation, A Multidisciplinary Approach.* Dubuque, IA: William C. Brown, 494.

Shivers, J. & Fait, H. (1985). *Special recreational services: Therapeutic and adapted.* Philadelphia: Lea and Febiger.

Stewart, J. (1978). *Parents of exceptional children.* Columbus: Charles E. Merrill.

Wehman, P. (1979). *Programs for the developmentally disabled persons.* Baltimore: University Park Press.

Wolfensberger, W. (1972). *The principle of normalization in human services.* Toronto: National Institute on Mental Retardation.

Wooden, W.S. (1995). *Renegade kids, suburban outlaws: From youth cultures to delinquency.* Belmont, CA: Wadsworth.

Chapter 4

THE QUALITY OF CHILDRENS' LIVES

ROBERT L. SCHALOCK

Major concerns exist today about the quality of the lives of children, amid fundamental changes in the American family and real threats to the health and well-being of increasing numbers of children. Note, for example, the following trends (Stark, 1992):

- The traditional nuclear family of a full-time, married housewife/mother, with children, represents fewer than 20% of all households today. More than 25% of all families are headed by a single parent. Some 60% of all children born today will live with a single parent, and 25% will live with a step-parent.
- Single-parent households represent 55% of all families in poverty. Fully 21% of all children in the United States live below the poverty level, which is three times as high among minority groups than non-minority groups.
- Thirteen million children are not covered by health insurance, and almost half a million are malnourished.
- One million students drop out of high school each year, and only one-third of all high school students have the entry skills necessary to find a job.
- Twelve percent of all preschool children have experienced child abuse.
- Child abuse and neglect have increased 74% in the past decade, involving 2 million children.
- Suicide rates have tripled among teenagers, and homicide is one of the leading causes of death among teenagers.

These trends underline the importance of discussing how childrens' quality of life (QOL) can be enhanced within both the home and community. Such is the purpose of this chapter. To assist our discussion, the chapter begins with a brief overview of current attempts to operationalize and measure one's quality of life. Thereafter, I will outline the parameters of a QOL model for children that can be used to guide our efforts to enhance childrens' quality of life. The chapter concludes with a brief discussion of our recent attempts to measure the quality of student life.

ATTEMPTS TO OPERATIONALIZE AND MEASURE QOL

Attempts to measure a person's QOL have thus far used one of two approaches: objective and subjective. The objective approach assesses external, objective social indicators such as standard of living, health, education, safety, and neighborhood (Andrews & Whithey, 1976; Campbell, Converse & Rogers, 1976). The subjective approach stresses the person's perception and evaluation of life experiences, focusing on factors such as physical and material well-being, relations with other people, community activities, personal development, and recreation (Flanagan, 1982; Schalock, 1990).

Within the area of exceptionality, both approaches have been used, generating a number of QOL measurement instruments that have provided the basis for the empirical investigation of the multidimensional nature of the QOL concept. Recent reviews (Schalock, 1994; Schalock, in press) of the empirical work based on QOL measurement suggests that the most common factors comprising the conceptualization and measurement of QOL for children include:

- home and community living
- educational opportunities and challenges
- possessions
- social integration (family, friends, natural supports)
- health and wellness
- safety
- personal control
- choices and decision making opportunities

A WORKING QOL MODEL FOR CHILDREN

In this chapter, quality of life is defined as a concept that reflects a person's desired conditions of living related to nurturance, education, and health and wellness. As such, QOL is a subjective phenomenon based on a person's perception of various aspects of life experiences, including personal characteristics, objective life conditions, and the perceptions of significant others. Thus, the central issues surrounding the examination and enhancement of a person's perceived quality of life involves understanding the relationship between objective and subjective phenomena.

One cannot enhance a person's quality of life in a vacuum or without a model that provides the guidance and direction to quality enhancement. Such a model is presented in Figure 1. The model, which reflects the multidimensional nature of the QOL concept, suggests that a child's perceived quality of life is related significantly to factors within three major life domains: nurturance, education, and health and wellness. Each of these three domains is discussed below and on subsequent pages.

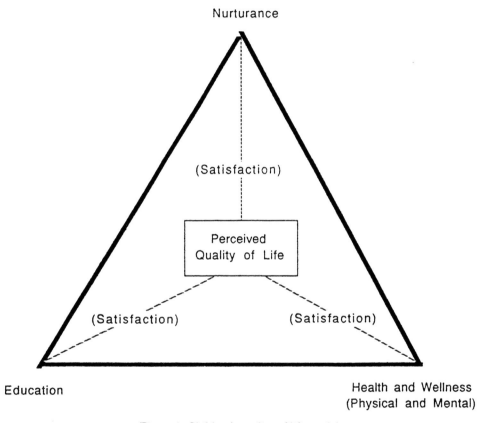

Figure 1. Children's quality of life model.

Nurturance

Children need to be nurtured, including the satisfaction of both physiological and psychological motives (Bee, 1995). I would suggest that in reference to childrens' quality of life due consideration should be given to three critical concepts: stages of psychosocial development, freedom from aversive controls, and social supports.

1. Stages of Psychosocial Development. Erickson (1980) in his book *Identity and the Life Cycle* discusses a number of critical psychosocial developmental issues that persons confront during critical life stages. How these are resolved affects not only one's quality of life, but one's adjustment as well. Briefly, these issues and their positive resolutions (presented in parentheses) include:

- trust vs. mistrust (trust and optimism)
- autonomy vs. doubt (sense of self worth and adequacy; internal locus of control)
- initiative vs. guilt (purpose and direction)
- industry vs. inferiority (competence)
- identity vs. confusion (self concept)
- intimacy vs. isolation (ability to form a close and lasting relationship)

Page constraints preclude discussing how these issues can be resolved successfully, and the interested reader is referred to Erickson and others (for example, Bee, 1995) for a detailed discussion. The critical point that needs to be made is that one cannot enhance the quality of childrens' lives without considering the vital role that one's early environment plays in the resolution of these issues. Nurturing and wholesome environments are, by definition, characterized as fostering well-being, promoting stability, and providing opportunities. They also result in the successful resolution of the six developmental issues listed above.

2. Freedom from Aversive Control. The trends listed at the beginning of the chapter indicate clearly that many children experience considerable aversive events in their lives. The impact of these events on both their quality of life and their growth and development are obvious. As suggested by Skinner (1971), the key to both a technology of behavior and enhancing childrens' quality of life is encompassed in contingencies of positive reinforcement, whose objectives are found in the values of those things that help others, and those things that help a culture survive.

When one is free from aversive controls, one is much more able to obtain the characteristics of self actualized persons whose characteristics have been described by Maslow (1968) to include:

- clear, efficient perception of reality and comfortable relations with it
- spontaneity, simplicity, and naturalness
- autonomy and independence
- feelings of kinship and identification with the human race
- strong friendships

- democratic character structure
- ethical discrimination between good and evil

3. Social Supports. There is currently considerable conceptual and practical interest in the use of social supports as an efficient and effective way to maximize a person's independence, productivity, community integration, satisfaction, and quality of life. This belief is exemplified in the current emphasis on supported employment, supported living, and regular-class support systems in education.

There are currently a number of ways to conceptualize the source of supports, along with their functions, intensities, and desired outcomes. Luckasson et al. (1992), for example, suggest that support resources include personal, other people, technology, and services; support functions include teaching, befriending, financial planning, employee assistance, in-home living assistance, community access and use, and health assistance; and the intensities of support can vary from intermittent to pervasive.

For children with special needs, supports need to be offered in both the home and at school. At home, House (1981) emphasizes the support categories of emotional, appraisal, information, and instrumental. School-based support can come from an "in-house" team of school personnel working with the principal and parents to: (a) address inclusion issues around individual students; (b) arrange schedules so integration occurs in all school activities, including academics; and (c) adjust teaching staff assignments. Such support allows special education teachers to plan and co-teach with regular education teachers and thereby assist in the individualization of programs for students with identified special needs. Additionally, peer support is perhaps the most powerful of all supports in building meaningful relationships, promoting advocacy and respect for diversity, and enabling students with special needs to have age-appropriate models, learn to cope with stress, and achieve positive psychosocial adjustment (Forest, 1991; Snell & Brown, 1993).

Education

The second component of the working QOL model for children relates to education. To say that there is turmoil in education today is understandably an understatement. Public (and private) education is being buffeted by strong social and political forces pertaining to educational funding, content, and outcome based evaluation (Baker, O'Neil

& Linn, 1993). For exceptional children, the conflicting forces are equally strong: inclusion vs. segregation, empowerment vs. dependency, community-based vs. school-based instruction, and outcome vs. process-oriented evaluation (Meyer & Eichinger, 1994; Meyer, Peck & Brown, 1991; Noddings, 1988; Schalock, in press).

Although a slow process, special education is seemingly moving in the right direction in reference to enhancing the educational opportunities afforded exceptional children, and by inference, enhancing their quality of life. The Individuals With Disabilities Act (P.L. 101-476) emphasizes the importance of early intervention and special education that is defined [Section 1401 (16)] as, "specifically designed instruction, at no cost to parents or guardians, to meet the unique needs of a child with a disability including instruction conducted in the classroom, in the home, in hospitals and institutions, and in other settings." Transitional services refer to "assistance in making the transition from school-based education to vocational training, competitive employment, independent living, and use of community resources to meet health, fitness, and leisure needs."

For all of this to occur, however, children with special needs must be given educational opportunities within integrated classrooms. Thus, the proof lies in quality inclusive education. Meyer (1994) and Meyer and Eichinger (1994) have recently suggested a number of program quality indicators including:

- Local education agency district indicators (e.g. home school enrollment, unified staff/faculty, staff assignments, regular class placement, and universal student outcomes).
- Building indicators (e.g. transportation, site-based management, enrichment/ extracurricular activities, team planning meetings, services in general education).
- Educational placement and related services indicators (e.g. daily schedule, general educational instruction, appropriate relevant modifications, student expectations, social relationships, support services, and transition).
- Individual student and program indicators (e.g. diverse curricular options, modified student outcomes, self actualization focus, general educational enrichment, daily routines).

Education is one of the primary vehicles to enrich one's quality of life. Hence, there is an increasing interest in assessing the quality of life of children in both regular educational programs (Epstein & McPartland, 1976; Flanagan, 1976, 1980, 1982; Willitis, 1988; Wilson, 1988) and in special education (Gartner & Lipsky, 1987; Sailor et al., 1988; Stainback

& Stainback, 1984; Wilcox, 1986). We will return to this issue in the final section of the chapter.

Health and Wellness

The third component of the working QOL model for children relates to one's health and wellness. Although this issue can fill volumes (Cf. Kaplan, Sallis and Patterson, 1993), four important aspects of health and wellness are related to an enhanced quality of life (Schalock & Kiernan, 1990): physical fitness, proper nutrition, healthy life style, and stress management.

1. Physical Fitness. Incorporating physical fitness training activities into childrens' lives is important primarily because they result in opportunities for interactions with peers, constitute normal leisure time activities, are pleasurable to the person, and result in enhanced gross and fine motor skills as well as improved mental and cardiovascular functioning.

2. Proper Nutrition. Evidence is accumulating that improper nutrition influences susceptibility to a variety of diseases and health problems, including:

- Obesity, which in turn has been related to increased risk of heart disease, hypertension, stroke, respiratory ailments, arthritis, and back problems.
- Elevated serum cholesterol, which increases the risk of heart disease.
- High blood pressure resulting from high salt intake.
- Diabetes, whose onset can be hastened by high sugar intake.

3. Healthy Life-Style. There is no simplistic standard against which one can evaluate a child's life style. But some general parameters do influence our perception of a life of quality. Among the more important:

- taking time to unwind and relax
- getting adequate sleep
- limiting the amount of medication
- being physically active, including exercise
- controlling excess weight
- eating well-balanced meals
- limiting intake of stimulants, sugar and junk food.

4. Stress Management. One is never too young to benefit from effective stress management techniques that are based on two premises: not all stress is bad; and stressors do not go away and therefore one needs to develop effective ways to cope with the stresses of everyday life. This coping process involves a number of principles that reflect good "copers" (Shafer, 1987):

- Know the importance of social supports including family, friends, church, and peers.
- Use anchors such as religious and personal beliefs, daily routines, enduring and meaningful objects, and favorite spots in nature.
- Take care of your body by practicing sound health and fitness habits.
- Get involved.
- See the world in a generally positive way, and view problems as opportunities and challenges.

Before leaving the issue of the relationship between health and wellness and one's quality of life, it is important to think briefly about what indicators might one use to evaluate whether this aspect of one's life is truly one of quality. A number of critical quality indicators for mental and physical well-being are summarized in Table 7, keyed to our discussion of Erickson's critical issues in one's psychosocial development and the preceding discussion of physical health and wellness.

Table 7. Critical Indicators of Psychological and Physical Health.

Psychological	*Physical*
Trust	Wellness Indicators
Optimism	Number Days Sick
Sense of Self Control and Adequacy	Number Days Missed School
Internal Locus of Control	Number Doctor Visits
Purpose and Direction	Medication Level
Competence	Number Hospitalizations
Positive Self Concept	Weight
Ability to Form Close and Lasting	Physical Fitness Indicators
Relationships	Strength
	Flexibility
	Agility
	Balance
	Cardiorespiratory Efficiency
	Activity Indicators
	In Home
	Out of Home

MEASURING THE QUALITY OF STUDENT LIFE

To conclude our discussion of childrens' quality of life, I would like to summarize briefly work that Ken Keith and I have done on measuring the quality of student life (Keith & Schalock, 1993, 1994, 1995). As mentioned previously, there is currently a strong interest in assessing the quality of student life in both regular and special education. The primary reasons for this current interest include:

- The concern about student satisfaction, and the relationship between students' perceptions of classroom environments and quality of school life.
- The focus on outcome-based education, with an increased quality of life being an important criterion measure of the relevance of education.
- The need to evaluate the effects of mainstreamed education in areas other than academic performance.

Development of the Quality of Student Life Questionnaire has been described previously (Keith & Schalock, 1993). Briefly, it involved rewording the 40 items of the Quality of Life Questionnaire (Schalock & Keith, 1993) into language suitable for an adolescent audience, with assistance and review by 25 junior and senior high school teachers. Subsequently, a field test was conducted with 400 junior high and senior high school students.

A principal components factor analysis was performed on the data from the field test sample. Four factors (satisfaction, well-being, social belonging, and empowerment/control) emerged in this analysis. Each factor contains 10 items, each scored on a three-point Likert scale. The following are brief descriptions of the factors and sample items from each:

Satisfaction. Personal opinions reflecting satisfaction with current circumstances, emphasizing school and school-related activities. Sample question: "Do you feel you receive fair grades for your effort?"

Well-Being. General view of the student's feelings regarding his/her life circumstances, including personal problems and some questions about family. Sample question: "Are there people living with you who sometimes hurt you, pester you, scare you, or make you angry?"

Social Belonging. Participation in activities, social contacts, and relations. Sample question: "Do you worry about what people expect of you?"

Empowerment/Control. Opportunity to exert control over one's life and to make choices. Sample question: "May you have a pet if you want to?"

Thus far, our work has been directed towards establishing norms across a number of parameters including special vs. regular education students, student age groups, and cross-cultural comparisons. Additional investigation of the reliability and validity of the questionnaire is in progress, and revisions of the instrument are likely as broader samples are studied. There is much more, of course, to the quality of a student's life than those items represented in the four factors and a brief questionnaire, but the questionnaire may be useful as one source of information about how students perceive the quality of the educational aspects of their lives.

In conclusion, this had been an enjoyable chapter to write. My interest in quality of life thus far has focused primarily on adults with disabilities, who are often the victims of the adage that "everyone loves a kitten and no one particularly likes a cat." But kittens become cats all too soon. Thus the earlier in one's life that quality becomes a guiding issue and principle, the greater will be the eventual pay off. The quality of life model presented in this chapter, with its three components of nurturance, education, and health and wellness, hopefully sensitizes the reader to the important role that early experiences play in the perception of a life of quality. The model will also hopefully help us to not forget Yogi Berra's admonition that: "The trouble with not knowing where you are going is that you might end up somewhere else."

REFERENCES

Andrews, F. R. & Whithey, S. B. (1976). *Social indicators of well-being. Americans' perception of life quality.* New York: Plenum Press.

Baker, E. L., O'Neil, H. F., & Linn, R. L. (1993). Policy and validity prospects for performance-based assessment. *American Psychologist, 48* (12), 1210–1218.

Bee, H. (1995). *The developing child,* 7th edition. New York: Harper Collins.

Campbell, A., Converse, P.E., & Rogers, W. L. (1976). *The quality of American life.* New York: Sage.

Erickson, E. H. (1980). *Identity and the life cycle.* New York: Norton.

Flanagan, J. C. (1976). Changes in school levels of achievement: Project TALENT ten and fifteen year status. *Educational Researcher, 5* (8), 9–12.

Flanagan, J. C. (1980). Changes needed in our educational system to improve the quality of life of Americans. *Education, 100* (3), 194–202.

Flanagan, J. C. (1982). Measurement of quality of life: Current state of the art. *Archives of Physical Medicine and Rehabilitation, 63,* 56–59.

Forest, M. (1991). It's about relationships. In L. H. Meyer, C. A. Peck & L. Brown (Eds.), *Critical issues in the lives of people with severe disabilities* (pp. 399–408). Baltimore: Paul H. Brookes.

Gartner, A. & Lipsky, D. K. (1987). Beyond special education: Toward a quality system for all students. *Harvard Educational Review, 57* (4), 367–395.

House, J. S. (1981). *Work stress and social support.* Reading, MA: Addison Wesley.

Kaplan, R. M., Sallis, J. F., Jr. & Patterson, T. L. (1993). *Health and human behavior.* New York: McGraw-Hill.

Keith, K. D. & Schalock, R. L. (1993). Assessing the quality of student life. *Issues in Special Education and Rehabilitation, 7* (2), 87–997.

Keith, K. D. & Schalock, R. L. (1994). The measurement of quality of life in adolescence: The quality of student life questionnaire. *The American Journal of Family Therapy, 22* (1), 83–87.

Keith, K. D. & Schalock, R. L. (1995). *The quality of student life questionnaire.* Worthington, OH: IDS Publishing Co.

Luckasson, R., Coulter, D. L., Polloway, E. A., Reiss, S., Schalock, R. L., Snell, M. E. & Stark, J. A. (1992). *Mental retardation: Definition, classification and systems of supports.* Washington, DC: American Association on Mental Retardation.

Maslow, A. (1968). *Toward a psychology of being,* 2nd edition. New York: Van Nostrand.

Meyer, L. H. (1994). Quality inclusive schooling: How to know it when you see it. *TASH Newsletter, 20* (10), 16–22.

Meyer, L. H. & Eichinger, J. (1994). *Program quality indicators (POI): A checklist of most promising practices in educational programs for students with disabilities,* 3rd edition. Syracuse: Syracuse University School of Education.

Meyer, L. H., Peck, C. A. & Brown, L. (1991). *Critical issues in the lives of people with disabilities.* Baltimore: Paul H. Brookes.

Noddings, N. (1988, February). An ethic of caring and its implications for instructional arrangements. *American Journal of Education,* 215–230.

Sailor, W., Gee, K., Goetz, L., & Graham, N. (1988). Progress in educating students with the most severe disabilities: Is there any? *Journal of the Association for Persons with Severe Handicaps, 13* (2), 87–99.

Schafer, W. (1987). *Stress management for wellness.* New York: Holt, Rinehart and Winston.

Schalock, R. L. (1990). Attempts to conceptualize and measure quality of life. In R. L. Schalock, (Ed.), *Quality of life: Perspectives and issues* (pp. 141–148). Washington, DC: American Association on Mental Retardation.

Schalock, R. L. (in press). *Outcome based evaluation: Application to special education, mental health and disability programs.* New York: Plenum Press.

Schalock, R. L. & Keith, K. D. (1993). *The quality of life questionnaire.* Worthington, OH: IDS Publishing Company.

Schalock, R. L. & Kiernan, W. E. (1990). *Habilitation planning for adults with disabilities.* New York: Springer-Verlag.

Skinner, B. F. (1971). *Beyond freedom and dignity.* New York: Alfred A. Knopf.

Snell, M. E. & Brown, F. (1993). *Systematic instruction of people with severe disabilities,* 4th edition. Columbus, OH: Macmillan.

Stainback, W. & Stainback, S. (1984). A rationale for the merger of special and regular education. *Exceptional Children, 51* (2), 102–111.

Stark, J. A. (1992). Presidential address 1992: A professional and personal perspective on families. *Mental Retardation, 30* (5), 247–254.

Wilcox, B. (1986). Review of integration of students with severe handicaps into regular education. *Journal of the Association for Persons with Severe Handicaps, 11,* 74–76.

Willitis, F. K. (1988). Adolescent behavior and adult success and well-being: a 37-year panel study. *Youth and Society, 20* (1), 68–87.

Wilson, M. (1988). Internal construct validity and reliability of a quality of school life instrument across nationality and school level. *Educational and Psychological Measurement, 48,* 995–1009.

CHAPTER 5

LAWS TO ASSIST PERSONS WITH DISABILITIES

LONNIE NOLTA

INTRODUCTION AND BACKGROUND

Whⁿen reviewing access to services and supports for children and adults with disabilities, it is essential to be aware of and understand the current laws and regulations which provide opportunities, options, and protection for individuals with disabilities, and their families.

This chapter will focus on selected laws, particularly those mandates which have had less visibility. As children grow into their youth, adulthood, and the aging stage, it is critical to do long-range planning and prepare for individuals' changing needs with appropriate resources. In this process, it is also important to understand the evolution that has taken place in concepts of services as well as in laws for people with disabilities. Many advancements have been made over the past years due to the incredible effort of individuals with disabilities, family members, progressive professionals, and advocates working together.

For hundreds of years, parents had been told by the medical community that their child with a disability (especially if they were diagnosed with mental retardation) would not be able to function in society and that the most humane course of action would be to place them in large medical facilities where they would have lifelong care. However, during the 1940s, families began to reject the idea that the only choice was placement in large institutions which generally had sterile environments. Many parents decided to keep their children at home to continue the nurturing process and provide training in basic self-help skills. This often resulted in remarkable developmental progress. Families soon realized that their children understood more than anticipated and were capable of performing many tasks.

One of the greatest dilemmas for parents was the lack of resources. There were few specialized medical or social service professionals who could provide information on human development and growth stages for children with special needs. Parent training, family support and services to aid them in maintaining children at home were nonexistent. The situation was complicated by social rejection, resistance to inclusion in the education system, cultural and philosophical differences, language barriers, and the absence of community-based training programs for their children as they grew older.

Parents began to join together to assist each other with child care and then to develop educational and training programs for their children. The real "disability movement" began in the 1940s and 1950s as families recognized the need for public information and education. They formed national organizations such as the Association for Retarded Citizens and the United Cerebral Palsy Association. They organized themselves and collectively identified needs and the resources necessary to assist the child and family unit. They dared to dream of a future for their growing children . . . education in public schools, sheltered workshops for day activities, work training, the potential for employment . . . and many held the belief that their children could live active and productive lives in local communities . . . just like other people!

Over the years, their commitment to ensure the availability of needed resources and supports has resulted in the enactment of many pieces of "landmark" legislation and the development of more reasonable and realistic regulations at the federal and state level. Over the past thirty years, there have been massive public education campaigns. We have seen changes in attitude and awareness about helping people with disabilities to gain acceptance, respect, and value as citizens. As children and adults with disabilities have become more visible in the education system, the workplace, and as neighbors, the general public is beginning to recognize their abilities and enrichment to all of our lives.

The struggle still exists and we all must continue to be vigilant and actively participate with people with disabilities and families to ensure full inclusion. We need to actively search and research advancements, new options, and opportunities to satisfy still unmet needs. Remember, the more we learn, the better we understand how much farther we have to go! On behalf of this effort, the chapter will also address basic techniques for effective advocacy to influence public policy.

Following are the main topics addressed in the chapter:

1. The "Individuals With Disabilities Education Act" (IDEA);

2. The "Technology-Related Assistance For Individuals With Disabilities Act";
3. The "Rehabilitation Act";
4. The Social Security Administration;
5. The Developmentally Disabled Assistance and Bill of Rights Act;
6. The "Americans With Disabilities Act";
7. Federal "Medicaid" resources;
8. Protection and Advocacy resources; and
9. A Blueprint For Effective Public Policy Advocacy.

INDIVIDUALS WITH DISABILITIES EDUCATION ACT (IDEA)

Probably the most commonly known and widely used resource in the United States is the *Individuals With Disabilities Education Act (IDEA)* (20 U.S.A. Sacs. 1400 and following), which was enacted in 1975. This federal law authorized special education and related services to children with eligible disabilities which include, but are not limited to: sensory (hearing, visual, or speech/language) or orthopedic impairments, mental retardation, autism, serious emotional disturbance, traumatic brain injuries, and other health impairments or specific learning disabilities.

Special education is instruction that is specially designed to meet the unique needs of students with disabilities at no cost to parents. This includes academic instruction in the classroom, in the home, or in hospitals and institutions; vocational education; physical education; and training in independent living skills. *Related services* include a broad range of support services that students require in order to benefit from their special education program, including assistive technology. Related services may include, but are not limited to: transportation, and such developmental, corrective, or other supportive services (including speech pathology and audiology, psychological services, physical and occupational therapy, recreation, including therapeutic recreation and social work services, and medical and counseling services. Support for medical services will only be for diagnostic and evaluation purposes, as may be required to assist a child with a disability to benefit from special education, and includes the early identification and assessment of disabling conditions.

In an effort to ensure that *assistive technology* would be available through the local educational system, the definitions from the federal Technology-Related Assistance For Individuals With Disabilities Act of

1988 (P.L. 100-407), were included in the reauthorization of the IDEA. Specifically, *assistive technology* in special education consists of devices and services necessary to assist a child select, acquire, or use an assistive technology device made available if required as part of the child's special education or related services, including specialized transportation equipment such as "special or adapted buses, lifts, and ramps."

The term *assistive technology device* means "any item, piece of equipment, or product system whether acquired commercially off the shelf, modified, or customized, that is used to increase, maintain, or improve functional capabilities of children with disabilities" (20 U.S.C. Section 1401(a)(25)). The term *assistive technology service* means:

> any service that directly assists a child with a disability in the selection, acquisition, or use of an assistive technology device, and includes: (1) the evaluation of needs, including a functional evaluation of the child in the child's customary environment; (2) purchasing, leasing, or otherwise providing for the acquisition of assistive technology devices by children with disabilities; (3) selecting, designing, fitting, customizing, adapting, applying, maintaining, repairing, or replacing of assistive technology devices; (4) coordinating and using other therapies, interventions or services with assistive technology devices, such as those associated with existing education and rehabilitation plans and programs; (5) training or technical assistance for a child, or when appropriate, the family of a child with disabilities; and (6) training or technical assistance for professionals, including individuals providing education or rehabilitation services, employers, or other individuals who provide services to, employ, or are otherwise substantially involved in the major life functions of individuals with disabilities.

Educational agencies are also required to provide assistive technology for students as a "reasonable accommodation" under the Americans with Disabilities Act (ADA) and Section 504 of the Rehabilitation Act of 1973. Students who are not eligible for special education under the IDEA because they do not fit into one of the defined categories or because their learning problems are not severe enough to qualify for special education, may still receive assistive technology to allow them equal access and the opportunity to participate with nondisabled peers.

Children who meet these criteria and who are between the ages of five years and eighteen years, inclusive, are eligible for special education. In addition, individuals between the ages of nineteen and twenty-one years who are enrolled in or are eligible for special education programs prior to their nineteenth birthday, and who have not completed their prescribed courses of study (or who have not met prescribed proficiency standards), are eligible for special education.

Children aged three to five years are eligible under the same criteria as school-age children, with the addition of one new category, "established medical disability." This medical condition or congenital syndrome must have a high predictability of requiring special education.

Infants and toddlers less than three years of age who are developmentally delayed or at risk of such delay, or who have low-incidence disabilities (visual, hearing, or orthopedic impairments), are also eligible for early intervention services under P.L. 99-457 (Part H of the IDEA).

The IDEA Act specifically requires that: "To the maximum extent appropriate, handicapped children including children in public or private institutions or other care facilities, are educated with children who are not handicapped, and that special classes, separate schooling, or other removal of handicapped children from the regular educational environment occurs only when the nature or severity of the handicap is such that education in regular classes with the use of supplementary aids and services cannot be achieved satisfactorily" (20 U.S.C. Section 1412(5)(B)). The burden of proof to show that the child will not benefit from regular classes rests with the school district.

The intent of the Act was not only to ensure that children with disabilities received an appropriate education in the least restrictive environment in accordance with their individual education program (IEP), but also to eliminate segregation and discrimination. The issue regarding "full inclusion" in regular classes remains the most controversial and emotionally charged mandate in the Act.

With overwhelming research supporting the benefits of integration for disabled and nondisabled children in all educational domains (social, language, academic and psychological) parents, teachers, and advocates began in earnest to have children with disabilities included in regular classes. However, due to the general misconception that these children could not benefit and that they would be disruptive to the learning of other students, negotiations with school districts often failed. As a result, we began to see parents pursue legal action during the early 1980s which resulted in major "landmark" court decisions.

Several cases are extremely notable and have helped clarify the issue. In *Roncker v. Walters,* 700 F. 2d 1058 (6th Cir., 1983), the Sixth Circuit Court upheld the right of a boy with mental retardation to remain in a special day class in a regular public school instead of being removed to the school district's proposed placement in a segregated "handicapped only" school. The court articulated a standard underscoring IDEA's presumption in favor of regular education placement and, in ordering the placement, stated: Where the segregated facility is considered superior, the court should determine whether the services which make that placement superior could be feasibly provided in a non-segregated setting. If they can, the placement in the segregated school would be inappropriate under the Act.

Daniel R.R. v. State Board of Education El Paso Independent School District, 874 F. 2d. 1036 (5th Cir. 1989), was the first major "full inclusion" case which involved the issue of mainstreaming children with mental retardation into regular education classes full time with special education support services. The court upheld the right of children with significant cognitive disabilities to attend regular education classes full time when the educational (academic and nonacademic) benefits for the individual child with a disability call for such placement.

In *Greer v. Rome City School District,* 950 F.2d 688 (11th Cir. 1991), the court considered whether the district was obligated under Section 1412(B)(5) to place a child with Down Syndrome who "functioned like a moderately mentally handicapped child . . . with significant deficits in language and articulation skills" in a regular class with nonhandicapped students at the neighborhood school. The court found that the school district violated the integration requirements of Section 1412(5)(B) by failing to consider the full range of supplemental aids and services which could assist her in the regular classroom. Nor had they considered the benefits of regular education placement by failing to modify the curriculum to accommodate the child and they had predetermined the placement without following the proper IEP procedures.

In *Oberti v. Board of Education of the Borough of Clementon School District,* 995 F.2d 1204 (3rd Cir. 1993), the Third Circuit affirmed a lower court decision that the school district failed to consider the appropriate factors in removing an eight-year-old boy with Down Syndrome from the regular classroom and placing him in a segregated special education class. In this case, the district maintained that he could not remain in a regular classroom because of his behavior problems. Even after any behavior difficulties abated in the following years, the school took no steps to mainstream him.

Another case of national significance is *Sacramento City Unified School District v. Rachel Holland,* No. 92-15608 (9th Cir. 1994). The case began in 1989 when the district refused the parents' request to allow Rachel, who has moderate mental retardation, to be included full time in a regular classroom. Rachel's parents felt that she would progress better through this type of program rather than splitting her time between a regular class and special education classes. The case involved the issue of whether Rachel could be educated satisfactorily full time in a regular class with supplementary aids and services. Factors considered in the decision included: (1) the educational or academic benefits for the child in the regular class as compared to the benefits of a special education classroom; (2) the nonacademic benefits of integration with nondisabled children; (3) the effect of the presence of the handicapped child on the teacher and other children in the regular classroom; and (4) the costs of supplementary aids and services. Following five painful years for the family, but with excellent representation by the Disability Rights Education and Defense Fund (located in Berkeley, California), the court ruled in favor of Rachel. During the trial, Rachel attended and progressed well in a regular classroom at a private school. Last year, she attended the Sacramento City Unified School District with full time participation in a regular classroom and successfully completed the fifth grade. This delightful and proud twelve year old is now looking forward to the sixth grade . . . with continued "full inclusion"!

TECHNOLOGY–RELATED ASSISTANCE FOR INDIVIDUALS WITH DISABILITIES ACT

The *Technology-Related Assistance For Individuals With Disabilities Act* of 1988 (P.L. 100-407) authorized competitive grants to states to facilitate access to, provision of and funding for assistive technology devices and services for individuals with disabilities. The *Tech Act*, as it is commonly known, was reauthorized in 1994 to continue the grant program for an additional five years. The Act does not provide funds for the direct purchase of technology. However, it requires states to produce permanent systems' change and advocacy activities that result in laws, regulations, policies, practices or organizational structures that promote consumer-responsive programs. In addition the Act promotes increased access to assistive technology devices and services and empowers individuals with disabilities (or their families if appropriate) to achieve greater independence, productivity, and integration within the community and the work force (29 U.S.C., Section 2202).

All states have received Tech Act grants and are in the process of implementing the federal mandates. Information on this effort should be available through the state departments of Rehabilitation, (K–12) Education, Aging, Employment Development, the agency responsible for developmental disability services, the designated protection and advocacy agency, or major disability organizations.

Each state is required to establish a steering or leadership council representative of all age groups and types of disabilities and which has a majority of persons with disabilities and family members. Other members come from the professional and advocacy community, private industry, and government. This group functions as "change agents" at the local and state level. The objective is to place individuals with disabilities and family members in a lead role to identify needs, resources, barriers to service, and to develop and implement solutions.

REHABILITATION ACT

The federal *Vocational Rehabilitation Act* of 1920 provided funding to the states and began the era of public support in providing a person with disabilities with counseling, vocational training, and job placement assistance. The Act has been greatly modified and expanded over the years and has become a major resource for adults with developmental and other disabilities through vocational rehabilitation, habilitation services, and supported employment. It is important to connect with your local state or district rehabilitation agency prior to the time an individual transitions from high school into higher education, specialized work training, or employment.

Under the Act, qualified individuals can receive counseling, enter into a variety of training programs and may receive direct assistance or counseling on the acquisition of work-related materials (e.g., books, special equipment, tools or clothing), vehicle modification, transportation services, assistive technology, job-site modifications, and job coaching.

Due to the popularity and large number of individuals participating in these rather high-cost programs, the federal government has now imposed a requirement that each state develop and implement an "Order of Selection." States must first provide services and supports to the most severely disabled individuals, as defined by the state. Unfortunately, due to funding limitations "waiting lists" may become necessary.

Some states have instituted a "loan guarantee" program to assist qualified low-income adults or families of young children with disabilities to obtain a bank loan for which the state program guarantees payment in the event of default by the borrower. A few states also have implemented a "low interest loan" program for which an individual can apply directly through the state rehabilitation or designated agency for assistance. This loan program usually has a lower interest rate than regular lending institutions and the flexibility to extend the repayment period if necessary.

These programs have been especially helpful to persons receiving financial assistance through the Social Security Administration (Supplemental Security Income (SSI), Social Security Disability Income (SSDI)) and to low income families.

SOCIAL SECURITY ADMINISTRATION: WORK INCENTIVES

Concern about the potential loss of Social Security benefit payments and health care resources has often created barriers to employment for persons with disabilities. Fortunately, there are a number of work incentive options available. These options are designed to assist the individual in obtaining gainful employment, either within the competitive work force or through a business in their own home, without a reduction or loss of monetary benefits or health care resources until the person can become partially or fully financially self-supporting. The fear of losing benefits and health care resources has been of major concern to individuals with disabilities.

The Social Security Administration has an excellent free publication entitled *Red Book on Work Incentives — A Summary Guide to Social Security and Supplemental Security Income; Work Incentives for People With Disabilities.* The book is very clearly written, divided into useful sections dealing with the various eligibility categories, and can be obtained through your local Social Security office. It is also available on audio cassette or in braille. The publication contains General SSDI (Social Security Disability Insurance) and SSI (Social Security Income) program information; an Overview of SSDI and SSI work incentives; work incentives which apply to both programs; those which apply specifically to each program; and special work incentives for beneficiaries who are blind.

There are training or work related expenses which can be deducted from gross earnings in figuring the substantial gainful activity (SGA) which relates to the performance of significant duties over a reasonable period of time in work for pay or profit, generally earnings averaging more than $500 per month for nonblind individuals receiving SSI or

SSDI, on which the Administration figures acceptable deductions and the potential reduction of benefits.

Impairment-Related Work Expenses may include the out-of-pocket cost (not paid for by any public or private agency) of certain items and services related to the impairment and which are needed to work (e.g., attendant care services; routine drugs and medical services; diagnostic procedures; medical devices; prosthesis; assistive technology; some nonmedical expendable items such as incontinence pads or elastic stockings; residential modifications; transportation; the cost of a guide dog including food, licenses, and veterinary services; work-related equipment and assistants) which can be deducted from earnings in determining if the person is engaging in SGA.

There are times when a subsidy may be allowed to support a person receiving assistance on the job which could result in more pay than the actual value of the services the person performs. SSA deducts the value of subsidies when determining SGA; however, subsidies do not reduce countable income for SSI. A subsidy includes giving the worker with a disability more supervision than other workers doing the same or similar job for the same pay, and/or giving the worker fewer or simpler tasks to complete than other workers doing the same job for the same pay. Only earnings that represent the real value of the work performed are used to determine if work is at the SGA level.

The disabled worker receiving SSI or SSDI may also have continued payment under a vocational rehabilitation program if he or she improves medically and no longer is considered disabled by SSA, if the person is actively participating in an approved state or nonstate public or private vocational rehabilitation program and completion or continuation of the program is likely to enable the person to work permanently. Cash payments and health insurance can continue until the rehabilitation services are completed or until the person ceases to participate in the program.

There is a Student Earned Income Exclusion which allows a person, under age 22 receiving SSI and regularly attending school, to exclude up to $400 of earned income per month with an annual maximum exclusion of $1,620. Regularly attending school means that the person takes one or more courses of study and attends classes in a college or university for at least 8 hours a week; or in grades 7–12 for at least 12 hours a week; or in a training course to prepare for employment for at least 12 hours a week; or for less time than indicated above for reasons beyond the student's control, such as illness. Under specific requirements a person may also be eligible if he or she is taught at home because of a disability.

Probably the most underused option is the *Plan For Achieving Self-Support* for persons receiving SSI benefits. A plan for achieving self-support (known as a PASS) allows a person with a disability to set aside income and/or resources for a specified period of time for a work goal. A person could set aside money for an education, vocational training, or starting a business. The plan can help a person establish or maintain SSI eligibility and can also increase the person's SSI payment amount. A PASS does not affect the SGA determination for initial eligibility decisions. Any person who is blind or disabled who receives SSI or could qualify for SSI can have a PASS. A person who does not need a plan now may need one in the future to remain eligible or to increase the SSI payment amount.

The PASS is fairly simple. It must: be designated especially for the individual; be in writing; have a specific work goal which the person is capable of performing; include a specific timeframe to reach the goal; indicate what money and other resources received will be used to reach the goal; show how the money and resources will be used; declare how the money set aside will be kept identifiable from other funds (such as a separate bank account); be approved by the SSA; and be reviewed periodically to assure compliance. Resources set aside under the plan are not counted towards the $2,000 resource limit. Anyone may help the person develop the plan, including a parent, vocational counselor, social worker, or employer. The SSA can assist the individual to put the plan in writing, then evaluate the plan and determine acceptability.

Other major work incentives are contained under Section 1619(a) and Section 1619(b). Section 1619(a) allows SSI beneficiaries, except for individuals who are blind, to receive SSI cash payments even when earned income (gross wages and/or net earning from self-employment) may exceed the SGA level. To qualify, the person must: be eligible for an SSI payment for at least 1 month before they begin working at the SGA level; still be disabled; and meet all other eligibility rules, including the income and resource tests. People earning above the SGA level can continue to receive SSI cash payments as long as they are still disabled and meet all other eligibility requirements. Payment amount will be calculated in the same manner as for someone who is not working at the SGA level and the person will remain eligible for Medicaid.

Section 1619(b) continues the health care coverage for most working

SSI beneficiaries under the age of 65 years when their earnings become too high for an SSI cash payment. Effective May 1, 1991, a person who is 65 years or older, who is blind or disabled, may also qualify for continued Medicaid coverage. To qualify, a person must: have been eligible for an SSI cash payment for at least 1 month; still meet the disability requirement and all other non-disability requirements; need Medicaid in order to work; and have a gross earned income which is insufficient to replace SSI, Medicaid and any publicly funded attendant care. SSA uses a threshold to measure whether the earnings are high enough to replace the SSI and Medicaid benefits. This threshold is based on: the amount of earnings which would cause SSI cash payments to stop in the person's state; and the annual per capita Medicaid expenditure for the state. If the gross earnings are higher than the threshold, the SSA can figure an individual threshold if the person has: impairment-related work expenses; blind work expenses; a plan to achieve self-support (PASS); publicly funded attendant or personal care; or medical expenses above the state per capita amount.

The following states use their own definitions of eligibility for Medicaid purposes which differ from SSI eligibility criteria: Connecticut, Hawaii, Illinois, Indiana, Minnesota, Missouri, Nebraska, New Hampshire, North Carolina, North Dakota, Ohio, Oklahoma, and Virginia. People in these states will continue to be eligible for Medicaid under Section 1619 (a and b) as long as they were eligible in the month before they become eligible for Section 1619.

There is also a special provision under Section 1619 for persons who must enter a Medicaid or other public medical or psychiatric facility on a temporary basis which allows an individual to receive an SSI cash benefit for up to two months. However, for it to apply, the facility must enter into an agreement with the SSA allowing the person to keep all of the SSI payment. This provision helps people who are hospitalized for a short period to maintain their housing resource.

THE DEVELOPMENTALLY DISABLED ASSISTANCE AND BILL OF RIGHTS ACT

In 1994, Congress passed the latest reauthorization of the Developmental Disabilities Assistance and Bill of Rights Act (P.L. 103-230). The law was originally enacted as Title I of the Mental Retardation Facilities and Construction Act of 1963 (P.L. 88-164).

The Congressional findings included recognition that in 1993 there were more than 3,000,000 individuals with developmental disabilities in the United States. Under the General Provisions—Part A, Congress also states that "disability is a natural part of the human experience that does not diminish the right of individuals with developmental disabilities to enjoy the opportunity to live independently, enjoy self-determination, make choices, contribute to society, and experience full integration and inclusion in the economic, political, social, cultural, and educational mainstream of American society."

Under the federal definition the term "developmental disability" means "a severe, chronic disability of an individual five years of age or older that: is attributable to a mental or physical impairment or a combination of mental and physical impairments; is manifested before the individual attains age 22; is likely to continue indefinitely; results in substantial functional limitations in three or more of the following areas of major life activity: self-care; receptive and expressive language; learning; mobility; self-direction; capacity for independent living; economic self-sufficiency; and reflects the individual's need for a combination and sequence of special, interdisciplinary or generic services, supports, or other assistance that is of lifelong or extended duration and is individually planned and coordinated, except that such term, when applied to infants and young children means individuals from birth to age 5, inclusive, who have substantial developmental delay or specific congenital or acquired conditions with a high probability of resulting in developmental disabilities if services are not provided."

Under Part A, the Act also states "the goals of the Nation properly include the goal of providing individuals with developmental disabilities with the opportunities and support to: (A) make informed choices and decisions; (B) live in homes and communities in which such individuals can exercise their full rights and responsibilities as citizens; (C) pursue meaningful and productive lives; (D) contribute to their family, community, state, and nation; (E) have interdependent friendships and relationships with others; and (F) achieve full integration and inclusion in society; in an individualized manner, consistent with unique strengths, resources, priorities, concerns, abilities and capabilities of each individual".

The purpose of the Act is to assure that individuals with developmental disabilities and their families participate in the design of and have access to culturally competent services, supports, and other assistance and opportunities that promote independence, productivity, and integration and inclusion into the community.

Under Section 110, Rights of Individuals with Developmental Disabilities, Congress makes the following findings: "(1) Individuals with developmental disabilities have a right to appropriate treatment, services, and habilitation for such disabilities; (2) The treatment, services, and habilitation for an individual with developmental disabilities should be designed to maximize the developmental potential of the individual and should be provided in the setting that is least restrictive of the individual's personal liberty; (3) The federal government and the states both have an obligation to assure that public funds are not provided to any institutional or other residential program for individuals with developmental disabilities that (A) does not provide treatment, services, and habilitation which is appropriate to the needs of such individuals; or (B) does not meet the following minimum standards: (i) Provision of a nourishing, well-balanced daily diet to the individuals with developmental disabilities being served in the program; (ii) Provision to such individuals of appropriate and sufficient medical and dental services; (iii) Prohibition of the use of physical restraint on such individuals unless absolutely necessary and prohibition of the use of such restraint as a punishment or as a substitute for a habilitation program; (iv) Prohibition on the excessive use of chemical restraints on such individuals and the use of such restraints as punishments or as a substitute for a habilitation program or in quantities that interfere with services, treatment, or habilitation for such individuals; (v) Permission for close relatives of such individuals to visit them at reasonable hours without prior notice; and (vi) Compliance with adequate fire and safety standards as may be promulgated by the Secretary."

The Act established and provides funding for three entities that work together to improve services for people with developmental disabilities and their families: Developmental Disability Councils in each state and U.S. territory; a protection and advocacy system within each state; and the University Affiliated Programs (UAPs) which provide professional and community training, information and technical assistance.

Under Section B of the Act, the federal government provides funding to the councils to promote, through systemic change, capacity building, and advocacy activities, the development of consumer and family-centered, comprehensive system and a coordinated array of culturally competent services, supports, and other assistance designed to achieve independence, productivity, and integration and inclusion into the community for individuals with developmental disabilities. Councils assist the state in identifying unmet needs, planning, coordinating, monitoring and evaluating services, and evaluating the state's implementation of both federal and state laws. They promote educational programs for the public and policy-makers regarding the capabilities, preferences, and needs of individuals and families.

Part C of the Act established and provides funding to support a Protection and Advocacy system in each state to protect and advocate the rights of individuals with developmental disabilities. The system may pursue legal, administrative, and other appropriate remedies or approaches to ensure the protection of, and advocacy for, the rights of such individuals; provide information and referral to programs and services addressing the needs of such individuals; investigate incidents of abuse and neglect of individuals if the incidents are reported to the system or if there is probable cause to believe that the incidents occurred.

Part D provides grants to university affiliated programs that are interdisciplinary programs operated by universities, or by public or nonprofit entities associated with a college or university, to provide a leadership role in the promotion of independence, productivity, and integration and inclusion into the community. Their primary focus is on the (1) interdisciplinary preservice preparation of students and fellows; (2) community service activities, including, training and technical assistance for or with individuals with developmental disabilities, family members, professionals, paraprofessionals, students, and volunteers; and (3) dissemination of information and research findings relative to (1) and (2) and which contributes to the development of new knowledge in the field of developmental disabilities.

Part E provides funds through grants and contracts for projects of national significance that support the development of national and state policy to enhance the lives of individuals with developmental disabilities.

California uses a "medical diagnosis" rather than the federal "functional" definition for "developmental disability" for eligibility for services and supports. With federal approval, it is based on the "medical diagnosis" contained in the Lanterman Developmental Disabilities Services Act. In accordance with that Act, a developmental disability means "a disability which originates before an individual attains age 18, continues, or can be expected to continue, indefinitely, and constitutes a substantial disability for that individual. As defined by the Director of Developmental Services, in consultation with the Superintendent of Public Instruction, this term shall include mental retardation, cerebral palsy, epilepsy, and autism. This term shall also include disabling conditions found to be closely related to mental retardation or to require treatment similar to that required for mentally retarded individuals, but shall not include other handicapping conditions that are solely physical in nature".

AMERICANS WITH DISABILITIES ACT

The Americans With Disabilities Act was signed into law by President George Bush on July 26, 1990. He commented: "Let the shameful wall of exclusion finally come tumbling down." The law impacts the lives of over 43 million disabled Americans.

This comprehensive law prohibits discrimination against persons with disabilities. It requires equal opportunity and access for individuals with disabilities in government and private sector employment services and facilities; bans discrimination on the basis of disability; and provides civil rights protection to persons with disabilities comparable to those in force for women and ethnic minorities for thirty years.

The five sections in the Act include:

- Title I—Employment: Employment practices cannot discriminate against qualified people with disabilities in the application, recruitment, hiring or any other terms of employment;
- Title II—Public Services: Prohibits state and local government from discriminating against people with disabilities or from excluding participation or denying benefits of programs, services, or activities;
- Title III—Access To Facilities: Private businesses must not discriminate in the goods, services, facilities, procedures, and privileges, advantages, and accommodations offered to the public;
- Title IV—Telecommunications: All common carriers of telephone services must offer nonvoice relay services which interface with voice services;
- Title V—Miscellaneous: Depicts the ADA's relationship to other laws; explains implementation of each title and notes amendments to the Rehabilitation Act of 1973.

Local protection and advocacy agencies; disability advocacy and service provider organizations; and state departments related to education, employment development, developmental services, mental health, or health services, and rehabilitation agencies can assist with the interpretation of the law and action for legal recourse if necessary.

Federal agencies directly responsible for assistance with specific issues include: *Employment issues* — the Equal Employment Opportunity Commission (Phone: 1-800-669-4000/TDD 1-8-800-3302; *Program, Building Access, and Miscellaneous* — the U.S. Department of Justice (1-800-514-0301/TDD 1-800-514-0383; *Telecommunication Relay Services* for persons who are hard of hearing, deaf, or speech impaired — the Federal Communications Commission (202-632-7260/TDD 202-632-6999).

The ADA is really about changing attitudes. It is about including people with disabilities into all aspects of the social, political, and economic mainstream of society. The Act requires us to change the way society thinks. It is no longer appropriate to focus on what people can not do, but, rather on what they can do!

FEDERAL MEDICAID AND MEDICARE RESOURCES

The federal Medicaid and Medicare programs (a part of the Social Security Act) have provided funding for a variety of health care services and other supports for eligible individuals of all ages, and includes those with disabilities, for years and is the most widely used resource by persons meeting specific economic and other eligibility criteria.

Unfortunately, for the average citizen trying to understand the many facets of the federal Medicaid program it is like a trip to the world of "Oz." The complexity of the program is mind boggling. First, for the most part the program is not really a program. It really is a listing of categorical funding resources available to states for the implementation of a variety of programs and services which include a description and limitations regarding what the funds can be used for to assist low or very limited income individuals and families. There are some entitlement programs and there are "waiver" programs. Under a "waiver," states may apply for funding for specific purposes and tailor the program to meet particular needs, sometimes for a specific population, as determined by the state within the guidelines of the federal government. Thus, the availability, eligibility requirements, services offered, and names of particular programs often differ from state to state. What may be available in one state may not be offered in another. For instance, in California, the Medicaid-funded health care program is known as "Medi-Cal," it is a mix of federal and state funding, and includes more benefits than are required under the federal government portion of funding. This section will briefly address a few of the major Medicaid components specific to persons with disabilities.

One of the most vital funding resources to states for children is the Early, Periodic Screening, Diagnosis, and Treatment (EPSDT) Program (known in California as the California Health and Disability Prevention (CHDP) Program). The funding is used by local health departments and schools to provide early identification of health care needs and treatment resources to prevent or alleviate disabling conditions to eligible children.

Screening programs focus on children from birth through age five years. If there is an identified health care need, the program has funding to assist with the treatment which may continue for the child over a period of years. Services include, but are not limited to: general and specialist care, medication, surgery, physical and occupational therapy, hearing aids, eye glasses, and other special equipment, assistive technology, and adaptive devices.

General health care programs are usually available to children and adults who are considered low income (within specific levels of the federal poverty guidelines) or if they are receiving SSI, SSDI, or Aid to Families with Dependent Children (public financial assistance to eligible low income families). States may also have resources for adults who are not receiving such assistance, but are indigent medically needy (e.g., unemployed without benefits or homeless). Again, states vary in eligibility, the type of treatment, and the duration of services.

Medicare is a program specific to elderly persons or in some cases younger individuals receiving Social Security Disability Income (SSDI) benefits. In some cases, an individual may qualify for both Medicaid and Medicare assistance.

Adults or families of a child with a disability should check with their personal doctor; the local health, social service or vocational rehabilitation department; Social Security office; or school district, as appropriate, for specific information and possible assistance.

Due to current shifts in philosophy at the federal congressional level, there will be major changes in the Medicaid and Medicare programs in future years. These programs are being considered for immediate funding reductions, more stringent eligibility requirements, and service type and time limitations. Thus, it is difficult to project what resources may be available even over the next few years.

PROTECTION AND ADVOCACY AGENCIES

If there is a need for legal advice or representation, individuals and parents should be aware that every state has a designated protection and advocacy agency. The agencies are mandated, and respond to specific issues, under the federal Developmentally Disabled Assistance and Bill of Rights Act of 1978 (commonly referred to as the D.D. Act), 42 U.S.C. 6000; the Protection and Advocacy for Mentally Ill Individuals Act of 1986 (the PAIMI Act), 42 U.S.C. 10801; the Protection and Advocacy of Individual Rights Act of 1992 (PAIR Act), 29 U.S.C. 794e; and the Technology-Related Assistance For Individuals with Disabilities Act of 1988 (TRAID Act), U.S.C. 2201.

In accordance with the D.D. Act, services are available to individuals aged five years and older, whose disability fits the following definition: (1) is severe and chronic; (2) is attributable to a mental or physical impairment or combination of mental and physical impairments; (3) is manifested before the person attains the age of 22 years; (4) is likely to continue indefinitely; (5) results in substantial functional limitations in three or more of the following areas of major like activity: self-care; receptive and expressive language; learning; mobility; self-direction; capacity for independent living; economic self-sufficiency; and (6) reflects the person's need for a combination and sequence of special, interdisciplinary or generic care, treatment, or other services which are of lifelong or extended duration and are individually planned and coordinated. Persons from birth to age five years are eligible for services if they have a substantial developmental delay or a condition with a high probability of resulting in a developmental disability.

Under the PAIMI Act, services are available to individuals with mental disabilities who have a significant mental illness or emotional impairment, as determined by a mental health professional, and have complaints involving matters which occurred within ninety days of discharge from a facility providing care or treatment.

The PAIR program protects the legal and human rights of individuals with disabilities defined in the Americans with Disabilities (ADA) Act, but who are: (1) ineligible for client assistance under the Department of Rehabilitation Client Assistance Program (CAP); and (2) are ineligible for protection and advocacy programs under the D.D. Act and PAIMI Act.

The TRAID Act provides some funds for the agencies to assist in assuring that new advances in technology which may assist persons with disabilities are made available to them.

The protection and advocacy agency can provide a variety of services, including:

- information about the legal and service rights of persons with disabilities, including the proper administrative appeal or litigation procedures and sources of assistance available to assure those rights;
- referral to other sources of assistance, including other agencies;
- technical assistance, training, and support to persons with eligible disabilities, their families, and advocates in the resolution of individual and systemic problems;
- direct representation of individuals with eligible disabilities, including: investigation of complaints of abuse, neglect, and rights violations, and legal representation in administrative and judicial proceedings to establish and enforce legal and service rights.

Due to the limited funding in all areas, the agency may consider several factors in determining whether to represent an individual, including: the merits of the claim; the individual's ability to self-advocate; the availability of other resources; whether the problem is identified as a priority in their three-year plan; and, the availability of agency resources. The agency does not charge fees for services; however, they do accept tax-deductible contributions to help cover the costs of providing representation.

Historically, these agencies have provided excellent counseling and legal representation. Their efforts have resulted in most of the successful "landmark" court cases which enable persons with disabilities of all ages to obtain necessary services and supports and to move forward with their lives.

Other legal resources include: Disability & Poverty Law centers, the Disability Rights Education & Defense Fund (DREDF) in California; local Legal Aid and Legal Services Foundation offices. There are also a few private practicing attorneys who have specialized in disability law who can be identified through the state bar associations.

If you have a Center for Independent Living (or Independent Living Center (ILC)) in your area, this is a good place to obtain general information and referral services. In some cases, they have an attorney on staff. This project began in Berkeley, California, is established throughout California, and has been replicated in many other states and countries around the world.

Experienced individuals with disabilities, family members, local disability associations, People First organizations, service provider agencies, and advocacy groups are usually an excellent resource for information and referral assistance.

BLUEPRINT FOR EFFECTIVE ADVOCACY

The majority of laws which ensure the provision of services and protect the rights of persons with special needs have come about because of the identification of need by an individual, family, or organization, and through active, effective political advocacy by individuals, family members, and advocates.

There are three major steps in the legislative process:

- the introduction, passage, and enactment of legislation into law;
- the development of regulations to implement the law; and
- the appropriation of funding, if necessary, through the budget process.

There appears to be a very real misconception among the general public regarding how laws are enacted. The average person does not seem to realize that their active participation in the democratic process can really make a difference. Sometimes they seem to think that some wizard in the U.S. Congress or state capitol is fully aware of the various needs of constituents and that they can develop a magic solution to perceived problems. Certainly, there are some very wise representatives in Washington, D.C. and in our state legislatures; however, most meaningful legislation comes about because of the identification of a problem and potential solution by an individual or group of people with the same problem who then turn to their representative for assistance.

Once the problem is identified, possible solutions need to be considered. It must then be determined what action needs to be taken to change the situation. Is there a need to (1) change the law, (2) develop new or modify existing regulations, (3) obtain appropriate funding, or (4) is it necessary to take legal action to enforce the law? If the need falls within the first three categories, the information should be communicated to your local representative and/or their staff member who works on those type of issue(s).

It is critical to get to know your local representatives at both the state and federal government level, inform them about the problem and need, and provide reasonable recommendations to solve the problem.

For most people this can be intimidating, so it is important to remember that legislators are really people just like everyone else. It can be important to be a good detective and to do a little investigation. Perhaps you have something in common with the representative which makes it easier to speak with him or her. Contact your local representative's office and ask for a biography/background sheet with information about the legislator. If you do not know the representative, contact the local office of the Registrar of Voters or the League of Women Voters. Give them your address and they can give you the name and phone number of your representatives.

The background material often gives a variety of information, including: the full name of the representative; their political party affiliation; the district (geographic area) they represent; addresses and phone/FAX numbers of federal or state, and district offices; legislative committees on which they serve or chair; where they were born; where they went to school/college; their professional background; if they are married and may list their children; if they are a military veteran; and special interests or organizational memberships. They print this information by the thousands and are just waiting to hear from you!

You may find that the representative was born in the same state or area where you originated, has a similar education or employment background. They may belong to the same civic or fraternal organizations. As a parent they may have been involved in some of the same organizations you have worked with or they serve on a legislative committee which is pertinent to your issue.

Once you have information about the representative, it is important to make the contact. You need to build communication and they need to have confidence in the information you provide. It is always nice to meet directly with the legislative representative; however, their schedules are usually very busy and it may be difficult to connect with them. It is probably more important to meet with and get to know the staff member or consultant who specializes in your particular area of interest. This usually is the person dealing with education or health and human service issues. You can telephone for an appointment with the receptionist, or ask when they might be in your locale. Often they are out in the community in conjunction with fundraising, so you may prefer to meet them in their office closest to you. When you call the office, ask to speak to the scheduling secretary for the member or to speak with the staff/consultant designated to work on your issue(s). Let them know that you are a constituent from the district, understand their busy schedule and would appreciate fifteen minutes of their time. They will be much more inclined to work you into the schedule with a shorter time-frame and may give you much more time once the meeting occurs.

When you meet with them, you need to be prepared. It is often helpful to have several people attend the meeting. You may want to take your child and include another parent, a supportive professional involved with your issue, or others friendly to your cause (e.g., a teacher, social worker, nurse, neighbor). Try to keep the number between three to five people. Going in like "gang busters" with twenty people making demands can also be intimidating to the representative!

Plan ahead. Think about who is going to introduce members of the group; take the "lead" to clearly articulate the problem; make suggested solutions; and provide historical and/or updated written material, including a list of people attending with their names, addresses and phone numbers. Make sure that everyone has a chance to speak to specific sections of the issue with which they are most familiar. Clearly identify the problem, research and document the issue as much as possible, recommend a reasonable solution(s), and let the representative know what you would like for them to do on your behalf. You should provide them with a short, three or four page, summary of this information. Do not take in a mound of paper. No one has time to read it. Make sure the information you communicate is current, factual, and can be validated. Remember, your most valuable asset is your "credibility"!

Following the meeting or telephone communication, be sure to send a "thank you" note. Thank the legislator and/or staff member for the time and effort on your behalf. Let them know that you are available to provide additional information, help organize the community, write letters, or testify at public hearings. Followup is critical to the success of the process. Let them know that you are there to help them. Do not just communicate when you need something . . . legislators have needs too! This effort has to be a partnership and you are a valuable resource for them. Followup is critical to the success of the process. Stay in touch!

If the issue is of major concern to a large number of people, it is wise to organize on a wider basis. This could include your local community, the county, state, multistate, or national level. This takes time, energy, and a monumental amount of effort, but it can be well worth every sacrifice. Without broad-based advocacy and grassroots community organization, we would not have most of the services and legal protection afforded by such laws as the Individuals With Disabilities Education Act or the Americans With Disabilities Act. It took thousands of people giving millions of hours of volunteer time, and incredible patience to make that happen! Progress can often be painful, but, the rewards can be everlasting.

Do not forget about the "regulatory process" after a bill is passed into law. The development of appropriate regulations and proper implementation is critical to ensure enforcement of the intent of the law to meet the needs of the people it is designed to assist. Proposed regulations are developed by the state agency or department responsible for implementation of the law. They are required to provide a notice of public hearing(s) and can send you a copy of the proposed regulations. In the case of "emergency regulations," they are usually filed and take effect before a public hearing. You may want to contact the appropriate department and ask to be placed on their regular mailing list for notices on proposed regulations.

Once the regulations are approved, it is important for you to help monitor activity at the community level for proper implementation. If you have concerns or feel that the regulations are being improperly implemented, you should contact the appropriate state department and voice your objection. If there is no response and you believe that the department is continuing to misuse the regulations, then you may want to take action and communicate with your local legislative representative in an effort to rectify the problem.

The other major issue is the passage of federal or state budgets which fund the various programs and services. It is important to actively participate in the process and communicate your needs and opinion. As with the legislative and regulatory process, telephone calls and letters in support or opposition are recorded. They really do influence the thinking of your representatives and the outcome of the process.

Get involved! Join with the established advocacy organizations. Participate in state council and protection and advocacy agency meetings. Contact state agency leaders who can and have a responsibility to help with issues affecting the lives of individuals and families. Attend legislative and government agency public hearings. Be present when you can and provide written or oral testimony. The legislature and various state departments publish notices of public hearings. The notices contain information on the focus of the hearing, date, time, and place. Again, make sure that you are on the mailing list. If you cannot attend, check the deadline for mailing written testimony. Let your views and voice be heard. You really can make a difference in the life of your child, family, friends, and community!

Note: Appreciation is given to the California State Council on Developmental Disabilities, Protection & Advocacy, Inc., and the Disability Rights Education Defense Fund in Berkeley, CA, for their assistance with resource information and to Joyce Berndt and Roberta Marlowe for their critique of the chapter.

Chapter 6

PROGRAMMING FOR LEISURE, RECREATION, AND PLAY

JESSE T. DIXON

Seeing all possibilities, seeing all that can be done,
and how it can be done, marks the power of
imagination. Imagination turns into reality. . . .
Wynn Davis

INTRODUCTION

This chapter is intended to help professionals or parents plan intervention with children that encourages play behavior. The two themes of this chapter will be facilitating playful experiences and developing the activity skills necessary for participation in leisure or recreation activities. Specific characteristics of leisure and recreation have been identified as guidelines for distinguishing therapeutic recreation service from other service contexts such as academia and vocation.

Problems with professional recognition of therapeutic recreation as a service may lie in the failure to emphasize the role of intervention. For example, professionals from other disciplines may believe that the activity is the sole reason for benefits to patients. As a result, this part-truth ignores the contribution of the therapist's skills, and the professional may be referred to as the "game person." Therapeutic recreation service provided by trained professionals involves the use of a knowledge base, critical thinking, and decision-making in regard to intervention with patients or clients.

Recognizing variables that professionals can assess and change to influence playful behavior should help professionals and parents to recognize the contributions of therapeutic recreation service efforts. A model illustrating a range of play-oriented and task-oriented behavior is presented and should help to explain and guide intervention that encourages playful behavior. In addition, several activity-related approaches to service are identified and sequenced as a reference for planning long-range intervention aimed at teaching participation skills.

Clarifying Terminology

Throughout the course of this chapter, the reader will note the use of the terms *leisure, recreation,* and *play.* Although readers can find varying definitions of these terms, this author has looked for instances of *similar usage* to provide an orientation to this chapter. In a manner similar to other authors of texts on leisure (Iso-Ahola, 1980; Chubb & Chubb, 1981), these terms will be acknowledged as inter-related. Distinguishing these terms is intended to clarify the theories offered and the programming suggestions contained in this chapter. The result is a suggested usage of the terms which acknowledges a relationship but separates each term when applications in service settings are explained to other professionals or to parents.

Leisure

The term *leisure* is typically used in referring to satisfying activities in the context of **non-work** hours (Chubb & Chubb, 1981; Iso-Ahola, 1980). Iso-Ahola (1980) and Kelly (1990) argue that **perceived freedom** or **freedom to decide** is the starting place for leisure. In other words, leisure is presumed to occur where there is no obligation factor in the origination of the behavior. For example across the lifespan, the category of leisure would *not* include career behavior or compulsory education where people purposely earn a wage, achievements, or recognition. This does not mean that people cannot enjoy their occupation or school work. In fact, many people choose satisfying careers or studies that are enjoyable and modify conditions in order to make them more enjoyable. The enjoyment of work behavior may tempt some people to label the work experience as *leisure.* However, Iso-Ahola (1980) would argue that people would probably make very different choices for work behavior if obligation did not originate with the behavior in the form of economic considerations, time limits, or accessibility. Kelly (1990) would argue that leisure behavior is not focused on external goals as task-oriented behavior appears to be influenced. Hence, in accordance with Iso-Ahola (1980) and Chubb and Chubb (1980), the author of this chapter will use the term *leisure* to identify enjoyable activities which occur in non-work hours and involve perceived freedom. In the case of children, there are opportunities for leisure where the activity is freely chosen and enjoyed for its own sake.

Recreation

Given that leisure originates differently than work or achievement behavior, there are some activities that people choose and enjoy that are **restorative, relaxing,** or **re-creative** in nature. Chubb and Chubb (1981), Iso-Ahola (1980), and Kelly (1990) would refer to such activities as **recreation.** As Iso-Ahola (1980) points out, a person must decide if a leisure activity results in restorative benefits, and is, in fact, recreation. In addition, Kelly (1990) argues that recreation represents *organized activity* which may be *programmed* for purposeful ends.

Play

The term *play* is used broadly with children and adults. Ellis (1973) suggested that people may play at their work or work at their play. These apparent contradictions make definitions difficult. Ellis's book *Why People Play* (1973) provides two important premises. First, play is behavior commonly not motivated by the end behavior or outcome (Ellis, 1973: p. 2). Second, when the enjoyment of an activity ceases to lie in the processes that provide arousing stimuli and depends on external rewards or goals, the activity becomes less playful (Ellis, 1973: pp. 142–143).

Describing play behavior using terms like *more* or *less playful* suggests that there are **degrees of playful behavior** (Ellis, 1973). Similarly, Kelly (1990) argues that play or leisure behavior refers to a quality of action. Qualifying degrees of play behavior makes the term *play* more useful as an adverb or an adjective than as a noun. That is, *play* describes *the way* people do an activity-**playfully.** Similarly, behavior that is **playful** will have characteristics that differ from behavior that is dramatically task-oriented (Kelly, 1990). This use of the term *play* fits with Nachmanovitch's description of play in his book *Free Play* (1990).

Nachmanovitch (1990) suggests that play refers to **an attitude** for exploration combined with action initiated for its own joy. For example, if a child is practicing a piece of music on the piano in an effort to perfect his or her performance, this is a task. The use of exercises and practice are emphasized to achieve an outcome. Playing with the musical piece, however, would involve an emphasis on pleasure. There may be improvisation and creativity, but decision-making would be oriented to preferences rather than the demand for a better outcome or product.

In this chapter, the use of the term *play* to describe children's behavior will characterize **the way participation occurs.** There will be degrees (the extent or quality) of play behavior in that children make choices and react to limits in play situations. Using professional intervention to make participation more playful will be one obvious value of therapeutic recreation services to children.

Therapeutic Recreation

In therapeutic recreation service, professionals program *leisure, recreation,* or *play* activities for patients or clients who demonstrate an impairment (Peterson & Gunn, 1984). **Assessment** is used so that activities offered fit within the measured preferences of the patients or clients. This use of **choice** serves to address the issue of perceived freedom for participation. In addition, treatment goals and objectives are usually designated to emphasize the value of the activity for the patient or client. Using the activity to address the impairment of the patient or client is **therapeutic.** Assuming that the leisure activities used have re-creative or restorative benefits, therapeutic recreation programming may be offered under more global service headings such as **rehabilitation** or **habilitation.**

RECOGNIZING PLAY BEHAVIOR, MOTIVATION, AND SERVICE

The Characteristics of Play Experiences

Rubin and Tregay (1989) suggest that professionals who intend to facilitate the play behavior of children should clarify their role with specific suggestions for **intervention** and clarification of the **play experience.** In addition, these authors suggest using terms that are different from other contexts of service such as education and vocation. Terms like *flow, positive addiction,* and *play* have all been used to label experience that occurs within the context of recreation and leisure (Csikszentmihalyi, 1975; Glasser, 1976; Nachmanovitch, 1990). In an effort to facilitate these types of experiences, it may be helpful to professionals and parents to avoid overlapping the terms "task" and "activity" within the context of recreation services.

As an example, Austin (1991) points out that there appears to be a repeated practice of identifying activity analysis within a behavioral framework. Austin (1991) cautions against oversimplifying analysis procedures to the point of equating the completion of behavioral requirements by an individual with a recreation or leisure experience. Nachmanovitch (1990) suggests that play is not *what* we do but *how* we do it. Similarly, Rubin and Tregay (1989) recommend that the context of play be distinguished from academia or other service areas. Recognizing the importance of **choice** in play, Rubin and Tregay (1989) emphasize the need for playful activity to be what children *want to do* rather than what they *have to do*.

Following a review of literature, playful activity that is leisure or recreation would appear to be distinguished by variables that are significantly different than the variables which determine desirable work or academic skill. These variables are as follows: the **orientation to choice**, the **irrelevance of time**, the activity **focus on the person**, the role of **unique ritual**, and the **nonlinear path** of the experience process.

The Issue of Choice in Playful Activity

In the context of therapeutic recreation service, children can be given a choice of activities based on an **assessment** of their interests. For example, a child's history of participation, his or her current favorite activities, and his or her desires for future participation can guide the recreation professional in program planning. Iso-Ahola (1980) and Kelly (1990) identify perceived freedom as a critical factor regulating feelings of leisure or recreation and maintain that choices and freedom in participation remain important throughout the entire life cycle for the context of recreation.

The perceived freedom within activity participation is useful to distinguish the orientation to choice from the orientation to obligation. Iso-Ahola (1980) maintains that when a person is deprived of the opportunity to make decisions regarding participation, the activity loses its recreation-like quality. Similarly, Glasser (1976) and Nachmanovitch (1990) stress the re-creative value of activity that is oriented to choice in contrast to participation that is obligated or necessary in some way.

The Irrelevance of Time

In therapeutic recreation services, professionals may need to adhere to a schedule and honor a specific time to end an activity period. The time for ending the activity, however, is not presented as part of the objectives of the activity. Children may or may not feel they are ready to finish an activity that has been initiated. The emphasis in service should be on the enjoyment of the activity. The need to continue or repeat an activity at a later date is consistent with the nature of playful activity (Ellis, 1971).

The issue of choice is also influenced by the relevance of time limits. Both Glasser (1976) and Nachmanovitch (1990) stress the need for enough time for the individual to become involved in the activity and to experience the irrelevance of time. In addition, Csikszentmihalyi (1975) argues that the goal or awareness of a time deadline may inhibit or diminish the experience for participants in a recreation activity. In short, the playfulness of participation can be inhibited if the participant is "watching the clock."

Participation Focus

As a part of therapeutic recreation service, children can make decisions within activities based on their preferences rather than externally imposed goals. For example in an art activity, children can be permitted to choose the colors they desire for depicting a tree rather than being asked to paint a *green* tree. Similarly within the concept of New Games, participants are encouraged to change the nature of suggested games as they desire. Permitting an activity to revolve around participant preferences (within realistic limits) focuses the activity on the individual.

Nachmanovitch (1990) and Csikszentmihalyi (1975) point out that vocational and academic settings frequently focus on the outcome or product generated by workers or students. Both authors acknowledge the feelings of sacrifice that participants experience in efforts to succeed and achieve. The role of choice in leisure and recreation, however, typically results in **a focus on the person** in terms of individual needs (Peterson and Gunn, 1984). That is, the activity revolves around the person rather than the objective (Kelly, 1990).

The Use of Rituals

As part of recreation participation, it is not unusual for a child to choose his or her friends to be together on a team for a game. During outings to a museum or the zoo, children may have a specific preference for the order of events viewed. In planning a party, a child may feel that a specific menu of food will contribute to the success of the event.

Glasser (1976) emphasizes that recreation participation is frequently **unique** for each person. Unlike vocation or academia, the second-hand experiences of others are not used to determine or measure successful participation for leisure or recreation. Generally, there is not a standardized perception for participation in activities. Rather than standardizing behavior, participants often modify an activity to satisfy their own needs to make the experience more interesting or enjoyable (Ellis, 1973; Nachmanovitch, 1990).

Rituals which are used to enhance the participation experience appear to tolerate inefficiency, ignore the logic of alternative behaviors, and focus on the mood of the participant. For example, selecting a friend to be on a team may not result in a win during competition, but participation will probably be more fun. Similarly, serving brand-name beverages and snacks is probably more expensive than serving generic-labeled economy food in institutional containers; however, the participants will probably appreciate the difference. In terms of work or academia, rituals appear to be more generalized. For example, ritual procedures are often designed to enhance performance outcome, characterized as "ways to succeed," or standardized to be the "best strategy" when applied to different people (Jonassen, Hannum, & Tessmer, 1989).

Morris and Blatt (1986) point out that the use of rituals in work or academia are important to the time and action economy. Nachmanovitch (1990) suggests that rituals within vocation or academia are often designed to enhance the efficiency and the economy associated with an outcome or production. In particular, there may be a standardization of behaviors and processes. For example in production, standardization is used to enhance performance outcome through efficiency, precision, certainty, and the avoidance of error (Morris & Blatt, 1986).

The Path of Experience

In leisure or recreation activities, a child may listen to a song or watch a video numerous times with apparent enthusiasm. Despite a knowledge of an event, a child may sincerely appreciate the numerous repetitions of participation. From a "bottom line" perspective, going backwards or digressing in a **nonlinear** fashion in an effort to repeat or continue playful behavior may appear inefficient or excessive.

Leisure, recreation, or playful activity is intended to be stress-free where detail can contribute to appreciation or exploration. For example, Nachmanovitch (1990) refers to the importance of taking the "scenic route" and using improvisation within playful behavior. Ellis (1971), in discussing playful behavior, argues there is usually a **continuation of behavior.** Overall, leisure, recreation, or playful behavior may involve excessive, exaggerated, or uneconomical behaviors which influence participation (Nachmanovitch, 1990).

For the sake of comparison, descriptions of the process for performing work or academic tasks appears to be very **linear** from beginning to end. Ellis (1971) suggests that there is an emphasis on the termination of behavior for achievement. In addition, Nachmanovitch (1990) suggests that there is an emphasis on compressing time and effort with the intent of reaching objectives quickly and efficiently. Hence, the phrase "Time is money." is very common in work settings.

The Origin of Behavior and the Degree of Experience

Figure 2 (see Figure 2) is intended to characterize two participation experiences which originate differently. The legend and terms used for Figure 2 were derived from the publications of several authors (Chubb & Chubb, 1981; Csikszentmihalyi, 1975, 1990; Ellis, 1973; Glasser, 1976; Kelly, 1990; Iso-Ahola, 1980; Nachmanovitch, 1990; Rubin & Tregay, 1989). Each **origin of behavior** is characterized by five variables which describe participation orientations. For example, one primary distinction is the orientation to choice for leisure behavior as opposed to obligation for task-oriented behavior. This author acknowledges that people may derive pleasure from participation in tasks that emphasize completion and/or achievement. Task and achievement related behaviors are characterized by conformity to obligations within the context of participation (Morris & Blatt, 1986). In contrast, Iso-Ahola (1980) and Kelly (1990) argue that leisure and recreation behaviors have to originate within a context of perceived freedom (choices). Behavior that originates from a perspective of **choice** emphasizes the *internal* motivation of the participant. Behavior that originates with a sense of **obligation** emphasizes the influence of *external* circumstances.

Figure 2 also suggests that the participation experience can occur within **degrees of behavior** whether the experience is oriented to task completion or leisure participation. Using degrees provides *a range of* *experience* (e.g. more or less emphasis on time limits) and is derived from Ellis's (1973) observation concerning work-oriented behavior and playful behavior. Ellis (1973) maintained that a person may play at their work or work at their play. In other words, whether a behavior originates as leisure or as a task, it may be modified to be *more or less* of that orientation.

Thus, Figure 2 provides three useful perspectives. First, leisure and recreation participation has an **origin** that is characterized by five named variables. People, as individuals, may choose to orient their leisure participation more or less (in degrees) to the named variables as a strategy to enhance enjoyment. One value of this figure to the professional or the parent is that *intervention* can be designed to address the origin of the behavior. For example, if a recreation experience is less than satisfactory, the professional or parent may want to encourage a change in the approach to participation. A child may be asked not to worry about a time limit, or a child may prefer to invite a friend along as part of the ritual to make the experience originate within an orientation to leisure.

Second, the use of **degree** as a legend in Figure 2 provides *directions for changing behavior* to modify participation experience. For example, the issue of degree can explain why some people may argue that their work is so enjoyable that it *is* leisure. This author acknowledges that in considering the degree or amount or orientation, it is possible to modify task-oriented behavior so that it is more enjoyable and appears more playful. Iso-Ahola (1980) would argue that such behavior is work; however, the reader can readily identify characteristics that "move" the experience away from a specific task orientation (see Figure 2).

Third, Figure 2 illustrates different experiences which can change in degree and may be **parallel.** As the model illustrates, the experiences do not overlap or intersect. For example, enjoyable work would not be labeled as *leisure.* Similarly, participation that originates with choice and provides enjoyment may be very structured but should not be labeled as *work* if the origins to the behavior are maintained.

The use of parallel boundaries also supports the data reported by Csikszentmihalyi (1990: pp. 157–153) and the assertion by Ellis (1973) concerning work and play. Csikszentmihalyi (1990) reported survey results that indicated flow situations were experienced in the contexts of *both* work and leisure. Ellis (1973) maintains that people may play at their work and work at their play. Although task-oriented behavior and leisure behavior may originate differently, both experiences may appear very similar if they are modified by degrees and moved towards each other in Figure 2. However, the origin of the participation would distinguish the behaviors for the purpose of labeling the behavior. It is interesting to note that Csikszentmihalyi (1990) also reported that people wished to be doing something else to a much greater extent when working than when at leisure despite the flow experience. Csikszentmihalyi (1990) speculated that the people surveyed were reacting, in part, to the origin of the behavior (freedom).

Overall, considering **the origin and the degree of participation experience** are intended to suggest intervention strategies with children within leisure participation. For example, a child may not enjoy a leisure (non-work) activity if the experience is too task-oriented with concerns for performance outcome and standardized behavior. Using Figure 2, recreation professionals may intervene by suggesting more of an emphasis on personal preferences for motivation (see Figure 3) and the use of improvisation which would "move" the degree of participation towards more of an orientation to leisure.

Intervening to Encourage a Leisure Experience

Therapeutic recreation professionals may not find it realistic to insist on or to plan a "pure" leisure, recreation, or play session. If participants are satisfied with participation that is positive behavior, then it may not be necessary to plan intervention. **However, professionals or parents will want to have strategies for making participation more playful when children do not seem motivated or satisfied.** Increasing the degree of playful behavior experienced in leisure or recreation participation is a valid intervention with children who are not motivated within an activity. The previously mentioned characteristics of playful activity are easily integrated within a leadership style and can be implemented within an activity session.

The following are sample suggestions the professional or parent may want to consider when planning intervention. First, providing the element of choice is a primary factor. Ultimately, if the child can elect participation and behavioral content, the participation is well into the leisure/recreation end of the scale (see Figure 2). A second modification is that the control of time can be deemphasized. Unless there is a

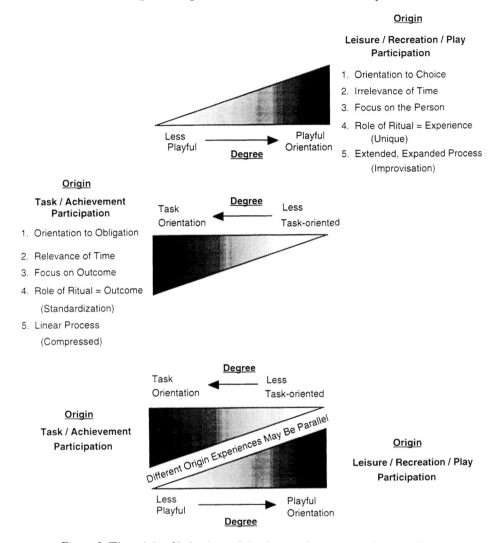

Figure 2. The origin of behavior and the degree of experience (Dixon, 1994).

competitive or mastery need expressed, participation does not need to be perceived as hurried or aimed at a deadline.

A third possibility of modification could be to manipulate the concern for mastery, and consider improvisation for the sake of experience. The concern for mastery will probably reflect the child's need for structure and certainty during participation. There is no "good" or "bad" in these considerations. If a child is happy with structure and objectives, there may not be a need for intervention. The child's preferences for participation should be a guideline for providing intervention. Given that a child is unmotivated or dissatisfied with participation, illustrating the process rather than the outcome as a source for satisfaction emphasizes the element of choice. Permitting a child to have choices for participation focuses the activity on the person rather than the outcome.

Fourth, if rituals are a part of the participation, they can be used to enhance the experience of participation rather than the certainty of the outcome. For example, serving snacks or providing music as part of travel during outings changes the nature of waiting. Identifying the role of rituals will serve to define the experience more clearly to a child.

Finally, participation does not have to be limited to achieving an objective or end result. If the activity is satisfying, the participant may want to extend, expand, or repeat the activity. The emphasis of participation can be on "doing" the activity as opposed to "completing" the activity. Ideally, some leisure or recreation activities may be positive enough to be requested at a future date and repeated on a maintenance schedule.

While the desire to achieve, produce, learn, and play may all be innate drives, the contexts of leisure and recreation activity appear to differ from task or work completion primarily in terms of the **fragmentation of the experience.** Rather than considering the person separately in order to focus on external incentives (critique, quality, criteria, obligation), leisure or recreation activity appear to require the participation to complement and orient to the individual. For example, being original does not mean being different for the sake of distinction within school or work contexts. Instead, the participant's action represents the **unique origin** of the behavior (Nachmanovitch, 1990). Recreation participation represents the individual in an on-going, evolving form of activity that stretches across the life span (Peterson & Gunn, 1984:4).

The following section will address four common orientations to motivation that people elect for participation. These choices are not definitive, but the choices may help the professional or the parent to recognize the preferences of individual children. In addition, these orientations may provide alternative suggestions for motivating children to participate in leisure or recreation activities.

Identifying Orientations to Motivation

One goal of the therapeutic recreation process is to increase the awareness and ability of a handicapped child so that he or she will make self-directed choices for independent leisure, recreation, or play (Peterson and Gunn, 1984, p. 51). Gold (1980) attributes informed choices to the **"content influence"** of activities. That is, the handicapped child has a knowledge of, belief in, or awareness for the value of participation.

Recognizing alternative preferences for participation may expand the content influence of leisure or recreation activities for handicapped children. For example, Rubin and Tregay (1989) warn therapists against talking children out of how they feel during play sessions. These authors emphasize the need to create an environment for playful activity as well as using the opportunity to teach information or skill. As strategies, Rubin and Tregay (1989) suggest the following alternative for motivating a child to participate in an activity:

1. The use of challenge, e.g., "Bet you can't do this."
2. The use of paradox, e.g., "Hold this hat, but don't put it on your head."
3. The use of prediction, e.g., "Sam usually runs ahead of everyone. Let's see if he helps pull the wagon this time."
4. The use of appropriate activity for inappropriate behavior—e.g. Introducing a piñata game to the child who wants to hit and break something for play. Note: For further discussion of these strategies and other interesting issues, this author refers the reader to the text by Rubin and Tregay (1989).

These alternatives, in effect, provide the therapist or parent with different ways to intervene and shape participation to the preferences of a child. One premise for these alternatives is that *the orientation to motivation may differ across children.* Individual preferences for motivation are important to consider when planning intervention whether the participant is a child or an adult.

Different categories of orientations to motivation are presented in the following paragraphs in an effort to recognize possibilities for "content influence." Recognizing preferences for motivation permits the **assessment** of an individual and can guide the intervention as suggested by Rubin and Tregay (1989). Recognizing alternative preferences for motivation also provides additional perspectives the professional or parent can use to educate a child about participation.

Four preference orientations to motivation are frequently observed for recreation participation and can be labeled as follows: **acquisition, prevention, maintenance,** and **serendipity.** In addition, the issue of certainty and the use of evaluation concepts are considerations which influence the preferences for recreation participation.

Acquisition

The concept of **acquisition** involves gaining something by one's own efforts (Guralnik, 1975). Commercial advertisements for recreation frequently suggest the acquisition of fitness, quality entertainment, and interesting information (Dixon, 1986). Children may be motivated to select recreation activities to develop art, music, or physical activity skills as well as to acquire new experiences.

When acquisition is the focus of participation, there is a degree of uncertainty due to the level of skill and the amount of effort necessary to achieve or complete an objective. For example, people frequently participate in recreation activities to acquire a level of fitness. Following an assessment, this could include a desire for weight reduction, an increase in cardiovascular endurance, or a change in muscle tone. Acquiring a level of fitness that is beyond the participant's assessed status would probably require skills in nutritional planning, exercise selection, and performance (Dixon, 1994). When fitness programs are appropriate, the degree or rate of acquisition are influenced by the participant's perception of their goals and their ambition for improvement. In therapeutic recreation service settings, professionals can provide leisure education to develop activity skills and influence the expectation for success of acquisition strategies. Human service efforts aimed at the rehabilitation of handicapped children frequently use the concept of acquisition.

Acquisition and Rehabilitation. Rehabilitation is an individualized process that is intended to reduce or eliminate the effects of disability and restore the functional capacity of a person (Rosen, Clark, and Kivitz, 1977; Shivers and Fait, 1985). The concept of rehabilitation assumes that a person lacks a significant ability and must acquire this ability to achieve a normal state of health. The rehabilitation process is designed to compensate the individual for functional problems following disease, illness, or injury (Shivers and Fait, 1985). For example, the child who experiences a visual impairment will require training in orientation and mobility skills in order to be aware of the environment and achieve some level of independent functioning. Otherwise, an extreme dependence on others may result in a very limited lifestyle. Similarly, the institutionalized child may need to acquire specific coping strategies to resume living in the mainstream of society.

Therapeutic recreation is a supportive service designed to contribute to a rehabilitation plan. For example in physical rehabilitation, a child may learn about opportunities for wheelchair sports and accessible outings. In psychiatric settings, the use of group recreation participation may be oriented to developing social skills, positive attitudes, and identifying personal life values (Shivers and Fait, 1985). In general, the use of recreation experiences to acquire skills and awareness can contribute to the physical or psychological strength of children and their ability to demonstrate a level of independent living in society.

Prevention

The concept of **prevention** suggests the need for activity or experiences to avoid negative consequences (Avedon, 1974; Glasser, 1976). Shivers and Fait (1985) recognize the concept of prevention as part of a healthy life-style for individuals to avoid dysfunction or illness. These authors recommend a balance between tension and relaxation with recreation opportunities. That is, recreation is considered to have the value of prevention for helping to cope with pressures that result in physical/mental illness or other forms of deterioration (Avedon, 1974; Shivers and Fait, 1985).

Therapeutic recreation programs frequently use a prevention orientation to motivate people to participate in activities and preserve a state of health. For example, warm-up exercises are recommended to avoid possible injuries and prepare children for excelling in active participation. Similarly, special diet plans, food information, and recreation activities can be presented to avoid problems with physical appearance, nutrition, and weight control (Dixon, 1994). Handicapped children may encounter numerous media sources which promote nutritional items, cosmetic products, and activity programs with suggestions to avoid injury, illness, or being unattractive. In addition, community recreation sources are frequently promoted to discourage social isolation and encourage children to be "where it is happening" (Burt, Meeks, and Pottebaum, 1980). In terms of prevention, therapeutic recreation programming may be a valuable resource for handicapped children who are concerned about physical health, appearance, and social opportunities.

Maintenance of Motivation

The concept of **maintenance** involves a continuation, rather than a termination of experience, and a satisfying process or outcome (Ellis,

1971; Kelly, 1990). Commercial media sources may suggest a maintenance orientation for the repeated use of a vacation site or the pleasurable use of beverages or foods. A maintenance orientation with regards to leisure, recreation, or play can be described as participation for the fun of it; that is, people seeking activities which provide pleasurable experiences (Havighurst and Feigenbaum, 1974). Perceiving recreation activities as pleasurable may help to explain the enthusiasm of individuals who *repeatedly* plan or seek opportunities for participation (Kelly, 1990; Shivers and Fait, 1985).

Some authors view recreation for pleasure as a basic human need that is vital to the life-style of well-adjusted and healthy people (Burt, Meeks, and Pottebaum, 1980; Peterson and Gunn, 1984). Therapeutic recreation professionals frequently encourage a maintenance orientation with an emphasis on *regular participation* for handicapped children. Recognizing the value of a balanced lifestyle that supports regular opportunities for play encourages children to be more aware of the play experiences and not be limited to outcomes such as winning, losing, or completing an objective (O'Morrow, 1980, p. 123).

Although the concept of maintenance is not limited to commercial sources of recreation, useful program ideas and alternatives may be learned from successful recreation businesses. For example, popular amusement parks appear to be very successful at providing unique and challenging environments, rides, and experiences that people rate as exciting, fun, thrilling, and educational. Apparently, such commercial recreation enterprises are designed to provide positive, entertaining experiences for patrons *and* encourage return visits for repeated participation.

The use of **novelty** and **complexity** to stimulate the human senses may be important factors for attracting and maintaining the future interest of children in entertaining recreation (Ellis, 1973). The application of novelty to recreation programming can include planning activities that *have not been experienced recently* as well as *"new"* activities. For example, discovering a new area for bicycle riding or reintroducing a neglected hobby such as stamp collecting can make participation seem more novel. Thus, assessing handicapped children for their recreation history will provide insights into the maintenance of program novelty for professionals or parents who are seeking alternative ways for planning new activities.

The use of complexity in programming recreation activities involves adding information to the recreation experience to make participation more stimulating for handicapped children (Ellis, 1973, p. 92). The use of complexity can include increasing the task difficulty of one activity skill to make it more challenging or increasing the number of skills required for participation to expand a game and prevent boredom. For example, permitting a child to adjust the distance of a target or to try ski slopes of different levels of difficulty may enhance the experience of participation.

Serendipity

The concept of serendipity involves the discovery or awareness of desirable things not sought (Isaac and Michael, 1971, p. 178). The term **serendipity** is derived from a Persian fairy tale about the three princes of the Isle of Serendip (Ceylon) who repeatedly travel to the mainland to complete specific tasks. During their travels they never complete their missions, but they always have other valuable discoveries or experiences. Hence, the term serendipity implies unplanned discoveries of a positive nature.

Chubb and Chubb (1981, p. 250) discuss quality recreation experiences in terms of serendipitous conditions. That is, individuals who participate in recreation without long-term goals or preconceived notions allow the elements of surprise and spontaneity to influence the experience. For example, the unexpected sighting of budding plants or active animals during nature outings could be serendipitous experiences (Chubb and Chubb, 1981, p. 250; Dustin and McAvoy, 1984, pp. 14–15). Serendipitous conditions require handicapped children to be perceptive of opportunities and to take advantage of them when they occur.

In therapeutic recreation service, serendipitous conditions can encourage handicapped children to make spontaneous decisions as part of participation. Avoiding a crowded restaurant or movie theatre could lead to the discovery of a new restaurant, type of food, movie, or another source of recreation that would have otherwise been ignored due to planning. A trip to a shopping center could lead to the discovery of an unexpected bargain or merchandise item. A movie outing can provide children with insights for coping with daily living within an entertainment experience. The use of serendipity as an orientation for participation can be stimulating for handicapped children. Serendipity, however, may require the professional, parents, and the children to be comfortable with initial **uncertainty.** In this event, assertive problem-solving or exploration may then lead to opportunities for positive experiences.

In summary, recognizing orientations for motivation in recreation participation provides parents and professionals with alternatives for increasing the awareness of handicapped children and encouraging some level of independence (see Figure 3). It is possible that the four orientations may be used in combination or alternately depending on the preferences of the children involved. In addition, parents and professionals need not be limited to the four orientations described here. Ideally, increasing the awareness of handicapped children may result in motivated choices for independent participation in recreation activities.

MOTIVATION ORIENTATIONS

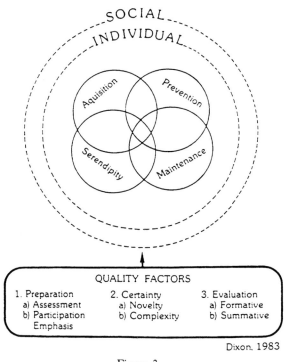

Dixon, 1983

Figure 3.

Discussion of Limitation

Intuitively, the concept of **acquisition** appears to require a child to be ambitious. In rehabilitation service, the patient is encouraged to restore or develop personal abilities which are reduced by a handicapping condition. In addition, the use of an assessment may clarify the absence of a specific ability. For example, wheelchair sport activities may be attractive to a child with paraplegia who desires wheelchair mobility skills and seeks participation in wheelchair sports. In contrast, it is possible for a child with paraplegia to show no interest in skilled sports participation and see no application to his or her personal lifestyle.

Similarly, a child in a psychiatric setting may be subject to group program planning to develop interaction skills and experience social opportunities. Such programming can provide model experiences for a transition or return to community settings. However, an individual child may elect a life style that is isolated compared to the objectives of parents or a treatment program. Parents and professionals may want to suggest prevention, maintenance, or encourage serendipity for children who are not oriented to acquisition.

The **prevention** orientation appears to be dependent upon the strength of a fear for motivating active participation. For example, a child's fitness efforts at reducing excess body weight may be motivated by avoiding the disapproval of a friend. If a child's feelings of affection terminate, however, the motivation for fitness may also decline. Similarly, in service settings for young legal offenders, a child may be motivated to participate in group recreation activities to avoid feelings of loneliness and develop social contacts. Unfortunately, a child's motivation for group interaction may diminish if he or she decides that a misunderstood and disruptive loner is a romantic and desirable image to project. In other words, a prevention orientation for recreation participation can be useful but is limited when fearful concerns diminish or can be rationalized by a child.

A **maintenance** orientation for recreation can be useful in therapeutic service settings where children are motivated to participate in recreation for fun. Emphasizing the pleasure associated with preferences for recreation is reinforcing for *continued* participation. In describing Positive Addiction, Glasser (1976) suggests that people may enjoy certain recreation activities so much they crave future opportunities for participation. Hence, it is essential for parents and professionals to be aware of the use of choices and opportunities to facilitate handicapped children to *repeat* recreation experiences. It is possible, however, for individual beliefs about recreation to inhibit the pleasure associated with participation. For example, there may be children who believe that too much pleasure is undesirable or is an undeserved reward (Havighurst and Feigenbaum,

1974). In this event, recognizing the concepts of acquisition, prevention, and serendipity may provide useful alternatives for motivation.

A **serendipity** orientation can be useful in situations where opportunities for spontaneity occur. Discovering new sources of interest, objects to observe, activities to experience, or changing a child's level of awareness can be positive benefits from recreation participation. Due to the spontaneous nature of the serendipity orientation, it is likely that a *summative* approach to evaluating recreation participation would be useful (Peterson and Gunn, 1984, pp. 141–142). That is, the inconvenience of problem-solving and dealing with uncertainty may require an evaluation of recreation participation within a framework of the total benefits.

One potential drawback for the use of serendipity as an orientation is that a child may choose to perceive opportunities as being externally planned by fate, powers, etc. The positive value of serendipity is related to the awareness of the child in responding spontaneously to experiences and discoveries. To suggest that serendipity involves preordained events deemphasizes the role of the child and implies an external locus of control (outside the person in participation). It is possible that a child could reduce his or her awareness for discovery and rely on external forces to establish positive discoveries or heightened awareness. For individuals who demonstrate a need for preplanned objectives and the certainty of outcomes, the use of acquisition, prevention, and maintenance could be emphasized with *formative* (progressive) evaluation strategies.

Distinguishing orientations for motivation in recreation participation is intended to suggest alternative ways handicapped children may recognize content influence. In addition, parents and recreation professionals can identify different values for activities which may contribute to the motivation of children with impairments. Ideally, planned intervention can increase the awareness of handicapped children and result in motivated choices for independent participation in recreation activities.

Orienting to a Model of Service

Developing a plan for action and programming activities for handicapped children requires a framework of therapeutic recreation service. For the purpose of discussion in the remainder of this chapter, the Gunn and Peterson model of therapeutic recreation service will be used to distinguish the emphasis of program planning. The model identifies three phases of service: rehabilitation, leisure education, and independent recreation (see Figure 4).

In the **rehabilitation phase** of service, the professional assesses a child to orient to his or her motivational preferences. Leisure activities are used as opportunities for activity that is enjoyable to the child. If there are goals or objectives specific to an impairment, then the intervention is intended to be therapeutic. If the participation experience is deemed to be habilitative or restorative in some way, then the participation is considered recreation (Kelly, 1990). **Rehabilitation** programming emphasizes the need to address the functional abilities of the child as a part of "therapy." This would include developing a rapport with a child to ensure effective communication and the development of physical and social skills that are prerequisite to many recreation activities.

Once prerequisite skills are demonstrated and the child's awareness and knowledge permit informed choices, **leisure education** is planned. The term *leisure* is appropriate because the activities used in programming represent participation opportunities outside of the contexts of vocation and academia. It is important for children to have options when participation is expected during leisure time. For example, when children choose one activity because it is the only activity they know, this is not a choice—it is a condition. Thus, recreation professionals frequently teach skills, provide knowledge of resources, and counsel with regard to awareness in order to encourage perceived freedom on the part of the individual.

The service phase, entitled **independent recreation,** is realistic when a child has some level of independence with regard to activity skills, opportunities for socialization, and a repertoire of activities to choose from for a personal leisure lifestyle. The recreation professional can serve as an important resource to a child who is independent by supervising participation opportunities with regard to accessibility. An accessibility guide for community recreation settings, innovative adaptations for recreation activities, and opportunities for integrating leisure experiences into personal growth plans are possible contributions. Recognizing these three phases of service can help to establish a linear contribution of service in the development of programs serving handicapped children.

COMPREHENSIVE LEISURE SERVICE MODEL
(Peterson and Gunn, 1984)

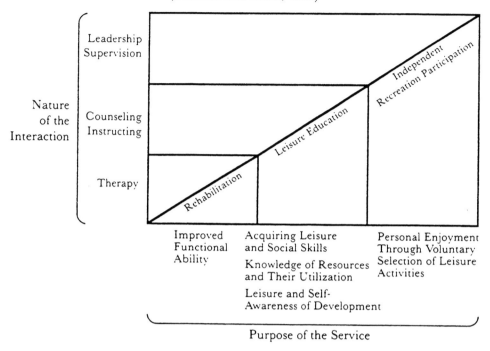

Carol Ann Peterson/Scout Lee Gunn, *Therapeutic Recreation Program Design: Principles and Proce-dures*, 2/e, c 1984, p. 12. Reprinted by permission of Prentice-Hall.

Figure 4.

TEACHING RECREATION SKILLS

Developing Abilities for Recreation Participation

Common goals of therapeutic recreation include improving the self-image of the participant and the way the participant is perceived by others (Kraus, 1983; Stein and Sessoms, 1977). In view of these goals, it would seem important for parents and professionals to be aware of the conditions and factors that influence the perceptual process when people systematically infer personal attributes on the basis of observable per-formances by themselves and others in recreation activities (Heider, 1944; Hastorf, Schneider, and Polefka, 1970). Perceived attributes can be personal qualities or conditions outside of the person which contribute to the outcome of participation in recreation activities (Hastorf, Schneider, and Polefka, 1970).

Based on an analysis by Heider (1958), causes for success or failure can be attributed to one or a combination of factors, including (a) ability, (b) effort, (c) task difficulty, and (d) luck. The factors **ability** and **effort** have been viewed as originating internally in the person during participation, whereas task difficulty and luck appear to be factors external or outside of people (Rotter, 1966). In terms of stability, the causal factors **ability** and **task difficulty** can be considered unchanging over time within a performance while effort and luck appear to be subject to unpredictable variance (Weiner et al., 1971). Hence, these causal factors can be viewed as *internal* and *external* as well as *stable* and *unstable*. Figure 5 illustrates the dimensions for these four causal factors.

DIMENSIONS OF CAUSAL ATTRIBUTIONS

Locus of Control

	Internal	External
Stable	Ability	Task Difficulty
Unstable	Effort	Luck

Figure 5.

The use of causal attributions appears to be learned (Katz, 1967; Coleman et al., 1966). In addition, the use of these causal factors as they are arranged in Figure 5 suggests a relationship between them. Perceiving failure as due to lack of ability (a stable factor) indicates that effort cannot reverse the performance outcome. However, failure attributed to effort, an unstable factor, suggests that the future outcome can be modified by exerting more effort.

When success is viewed as due to high ability (a stable factor), the probability of future success is supported. When success is attributed to effort (an unstable factor), any future outcome is subject to the variance of this trait (Bar-Tal, 1975). For example, a person who fails to return a volley in racquetball and feels that he or she did not have the racquet

skill to accurately hit the ball will not believe that running faster during a volley could enable successful hitting. In contrast, a child who feels that he or she did not hustle for correct body position in making a skilled return is likely to believe that he or she could have exerted more effort to succeed.

Success can also be viewed in terms of stability. A child whose racquetball skill is considered to be superior will likely be expected to succeed in future volleys with previously defeated players. However, when a child's success is attributed to someone else's fatigue or an unlucky break ("my foot slipped"), the outcome of future encounters will not be certain.

The usefulness of these attributions depends upon the insight gained concerning recreation service as it relates to handicapped children. The causal attributions ability, effort, and task difficulty are subject to the influence of therapeutic recreation intervention and have implications for a child's observed recreation satisfaction, self-concept, and the way they are perceived by others (Ellis, 1973; Weiner, 1974). Within the context of rehabilitation and leisure education, the use of successful intervention techniques suggests that training or education could be considered as additional external causal factors when explaining the recreation development of handicapped children (Dixon, 1979). When independent recreation participation is demonstrated by a handicapped child, he or she should receive credit in terms of personal abilities and efforts. The external use (outside of the child) of therapeutic recreation intervention as a causal factor should serve to reflect on the role and responsibilities of the parents and the professionals. Specifically, activities can be modified to encourage play behavior that is beneficial to the child in terms of his or her quality of life, health, and development.

Using Remedial References for Teaching Recreation Skills

Children who experience a handicap often do not exhibit appropriate recreation behavior (Ellis, 1973; Kraus, 1983). Some of these children have not had the same developmental experiences as "normal" children, nor have they been effectively facilitated through the developmental progression of motor skills (Wehman, 1977). As a result, handicapped children can appear to be slow or behind in their participation skills (Moran and Kalakian, 1977).

Motor activity, within the contexts of leisure, recreation, or play is viewed by many educators to be a potential medium for promoting skill development, fitness, social interaction, and intrinsic satisfaction (Bradke, Kirkpatrick and Rosenblatt, 1972; Kraus, 1983; Shivers and Fait, 1985). Therapeutic recreation programming sources typically include planning activity-related approaches which can serve as references in planning motor activities for remedial use with handicapped children. These remedial reference areas for motor skills and recreation participation include (a) **perceptual motor efficiency,** (b) **functional basic skills,** (c) **physical and motor fitness,** and (d) **rhythmic development** (American Alliance for Health, Physical Education, and Recreation (AAHPER), 1977; Council For Exceptional Children (CEC) and AAHPER, 1966; Institute For Physical Education, 1975; Moran and Kalakian, 1977). All four of the content areas involve physical movement and have a separate definition and rationale indicating their value as therapeutic recreation program content. Each of the four remedial reference areas are briefly defined and described as they appear in the literature.

Perceptual Motor Efficiency

The capacity to perceive sensory information from motor experiences when a child is participating in recreation activities includes the abilities to hear, see, and feel. The efficiency of this capacity will influence the quality of the play experience for children. When it is important for a child to demonstrate normative skills within a play environment or to respond to instruction, perceptual motor ability is an important variable. Perceptual motor ability is helpful to the individual in **organizing and systematizing the environment in order to make appropriate motor responses to sensory stimulation** (Moran and Kalakian, 1977). The following concepts are included in perceptual motor training programs (Bradley, Konicki, and Leedy, 1968):

1. Body image
2. Space and direction
3. Balance
4. Hearing discrimination
5. Visual discrimination
6. Form perception
7. Large muscle movement
8. Fine muscle movement

9. Symmetrical activities
10. Eye-hand coordination
11. Eye-foot coordination
12. Rhythm

During a perceptual motor training program one or more of these concepts may be emphasized during participation. For example, movement around the body's center of gravity (balance) and visually monitoring foot placement (eye-foot coordination) could be stressed while walking on a balance beam, a line on the floor, or playing hopscotch. Similarly, identification of body parts (body image) and moving correctly on command (space and direction) could be emphasized and developed during a game of "Simon Says."

Functional Basic Skill Efficiency

A number of traditional recreation activities as well as New Game activities involve the use of repeated or sequenced motor skills. The ability to exhibit motor skills which ordinarily develop instinctively (**phylogenetic skills**) and to learn additional motor skills necessary for participation in desired games (**ontogenetic skills**) can complement activities of daily living. A repertoire of basic skills has a strong application for functioning in an academic, a vocational, or daily living situation, e.g. walking, pulling, pushing, lifting. Many recreation activities include variations of learned skills such as running, throwing, catching, swinging, dancing and marching. Two major categories of basic skills are identified in Table 8.

A knowledge of basic skills is particularly useful for analyzing recreation activities and identifying the prerequisite skills necessary for participation. Many of the demands of daily living and opportunities for recreation are oriented to the phylogenetic and ontogenetic skill categories.

Physical and Motor Fitness

There is value in linking the concepts of fitness and playful activity as they relate to human health. Vigorous playful activity is considered to complement a person's fitness level. In addition, activity that is fitness-oriented and playful can balance with work and result in a healthy life style. This author prefers to go beyond the perception of fitness activity as obligated exercise. Playful activities which increase human fitness can

Table 8. Phylogenetic Skills (Instinctive).

Crawling	Jumping
Walking	Running
Kicking	Hopping
Throwing	Climbing
Pulling	Swinging
Pushing	Squatting
Rolling	Catching
Kneeling	Hitting
Hanging	
(The Illinois Program, 1972)	
Ontogenetic Skills (Learned)	
Marching	Surfing
Dancing	Skating
Bicycle Riding	Sailing
Car or Motorcycle Driving	
(Moran and Kalakian, 1977)	

Note: The skills listed in the two categories are intended to be representative rather than definitive.

represent fun, perceived choice, and exist within a maintenance orientation for recreation participation (Dixon, 1994).

Fitness refers to a bodily state which characterizes a person's ability to function in daily life (Wheeler and Hooley, 1976). Physical (**Organic**) fitness represents the *quantitative* capacity of the body tissues. For example, the strength or flexibility capacity of the body are measures of organic fitness. **Motor** fitness involves the body's *qualitative* capacity to move. For example, demonstrated balance or agility are measured within the category of motor fitness. Both balance and agility contribute to the appearance of movement that is skilled and well-timed. The components that are categorized under the organic and motor fitness headings are identified in Table 9.

The value of physical and motor fitness relates to the efficiency of bodily

Table 9. Physical and Motor Fitness Categories.

Organic Fitness	*Motor Fitness*
Strength	Balance
Flexibility	Agility
Muscular Endurance	Speed
Cardiovascular Endurance	Coordination
Reaction Time	
(Moran and Kalakian, 1977)	

function or movement and has desirable implications for self-concept, e.g. feeling good with one's own body (Wheeler and Hooley, 1976). The fitness level of children is often measured and developed during participation in recreation activities due to the level of demonstrated motivation.

Rhythmic Movement

Rhythm is a common element within recreation activities such as listening to music, dancing, or skilled participation in sports. The concept of rhythm is a connection of parts into a whole. Rhythmic movement involves energy, action, and control, as well as relaxation and release. Rhythm in action is demonstrated by coordinated movement patterns where parts of the body move in a timed sequence that appear smooth and controlled (Godfrey and Thompson, 1966).

Music and sound can also guide expressions of movement. For example, a person can respond to the rhythm he or she feels in his or her body through playing a musical instrument. Rhythm, in relation to motor performance, is classified into three categories distinguished by the character of the movements and the use of apparatus. All three of these categories can be utilized across recreation participation which involves human movement.

Nonlocomotor Rhythm. This category includes bodily movements that are made while the feet are stationary. This type of movement includes bending, stretching, swinging, twisting, swaying, and raising or lowering the upper parts of the body. Example: Many people enjoy listening to music and enjoy the beat without engaging in locomotor activity.

Locomotor Rhythm. This category involves bodily movement or travel from place to place. Locomotion requires a relocation or change of the body's base of support and includes walking, running, jumping, hopping, leaping, and handsprings. Example: Locomotion with an emphasis on rhythm is frequently associated with dancing (with or without music) and improving the performance of specific traditional sports skills. Due to the concern for control, coordination, and timing of locomotor movement, there would appear to be a qualitative measure used to evaluate locomotor rhythm. That is, the recreation experience of dancing or the level of achievement in performing an activity skill would be influenced by the perception of rhythm within locomotion.

Manipulative Rhythm. The category of manipulative rhythm is an important variable in recreation activities which require physical performance in relation to equipment. This category includes the movement or manipulation of items such as ropes, balls, wands, hoops, and musical instruments in relation to time. The physical manipulation of objects is observable and can be performed in a stationary position or in locomotion. The size and the nature of the objects will determine whether the movements utilize large or fine muscles. Sound or music can be used to assist or guide the participant in manipulative rhythms. When musical instruments are used, the sound or music created can be used to judge the quality of the motor involvement.

One value of rhythmic training is the efficient and skilled movement that results when a person is able to sense and accurately express rhythm. Examples: Skilled performances of activity skills that require the manipulation of equipment involve manipulative rhythm. Bowling, tennis, badminton, volleyball, and baseball are common activities which require participants to develop a sense of rhythm in manipulating the necessary equipment. The development of a comfortable rhythm will assist the participant in achieving consistency and accuracy during participation. In addition, the use of musical instruments, including percussion instruments, are obvious examples due to the production of a rhythmic product-sound. However, if an observer can view a skilled performance of music without focusing on the sound, the *movement* of the player will appear to be very controlled, coordinated, and timed.

Comments on Rhythm as an Activity-related Approach

The concept of rhythm is a very relevant variable in the analysis of leisure or recreation behavior. Whether participants are children or adults, authors agree that a certain sense of rhythm is necessary for people to develop skills or to move beyond functional levels of participation (Glasser, 1976; Nachmanovitch, 1990). For example, Glasser (1976) and Nachmanovitch (1990) suggest that skilled creativity is a direct result of developing a type of relationship with an activity that involves the equipment and results in a feeling of rhythm. This relationship helps to provide a sense of control as well as confidence for the participant. For this reason, the concept of rhythm should be acknowledged and encouraged where appropriate within recreation participation.

It should be noted that there may be some overlap for the development of rhythm with other remedial reference areas. The same movement or activity can be used in different remedial reference approaches; however, there may be a different purpose emphasized for participation.

For example, an individual may be asked to hop on one foot for a given distance as quickly as he or she can (fitness-speed). In contrast, a participant could also be requested to hop, in time, to the beat of a selected piece of music as part of rhythmic training (locomotor rhythm).

Overall, each of the four remedial reference approaches identify different motor abilities that have relevance for participation in recreation activities. These skills contribute to an individual's capacity to function in daily life situations, as well as to participate in leisure or recreation. The application of these remedial reference areas as a sequenced approach is addressed in the following section.

Recognizing a Hierarchy for Remedial References

The four remedial reference approaches may appear in the literature as separate content areas or be combined within selected activities (Braley, Konicki, and Leedy, 1968; Hackett, 1970). In therapeutic recreation service to handicapped children, any one of the remedial reference approaches could be justified as a module within an activity program. For children who experience a severe handicap, all four of the remedial reference approaches may be valuable and a necessary part of **long-range programming.** For parents or professionals who are programming establishing priorities or recognizing a **hierarchy** for these approaches may be helpful. Projected long-range goals for the use of the remedial references could help to guide the professional or the parent in systematically sequencing behavioral objectives and facilitating transitions in activity skill training with handicapped children. Based upon the nature of the content described for the remedial references, there is a logic for sequencing the four approaches in a therapeutic recreation program (see Figure 6).

Perceptual motor efficiency is identified first in Figure 6 because it is fundamental to a child's awareness of his/her own body, the ability to move, and the body's relationship to the environment. It is important for any handicapped child, in the context of a play activity or other daily living situations, to initially perceive and process stimuli correctly in order to make an appropriate motor response. If a handicapped child does not perceive stimuli during participation in recreation activities, then the personal feedback necessary for intrinsic motivation would be unavailable (Dixon, 1980). A handicapped child cannot be expected to efficiently perform basic functional movements if he or she does not perceive and correctly interpret information from other people, the environment, and movement experiences.

Given that a handicapped child can make the appropriate motor responses to sensory stimulation, functional basic skill efficiency is identified as a sequential approach in Figure 6. Therapeutic recreation service goals include teaching appropriate or normal leisure behaviors to handicapped children (Council for Exceptional Children and American Alliance for Health, Physical Education, and Recreation, 1966; Ellis, 1973; Wehman, 1977). Ideally, a repertoire of functional basic motor skills could be readily applied within the context of playing a game or a fitness activity. Children who experience a handicap should be competent in the necessary basic skills before he or she is encouraged to perform them as part of a fitness approach. Programming that is described as a fitness approach is sequenced third in Figure 6.

A reasonable amount of both physical and motor fitness is essential for handicapped children in educational opportunities and recreation activities where physical stamina and skilled motor ability are necessary for independent participation. A functional level of both motor and physical fitness should facilitate a feeling of well-being in the handicapped child and add to their quality of life (Wheeler and Hooley, 1976). The promotion of physical fitness in both the organic and motor categories is commonly achieved through the use of basic motor skills. For example, running is frequently used to develop cardiovascular endurance, lifting a weighted object can be used to develop strength, and walking on a line can be used to develop balance (Hackett, 1970; Moran and Kalakian, 1971).

Ultimately, the degree to which handicapped children can be successfully integrated into society will depend, in part, on their physical capacities and their competencies demonstrated to the public (Dixon, 1979). The demonstrated quality of movement often characterized as smooth or graceful is dependent upon the timed sequence of movements in accordance with the appropriate rhythm (Arnheim, Auxter, and Crowe, 1973). In recreation events such as the Special Olympics, participation may include running, throwing, or jumping and develop the rhythmic abilities of the participants. For informal group situations the rhythmic use of music and dance is popular and offers leisure choices for children during unobligated time. It should be noted that the programmed use of rhythmics does not have to follow perceptual motor, basic skill, and fitness training, since it could be encouraged at anytime for facilitating creativity with children. However, if motor proficiency is a *long-range* treatment goal, the other previously described approaches would complement and facilitate the success of handicapped children in rhythmic activities by first establishing prerequisite skills and physical capacities. Thus, the use of rhythmic movement, as a programming approach is sequenced fourth in Figure 6.

A Remedial Reference Hierarchy

A hierarchy has been illustrated which suggests a sequence for programming the four remedial reference approaches for use with handicapped children in recreation programming (see Figure 6). One feature of the model presented is that *play behavior* is a conceptual umbrella component. This is very important, in that therapeutic recreation service should emphasize exploration and facilitate intrinsic motivation during an activity period for each of the remedial reference approaches. This can be accomplished through the use of effective intervention techniques which provide opportunities for choice, deemphasize time limits, and orient participation to the individual child (see Figure 2). The author of this chapter has deliberately avoided an emphasis of achievement or exercise as reasons for participation. Although performance or participation benefits may include skilled participation or fitness, they are intended to be the results of a type of **elected participation** (see Figure 2).

Leisure education may use the hierarchy as a reference in planning programs and facilitating independent participation in a recreation activity. It is intended that this hierarchy be applied where an overall deficiency in motor performance ability is noted with handicapped children. The hierarchy presented is a suggested sequence for systematically presenting the four remedial reference areas in a long-range therapeutic recreation program.

The sequence in Figure 6 is intended to emphasize the value of having recognized prerequisite abilities for active leisure or recreation in order to plan for progressive and successful experiences. Ideally, each remedial reference approach would be programmed by the professional or parent to encompass both the treatment (participation) goals and the intrinsic needs (preference) of the children involved. The author assumes that the completion of each approach would be planned in accordance with specific objectives identified prior to implementation. Where handicapped children are considered to have an overall deficiency in motor

REMEDIAL REFERENCE MODEL
FOR THERAPEUTIC RECREATION SERVICE
(Dixon 1980)

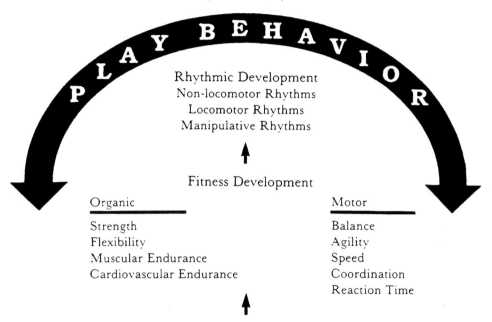

Rhythmic Development
Non-locomotor Rhythms
Locomotor Rhythms
Manipulative Rhythms

Fitness Development

Organic	Motor
Strength	Balance
Flexibility	Agility
Muscular Endurance	Speed
Cardiovascular Endurance	Coordination
	Reaction Time

Functional Basic Skill Development

Walking	Rolling	Squatting
Marching	Jumping	Catching
Kicking	Crawling	Kneeling
Throwing	Hopping	Hitting
Pulling	Climbing	Running
Pushing	Swinging	Hanging

Perceptual Motor Development

Body Image	Symmetrical Activities
Space and Direction	Eye-Hand Coordination
Balance	Eye-Foot Coordination
Hearing Discrimination	Form Perception
Large Muscle Movement	Rhythm
Visual Discrimination	Fine Motor Movement

Figure 6.

performance skills, the sequence of remedial references should help the professional or the parent to make program teaching decisions and to establish specific measurable objectives for therapeutic recreation content.

Activity Analysis Oriented to Intervention

Recreation professionals are expected to develop effective approaches for presenting recreation activities to special populations (O'Morrow, 1980). In the leisure education phase of therapeutic recreation service, teaching procedures help to communicate information about an activity to a handicapped child. It is important that the interaction between the teacher and the learner result in a mutual sharing of information. The learner can develop a greater awareness of the motivating characteristics of the activity or experience while the professional gains insight into the learning preferences of the handicapped child. A teaching-based activity analysis procedure can help to prepare the professional or parents to present recreation activities to children who experience a handicap with participation.

Activity analysis has been described as a procedure for examining an activity to understand motivational factors and qualities that complement professional treatment goals (Peterson and Gunn, 1984; Kraus, 1983; O'Morrow, 1980). This includes dividing an activity into component or behavioral requirements for participation and planning a systematic evaluation. However, activity analysis could include specific considerations which would assist the professional or the parent in actually teaching or presenting recreation activities effectively (O'Morrow, 1980). The author wishes to recognize the contributions of materials on task analysis by Gold (1980) and kinetic analysis by Shivers and Fait (1985). Both approaches contribute information which applies to the teaching of recreation skills to handicapped children (Carter, Van Andel, and Robb, 1985; Shivers and Fait, 1985).

This author applies many of the concepts of task analysis and kinetic analysis within the concept of activity analysis. This author feels it is appropriate to plan the intervention necessary for leisure education within the process of activity analysis. In addition, the distinction between the terms *playful activity* and *task* suggest that leisure or recreation activities originate within an orientation to choice (see Figure 2). In addition, leisure or recreation activities will involve experiences within the context of playful activity that are different from the context of work (see Figure 2). For these reasons, this author will refer to *activity analysis* rather than task analysis for use in teaching recreation skills to handicapped children. For a more indepth discussion of this issue, the reader is referred to paper by Dixon (1995) entitled "Task-oriented Versus Activity-oriented Intervention."

The identification of a teaching-based activity analysis procedure may encourage professionals and parents to be flexible in their teaching techniques. The concept of teaching flexibility includes consideration for the skills of the teacher as well as the handicapped child. Developing teaching alternatives should encourage the identification of techniques that ultimately result in successful interactions when recreation activities are presented. The three phases for developing a teaching-based activity analysis procedure include: (a) the demonstrated method of recreation participation, (b) the identification of recreation participation content which defines the method, and (c) the process of designing strategies for teaching the participation content.

The Method of Recreation Participation

The demonstrated method of recreation participation is an important consideration for ensuring access for the handicapped child. **Different methods for participation** are illustrated by the following approaches.

The Use of a Functional Device. The purpose of a functional device is to serve as *a tool* for assisting the handicapped individual to perform a recreation activity. Handicapping conditions can often be negated in recreation participation through the use of a handle, holder, an extension, or bracing materials. For example, handles attached to puzzle pieces may allow a handicapped child who is lacking in fine motor skills to manipulate the pieces with an open hand (see Figure 7). The use of a wheelchair facilitates mobility for the child with limb paralysis or motor spasticity. An extended handle can be designed for push-and-pull toy cars, trucks, etc., so the child using a wheelchair can have access to and control floor toys. Overall, it is important to emphasize that the use of a functional device within the concept of method refers to *use by the participant* rather than the professional or the parent during recreation participation.

The Use of an Alternative Stimulus. The purpose of using an alternative stimulus is to direct the feedback from recreation participation through *the accessible senses of the individual.* A handicap may be experienced in participation if the physical sense required for an activity

Figure 7. Adapted puzzle pieces.

is inaccessible. In the case of a visually impaired child, games that utilize color, knowledge of position, and other visual cues may seem inaccessible. One example of changing the method of participation with an alternative stimulus could be the adaptation of the game "Twister" by using tactile fabrics on colored areas or playing boards (see Figure 8). This adaptation is intended to motivate the visually impaired child to use the sense of touch to problem solve, manipulate game components, and monitor changes within a game.

Target games which traditionally use visual information may be adapted with materials that provide distinctly different auditory cues when struck by a coin, ball, etc. (e.g. tin foil, foam rubber, wood). Different auditory cues could reflect the accuracy of attempted throws. This method of participation (using an auditory stimulus) is intended to encourage visually impaired children to participate and to monitor their changing scores independently. Ideally, the use of an alternative stimulus in adapting recreation activities represents a service approach which can emphasize the abilities of a handicapped child.

Figure 8. Twister adapted.

Changing the Participation Technique. The purpose of changing the participation technique for a leisure activity is to acknowledge *alternative methods of performance.* The changes in participation technique may or may not involve a functional device but should reflect a level of independent recreation participation. There are occasions when changing the method or technique for doing an activity can facilitate the participation of children who would otherwise experience a handicap. For example, the method of using a fishing rod and reel with one hand instead of two permits individuals with hemiplegia to be independent (see Figure 9). Mouthwriting and footwriting also represent alternative methods for pursuing artistic painting for individuals who do not have the use of their hands.

Changing the participation technique for an activity requires the professional or the parent to have an understanding of the requirements of an activity and how the skills of the child can be substituted. For many years, participation in games and athletic sports from a sitting position has been a successful alternative method for individuals in wheelchairs. Rule changes have accompanied this adaptation, and the result has been international participation in recreation and sports activities by individuals who use a wheelchair.

Creating Transitional Recreation Experiences. The purpose of creating transitional adapted recreation experiences is to provide an opportunity for the handicapped child to learn useful *prerequisite knowledge and subskills* within the context of a program. For some children, a handicapping condition may be accompanied by a lack of prerequisite information or skill training necessary for independent participation. Independent participation can be facilitated in some cases by creating an adapted experience as a transition for learning information and developing awareness. For example, a fishing game can be useful for teaching children the prerequisite skills and purpose of using a fishing rod and

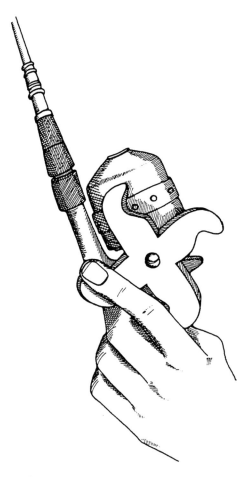

Figure 9. Hemicast adapted fishing reel.

reel (see Figure 10). This can occur as a part of leisure education prior to the introduction to an outdoor recreation environment. The objective of such a game parallels the fishing experience and allows for the introduction of safety rules and other concepts in preparation for a fishing trip.

Similarly, stuffed toys can be recognized as transitional toys for teaching body-part identification to handicapped children. The features of such toys are typically enlarged, easily identified, and can be associated with the child during a play session. An activity like Macrame can be introduced to handicapped children by initially teaching the prerequisite knot skills for using rope which would later be used for making plant hangers, wall decorations, etc. Utilizing transitional experiences with adapted activities is a useful method of participation where the concept of recreation is balanced with an emphasis on education.

Figure 10. Adapted fishing game.

During recreation participation it is the feedback a person receives from an activity that is reinforcing and increases voluntary movement at an independent level (Dixon, 1981; Shivers and Fait, 1985). Considering different methods for participation provides the professional or the parent with alternatives for making feedback more accessible to a handicapped child. In addition, the use of an alternative methods for participation may reduce the need for instruction.

Recreation Participation Content

Participation **content** refers to the **demonstrated behaviors that are required of the person to *complete* the method** of participation. For example, in bowling, the content can be listed as the following:

1. The grip of the ball
2. The three-step approach
3. The backswing
4. The delivery
5. The follow-through

The strategy of dividing an activity into parts so that each one can be learned separately and then integrated into the whole activity again has received mixed support in the research literature. Apparently, the nature of the activity can influence the way an activity is divided into parts for instruction. Schmidt (1976) provides a summation for use of the part method in teaching motor skills. Continuous skills such as swimming or riding a bicycle involve a time-sharing of movements. That is, there is an interaction between the movement components. To learn the timing and interaction, Schmidt (1976) recommends that continuous skills be taught and demonstrated as a whole. In contrast, a serial activity has a number of discrete or separate steps and allows the isolation of movements for teaching and practice. Assembling a puzzle, playing a game of chess, or operating a television set require a sequence of skills that can be isolated and taught as separate parts in a forward or a backward chaining procedure.

When the part method of instruction is used, the functional level of the child determines the number of steps or behaviors in participation content. For example, if the child's comprehension is severely impaired, the three-step approach in bowling can be divided into single steps or smaller units of learning. In contrast, a child with a high level of motor skill may be successful with the backswing, the delivery, and the follow-through of bowling combined into one step as a larger unit of learning. Recognizing potential problem areas in the list of content behaviors can be useful in preparing for the teaching process phase of activity analysis.

Gold and Pomerantz (1977) have identified two characteristics of learning situations that can help the parent or the professional to recognize and avoid confusion during leisure education. The authors make a distinction between bits of learning that are *informational* and *judgmental*. A leisure activity is considered **judgmental** if there are a variety of correct responses or non-specific feedback for completing an objective. For example, in archery the bow-string can be drawn at different lengths to release the arrow and hit the target, depending on the different procedures used for aiming. Similarly, a strike in bowling can be achieved by using a straight or curving roll of the ball. When an activity is introduced to a child, the objectives of leisure education can be clearly understood if the teacher identifies informational learning cues.

A recreation activity is **informational** for teaching if correct participation can be clearly identified and all other responses can be recognized as incorrect. For example, drawing the bow in archery might include touching the bowstring to the lips before releasing the arrow. Specifying this condition allows the participant to have immediate feedback on this aspect of their performance independent of the parent or the professional. That is, a handicapped child can recognize the objective and evaluate directly from his or her participation without intervention.

Similarly in teaching bowling, the use of a straight throw instead of a curve can focus initial attention on one method for throwing and making corrections in hitting the pins. Modifications of skilled attempts at rolling the ball should be more successful if there is consistency in the method used for throwing and fewer variables for the handicapped child to address in participation. In addition, the arrow markers in the lane near the foul line provide participants with early feedback regarding the accuracy of their throw and makes the learning process more informational. When learning is informational, it will be easier for the handicapped child to isolate the learning objective and to recognize guidelines for participation. The purpose of making judgmental aspects of content informational is to clearly identify what is right or wrong for achieving learning objectives.

In practice, the parent or the professional will find more resources for teaching and evaluating activity content that is informational. Limiting activity elements that are judgmental to clearly right or wrong decisions will provide the handicapped child with direct feedback from participation. As an impact of service, the handicapped child will be more independent and the likelihood of participation within a correct range of behavior (normalcy) will be increased (Gold and Pomerantz, 1977).

Planning the Process

The **process** of activity analysis refers to **the planned interaction between the teacher and handicapped child** when activity content is presented. Designing strategies for teaching activity content involves the following:

- Identifying desirable feedback for the learner
- Organizing and presenting the activity content
- Planning the type of interaction that will occur during the teaching process (Gold, 1976).

Recreation activities are motivating because of the desirable feedback the handicapped child receives during participation (Dixon, 1981; Shivers and Fait, 1985). Feedback from participation can include the demonstrated completion of an objective, the perception of stimulus such as music or a movie, and the nature of a social interaction with other participants. The feedback provided from recreation participation can be a reinforcer during the leisure education process. Hearing the song to be learned on an instrument, seeing art projects that belong to others who have completed instruction, or noting the degree of skilled improvement across a period of time are examples of using activity feedback from participation to motivate a learner. The motivation of handicapped children in a treatment setting will be directly affected by the accessibility of feedback during the leisure education process. Organizing the content and using an efficient format for presenting information should be planned around the motivation of a handicapped child.

Organizing and presenting the content of an activity will include selecting a group or individual setting for teaching (Gunn and Peterson, 1984; Kraus, 1983). Whether the setting is cooperative or competitive should depend upon the learning preferences of the handicapped child. Selecting a teaching format is also important. The use of forward- or backward-chaining techniques will depend on the nature of the activity.

Activities that provide the most motivating feedback upon completion should utilize a backward-chaining format whenever possible. For example, using a record player and assembling a puzzle are activities that permit the use of a backward-chaining format and emphasize the abstract feedback of the activity (as a whole) at the beginning of the learning process. There are many activities, however, that require a sequence of skill acquisition and logically require the use of a forward-chaining format. For example, throwing games such as darts or sequential movements in dancing are activities that involve prerequisite skills for independent participation to occur.

Social interactions or affective experiences that require social skills are probably taught most efficiently in the actual setting where the behaviors will be required rather than in artificial or practice situations. Ideally, the parent or the professional should use a strategic intervention that is supportive and constructive when identifying personal feelings or skill development in relation to the learning objectives.

Planning the Instructional Interaction. The interaction process planned for the activity analysis identifies how the parent or the professional will communicate information directly to the handicapped child. The teaching stimuli that can be used include **visual, auditory, tactile, kinesthetic,** and **abstract cues** (Dixon, 1981).

Visual Cues. Visual feedback is a common form of stimulus in recreation participation. When used to introduce a new leisure activity, the professional often demonstrates the activity to a child so that *he or she can see what participation would look like.* The visual demonstration is a valuable stimulus for communicating the nature of the intended activity as well as modeling appropriate behavior.

Auditory Cues. Auditory feedback is typically *experienced when listening* to records, tapes, or the radio. When used to educate a child about a recreation activity, verbal explanation or verbal direction as well as the sounds in the activity communicate information and feedback.

Tactile Cues. Tactile feedback is a valuable part of activities such as woodworking, making pottery, finger painting and other crafts or artistic pursuits. The ability to receive *information through the sense of touch* has proven to be of immense value for visually impaired children. Providing tactile feedback offers an additional stimulus by which the professional or parent can communicate information about a recreation activity to special populations.

Kinesthetic Cues. The *awareness of the body's position in space* is easily experienced in swimming where the water element and its properties of resistance give the individual sensation as he or she moves. Duplicating a basic movement in dance also requires a sense of body positioning as it relates to space. By assisting and guiding an individual's body through space or by calling attention to the position of the body (e.g. tying a ribbon to the body part), a stimulus for kinesthetic awareness is provided.

Abstract Cues. Abstract stimuli involve the role of the cognitive process in *conceptualizing the recreation activity as a whole.* If an individual has difficulty performing a physical skill in an activity, it is sometimes helpful to break it into parts and teach each phase or movement separately. After an individual learns an activity by the part method, it may help him or her to see the parts performed together as a whole and in the correct sequence. For example, bowling consists of the grip, the approach, the swing, the delivery, and the follow-through. Helping a child to understand how these parts fit together might include showing him or her these parts in their correct sequence and at a comfortable body rhythm. These kinds of cues show the individual how the separate parts of an activity fit together and help to convey a sense of timing necessary to ensure a skilled quality of movement.

These cues can be used separately or in combination. For example, auditory, tactile, and kinesthetic cues are appropriate for teaching the visually impaired child. Visual demonstration is a commonly used cue for hearing-impaired children. The selection of teaching cues depends on the learning preferences of the handicapped child. That is, the cues that are clearly perceived by the child should be used to communicate the teaching objectives.

In addition to effective communication, the teaching process should provide for a transition to a level of independent participation in the activity. The transition can be planned by identifying teaching cues which range from *strong to light intervention.* For example, physically manipulating a child's arm while teaching a swimming stroke is a stronger intervention than verbally guiding the rhythm of the movement. Similarly, physically moving a child's hand to the appropriate puzzle piece can be faded to a gesture of pointing to the correct vicinity.

Planning a transition from strong to light teaching cues allows the instructor to avoid a "sink-or-swim" feeling in the participant. The teacher does not convey an abrupt testing of the participant but promotes the mutual sharing of information and progression of skill development as a positive demonstration of learning acquisition. The degree of learning or level of independence will depend on the **criterion** used in the teaching process. Criteria are utilized within performance measures and are used to evaluate learning (Gunn and Peterson, 1984).

Determining criteria for learning one part of content or all of an activity is arbitrary. Peterson and Gunn (1984) suggest the least amount of the behavior that is still representative of the teaching intent for determining criteria. Gold (1976) suggests repeated performances of the skill in the setting where the activity will ultimately take place, e.g., in the community or the residential setting. In two separate studies by Dixon (1983, 1984) a 50 percent criterion level was used to teach a recreation activity to participants labeled as mentally retarded. Both of the studies yielded significant improvement in the skilled participation of the clients. The 50 percent level was selected in an attempt to create an intermediate level of novelty during the teaching process (Ellis, 1973). Negative effects on motivation were not observed in either study for this criterion level.

In general, the criterion level for teaching should be strict enough to ensure a level of independence and transition to other skills required for participation. To promote mainstreaming, a criterion level should go beyond sheltered situations and include the environment where the handicapped child is evaluated by society. For further information on alternative criteria, the reader is referred to materials by Gold (1976) and Peterson and Gunn (1984).

Distinguishing Content and Process for Programming and Evaluation

Leisure education programs for developing activity skills can directly affect the motivation of handicapped children during therapeutic recreation service. Gold (1980) has distinguished the **content** of skill development programs from the **process** used to communicate information about activities in order to clarify the impact of intervention in programming. In addition, recognizing the content and the process of leisure education can lead to a mutual sharing of information between the professional and the child during instruction or evaluations.

Recognizing Activity Content. Activity content refers to the list of observable behaviors that are required for the child to demonstrate a level of independent participation. Example: The activity of bowling includes (a) the grip, (b) the approach, (c) the backswing, (d) the delivery, (e) the ball release, and (f) the follow-through. Four benefits of identifying activity content are listed.

1. *The professional can recognize behaviors the child must demonstrate and identify teachable components.*
2. *The professional can plan the sequence of steps the child will complete and target potential problem areas.*
3. *The professional can recognize the child's ability level through the percentage of activity skills completed.*
4. *The professional can develop an awareness of how the activity parts fit together as a whole.*

A knowledge of what is to be learned provides the specialist with content behaviors for criterion-referenced instruction. As an additional part of leisure education, the how of instruction includes considerations for the skills of the specialist, the motivation of the child, and developing a level of independent participation. The term **process** refers to considerations for instructional intervention (**the *way* the activity content is taught**) (Gold, 1976).

Recognizing the Teaching Process. Planning the process of leisure education involves anticipating the interaction between the specialist and the child when an activity is presented. It should be noted that if a child is highly skilled and adaptive, the teaching process may appear to be of little significance. That is, the child may be able to participate successfully with a minimum of verbal instruction and visual demonstration. However, an emphasis on the teaching process used by a parent or the professional is intended to address problems that occur with a child's ability to understand and participate in recreation. Five benefits for planning the process of instruction are listed.

1. *The professional can develop a lesson plan for communicating information about an activity to a child.*
2. *Planning the process provides an opportunity for the professional to match his or her own teaching style and skills with the requirements of an activity.*
3. *In planning the teaching process, many decisions can be made in advance of the interaction with the child.*
4. *In planning the teaching process, the professional can anticipate transitional learning environments for the child.*
5. *Identifying learning objectives for the teaching process can help the professional to evaluate levels of independence and influence expectancies for client participation.*

In summary, the distinct characteristic of a teaching-based activity analysis is the planning of the interaction between the recreation professional (or parent) and the handicapped child. The practitioner should be aware of alternative methods for participation to develop accessible leisure activities. In order to introduce and actually teach activities, the professional or the parent should understand the content of the method for participation and plan strategies for teaching that content. This includes considerations for the motivation of the child, potential feedback from participation, the learning preferences of the child, and an effective format for teaching. An outline of this activity analysis procedure is included in Appendix I for assistance in preparing the presentation of activities to handicapped children.

The emphasis on professional preparation in therapeutic recreation service is motivated by three assumptions identified by Gold (1976). These assumptions about teaching are supported by the authors Hayes (1971), O'Morrow (1980), and the research experience of this author.

- First, the more a child experiences a handicap in recreation participation, the more the professional must know about teaching the activity.
- Second, the more the professional knows about teaching an activity, the less prerequisite skills are needed by the handicapped child. For example, the effective use of verbal, tactile, and kinesthetic cues in teaching an activity can eliminate the significance of a visual impairment.
- And third, the decision to teach or not to teach a recreation activity to a handicapped child must be based on whether or not that activity can be analyzed and effectively taught rather than on labels of impairment.

Developing Evaluation Strategies

The concept of evaluation in therapeutic recreation involves the collection of information in order to make useful judgments concerning the following issues:

1. The selection of leisure activities for program content.
2. The degree of intrinsic motivation and satisfaction demonstrated by the handicapped child during participation in recreation activities.
3. The benefits of recreation activities for children who experience a handicap (Peterson and Gunn, 1984; Kraus, 1983; O'Morrow, 1976).

Ideally, the evaluation process should be an integral part of a therapeutic recreation program. That is, the therapeutic recreation professional or parent should plan activities and design the conduct of a program with the intent of recording information about the children participating. Evaluation procedures can help to identify and clarify the value of a leisure experience in a remedial setting. The way handicapped children are portrayed in the evaluation process of a therapeutic recreation program will subsequently influence their independence in a recreation setting, their self-concept, and the way they are perceived by others. Thus, the professional or parents should determine the purpose of the evaluation process carefully during program planning.

The Purpose of the Evaluation Process

The evaluation of a handicapped child involves collecting information during an interaction with a professional, parent, or observing the child in a recreation experience. The purpose of the evaluation process may be **normative information, functional information,** or information concerning the **education and awareness** of a handicapped child.

Normative Evaluation. Normative evaluation generally compares the performance or behavior of a handicapped child with *cultural or developmental standards representing the majority of society.* In essence, this is a social comparison and reflects any deviancy from the norm. Normative evaluation is frequently used in recreation programming with mentally retarded children to determine age-appropriate behavior, etiquette, and desirable social or activity skills which are useful for achieving normalization and mainstreaming (see Figure 11).

Functional Evaluation. Functional evaluation does not use a social norm as a standard for making judgments about a child's level of participation in recreation. The demonstrated physical and mental skill of a child can be measured in relation to *the physical and mental requirements in a recreation activity.* For example, functional evaluation might be used with a physically handicapped child who does not have the use of a body part. An above-the-elbow amputee might require an adapted prosthetic device in order to operate both flipper buttons on a pinball machine. A functional evaluation would not focus on the physical difference of the individual from the majority of society. Instead, the evaluation information would be used to determine if the prosthesis was satisfactory for independence in the activity (see Figure 11).

Education-Awareness Evaluation. Education-awareness evaluation involves teaching and facilitating the handicapped child as part of recreation programming *before* judgments are made about his or her participation. The evaluation procedure does not use a social norm or a list of activity requirements for criteria. The programmed leisure experience is compared with *the remedial needs and personal interests of the handicapped child.* For example, certain **teaching cues** may be more appropriate for a child's abilities. Some children may prefer more kinesthetic and tactile cues for learning about shapes, whereas others may only require verbal direction. In addition, recognizing variables that characterize playful behavior and assessing a child's orientations to motivation (see Figures 2 and 3) may influence decisions for teaching or intervention. Preferences for learning are determined by the individual and can influence the participation in recreation activities if the motivation is recognized by the professional or the parent (see Figure 11).

Since the evaluation process in therapeutic recreation is a direct reflection of the person who experiences a handicap, it is important for the professional to clearly identify the evaluation purpose. This may involve isolating or combining the normative, functional, or education-awareness orientations to evaluation with respect to agency service goals or the individual needs of the child.

Developing Evaluation as a Part of Therapeutic Recreation Service

The following is a list of guidelines for developing the evaluation component of therapeutic recreation service for handicapped children.

A. Determine whether the patient or client is in need of the therapy, leisure education, or independent recreation phase of service (Peterson and Gunn, 1984).

B. Determine the intended purpose for conducting an evaluation of the handicapped child (normative, functional, education-awareness level).

C. Select the recreation activities to accurately reflect the purpose of the evaluation. (This is an intuitive process for the professional or the parent.) For example, determine whether the activities are desirable for encouraging social integration and normalization, developing functional mobility, or satisfying the program requests of the individual child.

D. Select the procedure for implementing the evaluation.

1. Identify your own strengths and preferences for evaluating the child.

2. Identify the strengths and preferences of the child.

E. Interpret the implications of the information collected in terms of the evaluation. This would include considerations for child's awareness of the evaluation purpose, the conditions of the evaluation, and the evaluation procedure.

THE PURPOSE OF EVALUATING A PATIENT OR CLIENT
IN THERAPEUTIC RECREATION SERVICE

Type of Evaluation Purpose	Comparison/Measure	Evaluation Result
Normative Evaluation	$=$ Patient or Client Behavior / A Cultural or Developmental Standard, e.g., Age appropriate behavior, etiquette, social skills.	Identifies patient or client deviances from the norm.
Functional Evaluation	$=$ Patient or Client Behavior / The Physical and Mental Requirements of an Activity, e.g., The ability to kick a ball in a soccer game.	Identifies skill deficiencies and competencies specific to an activity or situation.
Education-Awareness Evaluation	$=$ Necessary Professional Teaching or Facilitation Skills / Needs, Interests, and Abilities of the Patient or Client, e.g., Evaluate cardiovascular fitness in a group mile run. / Client prefers competition with other runners.	Identifies a facilitative basis for intervention with a patient or client in therapeutic recreation service.

Figure 11.

These guidelines are intended to emphasize the role of the therapeutic recreation professional or the parents in the evaluation of a handicapped child. There is insufficient standardized evaluation material for collecting information and making judgments about the recreation participation of handicapped children (Coyle, Kinney, Riley, and Shank, 1991). However until widespread procedures are adopted, clarifying the purpose and the process of *unique* evaluation efforts can provide parents and professionals with meaningful information concerning mainstreaming, functioning, and preferences for motivation.

Implementing Evaluation Within Recreation Activities

Ideally, evaluation can be a part of therapeutic recreation service if the process complements treatment goals and encourages the handicapped child to participate. Hopefully, the evaluation process will be a positive experience for the children being served. For example, a standardized procedure for evaluating mentally retarded children may need to account for individual differences in perceptual abilities. Some children may require more verbal direction or physical demonstration than others in order to clearly understand what is sought in the evaluation.

Enthusiasm should be exhibited and the spirit of fun should be promoted as a part of the evaluation process if evaluation is to occur within an activity. The therapeutic recreation professional or parents can model such an attitude and interact with the participants to make evaluation personal and non-threatening. If possible, it is also important for the handicapped child to have an awareness of the evaluation process and its purpose for him or her. This will encourage both positive and negative feedback regarding the evaluation process.

Finally, the result of evaluating children can emphasize the value of service and deemphasize a condition of impairment. For example, visual impairment may not be restrictive in a recreation activity if sufficient auditory, tactile, kinesthetic, and abstract cues are provided. The above-the-elbow amputee need not be excluded from activities that require two hands if a functional device can be substituted. Similarly, a hearing-impaired child can be included in activities that utilize auditory commands by including visual cues for participation, e.g. touch football. Interpreting evaluation information can identify considerations for facilitating independent participation in recreation activities rather than emphasizing individual differences. Ideally, therapeutic recreation programming should encourage the handicapped child to participate in evaluation rather than be subjected to it.

In order for therapeutic recreation professionals to be accountable for programming and administrative funding, evaluation procedures need to be well-planned and implemented. The role of evaluation in therapeutic recreation service will be directly affected by the purpose of the evaluation process. Evaluation can provide a social comparison, indicate a functional level of skill, contribute to the education and awareness of an individual, or be a combination of all of these factors.

It is important to know what you want, because if you try hard enough you are going to get it (Cox, 1979). This perspective on life has a strong implication for the role of evaluation. The way handicapped children are portrayed in evaluation of their recreation participation will influence their self-perception and the way they are perceived by society.

CONSIDERATIONS FOR COMMUNITY PROGRAMMING

Artificial Reinforcement and Motivation

If a child's level of independent participation is measured in an evaluation, the use of artificial versus natural motivators will be a concern. It is sufficient to recognize that when artificial motivators are used to influence participation behaviors, e.g., token rewards, they will have to be phased out at a later date for independent participation to occur. Ideally, professionals or parents can identify motivational factors that are part of *real* life rather than service settings in order to encourage mainstreaming and normalization (Datillo and Murphy, 1987).

Zero-Order Behaviors, Normalcy, and Recreation Participation

Zero-order behaviors exist with minimal outside support or no social reinforcement from external sources. The explanation for *these behaviors* is that they are expected by society and, therefore, *receive little or no attention until the individual terminates such a behavior.* Zero-order behaviors usually become a remedial concern when they are absent from a person's routine of daily living (Gold, 1980). The behavior of wearing clothing and personal hygiene maintenance skills are examples of zero-order behaviors. Appearing naked in public, failing to inhibit perspiration odor or neglecting to clean teeth prior to socializing attracts negative attention from other people.

The purpose of clarifying zero-order behaviors is to emphasize the absence of external social reinforcement for some behaviors in daily living. There may be some circumstances where people are expected to value certain behaviors without ongoing reinforcement (e.g. dressing and hygiene). However, if the value of recreation participation is treated like a zero-order behavior during childhood, children may find it difficult at a later date to sustain the long range development of recreation skills.

If normal play behavior is a treatment goal, parents and professionals should recognize the importance of regular opportunities for recreation participation. Leisure or recreation participation, like zero-order behaviors, is expected to be intrinsically motivated rather than externally directed. For parents of handicapped children, leisure participation may be a quality-of-life issue. That is, parents may want their child to initiate play. In treatment settings, however, appropriate recreation behavior will probably be programmed with remedial expectations (Kelly, 1990). When the treatment goals are reached, parents and professionals can avoid the zero-order status of recreation participation by *continuing* to reinforce the value of recreation in the lifestyle of handicapped children. Otherwise, recreation services may be treated as optional and only addressed *after* problems with motivation and life satisfaction occur.

A Least Restrictive Environment: The Most Appropriate Site

A least restrictive environment is probably best measured in terms of the handicapped child's ability to participate in recreation activities he or she prefers. Determining the least restrictive environment for a child's participation is crucial to a successful outcome. Understanding a child's abilities, likes, dislikes, and needs are all factors that influence program decisions regarding recreation participation. The decision to program segregated recreation experiences or mainstreamed recreation experiences will depend on the treatment goals of the professional and the parents as well as the personal needs of the child.

Examples of segregated therapeutic recreation programs include wheelchair athletics and the Special Olympics. Wheelchair athletics provide opportunities for physically handicapped individuals to compete in adapted sports, experience success, and demonstrate their motivation and abilities. Similarly, the Special Olympics program provides individuals labeled as mentally retarded with opportunities to participate in adapted sports and games within the forum of an organized event. Participation is the emphasis of the Special Olympics, and everyone is considered a winner. In segregated participation, the participants in these programs do not compete with individuals who are not labeled as impaired.

Two of the major contributions of these programs is that the participants are able to explore their abilities and clarify the nature of their impairment. In other words, a handicapped child can determine the nature of their own limitations through their own participation, observe the adaptations of other children with impairments, and seek to improve their capabilities for participation within the context of the programs. Such programs represent new experiences for many handicapped children and expand their awareness for the benefits of an active life style.

Segregated programs may call attention to the special characteristics of handicapped children (Wolfensberger, 1972), but they can provide a strong basis for the transition to mainstreaming experiences and achieving normalcy. Wheelchair athletics and the Special Olympics program may have been considered to be very unusual and outside of the mainstream when the programs were founded. Both programs, however, are currently conducted on an international level of participation and receive widespread media attention.

Mainstreaming implies success in the present system of therapeutic recreation services and other human services (Frein, 1976). It implies that all people can adequately develop and use leisure opportunities regardless of their place in society or the handicap they experience. Successful mainstreaming requires effective recreational services which result in adaptations or modifications to facilitate independent leisure participation for handicapped children. The concept of mainstreaming can be applied to therapeutic recreation service through the use of a continuum, with the conditions for independent leisure participation and impaired leisure behavior identified. Powell (1979) specifies five desirable conditions that would facilitate recreation participation of the handicapped child into the mainstream of society. These conditions are as follows:

1. The elimination of misconceptions about persons who experience a handicap with an emphasis on their acceptance and individual abilities.
2. The reduction of segregated settings and services with an emphasis on more integrated settings and services.
3. The conscious development of a less restrictive environment.
4. The movement of the client from a state of dependency to a state of independence.
5. A reduction of the emphasis on disabilities while increasing the potential and abilities of handicapped individuals.

It is doubtful whether any of these conditions can be achieved independently of each other. For example, achieving independence will require the development of ability. Acceptance of individual differences will be directly related to an integrated setting. Furthermore, the development of a less restrictive environment will depend on public attitudes, client participation, and the opportunity for integrated settings.

In graphically representing these five conditions on a continuum for therapeutic recreation service, it is necessary to include descriptions that relate to leisure satisfaction and independent recreation participation. Figure 12 illustrates the concept of facilitating a handicapped individual from a state of impaired recreation behavior to independent recreation participation. As an outcome, the handicapped individual demonstrates his or her independence in leisure participation in a least restrictive environment. Thus, society can become more familiar with special populations, and the potential for integration in recreation settings is increased.

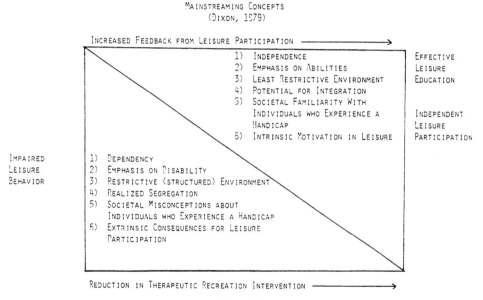

Figure 12.

CONCLUSION

Programming therapeutic recreation services for handicapped children involves the selection of appropriate activities, considerations for motivation, and the efficient use of intervention to develop activity skills and participation. This chapter was developed for practical application in programming recreation services for handicapped children. The information is intended for the parent, professional, or student who intends to develop leisure skills and encourage recreation participation. Ideally, playful behavior will occur spontaneously in treatment settings with children, but parents and professionals may recognize that intervention can improve the accessibility of recreation activities. The author has made an attempt to present material that is consistent with the terms *leisure, recreation,* and *play.* The material on teaching recreation skills was developed with an emphasis on a sequence and hierarchy for making programming decisions. The selection and development of material for this chapter has evolved from the author's own experience and professional preparation. It may help the reader to know that the selected content represents responses to questions posed in therapeutic recreation service settings with handicapped children.

REFERENCES

Arnheim, D., Auxter, D., & Crowe, W. (1973). *Principles and methods of adapted physical education.* St. Louis: C.V. Mosby.

Austin, D. (1991). *Therapeutic recreation: Processes and techniques.* Champaign, IL: Sagamore.

Avedon, E. (1974). *Therapeutic recreation service.* Englewood Cliffs, NJ: Prentice-Hall.

Bar-Tal, D. (1975). Individual differences and attribution analysis of achievement related behavior. Unpublished doctoral dissertation, University of Pittsburgh, Pittsburgh.

Bradtke, L., Kirkpatrick, W., & Rosenblatt, K. (1972). Intensive play: A technique for building effective behaviors in profoundly mentally retarded young children. *Education and Training of the Mentally Retarded, 7,* 8–13.

Braley, W., Konicki, G., & Leedy, C. (1968). *Daily sensorimotor training activities.* Mountain View, CA: Peek.

Burt, J., Meeks, L., & Pottebaum, S. (1980). *Toward a healthy lifestyle.* Belmont, CA: Wadsworth.

Carter, M., Van Andel, G., & Robb, G. (1985). *Therapeutic recreation: A practical approach.* St. Louis: Times Mirror/Mosby.

Council on Exceptional Children and the American Association for Health, Physical

Education, and Recreation (CEC and AAHPER). (1966). *Recreation and physical activity for the mentally retarded.* Washington, DC: AAHPER.

Chubb, M., & Chubb, H. (1981). *One third of our time.* New York: Wiley.

Coleman, J., Campbell, E., Hobson, C., McPartland, J., Mood, A., Weinfeld, F., & York, R. (1966). *Equality of educational opportunity.* U.S. Department of Health, Education, and Welfare.

Coyle, C., Kinney, W., Riley, B., & Shank, J. (1991). *Benefits of therapeutic recreation: A consensus view.* Ravensdale, WA: Idyll Arbor.

Cox, G. (1979). Excerpt from a conversation. Dallas, TX.

Csikszentmihalyi, M. (1975). *Beyond boredome and anxiety.* San Francisco: Jossey-Bass.

Datillo, J., & Murphy, W. (1987). *Behavior modification in therapeutic recreation.* State College, PA: Venture.

Dixon, J. (1979). The implications of attribution theory for therapeutic recreation service. *Therapeutic Recreation Journal, 8,* 1, 3–11.

Dixon, J. (1981). *Adapting activities for therapeutic recreation service:* Concepts and applications. San Diego, CA: Campanile Press.

Dixon, J. (1983). Teaching recreation skills to mentally retarded individuals using the whole and part methods. *Journal of Recreation and Leisure, 3,* 1, 5–11.

Dixon, J. (1984). Research on teaching recreation skills to adults labeled mentally retarded. *Society and Leisure, 7,* 1, 259–268.

Dixon, J. (1984). Recognizing orientations for participation in therapeutic recreation service. *Expanding Horizons in Therapeutic Recreation, 12,* 288–307.

Dixon, J. (1994). Therapeutic recreation, choice, and nutrition as factors in weight loss of overweight children. *Annual in Therapeutic Recreation, 4,* 1993/94.

Dixon, J. (1995). Task-oriented versus activity-oriented intervention in therapeutic recreation. *Expanding Horizons in Therapeutic Recreation, 16.*

Dustin, D., & McAvoy, L. (1984). Toward environmental eolothism. *Environmental Ethics, 6,* 13–18.

Ellis, M. (1971, August). Play and its theories re-examined. *Parks and Recreation,* 51–57.

Ellis, M. (1973). *Why people play.* Englewood Cliffs, NJ: Prentice-Hall.

Frein, J. (1976). Mainstreaming: Origins and implications. *Minnesota Education, 2,* 2.

Glasser, W. (1976). *Positive addiction.* New York: Harper and Row.

Godfrey, B., & Thompson, M. (1966). *Movement pattern checklists.* Columbia, MO: Kelly.

Gold, M. (1976). Task analysis of a complex assembly task for the retarded blind. *Exceptional Children, 43,* 78–84.

Gold, M. (1980). *Try another way training manual.* Champaign, IL: Research Press.

Gold, M., & Pomerantz, D. (1978). Issues in prevocational training. In M. Snell (Ed.), *Teaching the moderately, severely, and profoundly retarded* (pp. 1–15). Columbus, OH: Charles E. Merrill.

Guralnik, D. (Ed.). (1975). *Webster's new world dictionary.* New York: World.

Hackett, L. (1970). *Movement exploration and games for the mentally retarded.* Palo Alto, CA: Peek.

Hastorf, A., Schneider, D., & Polefka, J. (1970). *Person perception*. Reading, MA: Addison-Wesley.

Havighurst, R., & Feigenbaum, K. (1974). Leisure and lifestyle. In J. Murphy (Ed.), *Concepts of leisure* (pp. 117–128). Englewood Cliffs, NJ: Prentice-Hall.

Hayes, G. (1971). Activity analysis: Finger painting for the mentally retarded. *Therapeutic Recreation Journal, 5,* 3, 133–138.

Heider, F. (1944). Social perception and phenomenal causality. *Psychological Review,* 51.

Heider, F. (1958). *The psychology of interpersonal relations.* New York: Wiley.

Illinois Program. (1972). *Systematic instruction for retarded children: Motor performance and recreation instruction.* Springfield, IL: Office of the Superintendent of Public Instruction.

Isaac, S., & Michael, W. (1971). *Handbook in research and evaluation.* San Diego, CA: Robert R. Knapp.

Iso-Ahola, S. (1980). *The social psychology of leisure and recreation.* Dubuque, IA: William C. Brown.

Jonassen, D., Hannum, W., & Tessmer, M. (1989). *Handbook on task analysis procedures.* New York: Praeger.

Katz, I. (1967). The socialization of academic achievement in minority group children. In D. Levine (Ed.), *Nebraska Symposium on Motivation, 15.* Lincoln: University of Nebraska Press.

Kelly, J. (1990). *Leisure.* Englewood Cliffs, NJ: Prentice-Hall.

Kraus, R. (1983). *Therapeutic recreation service: Principles and practices* (3rd ed.). Philadelphia: W.B. Saunders.

Moran, J., & Kalakian, L. (1977). *Movement experiences for the mentally retarded or emotionally disturbed child* (2nd ed.). Minneapolis: Burgess.

Morris, R., & Blatt, B. (1986). *Special education: Research and trends.* New York: Pergamon.

Nachmanovitch, S. (1990). *Free play.* New York: Tarcher/Putnam.

O'Morrow, G. (1980). *Therapeutic recreation* (2nd ed.). Reston, VA: Reston Publishing.

Peterson, C., & Gunn, S. (1984). *Therapeutic recreation program design: Principles and procedures* (2nd ed.). Englewood Cliffs, NJ: Prentice-Hall.

Rosen, M., Clark, G., & Kivitz, M. (1977). *Habilitation of the handicapped.* Baltimore, MD: University Park Press.

Rotter, J. (1966). Generalized expectancies for internal versus external control of reinforcement. *Psychological Monographs, 80,* (1, Whole No. 609).

Rubin, P., & Tregay, J. (1989). *Play with them-theraplay groups in the classroom.* Springfield, IL: Charles C Thomas.

Schmidt, R. (1975). *Motor skills.* New York: Harper and Row.

Shivers, J., & Fait, H. (1985). *Special recreational services: Therapeutic and adapted.* Philadelphia: Lea and Febiger.

Stein, T., & Sessoms, D. (1977). *Recreation and special populations* (2nd ed.). Boston: Holbrook.

Wehman, P. (1977). *Helping the mentally retarded acquire play skills.* Springfield, IL: Charles C Thomas.

Weiner, B. (Ed.). (1974). *Achievement motivation and attribution theory.* Morristown, NJ: General Learning Press.

Weiner, B., Frieze, I., Kukla, A., Reed, L., Rest, S., & Rosenbaum, R. (1971). *Perceiving the causes of success and failure.* New York: General Learning Press.

Wheeler, R., & Hooley, A. (1976). *Physical education for the handicapped.* Philadelphia: Lea and Febiger.

Wolfensberger, W. (1972). *The principle of normalization in human services.* Toronto, Ont. Canada: National Institute on Mental Retardation.

Chapter 7

ASSESSMENT:
A NEED FOR FURTHER ATTENTION

AUBREY H. FINE

There is no known way of reaching
the depths of something without
going through the surface.
D. E. Berlyne

INTRODUCTION

Assessment represents a critical dimension in the overall provision of recreational services for children. Unfortunately, many therapists feel inadequately prepared for their roles in the assessment process. Furthermore, some have a limited understanding of incorporating complete assessment procedures. Consequently, they perceive their work as being unproductive and integrate assessment procedures primarily due to legislative compliance and employers' demands. This chapter is intended to provide a clearer perception of the value of assessment as well as some alternatives to incorporate into the assessment process.

Identifying hidden treasures has always been a rewarding experience. T. S. Elliott reminds us, "We shall not cease from exploration and the end of all our exploring will be to arrive where we started and know the place for the first time." Assessment (for our purposes with children) can be inferred as the process of discovery, which can help one understand clearly the strengths and limitations of a child. In fact, I sometimes view direct assessment as a series of mini-experiments, trying to derive new pieces of data in regards to a specific child.

Many practitioners view assessment as incredibly complicated and mystical. This appears partially due to the lack of familiarity with the possible procedures. However, assessment could be understood as similar to the process of putting a puzzle together. When one applies correct planning and insight, any puzzle is easy to complete. Simply stated, assessment is the gathering of information in regards to a specific client.

There are a variety of procedures available for the inquirer to secure the information desired. Such alternatives are in the form of paper-and-pencil questionnaires and tests, actual performance examinations (e.g. gross motor activities), interviewing, observations, history gathering, as well as the completion of rating scales.

Given assessment is such a large topic and has been somewhat neglected, it seems imperative that this chapter initially provide a global overview. It is the intention of this writer to provide the reader with a sufficient theoretical as well as practical understanding of the usage and application of the data generated by an assessment procedure.

The following outline has been developed to assist the reader in understanding the components within this chapter. I have formulated a series of questions as a method of organizing this outline. Hopefully, these questions will assist the reader in discovering the inherent values of thorough assessment procedures.

1. Assessment: What is it?
2. Why should I invest energies to assess?
3. What kinds of information does an assessment procedure yield?
4. What are some practical suggestions for conducting an assessment?
5. Why do I really need to know anything about test construction and, for that matter, what do I need to know?
6. What are some potential assessment alternatives?

QUESTION 1: ASSESSMENT—WHAT IS IT?

Wallace and Larsen (1978) suggest that assessments allow therapists to make decisions based on the data gathered during an assessment process. They provide a rationale for the inclusion of measurement procedures as an integral aspect of treatment. Some of their points of view are as follows:

(1) **To group children.** At times it is valuable to assess children so they can be placed in programs that fit their strengths and limitations.

(2) **To provide a framework to develop remedial instruction.** Therapists are encouraged to gather information germane to a child or a group so that program development can reflect this information.

(3) **To analyze the capabilities and accomplishments of clients.**

Measuring capabilities and accomplishments is the element which many view as being the primary purpose of a comprehensive assessment.

(4) **To measure the outcomes of instruction.** For quality assurance, it is imperative that the impact of implemented programs is analyzed. A major purpose of an integrated and consistent evaluation process is to provide feedback about the program. Consequently, the information derived can assist in modifying or stabilizing the effectiveness of service delivery. Therefore, the assessment process is not a one-time intake procedure but a related process of discovery, conjecture of need, measuring gains and then continually going back to analyze further or in-depth needs.

(5) **To provide material for research.** Although this element may be the least practical, the use of measurement devices are imperative in regards to research. Research impacts the field of treatment by enhancing the present body of knowledge through identifying positive and negative aspects of programs.

Fuchs and Fuchs (1986) suggest that assessment processes are employed to objectively describe children and their instructional environments, to generate hypotheses concerning alternative instructional methods, and to finally appraise, evaluate and inductively develop instructionally sound programs. Furthermore, Wehman and Schleien (1980) noted three additional goals of assessment in therapeutic recreation. They state that an individual's progress on specific skills should be frequently monitored so that staff can do the following:

1. Receive enough feedback to analyze the progress of a child. The more frequently a child's skills are diagnosed, the easier and more proficient the process becomes.
2. Make necessary modifications in the methods or materials being applied as well as ascertaining whether the sequence of instruction is effective or not.
3. Verify that objectives have been obtained.

While all of these aforementioned points are crucial, the primary purpose of the assessment process is to gather information that can be used in planning instructional programs. The data gathered during the process will help the therapist in further understanding a child's specific needs and suggest various instructional strategies and procedures.

Dunn (1984) points out that in regards to therapeutic recreation, assessment should be understood as a systematic procedure for gathering specific information which pertains to the individual. This information then can be integrated for the purpose of making programmatic decisions. Furthermore, Dunn (1984) stresses that the overall process must not only complement the client's needs but the agency's goals as well. For example, she points out that an in-depth analysis may be inappropriate for short-term-based programs. The writer is in agreement with this point of view only to the extent that the professional always considers the feasibility of an in-depth assessment. This is to say, the goals that are formulated for short-term interventions need to realistically project viable alternatives. It would be utterly ridiculous to expect a program to supply all the needed growth for a person when it was extremely short. Furthermore, short-term-based programs are usually ineffective if they are not tied into existing resources available in the community.

The assessment procedure can be viewed sequentially. Salvia and Ysselkyke (1985) conceptualize an assessment model that constitutes five phases. Table 10 lists the various components.

Table 10. The Five Phases of a Sequential Assignment.

1. Purpose of the assessment
2. Screening
3. Interpretation
4. Application
5. Program modification

The process begins with a referral or a purpose to the assessment. This is then followed by the actual screening or assessment of a child. Within this phase the actual collection of data is generated. However, as it can be easily seen, the four other phases either set the way for the collection or are the methods generated to analyze or apply the information obtained. The three final phases of the model relate to the application of the findings. The third phase represents the stage for the interpretation of the data. This is then followed with the final two stages which pertain to the incorporation of the findings in instructional planning and program modification. Both of these two steps are extremely crucial. Logically, instructional planning should be based on the identified concerns. Furthermore, instructional programs should be continually monitored to assess their overall effectiveness. All of these issues will be elaborated on in an upcoming section in this chapter.

Issues in Assessment Within Therapeutic Recreation

Dunn (1984) suggested several difficulties in the area of assessment within the field of therapeutic recreation. These difficulties will be used as a springboard for further discussion. The four areas are clustered as follows: general lack of assessment devices, inadequacies in test development, application deficits and staff training.

Lack of Assessment Procedures

Dunn (1984) strongly suggests that there is a significant void in assessment instruments solely developed for application in therapeutic recreation settings. She suggests that one alternative is to borrow instruments from other disciplines. The problem with this approach, Dunn points out, is that the findings do not always lead themselves to specific recreational interpretations.

Although this concern may be realistic in measuring generic leisure skills, the rubric of play behavior is dependent on various functional behaviors. These functional behaviors can be efficiently measured by several instruments on the professional market (e.g. gross and fine motor development, social skills, self-concept, self-help, language and cognition). If appropriate tests are applied to sample skills within these specific domains, an enormous amount of information can be secured and incorporated. Realistically, the dilemma may represent a lack of awareness within the field, in taking advantage of the most valid and reliable devices.

Inadequacies of Test Development

Many of the present-day instruments utilized in sampling recreational skills are unrefined and are so agency-specific that they are of limited value in other settings. Furthermore, there is a great difference between test construction and test application. Many practitioners develop tests solely for application and are not specifically concerned with the multitude of test construction problems. Dunn (1984) also suggests that these problems are further complicated because of the lack of an accepted or universal conceptual framework for leisure.

Problems of Utilization

There appears to be widespread abuse of test utilization as well as interpretation. Assessment cannot be looked upon telescopically. There is great diversity in the elements of an assessment. As a consequence, one should not be misled into believing that one instrument can answer all of the formulated questions. There is no simple answer. Information will have to be gathered through a multitude of sources.

Staff Qualifications

Until recently, professional preparation in the area of test and measurement has been significantly limited. However, with the ever-changing demands of the profession, recreational personnel have been required to initiate more comprehensive programs that incorporate an assessment process. Dunn (1984) suggests that there has been some progress made in this area both at the preservice (undergraduate) as well as professional level because of its perceived importance.

It is anticipated that in the future, professionals with a stronger background in the area of measurement will take the major role of supervising or initiating a majority of the measurement duties of their agencies. It is inappropriate to expect minimally trained persons to be responsible for conducting or interpreting and developing comprehensive assessments. The charge of this role should not be considered lightly. It is evident that greater emphasis must be placed in this area in undergraduate and graduate training programs. Attention also will need to be given to providing more comprehensive seminars to professionals in the field. These seminars will need to address practical concerns in addition to being extremely comprehensive.

QUESTION 2: WHY SHOULD I INVEST MY TIME ASSESSING?

The importance of assessment is supported in the philosophical position statement adopted by the National Therapeutic Recreation Society (1982). Within this philosophical statement is the assertion that programs should be developed by assessing the clients' needs and that strategies to monitor and measure clients' progress should be included. The implications of this revised definition will gradually have a significant impact on the field as a whole in addition to the direction in training at institutions of higher learning.

As can be interpreted by the following statement, assessment should be considered as a natural ingredient to program planning. When one does not complete a thorough intake, information in regards to the client's needs is insufficiently addressed. Consequently, the program goals generated eventually suffer and the outcomes attributed to program involvement are questionable at best!

As stated earlier, assessment is something we hear a lot about but remains an area in which some professionals feel inadequate. Some attribute a mystic quality to the field of measurement. However, there is nothing mysterious about it; most of the procedures merely require good judgment and specific training. Nevertheless, numerous assessment procedures really do have significant limitations! In fact, it is not the assessment instruments that lead to a thorough diagnostic impression but rather the professional's ability to glean from the data his/her judgments and interpretations. It is therefore imperative for an assessor to respect the integrity of the instruments applied and recognize that they are only tools by which one can uncover hidden treasures. The ultimate decisions are made by the individual, who synthesizes and interprets the findings and develops realistic expectations.

It is important to acknowledge that even the most reliable assessment instruments are sometimes misused. The art of assessment must not be conceptualized as the ability to administer tests or to observe behavior but, rather, to reveal the findings and apply them. Being able to synthesize and wisely incorporate the information obtained is the benefit of going through this process.

What Information Do You Usually Have At Your Disposal?

There is a wealth of information readily available at the therapist's disposal. I have always found this data helpful in augmenting assessment procedures that are incorporated. Again, let us return to my puzzle analogy. What I know about the design of my puzzle alters my expectations of how I proceed in completing the project. A similar assumption must also take place when analyzing a child's strengths and limitations. Take advantage of the obvious as well as what is already known from earlier situations. So let us briefly look at some of the pre-assessment information that is usually readily available.

(1) What Do You Know About the Client You Want to Assess?

Prior to incorporating formal or informal assessment procedures, efforts should be made to collect as much information about the child under investigation as possible. There are a variety of areas that could be pursued. For example, one should take advantage of collaboration with parents, significant others, and those who have previously worked with the child. All of these sources should be respected and not overlooked. In fact, all of these alternatives should be starting points, possibly in conjunction with the entire assessment procedure.

Numerous available questionnaires can be administered to families in addition to conducting a structured interview as methods to gain insight into the specific needs of a child. Families not only can give examiners a thorough orientation to their child, but they can additionally tell the therapists about their expectations. Parents are frequently the only individuals, aside from a few professionals, who see the child as a whole person. Furthermore, parents are able to observe how their child uses leisure skills for long periods of time in his/her natural environment. Obviously, information from family members should be respected and not overlooked.

Securing information from previous programs that a child was involved in represents another rich avenue for gathering input. Contacting these programs and reviewing pertinent data from schools attended are all excellent sources. Some will argue that it is too demanding to expect a professional to consult with this many resources to only gain a broader awareness of a child. This may not be the alternative of choice for each case under investigation. However, it may be an alternative for some children when more input is necessary.

(2) What Are the Behaviors Presently Being Displayed by a Child?

An enormous amount of information can be gathered through the informal use of observation. The astute observer appreciates the fact that through his/her eyes much of the world can be unravelled and understood. Observations represents an alternative method in gathering information. There are several formal and informal observational methods that can be applied. Further attention will be given to this area later within this chapter.

QUESTION 3: WHAT KINDS OF INFORMATION DOES AN ASSESSMENT PROCEDURE YIELD?

The process must provide the professional (for the purposes within the chapter, the use of the term **therapist, examiner,** or **instructor** may be used interchangeably with the term **professional**) with the information necessary for planning and measuring each child's program (Dollar and Brooks, 1980). Therefore, the included assessment process should: (a) be able to measure a child's current level of functioning so that the group will know where to begin; (b) be global and address all behavioral domains concentrated upon within the program (e.g., motor behaviors, language, social and recreational skills); (c) describe the conditions that are necessary for the facilitator to create the optimal learning environment; and (d) hopefully identify criteria that can later be used as a **measuring stick** for acceptable performance. The critical assumption relates to the position that assessment should be used as a "cornerstone for systematic instruction, uniting testing with instruction" (Dubose, 1979). Furthermore, as suggested earlier, this process must be an ongoing procedure, continually updating the body of knowledge formulated.

Sailor and Haring (1977) have identified four domains that they believe should be assessed from a developmental viewpoint. The four areas that they focused on were self-help, sensory motor, communication and social skills. On the other hand, there are others who suggest developing assessment procedures from an age-appropriate standpoint. Therefore, a couple of other areas that may need attention may pertain to domestic living, community functioning and more specific identification of leisure and recreational skills (Brown et al., 1979).

How can one gather information in some of the other behavioral domains? As was suggested earlier, there are a variety of options that an examiner can apply. The most common alternatives that have been cited can be sampled through criterion-referenced, norm-referenced as well as observational assessment. The following will briefly define each of the procedures for you.

Cautions in Collecting Assessment Information

It is very important for a therapist to recognize his/her role in not only interpreting the data but in addition how he/she can influence the outcome. Rapport must be established between the client and the examiner if any meaningful data will be generated. Furthermore, the examiner must realize that his/her expectations can influence another person's performance. For example, Rosenthal, in his pioneer work, found that a person's performance could be impacted by the expectations of the other individual. For example, if you were told that an individual was very bright, your findings and the way you interacted could be tremendously impacted. The obvious implication of this statement is that clinicians should be aware if they are communicating any underlying messages to the consumer which could impact the performance.

It is ironic that not only one's expectations can influence the outcomes, but in addition the degree to which the examiner likes the client and perceives him or her in a friendly manner. These issues can also impact the final performance.

Whenever anyone is testing or evaluating a child, the individual should be aware of the client's level of anxiety as well as motivation level. If the child is nervous and not feeling comfortable, the outcome could change just as easily as if they were not motivated.

Criterion-Referenced and Norm-Referenced Assessments

The measurement of performance, potential ability, achievement, and progress are crucial elements in the rehabilitation of exceptional children. Presently, an enormous amount of normative data is compiled to allow comparison of an individual's performance to a standard or group score (Wallace and Larsen, 1978). It is important, however, to realize that the primary purpose of a diagnostic workup is to provide professionals with pertinent information appropriately developed for an individual child (Johnson and Martin, 1980).

Typically, criterion-referenced tests use a specific population of persons as the interpretive frame of reference rather than a specific content domain. In this respect, instead of measuring an examinee's performance by comparing the findings with scores obtained by others on the same test (norm referenced), the examinee's performance can be reported in terms of specific skills s/he mastered or has difficulty with (Anastassi, 1976). Glaser (1971) stresses that criterion-referenced measures assess an individual's abilities that provide insight on the degree of competence attained by a child. This information is independent to the performance of others (which is usually secured by norm-referenced procedures). There are numerous researchers who point out the importance of qualifying what a child can or cannot do rather than just simply comparing the individual's performance to others. Holowinsky (1980), in his review of practices of the past, advocates for techniques that focus on individual growth and mastery.

Popham and Husek (1969) point out that it is sometimes literally impossible to tell a norm-referenced test from a criterion-referenced test simply by looking at them. They point out the advantage of the norm-referenced test is in its adaptability to make comparisons to a standard group. This is an asset when a degree of selectivity is necessary. On the other hand, criterion-referenced measures attempt to ascertain an individual's abilities with respect to a performance standard. Consequently, with this form of assessment, one would determine what an individual could or could not do. However, criterion-referenced procedures do not lend themselves to making reliable comparisons to others.

It seems only logical that both of these procedures should be utilized. Together, they can generate a reliable source of insight. In the initial intake process, it appears necessary to gather data which compares a child's performance to that of others (normative sample). However, after the initial assessment has been completed, there is very little applicability in applying standardized tests to make frequent measurements of a child's progress (Proger and Mann, 1973). As a rule, the information gained through normative tests is usually not precise enough for planning specific programs (Wallace and Larsen, 1976). This is where criterion-referenced procedures can play an important role. Criterion-referenced assessments can provide insight about instructional levels and mastery of concepts. Fuchs and Fuchs (1986) strongly suggest that the closer the assessment mirrors the actual learning environment, the more accurate and applicable the assessment data will be. Simon (1969) suggests that the distinction between the two discussed forms of measurement does not relate to the nature of the tests themselves but, rather, to the interpretation and use of the scores from the tests. Perhaps, the most important contribution of the integration of the criterion-referenced assessment in recreation is the probability of determining if a child has mastered the basic concepts explored in the program (Millman, 1970; Proger and Mann, 1973). Through consistent implementation of this procedure, the measurement of the development of skills as a consequence of programming can easily occur (Popham and Hasek, 1969).

As can be seen, there are advantages to utilizing both criterion- and norm-referenced approaches. Table 11 has been developed to illustrate concisely some of the strengths and limitations of both procedures.

Like all good things, criterion-referenced procedures can be misused. Johnson and Martin (1980) point out that similar to all new wine, criterion-referenced testing is in a developmental stage. They suggest

Table 11.
Liability and Assets for Norm-Referenced and Criterion-Referenced Procedures.

Procedure
Norm referenced.

Assets
Comparing individual's performance to a group.
Adaptability to make comparisons to a standard group.
When a degree of selectivity is necessary.

Liabilities
Not usually effective in frequently measuring a child's performance.
Sometimes not sensitive in measuring slight changes.
Not as effective in providing information about planning specific programs.

Procedure
Criterion referenced.

Assets
Reports data in terms of specific skills which a child has mastered or not.
Measures individual abilities with respect to a performance standard.
More accurate and applicable to programming.
Maximizes the probability of determining if a child has mastered the basic concepts explored
   by a program.

Liabilities
The tests do not lend themselves to making reliable comparisons to others.
There has been significant misuse of this term.
Some of these instruments are not psychometrically well developed.

that there are practices today which negate the value of the criterion-referenced model. A synthesis of their concerns follow.

Some professionals are now classifying many of their observational techniques and checklists as criterion-referenced testing. For example, in the recreation movement, there are in practice many leisure interest finders and behavioral checklists that could be misrepresented. Although, these instruments (e.g., Mirenda Leisure Interest Finder, Comprehensive Evaluation of Recreation Therapy) have their value, they should not be confused with a criterion-referenced approach. Although they note the merits in these approaches, Johnson and Martin (1980) believe it is not appropriate to suddenly begin calling them criterion referenced. They stress that by including such procedures as basic instructor-made checklists, which are not tests at all, the concept of criterion-referenced tests begins to lose its meaning. They also point out that various test constructors are borrowing the term from previously developed norm-referenced tests that may have been weaker psychometrically. This abuse should be considered unjustifiable and very misleading. The unsuspecting test users believe they are in the possession of an appropriate criterion-referenced test. To their dismay, they will eventually recognize that these tests will provide information that is similar to that derived from norm-referenced tests.

Those serving an exceptional child must become educated and aware of how to select and evaluate a useful criterion-referenced instrument. Ignorance due to not taking the time to investigate should not be used as an excuse for misusing an instrument. Attention should be given to how an instrument has been developed as well as its reliability and validity. A section on this topic will be incorporated later in this chapter. However, at this time I would like to discuss another assessment alternative: the area of observational assessment.

Observation: An Aspect of Assessment

The astute observer recognizes that much of the world can be unravelled through his/her eyes. When one is in search of information, one must take advantage of all available avenues. This basic truth applies within the domain of assessment. One alternative is through the use of observation. As Shakespeare once said, "We are creatures that look before and after: the more surprising is that we do not look around a little and see what is passing under our very eyes."

Assessment of overt behaviors can be accomplished in a variety of ways. As Kazdin (1980) points out, behaviors are usually assessed on the basis of separate response occurrences or the amount of time in which the response occurs. Nevertheless, there are a variety of observational techniques which are viable alternatives for the collection of data.

Before discussing formal observational techniques, brief attention will be given to the use of unstructured, non-systematic observation. In non-systematic observations, the observer simply watches an individual and takes note of anything of significance. The most basic type of observational technique is known as **narrative recording** (Cooper, 1981). In essence, the individual simply observes and records all the behaviors elicited by the observee in a specific time frame. Salvia and Ysselyke (1985) point out that nonsystematic observations tend to be anecdotal and subjective. When working with a specific child or a group of children, parents and professionals observe an enormous amount of behavior. For example, during a cooking activity, the following questions might pop into one's mind while the activity is going on:

1. Can each of the children complete the task being presented?
2. Is the length of the activity appropriate to maintain the interests of the children?
3. What are the social dynamics of the group?

In reality, all of these questions can be answered by just watching the interaction take place. One major advantage of informal observations is that the information obtained can enhance the productivity of the worker by giving that person some basic insightful information. Moreover, the time and effort expended by the clinician while observing are minimal in comparison to the amount of the information gathered. Nevertheless, the skills necessary to understanding or interpreting one's observations are a prerequisite of an astute observer. One must not only observe the occurrences but, additionally, question their relevance.

There are, however, significant limitations to informal approaches. Most notable is that only a certain amount of information can be gathered, and for that matter it is gathered very unsystematically. There are a variety of alternatives that can be used to systematize one's observations. Within systematic observations, the examiner sets out to observe a prespecified behavior(s). After specifying the behavior(s) to be observed, the examiner typically counts how often it was displayed and/or the duration or latency of the behavior. The following represents a brief overview of a few alternatives.

Frequency Measure

Obtaining frequency counts simply entails tallying the number of times the behavior occurs in a given time period. This is also known as the response rate. Frequency measures are particularly useful when observable behavior is discrete and takes a relatively constant amount of time to be performed (Kazdin, 1980). Therefore, behaviors such as smiling and talking are difficult to record by counting frequencies, because these behaviors may last varying amounts of time.

When measuring frequency of a behavior, one rule that must be followed is that the behavior should be observed for a constant amount of time, over several observational periods. Moreover, observations should also be made on a multitude of occasions at various time intervals. These time frames should sample the overall period that one works with a person. All of us recognize that children have times during the day when their performance is better than at other times. Therefore, we need to sample various time periods to ensure that our impressions are stable and reliable.

For example, consider a situation in which the observer is concerned with how involved a young boy is in a gardening program. Let us suppose that the boy is shoveling. It may be of interest to the therapist to find out how many times this child actually digs into the ground and shovels during a specified time frame. This may give the examiner some information relating to the boy's usage of time. The frequency measures can be obtained on a continual basis to assess if improvement in the usage has occurred.

Event Recording

The event recording represents the occurrence of a behavior itself as well as the relevant details of the behavior. When utilizing this procedure, the observer records the frequency, duration, and intensity of the behavior.

The process of utilizing event recording can be valuable in the initial evaluation as well as in an element within the treatment process. For example, when the relevant behavior which is desired is displayed, the therapist can get the client to discuss the behavior and his/her thoughts.

Discrete Categorization

Discrete categorization is a very straightforward observational procedure. In many ways it is similar to frequency measures. Discrete categorization is useful only with behaviors that have a clear beginning and ending. Its primary advantage is to classify responses into discrete categories such as correct/incorrect or performed/not performed. It is used primarily to measure whether several behaviors have occurred or not (Kazdin, 1980).

For example, let us focus on a group of six pre-teens cleaning up after preparing a snack for the group. A checklist can be developed to analyze how well the group cleans up after its program. The checklist may include behaviors such as washing the dishes, placing the garbage in the appropriate outlets, putting away the excess food and utensils and many other notable behaviors. Each behavior is then measured as being performed or not. Note that the behaviors incorporated within the checklist may constitute several different steps that relate to a completion of an entire task (Kazdin, 1980).

Interval Recording

The last observational format to be discussed is interval recording. In this approach, the focus is on the amount of time engaged in an activity rather than on specific behaviors per se. When using interval recording, a specified behavior is observed for a specific period of time. This block of time is then divided up into a series of short intervals. Observations are made during each of these intervals to assess whether the behavior has occurred or not. For example, a major goal of working with a child who is extremely impulsive may be to keep the child on task. One method of evaluating the effectiveness of a treatment program is through interval recording. The child can be observed a couple of times per day (once in the morning and once in the afternoon). The total observation period can take place within a 15-minute interval. This 15-minute interval can be further divided into 30-second durations. Consequently, an observer can merely articulate whether the designated behavior was displayed or not within each interval. To assist in the implementation of this procedure, a chart can be designed to keep track of the child's performance. For example, Figure 13 represents an interval recording sheet in which the observer merely circles whether the appropriate behavior was displayed or not within each interval. A plus sign (+) can be designated to indicate observed on-task behavior, while a minus sign (−) can be applied to indicate the child was off task.

INTERVAL RECORDING FORMAT

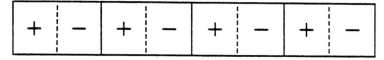

Examiners should circle the plus (+) if the behavior is observed
and circle the minus (−) if the behavior is not observed

Figure 13.

A variant of the interval recording approach is duration recording, which involves measuring how long a response was performed. This method is particularly useful for ongoing responses. Programs that attempt to increase or decrease the length of time of a response would profit from utilizing this approach. Again, we can observe the same child in regards to his on-task behavior, but this time address how long s/he was on task.

Before continuing any further, let us review the following information on the various observational paradigms. Table 12 will be utilized to illustrate the following information.

Basic Steps in Conducting Behavioral Observations

The following discussion of the steps in conducting behavioral observations is based on the work of McLoughlin and Lewis (1986). They suggest five steps within the observational process.

(1) **Describe the Behavior to be Observed.** Prior to conducting an observation, the behavior under investigation needs to be clarified. In other words, one needs to operationally define exactly what will be observed. For example, if one is focusing on disruptive behavior, it is necessary to clearly delineate exactly what one is considering under this heading (e.g. hitting, screaming, answering back).

(2) **Select a Measurement System.** Within this chapter, observational alternatives have been discussed. One of these alternatives should be selected. It has been suggested that with discrete (tangible) behaviors, frequency or duration measures are appropriate, whereas for nondiscrete behaviors (such as talking or on-task behaviors), an interval recording is more appropriate.

(3) **Set Up the Data Collection System.** This is a critical step in conducting the observation. Many questions need to be answered before making observations. For example, one must decide who will collect the data, when and where data collection will take place, how long the observations will last, and how the data will be recorded and analyzed. McLoughlin and Lewis (1986) suggest that observations should be scheduled at times and situations where the target behavior is most likely to occur. It is important to select alternate viewing periods so that one can more thoroughly observe the child.

(4) **Select a Data Reporting System.** The data collected should be charted and put on a graph. Graphs are extremely helpful in explaining data and illustrating if change has occurred.

(5) **Carry Out the Observation.** At this point in the process, the therapist is ready to carry out the observation and the analysis of behavior. Once the data is collected, the observer can determine if the behavior under investigation is a genuine problem or not. All too often, people assume that a behavior is a problem when in fact it is not. However, when the behavior is actually observed, they recognize that it

is not as significant a problem as they had assumed. However, a word of caution is in order. A significant limitation to the observational approach is that it is informal and thus there are not any norms to go by. Professional judgment or the development of local norms, where appropriate, are necessarily used as standards for comparisons.

Difficulties with Observational Data

Although there are several advantages to using observational procedures to assess the behavior of children, there are several disadvantages. The first difficulty pertains to time (Salva and Ysseldyke, 1985). Incorporating well-designed observational programs into a busy schedule can be difficult, and observers need to be prepared for this investment of time. Another disadvantage is that the very presence of an observer may alter a situation and may make an individual behave differently. If an individual is aware of being observed, the procedure is said to be obtrusive (Kazdin, 1980). However, there have been several studies that have indicated that the presence of an observer has little or no effect on behaviors that are observed (Mercatoris and Craighead, 1974). Nevertheless, the observer should be cautious while observing and should try to stay out of the way.

Finally, a word of caution needs to be incorporated in regard to observer reliability. Observers need to be trained so that they feel at ease with the data generated. Only when observers are appropriately prepared should they be permitted to actually collect data. This entails helping individuals develop the skills to initiate an observational assessment competently. Observers must have a clear understanding of what they are looking for. Furthermore, they need to consistently be able to observe the same phenomenon and record its presence. It is usually helpful if a couple of persons observe the targeted behavior. If they agree that the behavior has been generated, the interjudge reliability is positive. Having high interjudge reliability on what is being observed provides confidence that the observations are accurate. Unreliable data is useless and therefore precautions are necessary. Sometimes unreliable data is generated because of the observer's investment in the outcome. Consequently, what is documented may not be an accurate representation of the behavior under scrutiny.

Table 12. Liabilities and Assets for Various Observational Procedures.

Procedure
Non-systematic.

Assets
Simple to apply.
The procedure can provide an enormous amount of general insight.

Liability
Only a certain amount of information can be derived.

Procedure
Frequency data.

Asset
Particularly viable for behavior that is discrete and takes a relatively constant amount of time.

Liability
Reported data at times can be misleading. It is imperative that one collect data that is representative of a child's typical day.

Procedure
Discrete categorization.

Assets
Straightforward procedure.
Classifies responses into discrete categories such as correct/incorrect, performed/not performed.
Assists in identifying the various behavioral components within the entire task.

Liability
Useful only with behaviors that have a clear beginning and ending.

Procedure
Interval recording.

Assets
Useful when the focus is on the amount of time engaged within an activity rather than on specific behaviors.
Indicates relative frequency and duration.

Liabilities
Not appropriate for discrete frequency collection.
Requires ongoing observations in conjunction with time monitoring.
May not reflect an accurate representation of the overall frequency of the behavior under scrutiny.

Procedure
Duration recording.

Assets
Effective in measuring ongoing responses.
Often utilized in combination with other techniques.

Liabilities
Not appropriate for discrete frequency collection.
Cannot be used when several behaviors are being monitored.

Observing Play Behavior: What Information Can Be Derived?

Through play, a child can explore and experiment with his or her perceptions of the world. Play can provide an observer with significant insight into a child's life. However, without an awareness of how to interpret such behavior, the impressions would be worthless. An analogy would be similar to getting into a locked room. Without the key, one's entrance may be prohibited.

Thus far, a discussion of various observational paradigms have been presented. A clinician may even desire to tailor an entire play situation for purposes of gathering diagnostic information. Play is rich, revealing many levels of cognition as well as social abilities. Rubin (1983) and Belsky and Most (1981) suggest that research clearly indicates that observation of free play can be a reliable indicator of social, social-cognitive and cognitive competence in children.

Formal understanding of basic child development is imperative for generating accurate conclusions from one's observations. Several interpretations have been formulated as guidelines to follow. Nicholich (1977) as well as many other investigators (Sinclair, 1970; Lowe, 1975) have confirmed Piaget's developmental sequence of play. Table 13 lists a developmental sequence of cognitive and social behaviors as they relate to play. Furthermore, there have been others who have even specialized their interpretations so they specifically assess human functions. Nicholich (1977) has described procedures for assessing symbolic play maturity through the analysis of pretend play. The development of symbolic skills as manifested in play can provide a dynamic approach for assessing children's representational abilities and some of the cognitive prerequisites for communicative intentions of linguistic abilities. Westby (1980) succinctly describes the sequence of symbolic play and language stages and provides one method for interpretation: The Symbolic Play Scale. Table 14 illustrates several of the elements incorporated within the scale. The observer is also provided with an observation form to assist in the documentation of the elicited behavior.

The Play Observation Scale, developed by Rubin and his associates at Waterloo University, is another good example of how play can formally be interpreted. The Play Observation Scale has been used to derive developmental information on various areas. Several significant benchmarks have been identified with this scale (e.g. from three to five years of age,

Table 13. Developmental Stages of Play.

Levels of Social Play (Formulated by Smilansky, 1986)
Autistic play (onlooker play)
Solitary play
Parallel play
Cooperative play
Competitive play

Levels of Cognitive Play
Functional play (sensorimotor stage)
Constructive play (preoperational play)
Dramatic play (preoperational play)
Games with rules (associated with at least concrete abilities)

---

the frequency of parallel play decreases and group play is strengthened). Reports from various professionals who are acquainted with this instrument have been extremely favorable.

Rebecca Fewell, a respected scholar and educator, has spent an enormous amount of time studying the implications of play, cognitive, communicative, and social development (Fewell and Rich, 1987). Fewell has been instrumental in developing two useful devices that are valuable in assessing the abilities of preschoolers. The Play Assessment Scale (Fewell, 1984) consists of 45 developmentally sequenced items appropriate for children between the ages of two and thirty-six months. In addition, The Learning Through Play Checklist (Fewell and Vadasy, 1983) provides a guide for using a resource manual of play activities for infants and toddlers to the age of three.

As can be easily understood, a clinical interpretation can also be applied as a means of securing insight. To apply these approaches, one would be in need of some background training to develop both the skills of observation and data collection. These skills will also have to be thoroughly combined with a solid theoretical frame of reference on what this information represents.

QUESTION 4: WHAT ARE SOME PRACTICAL SUGGESTIONS FOR CONDUCTING AN ASSESSMENT?

Now that some of the basic material has been presented, it is only logical that emphasis be given to some practical methods for initiating an assessment. McLoughlin and Lewis (1986) and Salvia and Ysselyke

Table 14. SYMBOLIC PLAY SCALE

Play (Cognition)	*Language*
Stage I — 12 months	
Child has some awareness that objects exist when he does not see them. Crawls or walks to get things he wants. Will pull string toys. Does not mouth all toys. Uses some common objects appropriately.	No true language. Child may have some performative words, i.e. words that are associated with actions or the total situations, but are not true labels. Child may often vocalize when he wants something.
Stage II–13 to 17 months	
Child explores toys purposively. Discovers operation of toys through trial and error or hands toys to adults to operate.	Some children develop single words. These words are extremely context dependent, e.g. the child may use the word "car" when he is riding in a car but not when he simply sees a car. Words tend to come and go in the child's vocabulary.
Stage III — 17 to 19 months	
Child knows how to use most common objects. Engages in some autosymbolic play, i.e. child will pretend to go to sleep or pretend to drink from a cup or eat from a spoon.	Beginning of true communication. Child uses single words to refer to agents, objects, rejection, objects disappearing and objects or people recurring.
Stage IV — 19 to 22 months	
Child begins to play with dolls. Will brush a doll's hair, feed a doll a bottle, or cover a doll with a blanket. Child may perform actions on a doll, another child, and adult, and himself.	Child begins to use word combinations. Variety of semantic relations increases and child refers to objects and persons not present.
Stage V — 24 months	
Child plays house — is the mommy, daddy, or baby. REPRESENTS daily experiences. Objects used in play must be realistic and close to usual size. Pretend events are short and isolated. Block play consists of stacking and knocking over. Sand play consists of filling, pouring, and dumping.	Child uses short sentences. Present progressive "ing" markers appear on verbs, and plural and possessive markers may appear on nouns.

Play (Cognition)	*Language*

Stage VI — 2½ years

Child RE–PRESENTS events less frequently experienced or observed — impressive or traumatic events (doctor-nurse-sick child). Child in a school may play teacher. Child still requires realistic props. Roles shift quickly. Events still short and isolated.

Child responds to WH questions in context (who, whose, where, what . . . do). Child asks WH questions by putting the WH word at the beginning of a sentence. Child's responses to Why questions are inappropriate except for well-known routines, e.g., "Why is the doctor here?" . . . "boy's sick." Child asks why particularly in response to negative commands given by adults (e.g. "don't touch that").

Stage VII — 3 years

Continuance of pretend activities of stage V and VI, but now the play has a sequence — events are not isolated, e.g., child mixes cake, bakes it, serves it, washes the dishes; or doctor checks patient, calls the ambulance, takes patient to hospital, patient dies. Sequence EVOLVES . . . NO PLANNED. Child still dependent on realistic props. Associative play appears.

Child now uses past tense and future aspect (gonna) forms, e.g., "I ate the cake," "I'm gonna wash the dishes."

Stage VIII — 3 to 3½ years

Child begins to carry out play activities of previous stages with a dollhouse and Fisher-Price toys (barn, garage, airport). First use of blocks and sandbox for imaginative play. Blocks used primarily as enclosures (fences and houses) for dolls and animals. Play not totally stimulus-bound. Child is able to use one object to represent another.

Descriptive vocabulary expands as child becomes more aware of perceptual attributes. Uses shape, size, texture, color, and spatial relationship terms — not always correctly. Metalinguistic awareness develops . . . child uses language to talk about language. Will give dialogue to toy people.

Stage IX — 3½ to 4 years

Child begins to be able to problem-solve events he has experienced. He hypothesizes "what would happen if." Is becoming less dependent on realistic props.

Child verbalizes intentions and possible future events. May use modals (may, can, might, will, would, could); conjunction (and, but, so, if, because). NOTE: Full competence for these modals and conjunctions does not develop until 10–12 years of age.

Play (Cognition)	*Language*

Stage X—5 years

Child now *plans* a sequence of pretend events. Organizes what he needs—in both objects and other children. Coordinates more than one event occurring at a time. Can be highly imaginative—not dependent on realistic props.

Child begins to use relational terms such as "then, when, first, next, while, before, after." NOTE: Full competence does not develop until 10–12 years of age.

Observation Form

Onlooking	Solitary	Parallel	Associative	Cooperative	
					Game
					Symbolic Spontaneous
					Symbolic Imitative
					Practice

Definition of Play Behaviors for the Observation Form

Practice   —The child engages in gross motor activities such as running, riding on bikes or wagons, climbing, throwing balls. Child works puzzles, strings beads, stacks blocks and knocks them down, fills and empties containers, operates cause-effect toys such as music boxes, "busy" boxes, talking toys, etc.

Symbolic Imitative   —The child engages in pretend play, but it is initiated and guided by another child or an adult.

Symbolic Spontaneous—The child initiates the pretend activity.

Onlooking	—The child observes but does not participate.
Solitary	—The child plays without reference to other children.
Parallel	—The child's play is of a companionable nature with similar materials but with no personal interaction.
Associative	—The children's play is loosely organized around a common activity, shared interests, and materials.
Cooperative	—The play includes different roles, common goals, usually with one or two leaders, and is of relatively long duration and complexity.

The observers using the forms recorded a description of the child's behavior within the appropriate box on the form. If a child engaged in several different behaviors during a recording time, the behaviors were sequentially numbered.

From Assessment in Cognitive and Language Abilities Through Play by Carol E. Westby. In *Language Speech and Hearing Services in the Schools,* 1980, *11*(3), pp. 154–168. ° 1980 by permission of the author and the American Speech-Language-Hearing Association.

(1985) offer suggestions concerning this area of assessment. Their suggestions as well as some personal tips are now discussed.

Interviewing and Incorporating Test Data

As indicated in the beginning of this chapter, it is important to interview parents or significant others to gather information about a child. Too often, professionals do not take full advantage of the family as a source. Unfortunately, an enormous amount of information is therefore lost. The use of family and significant others is especially crucial when children are very young and information acquired through testing may be inaccurate.

If the information gathered is usually loosely put together, all of the facts may be difficult to weed through. The ease of interpretation generally depends upon the degree of structure imposed upon the data collection. It is therefore important for an observer to think through the questions asked in an interview as well as the order in which questions are presented. If the need for further clarification arises, one then can deviate from the original format. By developing a format, the therapist can obtain a great deal of insight. It is also suggested that an interview (when permissible) should proceed all direct assessments. By following this guideline, the clinician can apply the obtained information as input in devising the most accurate assessment process.

The reader may find it helpful to apply a screening device which will assist in gathering pertinent developmental and play history. A good developmental history will provide the examiner with basic intake information as well as pertinent information in regards to the acquisition of developmental milestones. Furthermore, there have been some professionals who have established a play history survey which is amenable to an interview. For example, Takata (1974) developed a play history instrument. The instrument assists the examiner in synthesizing incoming information about the preferred forms of play as well as a child's play skills. From the findings derived in the interview, the clinician can develop a summary about the child's needs and provide some insight on a prescription program.

In reality, assessments in recreation programs are developed for two purposes. One purpose is to identify the needs of a child and to try and develop programs that address those needs. Secondly, continual estimates of the child's progress serve as a method of quality assurance. It is important to know if the programs are effective. If the child has reached the desired goals, new goals must be set and programs should be altered. On the other hand, if the program is ineffective, modifications are imperative. Ongoing measurements should therefore be viewed as necessary and critical to overall program effectiveness.

Formulating Questions in Regards to Assessment Devices

The examiner should formulate several questions when selecting an assessment tool. For example, a basic question is usually, **Which assessment devices should I use?** Too often, people allow the availability or familiarity of assessment tools to dictate their selection. Of course, this procedure is erroneous. The approach, which could be either normative, criterion-referenced or observational, should be selected based on its advantages and disadvantages to the case in question. For example, one needs to know the type of information requested. If the goal is to answer questions about the child's abilities in comparison to others, the only logical selection is a norm-referenced test. However, if the information desired pertains to mastery of a certain task or specific behaviors, criterion-referenced tests, observations, and/or informal checklists may be the most reliable format.

The assessment tasks must be compatible with the skills of the child (McLoughlin and Lewis, 1986). A child should not be required to attempt tasks that are significantly above his/her ability level. Assessment procedures should capitalize on strengths rather than penalize weaknesses (McLoughlin and Lewis, 1986). Additionally, the examiner should also be concerned with how the procedure is presented. For example, is the child required to read, write, listen or look at pictures? What modality is used when the child responds (e.g. verbalizing the answer, writing the answer out, or for that matter darkening-in a box)? Other considerations may include whether the test is administered individually or in a group, and how long the test takes to administer.

Other variables need to be considered. Testing should be discontinued, and the child should be given a break if she/he becomes restless. Furthermore, if the examiner believes that the results obtained are a minimal estimate of a child's ability (due to lack of motivation, distractability, etc.), the examiner should not accept the results obtained. As indicated earlier, the examiner is the master of the process. He/she brings into the examination his/her greatest asset, i.e. clinical judgment. When results obtained do not appear to agree with previous impressions or other test findings, the examiner will have to use his/her judgment to interpret the discrepancy.

The selection of the instrument of choice is also dependent upon the skill level of the examiner. Tools should never be applied by untrained personnel. These individuals will have an enormous amount of difficulty not only administering the test but also scoring and interpreting the results.

Is the Selected Tool Adequate?

One must have confidence in the instruments administered. The test must be soundly constructed and have high reliability and validity. Furthermore, the clinician must also determine whether the selected approach can be efficiently administered and scored.

Understanding and Acknowledging Developmental History and Present Conditions

Prior to conducting a thorough appraisal of a child's skills, it is imperative that the clinician gather information about the individual's past history and current circumstances. An awareness of the child's medical and developmental history may provide clues for understanding present levels of involvement. Past history can reveal intuitive reasoning for activity involvement and skills developed. Salvia and Ysseldyke (1985) stress that it is not enough to only assess a child's current level of functioning; rather, the therapist must become more cognizant of how the past may have influenced and shaped current behaviors. Furthermore, examiners should take notice when children are not performing up to their capacity due to factors such as health, anxiety, or attitudes. If this occurs, the examiner must disregard the results obtained and re-evaluate on another occasion.

Controlling Variables and Providing Encouragement for Efforts

When testing children, attention should be given to eliminating as many extraneous variables as possible. The professional should find a quiet room that has the least number of distractions. There should not be a lot of supplies around, since these may pose as a distraction to the child.

Children should be reinforced frequently for their efforts. This is permitted even in standardized testing. While one cannot tell a child that he/she responded correctly, one should tell a child how happy he/she is because the child is trying hard and/or cooperating. Finally, it is critical to administer tests exactly according to the directions in the manual. Modifying directions or expectations of a standardized test invalidates the findings. This is because the norms formulated have been derived by applying the specified procedure. When this procedure is modified, even slightly, it may make a significant difference in the results.

Interpreting Results

When an individual is assessed, one is basically sampling the performance of that individual at a particular time. These results represent predictions of potential future ability. They represent inferences in which one may place specific levels of confidence.

Probably the most difficult and most important aspect of the measurement process is the explanation of the findings. Additionally, these findings should be translated into practical applications and should play a role in generating program ideas. So, in reality, the therapist must cautiously administer tests s/he understands and that can be useful in generating programming alternatives.

Initially, the data collected from each phase of the assessment process should be individually summarized (interview, developmental history, observations, and actual direct assessment). Within this summary, the major findings should be synthesized. With this structure in mind, it will simplify the next step, which involves incorporating all of the information generated and synthesizing the findings to take some action. The interpretation can be organized around the initial assessment questions formulated (McLoughlin and Lewis, 1986). The outcomes should be described in such a manner that they lend themselves to a simple correlation of why certain programs might be helpful and should be introduced.

The information should be organized categorically to specify mastered and unmastered skills. It is always helpful to have examples of correct and incorrect responses that illustrate a specific problem or strength.

When this has been completed, the examiner can begin to get closure on the results obtained and reach some conclusions. Goals can then be formulated for taking into account the information derived. In many ways, activities are usually selected to remediate the limitations found. Unfortunately, this is not always the best alternative. For some children, activities should initially be developed according to a child's strengths. This will hopefully build the child's level of confidence. As a consequence, the child will be better able to accept working on his/her weaknesses at a later time.

As we have seen, the process of assessment is complicated. A great deal of thought must be integrated if an effective measurement is to take place. The examiner will also have to become experienced in administering the various applicable tests. Experience will help develop more refinement in administration as well as enhance clinical judgment in interpretation.

QUESTION 5: WHY DO I REALLY NEED TO KNOW ANYTHING ABOUT TEST CONSTRUCTION AND, FOR THAT MATTER, WHAT DO I NEED TO KNOW?

Without accurately understanding the essential characteristics of a test, an examiner can inadvertently make many errors in regards to test selection and applicability. For this reason, attention will now be given to those characteristics. The reader is advised that if s/he finds this material somewhat difficult to review, time should be allowed to study some of the primary references incorporated within this section.

Characteristics Essential for Reliable Assessment: Reliability

Reliability is concerned with how much error is involved within the measurement (Wodrich, 1984). Wallace and Larsen (1978) suggest that the term **reliability** is used to refer to the consistency of the findings of a

given test. Kerlinger (1973) suggests that acceptable synonyms for reliability are accuracy, predictability, and stability. Reliability is determined
through the application of statistical procedures. Correlational techniques are the usual approach to studying reliability. The correlation
represents the relationship between two sets of scores acquired from the
same test instrument. A perfect positive relationship between the two
would be depicted with a coefficient correlation of 1.00. On the other
hand, no relationship would be indicated by 0.00. Reliability coefficients
somewhere in the 0.80s and 0.90s are generally considered acceptable for
tests (Wodrich, 1984).

There are several methods for determining the reliability of a test.
One of the most commonly used techniques is **test-retest** reliability,
which is also called the "coefficient of stability." To determine this type
of reliability, one administers the identical test to the same examinee on
two occasions and then correlates the findings. If the test is stable, the
findings on both administrations should be similar. Potential sources of
error could relate to remembering some of the subtests from the first
assessment as well as the possibility of the practice effect. For this reason,
it is important to have some delay between the administration of the two
tests. The most appropriate time interval between tests will depend
upon the type of test and how the results will be applied (Wallace and
Larsen, 1978).

Another form of reliability is **alternate forms reliability,** which is
also called the "coefficient of equivalence." As its name denotes, an
alternate, but equivalent form of the test is administered. Unlike the
test-retest format, one should give the two tests in immediate succession
when employing alternate forms (usually within a week).

Finally, the most frequently used procedure to determine reliability is
the **split-half technique.** Split-half reliability is also known as the
"coefficient of internal consistency." To determine this type of reliability,
the test is administered to a set of examinees and is then literally split in
half so that each examinee has two scores. The scores are then correlated
to estimate the instrument's internal consistency. This method is not
appropriate for determining the reliability of speeded tests, because a
subject's responses may not represent his/her actual abilities (if untimed).
The split-half method includes the differences in content sampling
between the two halves as error (exactly in the same manner as it is
assessed with the alternate forms method).

Factors Affecting the Reliability Coefficient

There are several factors that influence the reliability. For example, the longer the material is of a specific test, the higher the reliability may be. Furthermore, the reliability of a test appears to be dramatically influenced by the sample investigated. The more heterogeneous the set of examinees, the higher the reliability of the test. Finally, very easy or very difficult items generally lead to a reduction in the reliability coefficient.

Standard Error of Measurement

Whenever one assesses another, some error is expected. This error can be estimated by the standard error of measurement which is determined by retesting an individual and comparing the differences between the scores. This error in measurement represents the standard deviation of the scores generated, which is simply a statistical reflection of how disparate the test and retest scores are. The error would be small if the scores of the various administrations are similar, and vice versa. The standard error of measurement also reflects the range that one's true score probably falls within. For example, a person's standard score may be 107 ± 5, meaning that the actual score would probably fall between 102 and 112.

Validity

Whereas reliability refers to the stability of a test, validity represents the extent to which a test is useful. This is considered the most important element in evaluating the effectiveness of a test. If a test is not valid, it is not worthwhile using it. Three types of validity that are considered in most tests are content, criterion-related and construct validity.

Content Validity

Content validity reflects the extent to which a test adequately measures the subject matter under investigation. The test must contain sufficient items so that it is representative of the areas that it purports to have measured (Wallace and Larsen, 1978). Typically, content validity is determined by a thorough analysis and comparison with other relevant tests. Another method of measuring this form of validity is through the agreement of those considered as experts in the field. If the experts agree that the tests sample the subject matter adequately and sensibly, the test will probably have high content validity.

Criterion-Related Validity

Criterion-related validity reflects the degree to which test scores predict performance in relevant real-life activities. One uses a test with criterion-related validity to obtain an impression of the examinee's likely performance on another specific measure (i.e., the criterion). For example, if the purpose of a test such as the Scholastic Aptitude Test (S.A.T.) is to measure success in higher education, what really becomes critical is whether one's score on the S.A.T. predicts actual performance of that specific individual while in college. If a given test predicts success for an individual (and if indeed the individual becomes successful), then the test has criterion-related validity.

There are two types of criterion-related validity. **Predictive validity** is when the criterion measure is sampled some time after the test was administered. The example previously illustrated predictive validity. A high correlation coefficient would indicate that the test is an accurate predictor and that its continued use is worthwhile. **Concurrent validity,** which is the second type of criterion-related validity, is when the criterion measure is administered at the same time or even prior to the test. Therefore, the findings of the measurement either concur with or disagree with criterion. It appears that this form of validity is critical on a practical basis. One may want to give a test to determine if a person is capable of being involved in certain activities. If the findings are accurate representations of what one might expect, the analysis is worthwhile.

Construct Validity

Construct validity reflects the extent to which the test measures a psychological construct, such as a trait or an attribute. For example, if a test is said to assess leisure behavior, it is assumed that there is such a thing as leisure behavior. Furthermore, it is implied that the items on the test incorporate behaviors that are indicative of this trait. Most constructs are relatively abstract and sometimes are defined by a multitude of observable behaviors that are very difficult to measure. Because of this abstractness, there is a need to further refine and clarify our understanding of the trait. It is therefore necessary to determine the construct validity of tests that purport to measure specific attributes or traits. The determination of a test's validity will either confirm or contradict the examiner's belief that the test accurately measures the trait or attribute under investigation. It would be extremely dangerous and erroneous to draw conclusions from an invalid test.

Gronlund (1976) suggests that construct validity is determined by taking the following steps:

1. Identify the constructs (traits and attributes) that are presumed to influence the behaviors under investigation.
2. Develop hypotheses regarding the performance on a test from the theory underlying the construct.
3. Verify the hypotheses by applying various logical and empirical methods.

Construct validity by far is the most difficult type of validity to ascertain (Wallace and Larsen, 1976; Salvia and Ysselyke, 1985). In fact, it is the least reported of all forms of validity. However, it is probably the most important. It is critical that examiners are accurately measuring what they intend to measure. Professionals must not tolerate test constructors who do not report acceptable estimates of construct validity. Without such information, there is not any clear evidence that the test is valid.

Factors Affecting the Acquired Validity Coefficient

There are several factors that influence obtaining an accurate validity coefficient. First, the more homogeneous the sample of examinees, the lower the validity coefficient. Second, the reliability of a test affects its validity. Reliability is a necessary but not a sufficient condition for validity, i.e., a test can be reliable but not valid. However, on the other hand, a test cannot be valid if it is not reliable. This is shown statistically by the fact that the validity coefficient can never be higher than the square root of the reliability coefficient.

Needed Attention to Test Construction, Reliability and Validity

Many examiners do not review test manuals with a critical eye towards issues of reliability and validity, and yet it is the test user's responsibility to thoroughly review the test manual to ascertain the appropriateness of the instrument. Fine (1982) and Dunn (1984) stress that assessment procedures will not accurately provide the information needed unless they are valid and reliable. In many situations, we find professionals using instruments that are ineffectively developed. These same individuals become frustrated later when they do not understand the meaning of the obtained results. It is therefore the responsibility of a test user to meet the qualifications necessary to administer the selected instrument. It is suggested that practitioners take courses in statistics and/or test construction that would be helpful in administering and interpreting test findings. A practical understanding of statistics and the interpretations of the reliability and validity coefficients are essential. With this understanding, professionals can make educated decisions pertaining to the selection and administration of test instruments.

Summary on Reliability and Validity

In essence, a reliable test is one which yields **consistent** scores when a person takes two alternate forms of the test, or when s/he takes the same test on two or more occasions. The reliability and consistency of test scores is critically important in determining whether a test or, for that matter, a procedure can provide good measurement. As noted earlier, there are many factors which could influence test-retest reliability: specifically, the history (the influence of the time between the two testing procedures) and, for that matter, the child's reactivity to taking the test.

The validity represents the **correctness** of the inferences developed from the testing. If tests are not valid, the examiner cannot utilize the data in a realistic manner. It is therefore imperative that the examiner study tests that he or she utilizes to understand how they were constructed and developed. Lack of knowledge is not acceptable when deriving outcomes which are not valid.

Test Administration Tips

Before discussing various tests, it may be helpful to incorporate some basic tips for test administration. Administering direct testing devices requires both attention to detail and flexibility. Attention to the details of test administration must be accompanied with direct attention to the child under investigation. At times, inexperienced test administrators focus so intensely on the procedures inherent to the test that they at times lose sight of the fact that they need to observe and be involved with the client. The client's cooperation indeed depends on the rapport established between the therapist and the child. Simple courtesies such as comfortable seating and a pleasant working environment are critical. Examiners can use discretion to encourage a child for his/her efforts. It is imperative that words of encouragement are not based on performance but rather on areas related to effort and cooperation. Encouragement solely based on performance would be detrimental to children who were not doing well. In addition, one must be empathetic as well as cheerful. The worst thing a therapist can do in a testing situation is just **test.** I can recall when I started my professional career, when I was assessing I wanted to make sure I executed the procedures to the tee. Unfortunately, that appeared to limit my ability to interact with the child. I wanted the child to merely follow my directions and not detour from any of the procedures. I soon began to realize how this in fact limited my abilities to genuinely assess a child. I now spend a lot of time getting to know a child. We may play with some toys, do simple art, talk, tell jokes and even do a few magic tricks, all as aspects of the assessment procedure. I would highly encourage the reader to incorporate some of these traits in his/her assessment techniques.

Salvia and Ysselyke (1985) suggest that the length of testing will vary with the age of a child as well as the disabling condition. As a general rule, a testing session should not exceed more than forty minutes without some form of a break. When children become restless, distracted, or for that matter even disinterested, testing should be interrupted and the child given a break. Furthermore, if the child's performance appears to be a minimal estimate of his/her abilities, the examiner should make note of this and not take into significant account the data that was generated.

Tests must be administered at times when children's attention is optimal. Therefore, we must take into consideration when and where the assessment procedures are implemented. For example, children may not want to cooperate completely when they have been taken out of an activity that they wanted to be at. Schedules must be adjusted at times to account for this concern. Furthermore, the assessment environment must be free of distractions. A room should be found that is quiet, away from others, and not overly arousing with a lot of extraneous stimuli. This will assist the child staying on task.

The examiner should take careful attention to review the test document as well as the manual. Usually within the manual, directions are given on how to deliver the assessment procedures. However, the humanistic characteristics discussed earlier in the section are critical to apply.

Finally, the reader should be cautious about the cost of tests and recognize that s/he will have to review various instruments before purchasing them. The mailboxes of many allied health professionals are replenished weekly with numerous pamphlets from test publishers offering professionals instruments that are supposedly the answer to the testing dilemmas they encounter. I would be suspect to these advertisements and recommend spending the time reviewing the tests and personally making the decisions after being informed. Tests can range in prices from $15–$20 to devices that are several hundred dollars. The clinician should therefore make appropriate selections that will meet his/her general needs, both practically as well as financially. Salvia and Ysselyke (1985) suggest that test users must examine all the pros and cons of utilizing specific test instruments. This may entail evaluating the kinds of behaviors or skills to be tested, the kinds of questions that need to be answered, and the extent to which commercially developed tests ought to be used. As can be seen, while performing assessments, therapists must attend to all details, reason carefully and make realistic decisions based on the client's and the professional's best interests. The following section will provide the reader with some basic information about various test instruments that will help in making appropriate and educated decisions.

QUESTION 6: WHAT ARE THE POTENTIAL ASSESSMENT ALTERNATIVES?

The final section of this chapter will be devoted to reviewing various tests which sample the broad base of behaviors influencing the acquisition of leisure skills. For your convenience, the following will be subdivided into four sections: (A) developmental profiles, (B) motor skills and psychomotor tests, (C) behavior rating scales, and (D) leisure interest and skill instruments. Because of the space constraints, only a limited number of tests could be cited in the document. There are many others that unavoidably had to be left out. The incorporated information is a representation of several viable alternatives.

Part I: Developmental Profiles and Interviews

When working with young children with disabilities or with the severely and profoundly handicapped, the developmental profiles and interviews to be discussed are useful in providing an enormous amount of practical information.

The Developmental Profile II

Purpose. The Developmental Profile II (Alpern, Boll and Shearer, 1980) is an inventory of skills designed to assess a child's development from birth through the age of 9 1/2 years. The profile is comprised of 186 items that are designed to assess a child's functional developmental age level. The instrument is administered by interviewing a person well acquainted with the child. Direct observation of the child may be incorporated if necessary (i.e., if the interviewee cannot answer all questions).

Description. The scale is divided into five areas. The five areas yield developmental ages for the child's physical, self-help, social, academic and communication levels. The items within each area are arranged into age levels expressed in terms of years and months. The age levels are presented at six-month intervals from birth to age three-and-a-half and proceeds from there by year intervals until the age of nine years, six months. Most age levels within the profile contain three questions. Items are scored as either being passed or failed, simply by determining whether the child has the skill described in each of the items proposed on the five scales. The scale was set up so that each item passed is credited in terms of a given number of months. The number of months reflecting the items passed is totaled, which represents the child's developmental age in each of the five areas tested.

To summarize one's findings on the profile, the results are then transferred to a profile sheet, graphically displaying the five areas and comparing level of development to the child's chronological age. The results of the profile clearly display if the child has a particular strength or delay in each of the five domains tested. This information can then be translated into instructional goals.

Before administering the instrument, the user should become familiar with the standardization, theoretical rationale, and psychometric properties of the evaluation tool. The author has found this instrument to be a useful method to incorporate into clinical interviews. Furthermore, the

Developmental Profile II can be easily applied and used to assess progress via pre- and posttest comparisons.

Learning Accomplishment Profile—Diagnostic Edition (LAP–D)

Purpose. The LAP–D is one of the instruments established by the Chapel Hill Training—Outreach Project. The final version of the test consists of a commercially produced and marketed assessment kit published by the Kaplan School Supply Corporation. The instrument has excellent inter-rater reliability.

The test is criterion-referenced and was developed with a solid research base describing normal child development. What is unique about this test is that the findings are easily translated into appropriate instructional goals.

Griffin and Sandford (1975) describe activities that can be applied to remediate potential deficits. The test is composed of five scales and thirteen subscales. The profile was developed utilizing a task analytic approach, whereby tasks are presented in order from simple to progressively more difficult.

As indicated in the test manual, all of the necessary materials needed to facilitate the administration of the test are found in the LAP–D kit. The following are the scales and the subscales under investigation:

Fine motor
Manipulation
Writing
Cognitive
Matching
Counting
Language/Cognition
Naming
Comprehension
Gross Motor
Body Movement
Object Movement
Self-Help
Eating
Dressing
Grooming

Toileting
Self-direction

As can be seen, many of these subtests are critical to recreation participation. Although this scale does not directly measure recreation skills, significant attention is given to the developmental skills which are the foundations of recreation skills.

Administration. The test is designed for infants to children six years of age. However, the test is very practical for older children with developmental disabilities. The examiner begins the LAP–D with items designated for the child's chronological age. However, the test developers suggest that when working with a child with a disability, the starting point should be half of the child's chronological age.

A basal level is determined so that the entire early items of the test do not have to be administered. The **basal** is the item below which it is assumed the child is able to pass all preceding items. When the child passes his/her first three items in a row, the basal has been achieved. If this does not occur immediately, the examiner is required to work backwards until the basal is achieved or the first item on the test is administered. The examiner then continues testing a child (on the specific subscale) until the child fails three items in a five-item span. This is known as the **ceiling level.** One makes the assumption at this point that the child is not capable of accurately responding to questions past this point. A plus sign (+) is recorded in the test protocol for items passed, while a minus sign (−) is displayed for a failure. Raw scores can be converted to percentages as well as developmental ages. It would be extremely difficult to administer the entire test in one sitting. In fact, one does not have to administer all 13 subscales. One may administer only those subscales that appear to be appropriate for a given child. The test is also extremely amenable to pre posttest evaluation.

The Brigance Diagnostic Inventory of Early Development

Purpose. The Brigance is designed for children from ages birth to seven years. In many ways, this test is very similar to the LAP–D. The following are the areas addressed by the diagnostic inventory.

a. Preambulatory motor skills and behaviors
b. Gross motor skills and behaviors
c. Fine motor skills and behaviors

    d. Self-help skills
    e. Prespeech
    f. Speech and language skills
    g. General knowledge and comprehension
    h. Readiness
    i. Basic reading skills
    j. Manuscript writing
    k. Basic math

Brigance (1978) lists five functions of the inventory. As an assessment instrument, it (1) determines the developmental level of the child, (2) identifies weaknesses and strengths, and (3) identifies instructional objectives. As an instructional guide, the inventory (4) lists objectives in a functional and measurable manner, and (5) it represents a valuable recordkeeping system in addition to a tool to develop an effective individualized program plan. However, it is suggested that when remediating a child's deficits, the clinician should take care not to promote parroting of the correct response. That is, the child should be taught the real meaning of each desired behavior, rather than just going through the motions in a perfunctory fashion. Finally, the findings attained from the inventory represent a body of knowledge that can be utilized to train parents and other professionals.

Administration. Just like the LAP–D, the Brigance is too comprehensive to be administered as a whole. Therefore, one should consider the reasons for the assessment in order to select the appropriate skill sequence. Furthermore, the assessment should be spaced over a period of time that takes the child's age and attention span into consideration.

In the test manual, Brigance clearly spells out the procedures. Recommendations for more effective use of the inventory are also provided. An example is "Rephrase verbal direction if it helps to check the skills or behaviors being assessed" and "Do not coach, but be prepared to reword the direction if the child has difficulty because of the vocabulary or form of the direction." Brigance also lists questions frequently asked about the inventory and provides a response to each.

As a criterion-referenced test, this inventory is based on observable functions sequenced by task analysis and correlated with child development and curriculum objectives. The skills are based on numerous references which contain published normative data for infants and children who are below the developmental age of seven.

Vulpe Assessment Battery

Purpose. The Vulpe Assessment Battery is a comprehensive tool for obtaining and organizing the pertinent information necessary to plan and develop a learning program for a child (Vulpe, 1979). The battery provides a developmental assessment for atypically developing children from birth to the age of six years. It may also be appropriate for older children who are severely disabled.

Description. The battery is divided into eight behavioral domains as well as one environmental domain. The domains include basic senses and functions, gross motor behaviors, fine motor behaviors, language, cognition, behavior, activities of daily living, and basic information about the environment. There are approximately 1,127 items on the test, and the items administered will vary from child to child. For older children, one would have to allow for a couple of assessment sessions, allocating about three hours to complete the entire analysis. The test appears to be more helpful for assessment of the preschool child than the five- and six-year-old. The battery is administered in the same way as many of the other developmental profiles, and the directions for administration are clearly presented in the manual.

Comments. Although the test is very comprehensive, it seems that few statistical evaluations of validity and reliability were conducted. Test items were selected from the developmental literature indicating appropriate age expectations, but field testing was not comprehensive. This appears to be one of the major limitations of the scale. However, this author has found this test interesting and would suggest that professionals working with the developmentally disabled review its contents. Furthermore, just like the other developmental profiles, one uses select parts of the battery for a given assessment. There appears to be a great deal of information gained from this test, and it appears useful in planning and measuring individualized goal-oriented programs.

Part II: Motor Skills and Psychomotor Tests

Measurement of motor skills has become a highly specialized discipline. There are several tests that can be applied. The intent of this section is to globally review a few instruments and discuss in more detail two basic administered scales. It is suggested that those interested in developing skills in this area take classes in motor development or review several texts that present a variety of test instruments.

Purdue Perceptual Motor Survey

One of the earliest examples of a motor skills assessment scale is the Purdue Perceptual Motor Survey. It is not truly a test but rather a survey that allows others to observe a variety of motoric behaviors within a structured situation. The survey diagnoses five types of motor skills: balance and posture, body image and differentiation, perceptual motor match, ocular control and form perception. The manual contains all the necessary information for administering and scoring the instrument.

Bruiniks-Oseretsky Test of Motor Proficiency

A commonly used measure of motor development is the Bruiniks-Oseretsky Test of Motor Proficiency. This test is a norm-referenced, individually administered test for children between $4\frac{1}{2}$ to $14\frac{1}{2}$ years of age. The test is divided into the following three major areas and eight subtests.

Gross Motor Skills

1. Running speed and agility
2. Balance
3. Bilateral coordination
4. Strength

Gross and Fine Motor Skills

5. Upper-limb coordination

Fine Motor Skills

6. Response speed
7. Visual motor control
8. Upper-limb speed and dexterity

This test produces two scores for each subtest. The first is a standard score and the second represents an age equivalent. Furthermore, composite scores are available for gross and fine motor performance as well as a total battery score. The test has a very positive reputation and is extremely well constructed. A representative standardization sample was utilized in field testing, and the inter-rater reliability and the level of content validity of this instrument appear satisfactory.

An overview of additional measures of motor skills that have been widely used are presented below.

Ohio State University Scale of Intra Gross Motor Assessment (OSU–SIGMA)

Purpose. The OSU–SIGMA was developed by Michael Loovis and Walter Ersing in 1979. It is a criterion-referenced test that qualitatively measures 11 basic motor skills of children ages two and a half to fourteen. The 11 skills addressed in this instrument are as follows: walking, stair climbing, running, throwing, catching, kicking, jumping, hopping, skipping, striking and ladder climbing.

Procedures. Each skill is assessed on a possible four-level scale, with level one representing the least mature and level four the most mature. The examiner merely observes the child in a natural setting and rates a child on each of the eleven skills. The criteria for evaluating each level has been operationally defined. This test is relatively easy to learn, and, most importantly, it represents a logical starting point to begin evaluating and eventually assisting a child's motor development.

Hughes Basic Motor Assessment Purpose. The test was developed by Jeanne Hughes in 1979. The test is norm referenced, with norming tables for children ages 6–12. There are ten basic motor skills covered in the Hughes Assessment: static balance, stride jump, tandem walk, hopping, skipping, target, yo-yo, catching, throwing, and dribbling.

Procedures. Each skill is given a score from 0–3, with 0 indicating the child was unable to perform the task or there was a minimum of three observed difficulties, 1 point indicating two observed difficulties while performing the task, 2 points indicating one observed difficulty, and 3 points are awarded if the child did not display any difficulties performing the task. This test is easy to administer and interpret. The total time for administration is about 15 minutes.

As can be seen, the measurement of psychomotor skills can become very involved. It is suggested that a comprehensive workup should include a test of psychomotor skills. The instruments reviewed above should provide a strong foundation.

Part III: Behavioral Checklists

A widely accepted approach to rating children's behavior is through behavioral rating scales. These scales are generally completed by a significant other (e.g., parent, group leader, or teacher) who is very aware of the child's behavior patterns. Most of these scales are checklists that are designed to identify whether the child demonstrates appropriate or negative behaviors. There are many such checklists presently on the professional market. Several checklists that were designed specifically for therapeutic recreation are presented below.

The Comprehensive Evaluation in Recreational Therapy Scale (CERT)

Purpose. The CERT was developed by Parker and his associates (1975). The scale was presented and described in the **Therapeutic Recreation Journal** and a separate test manual is not available. However, the procedures for administration are quite clear and easy to follow. The CERT provides a systematic format for observing behavior in a recreation setting. It was originally designed for patients in a short-term psychiatric setting. However, since its original development, there now is another version developed for persons with physical disabilities. The author believes that the test is appropriate for application with a multitude of special populations.

Description. The CERT is divided into three categories and addresses 25 behaviors related to recreational involvement. The three major domains covered are as follows:

(1) *General.* Attendance, appearance, attitude toward recreation therapy, coordination of gait, posture.

(2) *Individual Performance.* Response to therapist's structure, one to one, decision-making ability, judgment ability, ability to form individual relationships, expression of hostility, performance in organized activities, performance in free activities, attention span, frustration tolerance level, strength and endurance.

(3) *Group Performance.* Memory for group activities, response to group structure, leadership ability in groups, group conversation, display of sexual role in the group, style of group interaction, handles conflicts in group when indirectly involved or directly involved, competition in group, attitude toward group decisions.

Procedures. The 25 behaviors are rated from zero to four, with a high score indicating problem behavior. The author has found this test to be very useful, although it should be kept in mind that the reported inter-rater reliability of the CERT is relatively low. Reliability should increase if operational definitions of the various behaviors are spelled out more clearly. It is suggested that testers spend time together practicing with this scale so that inter-rater reliability is increased.

The Haring and Phillips' Scale (Adapted Version)

Purpose. The scale was initially designed to provide educators with an alternative method for assessing children with behavior problems. The scale was published in the book **Educating Emotionally Disturbed Children** and was published by McGraw-Hill in 1962. Fine (1982) adapted this instrument for some of his research in measuring the effects of therapeutic recreation programs for children with spina bifida and learning disabilities. It appears that the scale can also be used for other special populations such as the severely disturbed and other physical disabilities.

The scale assesses numerous social interactional skills that play a role in a recreation therapy program. Areas such as group interaction, responsibility, cooperation, communication, ability to comply to adult and group norms are each rated on a 7-point Likert scale. A low score on this test indicates possible difficulty. It is believed that many practitioners will find this instrument useful in providing good clinical and practical insight. The inter-rater reliability for the entire survey was 0.81.

The author found it critical to train his observers so that they completely understood each of the questions. Table 15 illustrates the various questions incorporated within the rating scale.

Burke's Behavior Rating Scales (BBRS)

Purpose. The BBRS are designed to identify patterns of pathological behavior problems in some children. The scales consist of a short four-page booklet containing 110 questions. A respondent who knows the child is asked to rate the child on each question using a prescribed 5-point Likert. One indicates that the respondent has not noticed this behavior at all, while a five indicates that this individual has noticed this behavior to a very large degree.

Factor analyses indicated found that the 110 items cluster into 19 groups. They are: (1) excessive self-blame, (2) excessive anxiety, (3)

Table 15. THE HARING AND PHILLIP'S SCALE (Adapted Version)

1. Child's ability to stay with group activities and remain integral to them.

Impervious to group.	Hardly knows others are near.	Sees others but is indifferent to them.	Some response to others on occasion.	Takes others into consideration when he wants to.	Usually takes one or many others into regard.	Amenable to and ready to consider others at any time.

2. Child's ability to concentrate on and finish (follow through on) tasks given him.

Extremely flighty.	Flighty most of the time.	May or may not stay with task; not dependable.	Stays with task if supervised some.	Can stay with task on own to some extent.	Stays with tasks very well even against will.	Fine ability to concentrate and stick with requirements.

3. Child's ability to get along with peers.

Fights, or in conflict almost all the time.	In conflict often or most of the time.	Usually has too much conflict for his and others' welfare.	Conflicts coming under some control.	Makes an effort to control discord.	Gets along well nearly all the time; controls self well.	Little or no conflict at all; under good self-control.

4. Child's ability to comply with adult direction.

Defies adult at all turns.	Usually defiant and uncooperative.	Defiant and cooperative in random ways.	Some cooperation under some conditions.	Cooperative if he feels you mean business.	Usually cooperative and dependable.	Seldom or never uncooperative.

5. Child's ability to change to new activity under guidance or direction.

Won't change except under strong pressure.	Usually very reluctant to change; opposes it.	May or may not change; depends on "whim."	Changes with some effort; not willing.	Changes slowly but with some willingness.	Changes reasonably well and willingly in most cases.	Changes and complies well in all or nearly all instances.

6. Child's ability to meet and adjust to new situations.

Can't face or meet them.	Faces them with great difficulty.	Faces them only with specific adult help.	Meets and faces some new situations.	Can face and cope with several new situations.	Usually faces them well and readily.	Relishes new demands and copes readily and well.

7. Child's ability to act fairly and take his turn in appropriate settings.

Always wants to be first; demands it.	Rushes in to be first but can be stopped.	Will take turns if reminded in advance.	Goes first no more often than others.	Goes first only if asked or chosen.	Suggests taking turns; is cooperative and pliable usually.	Very mature; takes normal charge in fairplay terms; very reliable.

8. Child's pleasant and courteous attitude toward others.

Very rude and indifferent; seems to do so with intention.	Usually rude and discourteous.	Rude or not in random, unpredictable ways and at unpredictable times.	Somewhat considerate of others.	Considerate if situation is clear to him.	Usually considerate; a dependable person in this way.	Very considerate, but not artificial or insincere.

9. Child's attitude toward those less capable, younger, or handicapped.

Very rude and indifferent; seems to intend it.	Usually rude and discourteous.	May or may not be rude; is unpredictable.	Considerate of others at times.	Considerate if he is in tune with the circumstances.	Usually considerate and dependable.	Very considerate; highly courteous without falseness.

10. Child's ability to share materials and equipment with others.

Wants all for himself always or nearly always.	Is hard to get him to share.	Shares only if cautioned in advance.	Shares in some ways or at some times.	Usually shares well.	Can be depended on to share in nearly all instances.	Shares and takes responsibility for others readily and always.

11. Child's ability and willingness to help others.

Never helps others.	Helps others only under pressure.	Sometimes helps others.	Helps others if he likes them or what they are doing.	Helps others in many instances.	Usually readily helpful in attitude and action.	An excellent help to others; readily and cheerfully helpful always.

12. Child's care of camp property.

Seems to destroy willfully and gleefully.	Usually destructive.	Destructive now and then, more by accident and carelessness.	Fairly careful in most ways.	Often careful and saving.	Quite careful and dependable.	Excellent carefulness; points out caution to others.

13. Child's ability to face own failures and shortcomings.

A very bad loser; always makes excuses.	Usually a bad loser and excuse maker.	Loses badly now and then; may face it well sometimes.	Usually a fairly good loser.	Faces losses and shortcomings on most occasions.	A really good loser; faces shortcomings well.	Excellent loser but not indifferently; seeks correction of weaknesses.

14. Child's willingness to abide by general rules.

Breaks rules right and left.	Generally breaks rules.	Breaks rules and follows them in seemingly random ways.	Abides by rules if held up to him.	Can be depended upon in many ways to follow rules.	Generally follows rules well.	Excellent; very dependable and willing.

15. Child's ability to accept disagreement.

Can't accept disagreement ever.	Accepts disagreement badly.	May accept it on occasion.	Accepts disagreement if well presented.	Can accept it fairly well.	Accepts it well.	Accepts it with openness; ready to improve or change.

16. Child's ability to accept constructive criticism.

Fights it bitterly.	Hates it but is passive.	Accepts it or not in inconsistent ways.	Accepts it under some circumstances.	Accepts it usually.	Takes it in good faith most of the time.	Accepts it readily; asks for it.

17. Child's concern for the welfare of the group as a whole.

Hostile to group and its welfare.	Often opposes and is hostile to group.	Unpredictably hostile and cooperative.	May accept group welfare, objectives at times.	Accepts group welfare on many occasions.	Takes group welfare as important.	Can be depended upon faithfully to do this.

18. Child's willingness to credit other members of group.

Hostile to credit given others.	Opposes credit to others.	May give credit or not.	Gives credit to others in some ways.	Willing to give credit to others.	Gives others credit most of the time.	Very fair and reliable this way.

19. Demonstrates self-confidence.

Utterly lacking.	Lacks it most of the time.	Shows it now and then; lacks it at random times.	Shows self-confidence in some ways.	Shows self-confidence in most ways.	Comfortably confident in most ways.	Very confident without bravado in all situations.

20. Child's acceptance of his share of responsibility.

Utterly irresponsible.	Very lacking in responsibility.	Shows it or not in unpredictable ways.	Accepts it in some ways.	Accepts it in many ways.	Very accepting.	A model of acceptance.

21. Child's refraining from violent temper outbrusts.

In a temper all the time it seems.	Frequent temper displays.	Shows temper in unpredictable situations.	Controls temper on some occasions.	Usually hard to provoke.	Very fine self-control.	Never see temper; solves problems effectively.

22. Child's restraint from show-off behavior.

Shows off all the time.	A bit show-off usually.	Shows off and is restrained in random ways.	Avoids show-off behavior on some occasions.	Usually controls self pretty well.	Shows good control most of the time.	Always under healthy self-control.

23. Child's display of anxiety/apprehension.

Under constant anxiety.	Shows anxiety much of the time.	Is anxious now and then.	No anxiety on some occasions.	Anxious on a few occasions.	Rarely shows anxiety or apprehension.	No anxiety noticed at all.

24. Child's dependency on Counselors for help/attention.

Always seeks help or attention.	Often seeks one or both.	Seeks both in random ways.	Able to get along on own on some occasions.	Gets along on own much of the time.	Very resourceful, usually on own.	Very independent and resourceful.

25. Child's popularity with other children.

Very unpopular.	Unpopular in most respects.	Popular-unpopular in hard-to-tell ways.	Popular with others in limited ways.	Fairly popular with others.	Very popular.	Probably most liked and popular.

26. Child's ascendency in meeting others, contacting others.

Most retiring and shy.	Usually retiring and shy.	Some ascendence in odd ways and times.	Somewhat ascendent at times.	Fairly ascendent and resourceful.	Very ascendent.	Most able and responsible here.

N. Haring and E. Phillips. (1962). *Educating Emotionally Disturbed Children.* Reprinted by permission of the authors and McGraw-Hill.

excessive withdrawal, (4) excessive dependency, (5) poor ego strength, (6) poor physical strength, (7) poor coordination, (8) poor intellectually, (9) poor attention, (10) poor impulse control, (11) poor academics, (12) poor reality contact, (13) poor sense of identity, (14) excessive suffering, (15) poor anger control, (16) excessive sense of persecution, (17) excessive aggressiveness, (18) excessive resistance, and (19) poor social conformity.

Procedure. The BBRS is simple to score. The items are arranged so that boxes in which the scores are entered descend in a column for each of these 19 categories. When one lays a straight edge adjacent to the column of scores, the numbers in a specific column can be added and the total can be transferred to the appropriate location on the profile sheet. When plotting the data on the profile sheet, three levels are indicated. The first level for clusters with low scores indicates that there is not a significant problem. The second level indicates cause for concern, and the third level indicates very significant problems in the child.

Comments. The BBRS provides parents and professionals with a great wealth of information. It can be used repeatedly over a period of time to assess if changes have occurred in behavior patterns. The scale has undergone significant test development and standardization. Research has yielded acceptable levels of reliability and three types of validity (criterion-related validity, content validity, construct validity).

Experience with the BBRS indicates that it is helpful to get two people who are aware of the child to complete the document. In this way, one can maximize the probability of obtaining an accurate picture of the child. After the checklist is scored, it is helpful to discuss the child's problem with the rater. While discussing these concerns, the raters can elaborate on their perceptions and possibly provide the evaluator with some behavioral examples. Recently, a remediation guide was prepared as an adjunct for the test. The purpose of the handbook is to serve as a guide for clinicians using the BBRS. The handbook provides some innovative assessment techniques and intervention strategies that have worked with many children.

The Devereux Child Behavior Rating Scale (DCB)

Purpose and Procedures. The DCB scale was designed for use with children ages eight to twelve. The scale provides a profile of potential behavior problems. It has been researched extensively and has yielded acceptable reliability coefficients.

The DCB is very similar in purpose to the BBRS. The DCB is intended to be completed by anyone who has had the opportunity to observe the child in a variety of daily situations. This is usually someone who lives with the child. The instructions for making the ratings are clearly defined on the cover sheet of the DCB protocol, and scoring is straightforward and explained clearly in the manual.

Summary of Behavioral Checklists

As can be seen, a wealth of information can be obtained via behavioral checklists. Some of the scales discussed can be completed by the therapist, while others have to be completed by significant others who are familiar with the child's behavior.

The third behavioral checklist is the **Behavior Assessment System for Children (BASC),** which was developed by Reynolds and Kamphaus. The BASC is published by the American Guidance System and is a viable instrument. The scale has different versions for both the parents and the therapist as well as for distinctive age groups (e.g., preschool, elementary age and adolescence). Lastly, the author would also like to recognize the **Parent Stress Index** by Richard Abidin as an excellent source of information about the child-parent relationship. All of these instruments require extensive training for proper interpretation.

Part IV: Leisure Interest and Skill Instruments

A variety of instruments have been utilized over the years to measure preferred leisure interests and perceived leisure competence. For this reason, one should be very cautious in selecting tests.

The following is a brief review of a few actively applied instruments.

Leisure Diagnostic Battery (LDB)

Purpose. The LDB is the first major assessment tool to thoroughly investigate leisure abilities. No other instrument of this complexity currently exists.

The Leisure Diagnostic Battery (LDB) represents a collection of instruments that were designed to assist in the assessment of disabled and abled-bodied persons.

Witt and Ellis (1987) suggest that the most unique feature of the LDB is its overall theoretical conceptualization. They point out that the battery was based on a more holistic view of leisure with its emphasis on leisure as a state of mind. In essence, the LDB attempts to measure a person's perceived freedom in leisure and factors that are potential barriers.

Witt and Ellis (1982) suggest that the battery has four major purposes:

1. To assess an individual's current leisure functioning level.
2. To determine areas where improvement of current leisure functioning is indicated.
3. To determine via post-assessment the impact of offered services on leisure functioning.
4. To facilitate research on the structure of leisure functioning to enable a better understanding of the value, purpose and outcomes of leisure experiences.

Description. There are several versions of the LDB. Both long and short forms of most of a family of instruments forming the battery have been developed. Both version A's of the long and short form have been applied with individuals nine to eighteen, either handicapped or nonhandicapped. The short version consists of 25 items taken from the batteries' first five scales.

The LDB is intended to allow an examiner the ability to identify an individual's perception of freedom in leisure as well as to further clarify the causative factors limiting this perceived freedom. Consequently, each of the battery's subtests has a distinct function in securing this data. The scales in Section 1 (A to E) are designed to provide the examiner with an indication of the individual's perception of freedom in leisure. Witt and Ellis (1987) point out that the sum of scores across those scales provides significant information in regards to the individual's level of perceived freedom. Table 16 provides a brief description of each of the subtests.

Witt and Ellis (1987) go to great lengths to list the findings of various studies which provide evidence of the reliability and validity of the LDB. Overall, scales A to F and the total perceived freedom in leisure show acceptable psychometric properties. Witt and Ellis (1987) suggest that extreme caution be exercised while using the knowledge test and preference inventory in some setting.

Administration. The instrument is easy to administer and score. All but two of the scales contain about 20 questions. These questions require the examinee to respond in one of the three ways: "sounds like me," "sounds a little like me," or "doesn't sound like me." Each of these responses is given a specific numeric score. The Leisure Preferences Scale and the Knowledge of Leisure Opportunities were designed differently. The preference scale is a 60-item forced-choice questionnaire. The responses to these questions are then clustered into specific categories to ascertain categorical interests. The knowledge subtest is a multiple-choice test focusing on general leisure opportunity knowledge. The test can be administered to an individual or group. Scoring the battery is clearly explained in the manual and involves adding all the subtest scores together to obtain an overall total. Scores falling within a given range indicate whether global leisure problems are present or not. It is helpful for the examinee to examine each subtest individually to ascertain whether there are specific problem areas. This examination of subtest scores is critical to a total understanding of the test results.

Resources. A variety of materials come with the LDB, including a user's guide, a user's manual, a manual explaining the instrument's background and structure, and a useful remediation guide. The test can be administered as an entire battery or specific subscales can be selected. The writer has found the descriptive/qualitative information yielded by the test as important and helpful as the quantitative data obtained. This test is highly recommended as an integral part of an assessment battery.

Table 16. PURPOSES AND DOMAINS FOR LDB COMPONENTS

Component	Purpose	Domains
Perceived Freedom (sum of scales A–E)	To enable the measurement of perceived freedom in leisure.	A scale is obtained by summing across all items of scales measuring "perceived freedom"
A) Perceived Leisure Competence	To enable the measurement of perceptions of the degree of personal competence in recreation and leisure endeavors.	1. Cognitive competence 2. Social competence 3. Physical competence 4. General competence
B) Perceived Leisure Control	To enable the measurement of degree of internality, or the extent to which the individual controls events and outcomes in his/her leisure experiences.	Each item is designed to reflect the presence or absence of an internal stable attribution tendency.
C) Leisure Needs	To enable the measurement of abilities to satisfy intrinsic needs via recreation & leisure experiences.	1. Relaxation 2. Surplus energy 3. Compensation 4. Catharsis 5. Optimal arousal 6. Gregariousness 7. Status 8. Creative expression 9. Skill development 10. Self image
D) Depth of involvement in leisure	To enable the measurement of extent to which individuals become absorbed, or achieve "flow" during activities.	Each item reflects an element of Csikzentmihalyi's "flow" concept: 1. Centering of attention 2. Merging or action and awareness 3. Loss of self consciousness 4. Perception of control over self and environment 5. Non-contradictory demands for action with immediate feedback
E) Playfulness	To enable the measurement of individual's degree of playfulness.	Based on Lieberman's work with the playfulness concept: 1. Cognitive spontaneity 2. Physicial spontaneity 3. Social spontaneity 4. Manifest joy
F) Barriers to Leisure Experiences	To determine problems that an individual encounters when trying to select, or participate in leisure experiences.	1. Communication 2. Social 3. Decision making 4. Opportunity

Component	Purpose	Domains
		5. Motivation
		6. Ability
		7. Money
		8. Time
G) Leisure Preferences	To determine the individual's patterns of selection among activities. In addition, this scale measures preference for mode or style of involvement.	*Activity Domains* 1. Outdoor/Nature 2. Music/Dance/Drama 3. Sports 4. Arts/Crafts/Hobbies 5. Mental Linguistic *Style Domains* 1. Individual/Group 2. Risk/Non-Risk 3. Active/Passive
H) Knowledge of Leisure Opportunities	To determine the individual's knowledge of specific information concerning leisure opportunities.	1. Cost 2. Who can participate 3. Where 4. When 5. What

From the *Leisure Diagnostic Battery: Users Manual* by Peter Witt and Gary Ellis. Reprinted by permission of the authors.

Leisure Activities Blank

Purpose. The most widely used leisure interest finder is McKechnie's (1975) Leisure Activities Blank (LAB). The purpose of this test is to explore patterns of leisure interests and to explore the psychological meanings and implications of the reported leisure interests.

Procedures. This test consists of 120 forced-choice questions that gather information about past and expected future interests. The questions are rated on two different dimensions. First, each question is rated on a four-point rating scale for present and past involvement. Second, upon examination of each question, the respondent must indicate future intentions about being involved with selected activities.

The manual clearly articulates guidelines for interpreting various scores. Like the LDB, a major asset to the LAB is its strong psychometric development and field testing. The qualitative results from the test provide added information about leisure-time interests. The test seems much more appropriate for older children and adolescents.

Mirenda Leisure Interest Finder (MLIF)

Purpose. Another frequently utilized measure instrument is the Mirenda Leisure Interest Finder (MLIF), developed by Joseph Mirenda. The MLIF is part of a Leisure Counseling Media Kit, which consists of the leisure interest finder, leisure inventory file, and the leisure activity file.

Mirenda and Wilson (1975) describe the finder as a series of 90 questions based on activities in nine areas: games, sports, nature, collection, crafts, art, music, education and culture, volunteer services and organizational services.

Procedures. Following each of the activity statements is a five-point rating scale that indicates the degree of preference for the activity ([1] dislikes very much to [5] likes very much). The responses are then profiled, and questions that are related are clustered (e.g. sports, nature). Each of the nine categories is subdivided, yielding a total of 18 subscales. A profile sheet is used to graphically project the outcomes on each subscale. The most interpretable profiles are those where the questions within a cluster are all rated high or low. For example, all of the questions pertaining to involvement in group sports could be rated with four's and five's. This information would lead the examiner to believe that the child enjoyed active group sports. However, this perfect kind of flat profile does not always occur. There may be a great deal of scatter on various subscale profiles. In this case, although there would not be any general patterns noted, the examiner could determine specific interests.

Other Leisure Interest Finders and Play Scales

There are many other useful leisure interest finders. A few worth noting are the Leisure Interest Inventory (Hubert, 1969), the Constructive Leisure Activity Survey (Edwards, 1978), the Avocational Activities Inventory (Overs, Taylor and Adkins, 1977) and the Self Leisure Interest Profile (McDowell, 1973).

There are a couple of play scales and inventories that the reader may find helpful. The Knox Play Scale (1974) may be found useful in the assessing of the psychosocial parameters of children in play situations. The scale has been found to be helpful in identifying various play experiences which may be used in enhancing development. Furthermore, the reader may want to acquaint himself/herself to Hurff's (1974) Play Skills Inventory. The inventory provides a description of play in four general areas (perception, intellect, sensation and motor abilities).

In addition, there are a few techniques established that have been developed specifically for persons with disabilities. The Mundy Recreation Inventory for the Mentally Retarded evaluates leisure skills in the psychomotor and cognitive domains (Mundy, 1981), while Berryman and Lefebvre (1979) developed the Recreation Behavioral Inventory designed for recreation therapists to use with persons with a multitude of disabilities.

Additionally, there have been tests developed that attempt to measure a leisure state of mind. Probably the two best known are the Walshe Temperament Survey, in addition to McDowell's (1979) Leisure Well-Being Inventory. Both of these instruments are easy to administer, but both lack any substantial normative data. The author does not feel that these tests would be useful when assessing young children. However, they could be of some value when dealing with adolescents with at least average intelligence.

Finally, there are a variety of other ways to measure attributes that pertain to leisure interests and well-being. The use of incomplete subjective sentences provides an enormous amount of information. For example, let us examine the following two sentences: "I like . . . "; "When I am at home alone I like to . . . ." While assessing a child's leisure interests, a great deal can be learned from a child's completion of such sentences. It is imperative that the therapist not make any comments to any of the responses until the entire interview is complete. At that time, one can ask a child to elaborate or discuss certain responses. All too often, examiners interrupt a child while s/he is talking. This may cause the child to become self-centered and nervous.

SUMMARY

The process of measurement is a comprehensive and important task. Assessment should not be considered simply for gathering entry data but rather as an integrated aspect in the entire recreational treatment process.

Within this chapter, technical as well as practical suggestions were interwoven together. This was done to provide a basic understanding of how to develop the skills necessary to become a perceptive reviewer. Assessment should not only be considered as paper-and-pencil activities;

indeed, we have seen a wide variety of approaches to gathering information about the child. Dowd (1984) elegantly stated that to merely rely upon a paper-and-pencil test is to miss the richness of information to be gained from a candid conversation or an observation. We need to learn how to take advantage of all the information that is around us.

However, I want to caution those who feel that a little information is all that is necessary to get by. This is an inappropriate point of view and is unfair to the child in question. One must understand that integrating assessment procedures into one's battery of skills is just as important as actually leading the selected activities.

We must judge the relative merits of different assessment instruments by first understanding variables such as reliability and validity (Dowd, 1984). For this reason, attention was spent attempting to explain the meanings of these variables. As test users, we need to meet the requirements to deliver an assessment that is safe and accurate. Accuracy also depends on the tester's ability to understand the purposes as well as strengths and limitations of a certain approach.

Assessment procedures need to be clearly linked to the examiner's methods in working with children. One needs to want to gather certain information, with the hope that it will assist in answering the proposed questions. Seneca once noted, "When a man does not know what harbor he is aiming for, no wind is the right wind." An assessment begins with the clinician knowing what information s/he needs to be answered. This is then followed by selecting the best available strategies to treat the prevailing problems. Clinicians' roles can in some ways provide as much excitement as being detectives. Not only will solving the mysteries challenge us, but we (as well as those we serve) will be rewarded by the implications of our findings.

REFERENCES

Alpern, G.D., Boll, T.J., & Shearer, M.S. (1984). *Developmental profile II.* Los Angeles, CA: Western Psychological Services.

Anastasi, A. (1976). *Psychological testing.* New York: Macmillan.

Belsky, J., & Most, R. (1981). From exploration to play: A cross-sectional study of infant free play behavior. *Developmental Psychology, 17,* 630–639.

Berryman, D.L., & Lefebvre, C.B. (1979). *Recreation behavioral inventory.* Unpublished manuscript (available from C.B. Lefebvre, 2225 East McKinney, Denton, Texas 76201).

Brigance, A. (1978). *Brigance diagnostic inventory of early development.* North Billerica, MA: Curriculum.

Brown, L., Branston, M., Nietupski, S., Pumpian, I., Certo, N., & Gruenweld, L. (1979). A strategy for developing chronological age-appropriate and functional curricular content for severely handicapped adolescents and young adults. *Journal of Special Education, 13,* 81–90.

Burk, H. (1985). *Diagnosis and remediation of learning and behavior problems in children using the Burk's rating scales.* Los Angeles: Western Psychological Services.

Cooper, J.O. (1981). *Measuring behavior* (2nd ed.). Columbus, OH: Charles E. Merrill.

DiNola, A., Kaminsky, B., & Sternfeld, A. (1978). *T.M.R. performance profile.* Ridgefield, NJ: Educational Performance Associates, Inc.

Dollar, J., & Brooks, C. (1980). Assessment of severely and profoundly handicapped individuals. *Exceptional Educational Quarterly, 1*(3), 87–101.

Dowd, E.T. (1984). *Leisure counseling: Concepts and applications.* Springfield, IL: Charles C Thomas.

Dubose, R. (1978). Identification. In M. Snell (Ed.): *Systematic instruction of the moderately and severely handicapped.* Columbus, Ohio: Charles E. Merrill.

Dunn, J.K. (1974). Assessment. In C.A. Peterson and S.L. Gunn (Eds.), *Therapeutic recreation program design* (pp. 267–320). Englewood Cliffs, NJ: Prentice-Hall.

Edwards, P.B. (1978). *The constructive leisure assessment survey II.* Los Angeles: Constructive Leisure.

Ellis, G.D., Witt, P.A., & Niles, S. (1982). *The leisure diagnostic battery remediation guide.* Texas: Division of Recreation and Leisure Studies.

Fewell, R., & Rich, J. (1987). Play assessment as a procedure for examining cognitive, communication, and social skills in multihandicapped children. *Journal of Psychoeducational Assessment, 2,* 119–137.

Fewell, R. (1984). *Play assessment scale.* Unpublished manuscript. Seattle: University of Washington.

Fewell, R., & Vadasy, P. (1983). *Learning through play.* Hingham, MA: Teaching Resources.

Fine, A. (1982). Modification of the Haring and Phillips' Rating Scale. Cincinnati: University of Cincinnati.

Fine, A. (1982, October). Assessment: Where to begin and what to do with handicapped children. Paper presented at the 1982 National Therapeutic Recreation Society, Annual Meeting in conjunction with the Congress for Recreation and Parks, Louisville, Kentucky.

Fuchs, L.S., & Fuchs, D. (1986). Linking assessment to instructional intervention: An overview. *School Psychology Review, 15*(3), 318–323.

Garvey, C. (1977). *Play.* Cambridge: Harvard University Press.

Glaser, R. (1971). A criterion-referenced test. In J. Popham (Ed.), *Criterion-referenced measurement.* Englewood Cliffs, NJ: Educational Technology Publications.

Gronlund, N.E. (1976). *Measurement and evaluation in teaching.* New York: Macmillan.

Haeussermann, E. (1958). *Developmental potential of preschool children.* New York: Grune and Stratton.

Haring, N., & Phillips, E. (1962). *Educating emotionally disturbed children.* New York: McGraw-Hill.

Holowinsky, I. (1980). Qualitative assessment of cognitive skills. *Journal of Special Education, 14,* 153–163.

Hubert, E.E. (1969). *The development of an inventory of leisure interests.* Unpublished doctoral dissertation, University of North Carolina at Chapel Hill.

Hurff, J. (1974). A play skills inventory. In M. Reilly (Ed.), *Play as exploratory learning: Studies of curiosity behavior.* Beverly Hills: Sage.

Johnson, D., & Martin, S. (1980). Criterion referenced testing: New wine in old bottles?. *Academic Therapy, 16,* 167–173.

Kazdin, A. (1980). *Behavior modification in applied settings.* Champaign, IL: Dorsey.

Kerlinger, F.M. (1973). *Foundations of behavioral research.* New York: Holt, Rinehart and Winston.

Knox, S. (1974). A play scale. In M. Reilly (Ed.), *Play as exploratory learning: Studies of Curiosity behavior.* Beverly Hills: Sage.

Lemay, D., Griffin, P., & Sanford, A. (1977). *Examiner's manual: Learning accomplishment profile diagnostic edition.* Chapel Hill, NC: Kaplan.

Lowe, M. (1975). Trends in the development of representational play in infants from one to three years: An observational study. *Journal of Child Psychology and Psychiatry, 16,* 33–47.

Loesch, L.C., & Wheeler, P.T. (1982). *Principles of leisure counseling.* Minneapolis: Educational Media.

McDowell, C.F. (1979). *The leisure well-being inventory.* Oregon: Leisure Lifestyle.

McLoughlin, J., & Lewis, R. (1986). *Assessing special students.* Columbus: Charles E. Merrill.

McKechnie, G.E. (1974). *The structure of leisure activities.* California: Institute of Personality Assessment and Research.

Mercatoris, M., & Craighead, W.E. (1974). Effects of nonparticipant observation on teacher and pupil classroom behavior. *Journal of Educational Psychology, 66,* 512–519.

Millman, J. (1970). Reporting student progress: A case for criterion-reference marking system. *Phi Delta Kappan, 52,* 226–230.

Mirenda, J.J., & Wilson, G.T. (1975). The Milwaukee leisure counseling model. *Counseling and Values, 20*(1), 42–46.

Mundy, C.J. (1981). *Leisure assessment instruments.* Unpublished manuscript (available from Dr. C.J. Mundy, Department of Human Services and Studies, Florida State University, Tallahassee, FL).

National Therapeutic Recreational Society. (1982). Philosophical position statement. In C.A. Peterson and S.L. Gunn (Eds.), *Therapeutic recreation program design* (pp. 321–323). Englewood Cliffs, NJ: Prentice-Hall.

Nicolich, L. (1977). Beyond sensorimotor intelligence: Assessment of symbolic maturity through analysis of pretend play. *Merrill Palmer Quarterly, 23,* 89–99.

Overs, R.P., Taylor, S., & Adkins, C. (1977). *Avocational counseling manual: A complete guide to leisure guidance.* Washington, DC: Hawkins and Associates.

Parker, R.A., Ellison, C.H., Kirby, T.F., & Short, M.J. (1975). The comprehensive evaluation in recreation therapy scale: A tool for patient evaluation. *Therapeutic Recreation Journal,* Vol. 9, 143–152.

Popham, J., & Husek, T. (1969). Implications of criterion-referenced measurement. *Journal of Educational Measurement, 6,* 1–9.

Proger, B., & Mann, L. (1973). Criterion-referenced measurement. The world of gray versus black and white. *Journal of Learning Disabilities, 6,* 19–29.

Rubin, R. (1985). Play peer interaction, and social development. In C. Brown and A. Gottfried (Eds.), *Play interactions: The role of toys and parental involvement and children's development.* Skillman, NJ: Johnson and Johnson.

Rubin, K. (1982). Non-social play in preschoolers: Necessarily evil? *Child Development, 53,* 651–675.

Rubin, K. (1982). Social skills and social-cognitive correlates of observed isolation behavior in preschoolers. In K. Rubin, and H. Ross (Eds.), *Peer relationship and social skills in childhood.* New York: Springer.

Salvia, J., & Ysselyke, J. (1985). *Assessment in special and remedial education.* Boston: Houghton-Mifflin.

Simon, G. (1969). Comments on implications of criterion-referenced measurement. *Journal of Educational Measurement, 6,* 259–26•••.

Takata, N. (1974). Play as a prescription. In M. Reilly (Ed.), *Play as exploratory learning: Studies of curiosity behavior.* Beverly Hills: Sage.

Vulpe, S.G. (1979). *Vulpe's assessment battery.* Toronto: National Institute on Mental Retardation.

Wallace, G., & Larsen, S. (1978). *Educational assessment of learning problems: Testing for teaching.* Boston: Allyn and Bacon.

Wehman, P., & Schleien, S.J. (1980). Relevant assessment in leisure skill training program. *Therapeutic Recreation Journal, 14*(4), 9–20.

Westby, C. (1980). Assessment of cognitive and language abilities through play. *Language Speech and Hearing Services in Schools, 11,* 154–168.

Witt, P., & Ellis, G. (1987). *The leisure diagnostic battery: Users manual.* State Park: Venture.

Witt, P.A., Connolly, P., & Compton, D. (1980). Assessment: A plea for sophistication. *Therapeutic Recreation Journal, 14*(4), 5–8.

Witt, P.A. (1982). *The leisure diagnostic battery user's guide.* Texas: Division of Recreation and Leisure Studies, North Texas State University.

Wodrich, D.L. (1984). *Children's psychological testing: A guide for nonpsychologists.* Baltimore: Brookes.

Chapter 8

BROADENING THE IMPACT OF SERVICES AND RECREATIONAL THERAPIES

AUBREY H. FINE AND JULIE LEE
SUSAN ZAPF, SHERRY KRIWIN, AND KATHLEEN HENDERSON
FRANK GIBBONS AND AUBREY H. FINE

Editor's Note

Due to the breadth of this chapter, the editors have elected to divide the readings into three concrete sections. The first section of this chapter pertains to play facilitated therapies which include various forms of play therapy, art therapy and bibliotherapy. This section of the chapter was written by Dr. Aubrey H. Fine and Julie Lee. The second section of this chapter pertains to unique applications of animal-assisted therapy with children. The section on animal-assisted therapy was prepared by Susan Zapf, Sherry Kirwin and Kathleen Henderson who were requested by the **Delta Society** to prepare this portion of this chapter. The final segment of the chapter was prepared by Dr. Frank Gibbons and Dr. Aubrey H. Fine and focuses on the application of Horticulture therapy.

> *All the world's a stage*
> *And all the men and women merely players.*
> *They have their exits and their entrances*
> *And each man in his time plays many parts.*
>
> William Shakespeare

INTRODUCTION

There is still a persistent misconception to contend with in our profession: that recreation is totally synonymous with physical activity and sport. As a consequence, certain stereotypes inevitably developed over the years concerning what one should expect from a recreational professional. These stereotypes, unfortunately, have often restricted what recreational personnel perceived as their domain or expertise. Corbin and Williams (1987) asserted that due to this myopic perspective and outlook, recreation leaders have not adequately explored, or have not even been allowed to pursue, a multitude of potential options in recreation and related fields.

Many energetic new professionals are socialized into these roles, adjusting themselves to the expectations of their peers or to what they perceive to be the scope of their position. While these perceptions are not wrong, they obviously limit out potentials. As a relatively recent profession closely allied with mental health, recreational therapy can impact the lives of many children with disabilities. However, if we equip ourselves only with what has been traditionally accepted, indeed prescribed, as our "domain," we might limit drastically our own scope and effectiveness.

In a traditional sense, the parameters of services provided by a recreational therapist incorporate a comprehensive array of recreational systems, techniques, and options. This chapter will focus on broadening the perceptions of what recreational services should consist. It will, additionally, offer suggestions of several alternative recreational modes that will enhance the therapeutic value of the services rendered to exceptional children.

Among the many options, there are several unique methods and activity processes that can be incorporated by a recreational therapist while assisting children. In fact, the intent of this brief exposé is to provide insight into some viable alternatives and to suggest some practical points for implementational purposes with various special populations. Since this chapter, by its nature, cannot be more than a mere overview, the interested reader should seek additional training in any of the listed alternatives prior to implementing them. Even if some of these procedures may at first glance appear simplistic to apply, lack of training may hinder progress as well as overall effectiveness. As we are aware, it is unethical to ascribe competence to a specific area of training when experience is limited.

SECTION 1: PLAY THERAPY

One of the most frequently perpetuated confusions in the minds of lay persons is between recreational therapy and play therapy. There are, indeed, significant differences between these two. But, for our purposes, both recognize the importance of children's play. That many recreational therapists have not taken advantage of some of the unique benefits of play therapy is, to say the least, unfortunate. They would definitely find some of the approaches useful while interacting with children and helping them work through and master quite complex psychological difficulties within their lives.

Play therapy is an important component of an overall, integrated treatment program. While play that takes place during therapy differs significantly from naturally occurring play, the most distinctive difference being the therapist's (professional or lay) involvement, it only impacts the child's natural willingness for spontaneous play. In spite of this drawback, through play, children can be assisted in divulging and possibly resolving any disturbing conflicts and trauma, as Schafer and O'Connor have suggested (1983). Others joined this notion by noting that play techniques and discovery approaches allow children to expose themselves in a nonthreatening manner. It must be understood, also, the play therapy must be playful and enjoyable to the child involved. Young people really find it easy to communicate feelings about themselves through play rather than through direct conversation (M. Bijou: personal communication, November 8, 1986). The use of this medium provides the professional with an insight into the child's world; almost any form of child's play can provide a professional with data for understanding, for fantasies, conflicts, anger, and joy can be acted out by children in play situations. It can be used to promote rapport between child and the therapist, for the latter can become more readily accepted in the child's world of feelings and thoughts while engaging in diversional play experiences. A skilled therapist can use this information as insight into the child's mode of feeling (Muro & Dinkmeyer, 1977). F. Amster, the noted psychologist, synthesized succinctly the positive contribution of play therapy in understanding the child:

1. While observing a child playing, one can develop a clearer diagnostic understanding of the child.
2. The medium of play enhances the therapeutic relationship in addition to helping a child verbalize certain conscious-associated feelings.
3. Play can also be used therapeutically to help a child act out unconscious material and, consequently, relieve underlying tensions. (Amster, 1943)

Play therapy has a long history encompassing several theoretical orientations. Anna Freud and Melanie Klein were among the first professionals to promote the use of play in psychotherapy with children. Freud incorporated play into her work primarily as a way of developing rapport and making children feel more at ease. Games and toys were used to encourage the child's involvement. Klein, on the other hand, is considered to be the first to incorporate play as a substitute for a child's verbalization (Klein, 1932). This is particularly important for younger children who are less capable of expressing themselves verbally. Due to both Klein's and Freud's theoretical orientations, play therapy took on a strong psychoanalytic framework. Specifically, it was appreciated for its cathartic value, since it appears that a child's own play efforts can indeed be self-healing. A further development was initiated by Levy, who established a new approach which he termed release therapy (Levy, 1939). This approach was aimed primarily at children who were victims of trauma. It was believed that if a child was given enough support, s/he would be able to recreate a traumatic event and get his/her feelings out in the open. In recent years, mastery play therapy has been successful in treating trauma victims (Schaefer, 1994). It combines several therapeutic strategies such as abreaction, cognitive reappraisal, a supportive relationship, and crisis-intervention principle.

An eminent play therapist, the humanist Virginia Axline, in the 1940s, incorporated key elements of client-centered counseling into her perspective of play, such as empathy, understanding, warmth, and acceptance. The child is regarded as the center of attention, and as such, playing is regarded as an opportunity for the child to experience growth under conditions that are unrestrictive and favorable to the child. An array of play opportunities are provided, but the child has the ultimate choice of what to play with. In fact, no directions are given to the child, the child takes the lead, and the facilitator takes a nondirective observational role. Axline explained that by playing-out their feelings, children bring their feelings to the surface, face them, learn to control them, or abandon them. Through play, children also realize the power within themselves to be individuals in their own right, to think for themselves, to make their own decisions, to become psychologically more mature, and, by so doing, to realize self-hood. The ultimate goal of Axline's orientation, thus, is to facilitate the child's self-direction and self-growth (Axline, 1947). While not differing in the basic rationale, Crocker Peoples modified some of the principles espoused by Axline by suggesting that the play therapist should become more directive at times and take the lead to ensure that the child engages in productive and meaningful play. This orientation is referred to as **Fair Play Therapy** (Peoples, 1983).

Applications with Special Populations

Play therapy is also one of several methods to help children with developmental and health disabilities to develop a sense of strength and competency (Carmichael, 1993). By expressing themselves through music, poetry, prose, and art, these activities provide a view to their inner world of fears, strengths, and weaknesses. In turn, therapist can help them deal with these issues in a therapeutic way. Children with mental retardation who experience emotional problems can benefit through play therapy (Hellendoorn, 1994). Working with this population requires the therapists to use individualized therapeutic goals because the diversity of problems and goals as well as the variability in age and mental level. For children with mental retardation, play-based interventions "can enhance the development, can overcome language problems, and can enhance their cognitive maturity" (McConkey, 1994). Imaginative play training has also helped children with special needs to develop play skills (Hellendoorn, 1994). Other developmental play games, such as jumping and skipping games, throwing at a target, or pretend games can help these children learn important everyday life skills (McConkey, 1994). With physically ill children, several different kinds of play therapy techniques have been utilized. Sand play, photographs, and the use of seeds, plants, and gardening have been very effective with this population as a way of contracting their own frustrations about their illness (Webb, 1991).

Play Therapy and the Hospitalized Child

When working with children in hospital settings, there are a variety of play therapy techniques that will be of obvious benefit for both the child and the therapist. Play can lessen the negative impact of hospitalization for children through expression of feelings, reversal of roles, and control of materials, concepts, and actions (Bolig, 1990). Dictated by the severity and the type of their illnesses, differing play therapy techniques should be implemented to different groups. Chronically ill children, children with terminal or progressive illnesses, and other children who face lengthy hospitalization (i.e., greater than a week) usually benefit more from individual play with a facilitator than children with shorter hospital stays. The stresses of hospitalization are intensified by the extended hospital stay, and thus a one-on-one play situation can promote rapport and trust between the facilitator and the children (Fine & Siaw, 1987). Thus, in order to normalize the experience for the child, one of the most widely-used play therapy techniques in the hospitals is the puppet play. The puppets are used to demonstrate feelings common to hospitalized children. Through puppet play, children can express thoughts and feelings that the child cannot express directly (Webb, 1991). Video games have also been used with children as a diversion from the side effects of such illness as cancer chemotherapy (Phillips, 1991).

Group play also has benefits for children who are in the hospital for extended stays. In particular, group play is important for the school-aged child, whom Erikson (1963) describes as defining him/herself by comparisons with peers (i.e., the industry versus inferiority normative crisis in Erikson's theory). One of the common denominators, as Golden points out, can be also an opportunity to interact with peers who have undergone similar medical procedures, a valuable means of social comparison with others. But the most important contribution is that group play provides children with a time for social interaction with peers; indeed, developmental research shows that peer interactions are especially important during middle childhood, where social interaction is deemed developmentally critical. Further, play provides a way to foster normal development in the face of the disruption of a hospital stay (Baron, 1991). In addition, a one-on-one play situation, especially in the case of lengthy hospitalization, not only promotes a rapport and trust between the children and facilitator, but it also helps them to "venture symbolic exploration of anxieties, and the necessity for structuring various specific procedures" (Golden, 1983, p. 222).

In this context, a facilitator can also utilize the group play therapy as a vehicle for observing how children interact with others. Children with chronic illnesses are often socially immature because of what has been called by Boone and Hartman the "benevolent overreaction syndrome." The benevolent overreaction occurs when parents overprotect their child to the point of retarding the child's social development, and thus the ill child does not know how to interact with same-age peers. Many chronically ill children spend a significant amount of time with adults (e.g., their parents and medical personnel) and are inevitably limited in social experiences with peers. In one case, an early adolescent with cancer attended a special camp for children with cancer. This was the child's first separation from his parents and a rare opportunity to spend a significant amount of time with peers. The child had been overprotected by his well-meaning parents and had never learned how to tie his shoes because his mother had always done it for him. The other campers thought this was funny and unfortunately made fun of him. Thus, the facilitator was able to recognize this child's social immaturity by observing him separated from his parents in a peer group situation. Problems such as social immaturity due to the benevolent overreaction can be tackled via various play therapy strategies (Boone and Hartman, 1972).

Play Therapy and Ethnic Minority Children

Working with ethnic minority children in play therapy requires special modification by the therapists due to the fact that these children encounter different experiences than the nonethnic children. For instance, with majority of the Hispanic children, their lives are influenced by the political, racial, and social factors which are different from other children. Thus, therapists need to be aware of these issues and be sensitive when conducting play therapy with this group or any other ethnic minority groups.

Martinez and Valdez (1992) identified issues to a model of play therapy with minority children:

1. Therapist facilitated where the therapist actively introduces relevant cultural and contextual elements into play therapy.
2. The play therapy environmental setting is structured with cultural and sociocultural themes.
3. The therapist is knowledgeable about the real-life sociocultural context that the child lives in.
4. The therapist advocates to find healthy strategies, defense mechanisms, and methods to deal with sociocultural context of minority children.

Some of the materials they identify in play therapy are toys that all children use, but it is specifically modified for the minority children. They suggest that the room decor should reflect cultural diversity because it provides an environment where the children feel welcome to explore a multicultural play environment. Having dolls targeted for minority group children is also important in providing an opportunity to incorporating their own cultural world into their play. Coloring books that depict different ethnic folklore and legends can be used also. The presence of map or globe in the play environment can facilitate children to discuss their emigration experience or the family's place of origin.

SPECIALIZED TECHNIQUES IN PLAY THERAPY

Theraplay

One of the unique forms of play therapy, applied with a wide range of exceptional children, is known as Theraplay. The approach was first proposed by Austin Des Lauriers when he discovered its value with children with autism and schizophrenia. The goals of treatment are to help children to become alive. Theraplay, as it was defined by Des Lauriers (1978):

> emphasizes the central factor of high affective impact in all stimulating contacts or communications with the autistic child; this is done through play, games and fun. In this relaxed atmosphere, no special effort is made at teaching the child anything; there are no specific special education methods or tools utilized. What the child learns first is that it is good to be human with another human being: that it is fun to be a member of the human race and that grown up human beings are worth having around to make life pleasant. (P. 317.)

Recently, the internal constructs of Theraplay have been closely aligned to Hayley's cognitive problem-solving therapy in which the responsibility for change belongs to the therapist. S/he is expected to plan a strategy of change to bring about what the patient is attempting to achieve. Within Theraplay, the therapist structures, challenges the child, intrudes and nurtures the relationship. Furthermore, this technique provides an element of fun and the focus of body contact, whether it be vigorous, playful, and/or competitive (Hayley, 1972). It is a viable approach for children with emotional, social and developmental problems. These are usually children who usually have little confidence in themselves and trust in their perceived worlds. The term itself, **Theraplay,** describes a process which "is insistently intimate, physical, personal, focused and fun; a form of treatment that replicates the structuring, challenging, intruding and nurturing interest in the mother-infant relationship" (Jenberg, 1979, p. 26).

Theraplay differs from conventional play therapy, in that the therapist is significantly more directive within this approach. Furthermore, within Theraplay, the environment is not stocked with a multitude of toys such as dolls and crayons but rather a room which is almost virtually bare. The major prop for the child to interact with is the play therapist. Ann Jenberg (1979) prepared a list of do's and don'ts as guidelines for implementing this approach. The foundation for this list was laid down over years of clinical experiences with hundreds of children. While I have taken the liberty to modify and cluster her thoughts, conforming to my own ideas, the following list basically represents a synthesis of Jenberg's suggested guidelines:

The Do's and Don'ts of a Theraplay Therapist

1. The therapist should appear confident and take advantage of his/her leadership skills.
2. S/he should be responsive and empathic in addition to being willing to take charge of all sessions.
3. Assures that eye and physical contact are established.
4. Attempts to project to the child that s/he is a unique and special person.
5. The therapist should be utilized as the primary play object.
6. The focus of the entire session should be upon the child.
7. The activities incorporated should impose limited frustration, challenge and discomfort on the child.
8. The therapist initiates rather than reacts to the child's behavior. Therefore, sessions are specifically structured so specific issues are clarified and articulated.

Over the years, Theraplay has been applied with several special populations, including the mildly handicapped. For example, Jenberg illustrates vividly the importance of this approach with children with learning disabilities. She feels that Theraplay can assist children in developing their self-esteem as well as building a sense of trust in others. She illustrates clearly some of the remarkable changes she has seen in children over time when they were assisted with this process. Practitioners from a variety of academic disciplines have incorporated aspects of Theraplay within their own repertoires. For instance, Sally Bligh described how she applied activities of Theraplay with 17 children who had a severe language delay. She credited Theraplay with precipitating and facilitating changes, i.e., improvements, with these children.

Rubin and Tregay (1989) state that there are many advantages of applying theraplay in the classroom. First, a Theraplay group is a way for many adjustment, social, and security needs to be addressed with all involved. It gives them the opportunity to express feelings and lets children know that it is okay to let them out. Second, it can increase the children's tolerance of differences by being more aware of each other's unique and special qualities. Third, children can learn to get along with others and to care about each other. And most importantly, it allows children to learn something while playing, which provides a relief from typical school routine. Rubin and Tregay also suggest qualities to bringing fun to the Theraplay groups in the classroom:

1. LET YOURSELF GO!
2. Having fun is being spontaneous.
3. It is being faster paced than you typically are.
4. It is being excited, yet it is being relaxed.
5. It is being "silly".
6. It is being in charge yet at the same time being a participant, joining right in with the children and enjoying the group yourself.
7. It is feeling comfortable with intimacy and play.
8. It is going back to how you felt as a kid yourself, playing with exuberance, excitement, and with little inhibition.
9. It is being playful.
10. It is having a twinkle in your eye.
11. It is being unpredictable.
12. It is saying to yourself, this group is going to feel totally different from school. This will be a pleasant haven for all of us to relax and let go of the controls that we must have to be students. Now we can be people, friends, playmates. Let's just enjoy each other!

Table 17. Two Potential Theraplay Activities.

Hand Prints

Materials: Finger paint and finger paint paper.

Procedures: Therapist covers the child's palm and fingers with paint and then presses child's hand firmly to paper. All four hands make interesting paintings and good souvenirs of terminating session.

Pillow Bump

Materials: Six pillows (24" × 24")

Procedure: Depending on the size of the child, three to six pillows are stacked on top of the other. Child and therapist stand back to back with the pillows between them. At the count of three both participants rush to claim the largest area of pillow space. Then both stand up, remove a pillow and the contest begins again. This process is continued until all pillows have disappeared.

Mutual Storytelling Techniques

The use of children's stories has always been informative to clinicians. Mutual storytelling takes advantage of children's self-created stories. One of its founders and a major proponent of this approach, Richard Gardner, saw the efficacy of storytelling in its quality for imparting and transmitting important values. It utilizes a story that is designed to be specifically relevant to a particular time. The stories are specifically elicited by the therapist at each session from the child. This usually ensures the likelihood that the activity will be attended with receptivity and incorporated into the child's emotional being (Gardner, 1986).

Mutual storytelling can also be used in diagnostic purposes. An analysis of the repeated themes in stories provides diagnostic information which is related to the child's conflicts and feelings (Webb, 1991). This is especially the case for children in crisis.

The Basic Technique

As previously noted, the clinician elicits a self-initiated story from the child. This event is then followed with a summary story generated by the clinician incorporating some of his/her own perceptions. In Gardner's view, through the therapist's interpretations, a healthier resolution and adaptation can be achieved to the conflicts presented in the child's story. Mutual storytelling technique can be modified by utilizing drawings, dolls, puppets, and other toys (Gardner, 1993). These materials can facilitate the child to express his/her feelings into a story. Further, a tape and/or video recorder is recommended to be used, which can enhance significantly the child's motivation to participate. Although these tools might not be regarded as crucial, when they are applied, the therapeutic message can be consistently reiterated.

Mutual storytelling usually begins by letting the child know that s/he will be the major start of make-believe television program (if a video camera is being utilized). The child is then encouraged to make up a story completely from his/her imagination. The facilitator should simultaneously emphasize that it is against the rules to tell stories that really happened either to the child or anyone else s/he knows. This, in turn, usually helps in relaxing and putting the child at ease. The therapist also should discourage the child from revealing a story about things that have been read, heard, or seen in movies or television.

After this brief introduction, it is explained to the child that, like all stories, the presentation must have a beginning, middle, and end. When the story is completed, the child is then requested to explain the lesson learned as well as the moral derived. This is followed by the clinician's formulation of a similar story with a discussion about the conclusions drawn from both. If the child is hesitant, which happens often, the clinician can use numerous approaches to encourage a more willing participation. One easy way to accomplish this goal is to suggest that early on, the child share a generated story with the clinician. Then s/he is told the clinician will begin the story and the child will eventually be invited to join in. The approach is usually successful in eliciting stories from a majority of children.

Mutual storytelling should be applied only on an individual basis. One of the major reasons is that children may feel uncomfortable with others listening in. It is also imperative that the clinician be actively listening (it is appropriate to spend time jotting down notes) with a dual aim: (1) to foster the child's involvement in the activity and (2) s/he can help formulate better conclusions. The follow-up of requesting a child to elicit the lesson derived from the story is intended to obtain additional details.

Obviously, the therapist is in no position to create a follow-up story unless s/he has an understanding of the original presentation. Again, as suggested earlier, the more training and experience the facilitator acquires, the better position one will be in applying various play therapy techniques. Several excellent resources are available to assist the reader in exploring this technique as well as derivative activities applying similar procedures (see Gardner, 1971, 1986; Schafer and Reed, 1986). Furthermore, several other games that encourage dramatized clinical storytelling are the Board of Objects Game (Kritzberg), the Bag of Toys Game (where a child is encouraged to generate a story about an object selected from a bag), and the Feel and Tell Game.

All these activities and techniques are usually appropriate for children ages four to twelve. It seems that children at this age are more candid and less aware that their stories may reveal unconscious feelings. With older children, more age-appropriate strategies can be utilized such as the Talking, Feeling, Doing Game or the commercially available Ungame. Personally, I have used many of these activities when working with behaviorally disturbed and learning disabled children. It will be perhaps instructive to share some of my observations with the reader. Through dramatized storytelling, children can gain a better understanding of their feelings and an ability to be able to deal with them more effectively. Thus, I have developed several similar game-like alternatives which allow children to respond to their internal feelings. Probably the most critical ingredients that I have found to be helpful pertain to the elements of trust and communication. Children will not open up completely if they feel uncomfortable.

One example of a dynamic approach that I have developed is a game that I call Secrets (Fine, 1985). Basically, within the game, all participants make up questions, which must be honestly answered and which is one of the most important rules by the person who draws that specific slip. While the rules are discussed prior to playing the game, the game format is ever-changing. Initially, as the child begins playing the game, the questions are very superficial. However, as the therapeutic relationship is established, the questions become more and more deep rooted. What is established, the questions become more and more deep rooted. What makes Secrets so special? It is the genuine relationship that is formulated with the therapist and the child. Consequently, the approach becomes a catalyst for further interaction and possible discussion.

The Talking, Feeling, Doing Game

This game was also developed by Richard Gardner with the intent of assisting uncooperative children in exploring their feelings. The game includes a **normal appearing** playing board, a set of dice, playing pawns, a spinner, reward chips, and cards that are drawn from the center of the board. It is similar in many ways to most table games. Nevertheless, the core is derived from the directions and questions formulated on each of the cards. Although most children participate due to the competitive nature of the game, children are reinforced for revealing psychodynamically meaningful material for therapeutic utilization (Gardner, 1973). Within this game, according to Gardner, the Talking cards assist the child in making comments that are primarily intellectual in nature, while the Feeling cards focus on emotional issues. Finally, the Doing cards require the child to engage in some sort of play activity or acting. There are 104 cards in each stack and range from very non-threatening to moderately anxiety-provoking questions (Gardner, 1983).

Although the game was devised to interact with resistant children, it has been shown to be useful with defensive children as well. As an additional benefit, this game is very useful and appropriate for groups.

The majority of questions are designed to elicit information (talking, feeling or doing) in regards to the fundamental problems of life with which children at some point in their lives may be confronted. In order to acquaint the reader with the essence of this game, Table 18 illustrates a few sample questions from each of the three domains. The readers should also be informed that there are several other games that have been formulated with a similar purpose in mind (i.e., the Changing Family Game, Assertion Game, Classroom Survival Game).

Table 18. Sample Questions From the Talking, Feeling, Doing Game.

Talking Cards
Question: What sport are you worst at?
                 What things come into your mind when you cannot fall asleep?
                 Suppose two people you know were talking about you and they did not know you were listening. What do you think you would hear them saying?
                 Tell about something you did that you are ashamed about.

Feeling Cards
Question: A boy's friend leaves him to play with someone. How does the boy feel? Why did the friend leave?
                 Tell about an act of kindness.
                 What is something you could say that could make a person feel good?

Doing Cards
Question: What is the most selfish thing you ever did? Make believe you are doing that right now.
                 You are standing in line to buy something and a child pushes in front of you. Show what you would do.
                 Make believe you have just met a bully. Show what you would do.

Applications of Other Common Table Games

Among the many games, the table games were found useful as an opportunity for children to deal with aggressive and competitive urges in socially acceptable ways. One of the first recognized pioneers of the therapeutic utilization of games has been E. Loomis. While using checkers in therapy, he recognized the potential application of the game as a vehicle for expression of resistance and unconscious conflict. The game was seen as a safe environment where the child lets loose of his/her defense (Loomis, 1957). Other scholars found that these games might provide opportunities for social learning as well as helping children to communicate, cooperate, learn to respect governing rules and to control anger while in competition. Finally, table games can be applied to help children learn how to deal with power and autonomy. While there are now many games solely developed for purposes of therapy, it has been suggested that several commercially available games are also suitable for prominent therapeutic goals (Schaffer and Reed, 1986).

Sutton-Smith and Roberts, two distinguished play theorists, established three classifications of games that can be purchased in most retail stores. (1) Games applying physical skills, such as Tiddily Winks, Pick Up Sticks, and Operation, can help children with their eye-hand coordination. (2) Games of strategy attempt to enhance cognitive skills which also allow an observer to informally gather insight on a child's problem-solving abilities. Games such as backgammon, checkers, chess, word games, and Connect Four all fit into this category. (3) Finally, there are games of little strategy, which merely involve chance. These games are usually beneficial because they neutralize the adult's superiority in intellect and skill. Games that fit under this category are Chutes and Ladders and several card games, such as War (Sutton-Smith and Roberts, 1971). As for their therapeutic benefit, these games can be further classified into four areas of orientations: (1) communication games (such as the Talking, Feeling and Doing game), (2) problem-solving games, (3) ego-enhancing games, and (4) games that promote socialization. A brief description of these games to acquaint the professional with these classifications is obviously important.

Communication Games

Through games, just like through other play therapy techniques, one can create a nonthreatening and permissive atmosphere that encourages self-expression. In working with a variety of children, I have applied several table games for this specific therapeutic benefit in the strong belief that if goals are set and developed prior to application usage and the therapeutic benefits are identified, games can become a dynamic resource for the practitioner. Most communication board games allow children to project certain aspects of themselves. Children over the age of five are usually prepared for this orientation. The most well-known games are the Ungame (Zakick, 1975), Reunion (Zakick and Monior, 1979). Scrabble for Juniors (Gardner, 1975), Self-Esteem Game (Creative Health Services, 1983), Social Security (Burten, 1976), and The Story Telling Card Game (Gardner, 1988).

The Ungame and Reunion are probably the best known of all listed. Both are noncompetitive and encourage the child to explore attitudes, feelings, values, and, in general, the self. For example, in Reunion, children might be asked to remember a time when they had their best day. A unique feature of most of these games is that they do not usually have a natural ending. The games are discontinued when the leader and the child decide to stop.

Scrabble for Juniors was adopted by Gardner (the developer of the Talking, Feeling, Doing game). Therapeutically selected words are presented on a game board. The child then goes ahead while taking turns covering the game board with letter chips s/he has drawn. When a word is spelled out, the player must say a little about their term. If the child recounts a personal experience, incorporating the word, s/he receives more points. The person with the most points at the end of the game is the winner. The Self-Esteem Game is appropriate for children who are about eight to twelve years of age. My experience has found this game enjoyable to play and well received by most children. But, most of all, these games help children learn how to deal with interpersonal setbacks.

Social Security game involves drawing a card with the instruction to make a sad face or to jump up and shout. This game allows for free expression of feelings and thoughts. Finally, in the Story Telling Card Game, children are encouraged to create stories based on pictures that portrays common scenes, which promotes expressions of deeper unconscious feelings.

Games for Problem Solving

Many of the games that can be purchased for children required some level of problem solving. Indeed, games under this category are intended to encourage children to apply problem-solving skills. One of the observations made by Schafer and Reed is that games found under this heading usually encourage the process of logical thinking. It appears that many children with behavior problems do not take their time in thinking through problems. They tend to react quickly and do not appear to absorb the consequences of their actions. This is also true of children who make poor choices socially as well as academically. They assist children in focusing more on the logic they need to apply. Children and leader may act as role models to each other displaying appropriate problem-solving mechanisms. I have found games of this nature to be effective with children with learning disabilities and emotional disturbances. These games can promote abilities to use reliable critical thinking strategies. Games such as checkers and backgammon are two prominent examples. Checkers has been used to enable a child to learn prosocial behaviors such as learning to take turns, to cooperate, and to win and lose with grace (Singer, 1994); however, it can have relatively low psycho-therapeutic benefit (Gardner, 1993). It can be used for decompression purposes at the end of a tension-laden session. After the game has been complete, it is suggested that attention be given to what has occurred which, in turn, may ascertain if a transfer of learning has occurred (Schafer and Reed, 1986).

Gardner (1993) found that Nintendo is another tool for observing problem-solving strategies of the child by the therapist. Others observed that benefits of Nintendo are the release of aggression and control, for example Kung Fu, and ability to develop appropriate methods of dealing with victories and defeats in sport-oriented arenas (ex. Techmo Baseball and Football). Gardner also found that Nintendo has been an excellent ice-breaker and rapport-builder. It is generally helpful for the therapists to be intact with the trends of the times. By being aware of video games such as the Nintendo, a therapist can convey a message to the child clients that they are "cool." Further, Nintendo games were the most useful factors in the child's improvement in therapy.

Ego-Enhancing Games

Under the rubric of ego-enhancing games, there is a host of activities that focus on a multitude of personality traits, including perceived competence, impulse control, frustration tolerance, and concentration. Many games such as Sorry, Connect Four, Monopoly, and Risk can relate to goals achieved under this category. Bruno Bettelheim, the noted psychologist, suggests that within the game of Monopoly several emotional feelings can come into account, such as the feelings of helplessness, the need to feel powerful, and aggressiveness (Bettelheim, 1972).

There are several other games that have proved useful in helping children with attention deficit disorders to improve their self-control. For instance, the manifested purpose of the game Beat the Clock is for the child to outlast the clock, so that s/he is actively engaged in the activity while the buzzer goes off. A practitioner who is interested in finding additional games of this nature may consult Margie Golick, who has prepared a book entitled **Deal Me In** which lists a number of card games and their therapeutic application (Golick, 1973).

Another technique used for helping children who are behind in others in attention span is water play (Hartley, Frank, & Goldenson, 1993). Water play suffices a need for the expression of aggressive impulses. Further, some aspects of this technique, such as blowing soap bubbles, offer tremendous opportunities for ego building. The game Dungeons and Dragons has also been effective in enhancing ego development in a patient with psychiatric disorders (Blackmon, 1994). Play and fantasy aspects of this game were used to foster an ego-building relationship for patients.

Socialization Games

In ancient Greece, Plato recommended that in working with children, it is advantageous to allow children to learn while playing. Socialization games are used in this context by helping children, dependent on their chronological and mental ages, to practice various social behaviors such as group cooperation and sharing. Several table games and group activities (New Games, Cooperative Games) can be selected to influence or alter a certain behavior. Active games such as blanketball, knots and the log roll can all be exercised to encourage cooperation and the mere joy of participation.

The contributions of game play to recreational therapy are obvious and, as we have seen through the preceding pages, recreators, teachers, and parents can naturally take advantage of the underlying benefits of game play. This is an area that has not been exhausted, and the contributions to pediatric therapy are endless.

TECHNOLOGY AND FUTURE AVENUE AND ITS APPLICATION TO PLAY THERAPY

New technological advances have created an impressive avenue for professionals working with children. Technology has played a vital role with children in clinical settings, therapeutic practices, and schools. One of the most widely utilized technologies is the computer. The computer in the past had been solely used in the science fields. Today, it is used in many other professions as well as among families and individuals. The creation of the Personal Computer (PC) and available software has allowed virtually every individual to have access to all kinds of programs that are in the market.

Recently, computer companies have developed software specifically designed for children. This software is very popular in schools for educational purposes. Many schools and daycare centers have included computer usage in their curriculums to enhance learning with students. It provides children with teaching methods that go beyond traditional school approaches. Some of these programs are useful in teaching children about mathematics, writing, as well as social skills. For example, a computer program called a Personal Problem Solving Guide teaches children social decision making and problem solving and provides guidance for managing conflicts (Elias, Tobias & Friedlander, 1994). The computer has also been a very effective tool for children with disabilities. It is an important instrument that provides access to things that they would normally not have access to. The following are few examples of many applications of the computer with special populations: children with hearing impairments learn vowel sounds through the computer (Pratt, Heintzelman, Deming, & Ensrud, 1993); it enhances writing skills for students with Down syndrome (Steelman, Pierce, & Koppenhaver, 1993), in improving reading comprehension with students with dyslexia (Elkind, Cohen, & Murray, 1993), and many other ways.

The computer has many other therapeutic values. There are many software programs in the market that are specifically designed to increase or enhance certain desirable or therapeutic behaviors and skills. A computer-assisted social skills intervention program such as "I Found a Solution" contains social conflict scenarios and adventure games that enhance cooperation and assertion with children with developmental disabilities (Margalit, 1991). Other studies show that computers are an effective tool for working with children with emotional and behavioral difficulties (Hopkins, 1991). It was found that computers increased motivation, improved concentration and attention span, and improved self-image and self-esteem. For example, Sandford and Brown have developed a program called Captain's Log which is a compilation of numerous cognitive games and skills for children with attention deficit hyperactive disorder.

Another modern technology that has added new dimension in play therapy is the internet. Internet is a vast network that allows people to interact with other people by using electronic email. Electronic email, part of the new information superhighway, is similar to post office boxes where people can send messages to one another through email addresses. Further, these sent messages are received in less than an hour anywhere in the world. Currently, the most widely used online service on the internet is the America Online. This is an online service that allows users to talk to other online users all across the country. Unfortunately, there is no direct online services specifically for children's use only.

Despite of the recent controversy with children using the internet, there appear to be many therapeutic values. Because the internet is very accessible, it allows children to interact with other children all over the country. Some children, especially children with disabilities, may face alienation from other children. These children can make friends or interact with other children without having their disability "handicapping" them. Using the electronic mail system can be like a modern-day pen pal system where children can communicate with one another through the internet. Sending and receiving messages through email can be exciting for the children because it makes children feel "grown-up." It also can help children correspond with others and express their feelings in a constructive fashion.

There is a great need for computer software and programs as well as the internet services specifically designed for children. The authors are certain that this new arena will be tremendously enhanced over the years to come.

SUMMARY OF THE VALUE OF PLAY THERAPY

The applications of play therapy are far-reaching. The procedures have been applied with many special populations, including the physically disabled, emotionally disturbed, mentally retarded, and learning disabled. The procedures incorporated are applied to help children conceptualize their internal conflicts and feelings. In many ways the advantage of this procedure is the knowledge of what to watch for while playing with children, in addition to knowing how to enhance the therapeutic play opportunities for children.

ART THERAPY

There are some who would say that play is the art of childhood and art is a natural form of play. Gerson, a professor of recreation, suggests that at times we reserve the name play for those activities which are pursued with the conscious intent of realizing pleasure. This is likewise true in art. In this regard, there is also complete agreement between both of these two activities.

Recreation therapists are not psychotherapists, and complex, deep-seated interpretations of art are generally beyond the level of training of most practitioners. However, it is appropriate to listen to children and synthesize what they say about their art, for they can provide revealing clues about the children themselves, their feelings and their personalities. Dinkmeyer and Caldwell state that through artwork the child may be able to project meanings only dimly revealed in his/her verbal expression (Dinkmeyer & Caldwell, 1970, p. 366).

Art therapy is the use of art for personal expression of feelings rather than primarily for the creation of aesthetically pleasing products. It has been employed as a significant self-expressive therapeutic approach with people of all ages, but through art a child can reveal hidden concerns more willingly and easily than may be possible through verbal communication (Liebmann, 1986). We must be aware that art therapy is a huge umbrella concept, encompassing the use of art expression for many purposes with several distinctive philosophical approaches. The three major theoretical orientations are: (1) the psychoanalytic orientation, where art is used in conjunction with psychotherapy and takes into account many of its principles; (2) the creativity approach, which sees art as inherently therapeutic and is applied to allow the child to display and explore his/her talents; and (3) the humanistic orientation, in which art is used as a means of establishing one's identity.

Indeed, art as a form of communication can also facilitate communication even when children are not able or willing to interact with others. While many of them do not engage in art activity for its cathartic value, there are times when children are worried, and art can allow them the opportunity to express their feelings. It can be used to help children feel better about themselves by promoting feelings of success, and the completion of the project can bring much joy to a child.

The use of art therapy was refined in the 1940s through the pioneering efforts of Margaret Naumberg, who relied heavily on her psychoanalytic orientation in encouraging her clients to associate freely through drawings (Wadeson, 1980). Edith Kramer, on the other hand, placed emphasis on an alternative direction; more toward a humanistic approach. Her work with children emphasized the healing properties of the creative process. In this scheme of things, art therapy obviously differs greatly from psychotherapy, for the therapist and/or teacher does not engage in interpretations but rather encourages an artistic experience. According to Kramer, then, art therapy presents the individual with satisfaction and pleasure which can be generated through creative production (Kramer,

1971; Fleshman and Fryrear, 1981). Several artistic methods are incorporated into this orientation. Some examples of procedures include the following:

1. **Automatic Drawing.** This technique is also known as the scribble technique. It is here that the individual is allowed to free draw. In free drawing, the client is encouraged to express him/herself using any form of art media.

2. **Color Exploration.** The child may produce a piece of artwork using his/her least and most preferred colors. The child is then asked to discuss how the colors interact. Furthermore, this approach can be refined to also incorporate exercises where a child can draw pictures expressing feelings. Each of the feelings are captured by incorporating a specific color. Again, as the example previously elicited, the final product is then discussed.

3. **Drawing Completion.** The child is presented with a few lines or shapes. S/he is then requested to make a picture using all of the elements. Denny (1972) suggests various techniques that can be applied to increase the child's self-awareness. For example, the child may be requested to paint and discuss the phrases "I feel" or "I am." They could also be asked to draw three figures which would include the ideal self, the real self, and the way others perceive them. Another example is the Squiggle Game (Winnicott, 1971), which is particularly useful as an icebreaker and as a means for identifying hidden concerns that a child may have. In this game, the facilitator draws a small figure (e.g., a curve, straight line, or other ambiguous figure) and the child is asked to create a picture out of the figure. This task is enjoyed by most children, it encourages creativity, provides a stimulus for conversation, and may uncover hidden concerns.

Adaptations of equipment for art activities may be necessary for children with some form of limitations. These limitations are obviously wide-ranged, from a child confined to bed, to those with physical or other disabilities. Wilson, for example, described a badly burned child who chose to finger paint the only way she could: with her feet. In addition, she devised a variety of methods, in effect overcoming her handicap, such as the use of "prism glasses, vertical lapboards with clips to hold drawing paper, horizontal mirrors suspended amidst traction and long tongs to allow for reaching" (Wilson, 1964, p. 218).

Art therapy has also been utilized with children with a variety of developmental and emotional problems and chronic illnesses. One of the advantages of art activities is that they are usually best initiated in groups, because it appears that children inspire one another. There are many types of supplies that can be applied or utilized in art, and a therapist must be aware of what materials need to be selected with well thought purpose and with the child's needs in mind (Robbins and Sibley, 1976).

BIBLIOTHERAPY

Bibliotherapy is a natural and effective intervention technique for helping children in a therapeutic setting. After all, most children enjoy reading or having some read to them. It is an approach that is being increasingly utilized by recreational personnel, child life specialists, nursing staff and psychologists. Through careful selection of material relevant to a given child, the facilitator helps the child to understand and accept him/herself. The reading materials serve as a springboard for discussion of sensitive issues while at the same time giving the child an opportunity to explore these issues in an indirect and more comfortable manner.

One of the latent benefits of this method is that there are many messages that can be transmitted from literature without the child even knowing. Bibliotherapy allows an issue to be exposed to a child in the least threatening manner. It also provides an opportunity for youngsters to identify with characters having problems similar to theirs. Moreover, this approach promotes an awareness that no man is an island and that problems are universal (Malkiewicz, 1970). Many stories have nonhuman main characters, such as animals or objects (e.g., bears, trains, balloons). These non-human characters are most valuable in their capacity to serve as a model without regard for gender or age. Melamed and Siegel, and others as well, suggest that a seven-year-old male main character may serve as an acceptable and effective model for children of both sexes and different age groups (Melamed & Siegel, 1975). The following represents some guidelines for applying bibliotherapy. These suggestions represent my thoughts and experiences as well as the insights of many authors:

1. Make sure you know the reading level of the child or group as well as the content of literature used. Although this suggestion may

seem simplistic and certainly a step that should be routinely employed, it is ironic that this position is often overlooked, especially the review of the text. I feel it part of a professional obligation to preview the material my students will be given. The most significant reason for following this procedure pertains to the content of the material integrated. One must completely understand the plot of the book if it will be applied appropriately with children. There are times when books appear on the surface to be well suited for the targeted child; however, after considering the material at a more in-depth level, the professional may sense that the story is inappropriate for the given situation. Other factors that should be taken into consideration prior to the selection of a book can be divided into two categories: child factors and book factors.

Child Factors
• Child's age
• Sex
• Why bibliotherapy is being applied
• Reading abilities
• Reading preferences

Book Factors
• Type of book
• Plot
• Difficulty level
• Appropriateness for child

2. A child can participate in the selection of stories. Presentation of choices of relevant books allows the child to feel some control. Whenever a book is suggested to a child, the child should always have some input on the final selection. I have found it helpful to have a few books to choose from. In this way, the child feels some autonomy and control over the situation. Sometimes, a child may not be willing to read a book on a sensitive subject. If this is the case, there is no justification to push the child at that time. If you meet with resistance after several prompts on your part, it is wise to wait awhile and make suggestions at a later time.

3. The selection of short material is especially critical for young children. Zaccaria and other scholars highly recommend using brief articles, poems, short stories and, for that matter, even chapters from a story. Brief passages allow the child to get to the heart of the point, thus allowing the child to focus his/her attention on the area of concern and then to talk about it immediately. After the reading is completed, the leader should then facilitate a conversation. Questions should be open-ended and should initially only center on the story. As the child becomes more

comfortable, s/he may begin to self-disclose. There are a variety of ways to encourage self-disclosure after reading a passage. I have found it quite helpful to center the locus of attention on the principal characters in the story. If the child is comfortable, s/he will alter the focus and discuss him/herself. With younger children, as a child ages, a more direct approach is feasible. Realistic stories about non-fictional situations should be presented sensitively and directly. In addition, I have found it helpful to draw feelings generated from the theme of the story. All of these techniques seem to allow a child the security to begin opening up and sharing feelings.

When stories are selected to encourage a child, it is likely that children will be more willing to share their thoughts and generalize conclusions. The writer has found such situations to be the most rewarding. All children, including children with disabilities, typically enjoy discussing stories with happy endings. Furthermore, there are many stories that are inspirational. The conclusions drawn can enhance a child's perceived competence and additionally may make the child more willing to try and change (Zaccaria, Moses, & Hollowell, 1978).

Some scholars, such as Rubin (1978) and Peller (1962) noted that young children can be significantly affected by stories because they nurture their dreams. They also found that animal characters are especially useful in helping young children to explore their feelings. Animal characters are useful because the elements of sex, age, and race are not involved.

Although there are several advantages to selecting books for therapeutic purposes, there are disadvantages. For example, there are many books that children enjoy but which make adults very uncomfortable (e.g., books on sexuality, divorce).

4. Bibliotherapy should be combined with other recreational therapy procedures, since it can be incorporated easily by a recreational therapist in programs that serve a wide range of children. That is to say, bibliotherapy must be integrated and utilized in conjunction with other techniques such as drama, art or other activities that might help the child act out, enact or express (i.e. through art) what the moral is suggesting.

5. A facilitator who does not possess adequate experience should utilize already available published literature. Bibliographies of

stories focusing on specific affective areas are available (e.g. Fosson and de Quan, 1984). With increased experience and effectiveness, however, many facilitators have found it useful and easier to develop their own stories that are individually tailored to a specific child's situation (e.g., Fosson & de Quan, 1984).

The previously cited texts should be used as a starting point for selecting children's books. However, it is not a substitute for personal reviews of books. The therapist should still take the time to review specific texts to make sure they are appropriate for a given situation. A comprehensive and useful resource book is **The Bookfinder,** published by the American Guidance Services. In addition, several of the major texts on bibliotherapy include a comprehensive listing of appropriate outlets (see Zaccaria et al., 1978; Rubin, 1978).

As we demonstrated here, bibliotherapy can be applied as a unique and very effective strategy with children. Depending on the specific disabling conditions, bibliotherapy can be utilized to supplement and enrich the ongoing activity programming in a wide variety of ways. For instance, the specific utilization of bibliocounseling for chronically ill children who are hospitalized is only one of the many promising and viable areas that might incorporate this technique into the repertoire of therapeutic techniques (Fine and Siaw, 1987).

There are at least two other ways this approach can be applied. First, if a child is residing in a hospital or another institutional setting, the parents can record stories on audiocassette or even videocassette so that the stories can be played by the child in their absence. A second variation of bibliotherapy involves having the child record stories. This is best illustrated by the following case example: Bobby, a nine-year-old boy with spina bifida, was hospitalized for an extended period of time. While in treatment, Bobby's perceived competence, which was low to begin with, decreased. This sense of helplessness appeared to be directly related to the loss of control he felt in the hospital environment that was structured for him by others. As we already noted, this **benevolent overreaction** syndrome often occurs in chronically ill children (Boone and Harman, 1972). The hospital's recreational specialist tried numerous therapeutic play strategies to boost Bobby's morale. Stories about kids like himself who overcame barriers and became successful were well received and seemed to have a positive influence on Bobby. He came to the realization that he was capable of many things, which propelled him to begin to take more responsibility for his actions. Bibliotherapy, however, assisted this child in other, somewhat non-traditional ways as well. The therapist asked Bobby to read simple stories for a visually impaired child. The therapist practiced the stories with him and then Bobby tape-recorded the stories for a visually impaired child. With the knowledge of having made a useful contribution, Bobby's perceived competence increased significantly.

SECTION 2: ANIMAL–ASSISTED THERAPY

History of Animal-Assisted Therapy

The human-animal bond is the interaction and interrelationship that exists between humans and animals. Animals have served the needs of their human companions for thousands of years. This certainty about the importance of the human-animal bond has evolved to such an extent that the medical and educational communities have researched and developed animal assisted therapy. Animal-Assisted Therapy (AAT) programs are being used in clinical, community, and residential settings as part of an overall therapeutic program. These programs are generally conducted under the direction of a healthcare professional who is trained in the selection and application of different modalities for therapeutic intervention. Among those professionals who use AAT are psychologists; social workers; nurses; and physical, occupational, recreational, and speech therapists. The use of AAT in treatment sessions may facilitate spontaneous expression of emotion, increased socialization, improved functional abilities, improved self-esteem, diversion from pain, and improved quality of life during hospitalization and rehabilitation.

The history of AAT emerges from man's early relationships with animals. The first species domesticated by man was the wolf, ancestor of the dog. Earliest evidence of this relationship surfaced in 1978 at an archaeological site in northern Israel. In a tomb from a late Paleolithic era, a human skeleton rested with the skeleton of a five-month-old domesticated dog, the human's left hand rested on the puppy's shoulder. According to James Serpell (1986), in his book *In the Company of Animals,* this strongly implies "that man's primordial relationship with this particular species was a deeply affectionate one." Nathaniel Shaler notes the presence of domesticated plants and animals as one of the three primary developments contributing to man's more civilized existence. He repeatedly equates a higher level of civilization with an appreciation for animals, believing that the success of civilization depends on the human-animal relationship. Shaler, the Dean of Harvard University's Lawrence Scientific School, believed that "the process of domestication has a far-reaching aspect, a dignity that few human actions possess."

Animals have lived in myth, legend, religion, art, and literature throughout history. The Shawnee believe that a dog is responsible for maintaining the state of the world. They see Kukumthena, the Grandmother, as responsible for creation, along with her dog. Kukumthena weaves a great basket and the world will end when it is completed, but each night, according to the legend, her little dog unravels her work, thus assuring another day of life.

The earliest known representation of animals in art are the Paleolithic cave paintings in Spain, France, Italy, and Central and Eastern Europe, dated 30,000–27,000 B.C., which depict early hierarchy in the arrangement of animals. These images are decorative, ritualistic, and symbolic. The Greek Temple of Aesculapius was dedicated to healing, where dogs licked wounds and were considered important in treatment. Methology suggested to dream of a dog signified the cure of the suppliant and its tongue was credited with healing powers.

The first contemporary therapeutic use of animals occurred at the York Retreat in England. It was founded in 1792 by the Quakers for humane treatment of individuals with mental illness. The patients helped care for the animals on the grounds which influenced improvements in the patients' behavior. In 1867, Bethel was founded in West Germany as a home for persons with epilepsy. Patients had birds, cats, dogs, horses, and a wild game park. Bethel operates today as a 5,000 patient facility for the treatment of physical and mental disorders, with two farms, horseback riding, and many companion animals. In 1942, a therapeutic program with dogs was implemented at Pawling Air Force Convalescent Hospital in New York to help patients in their rehabilitation. The soldiers worked with farm animals and a wildlife program. The successful program was discontinued after World War II.

The concept of using pets in therapy can be traced back to the early work of the late Dr. Boris Levinson. He was a psychotherapist and a professor of psychology at Yeshiva University. Dr. Levinson (1969) coined the term "pet therapy" after observing patient response and documented progress with his own dog, Jingles, during several therapy sessions with his patients. Dr. Levinson's book, *Pet-Oriented Child Psychotherapy*, discusses specific ideas and methods on how to utilize pets with children in therapy. Many professionals in medicine, psychology, social work, and related health care fields use this book as a guideline in developing their own therapeutic methods of using animals in their practice.

Today, the study of the AAT continues to emerge as articles in various healthcare publications (*American Journal of Occupational Therapy, OT*

Week, Child Psychology Journal, Holistic Nursing Practices) are beginning to document the benefits of AAT as a therapeutic modality. Dr. Bernie Siegal, M.D., writes of patients with terminal cancer whom he observed accepting their disease to a better degree in the presence of an animal. Newspapers, national magazines, and television talk shows have also contributed to the growing popularity of understanding the human-animal bond. Disney movies continue to portray the importance in the human-animal bond in recent top movies, *Homeward Bound, The Return of the Yellow Dog, Lassie,* and *The Jungle Book.*

A growing network of professional organizations and resources support AAT professionals. The Delta Society, a national, nonprofit organization, based in Renton, Washington, promotes the benefits of interactions between people, animals, and nature. The multidisciplinary membership includes physicians, veterinarians, therapists, nurses, social workers, educators, and scientists. The Delta Society awards research grants, provides access to current data, and conducts conferences and workshops, both nationally and internationally. National journals, including *Anthrozoos* (a scientific multidisciplinary journal) and *Interactions* (a quarterly publication) provide information on the interactions of people, animals, and nature. Both are available through the Delta Society. Other resource centers include the Human-Animal Program at University of California-Davis, Censhare (Center to Study Human-Animal Relationships and Environments) at the University of Minnesota, and the Center for the Interaction of Animals and Society at the University of Pennsylvania.

Literature Review on the Use of Animal-Assisted Therapy

The Benefits of Companion Animals

The importance of companion animals in the everyday lives of people is just now being understood. In a survey of pet owners in 11 states, the results indicated that 87 percent of the respondents considered their pets to be members of the family; 36 percent stated they treated their pets as people. Another survey indicated that almost half of the households in the United States have some kind of pet (Friedmann, Katcher, & Meislich, 1983). Pets have been theorized to serve as "clocks" for humans, providing a sense of order and a daily ritual for people who may lack in organizing daily routines. They provide a way to enjoy living in the "here and now" instead of focusing on the past or future of unfinished business. Pets also have been described as psychologically "safe" zones, nonthreatening and nonjudgmental companions. "Pets are a source of comfort that can be scheduled on demand of owner, in almost any quantity without bargaining" stated Katcher and Friedmann (1980). Their study, done through the University of Pennsylvania, suggests that stroking a pet lowers blood pressure in people in a way that human interactions do not. They found that in most situations, initial contact between humans resulted in increased blood pressure, respiration, and heart rate. However, when using the same human subjects with friendly and familiar animals, petting these animals reduced blood pressure levels in the subjects, relieved tension and anxiety, and made the humans appear more relaxed. The researchers also noted that observing the movements of tropical fish in an aquarium can also have an effect on lowering blood pressure.

An earlier study conducted by Friedmann and Katcher (1978), at the University of Pennsylvania, followed 92 recovering heart attack victims to determine the influence of social factors on their first year of survival. Significant data indicated that the survival rate of pet owners was higher than that of non-pet owners. The data concluded that pet companion-ship helped reduce feelings of isolation and stress on the owners. Pets can also enhance the therapeutic milieu and enrich the educational curriculum. They provide tactile gratification and therapeutic value to the physical, emotional, and social well-being of humans.

As pet ownership can enhance health benefits, it also may provide difficulties for sick and hospitalized owners. A survey was conducted to explore pet-related problems with hospitalization by Friedmann, Katcher, and Meislich (1983). They surveyed 100 patients about their pet owner-ship status. Pet owners indicated that family or friends cared for their animals when the owners were hospitalized. Owners said that difficulties placing pets did not affect their hospitalizations. Evidence indicated that the pets remained both a major support and concern for their hospital-ized owners and the owners required frequent reassurance about their pet's welfare. The pets also provided a sense of being needed and elicited a speedy recovery for the patients.

The Use of Animals in Therapy

The use of animals in therapy can provide a creative and effective media to elicit various patient/client treatment outcomes and enhance traditional therapy concepts and theories. George (1988) compared the use of animal-assisted therapy in five types of psychotherapies. In Logotherapy, animals can help people experience and accept the life process of birth and death and provide meaning to life. The practical use can be utilized through the care of animals during the process of life. The use of animals in Child-Centered Humanistic Therapy can help people see harmony in self and nature, experience self-worth and empathy, and provide metaphors of life. The practical use can be through interviews with the animal, sharing animal's feelings and dreams. In Gestalt Therapy, the animal can give contact with the environment, provide responsibility, the needs of others and to focus on the "here and now." The practical use can be through providing care and meeting the needs of the animal, reality orientation with focusing on the moment with the animal. In Reality Therapy, the animal can fulfill the need for love and unconditional love, self-esteem, learning to develop acceptance of others, and learning to master situations which facilitate independence. The practical use can be the child setting limits with the animal (e.g., training the animal) and sharing and accepting feelings. In Rational Emotive Therapy, the animals can facilitate recognition of self awareness and individuality, rights of others and provide opportunities for behavior management. The practical use can be obedience training/behavior management, understanding the rights of animals and nature, and learning self-acceptance.

Levinson (1970) contributed several studies and literature on using animals as a therapy tool in child-centered therapies. In an article titled "Pets, Child Development and Mental Illness," he discussed the interrelationship between the factors of child development, emotional disturbance, and the presence of a pet. Levinson believed that a pet is an influential factor in a child's life after age 6 months, because this is a time when the child begins to differentiate the self from the external world. The pet also influenced the child's learning process, emotional development and interpersonal relationships. In another article, "Pets: A Specific Technique in Child Psychotherapy," Levinson (1964) recommended that pets should be incorporated in the treatment plan for some children. This was especially true for children with autism because the animal strengthened the children's contact with reality. Levinson indicated that specific types of animals should be suited to meet specific needs of the child. The responsibility of the therapist using the animal in therapy is to assure that the appropriate type of animal will be used to help facilitate the patient's treatment. Therefore, it is important for the healthcare professional using animal-assisted therapy to have knowledge of different breeds of animals and animal behavior.

Animals help children learn responsibility for their own actions and assist in the cognitive development of the child. In a study done by Kidd and Kidd (1985), "Children's Attitudes Towards Their Pets," they studied 300 children and found that 90 percent of the children owned pets and 99.3 percent wanted some type of animal. They also compared Piaget's cognitive stages with children's attitudes about their animal. The results indicated that a child's attitudes of the animal had a significant correlation (x = < .05 level) with the current cognitive level of the child. They found that 51 percent of all the children stated that their pets were capable of understanding what they were attempting to communicate to the animal. Older children reported this more frequently than younger children. Children in the concrete operations stage, from 7 through 11 years, no longer confused the animal's and human's thoughts and they reported significantly more that they were able to read and communicate more often with their pets through body language. The 13-year-old children entering the formal operations stage showed no significant differences from the children in the concrete operations stage except for empathy; 25 percent of girls and 15 percent of boys attributed empathy to their pets and indicated that empathy provided for two-way communication. In regards to affective elements, 95 percent of the children reported that their pets loved them, 94 percent stated that they loved their pets, and 91 percent stated that they missed their pets when separated from them. Another study done at the University of Virginia on "Pets and Dreams" showed that in a group of children under the age of ten, 30 to 50 percent of the children's dreams concerned pets. A study done at the University of California-Davis found that of school-age children who owned pets, 85 percent thought about and missed their pets when daydreaming during school hours.

Animals can help children and adults deal with the stressful events that they may encounter daily. Fine and Fine (1995) found that animals play different roles in the lives of children. Depending on the child's stage of development, an animal can help the child meet his/her needs by representing a parent, sibling, or self. Katcher (1981) states that animals can help decrease depression, loneliness, and social isolation by providing opportunities for the child to care for something. Animals also assist in facilitating behavior management with children by providing opportunities to learn to control actions and follow through with responsibility. A recent study by Katcher and Wilkins (1994) on "The Use of Animal Assisted Therapy and Education with Attention Deficit Children and Conduct Disorders," indicated that animals immediately drew the attention of the children, lowering the level of psychological arousal, calming the child and reducing the opportunity of more impulsive behaviors. The animals also helped the children plan their actions; the children were attracted to the animal but were uncertain that this situation produced attraction—avoidance situation which inhibited the impulsive behavior and demanded the child to know more about the environment.

Animals also help the elderly in dealing with stressful events in their life and the aging process. Levinson (1969) studied the effects of using animals with the elderly population. In the article "Pets and Old Age," he rated that animals can provide affection, increase physical activity and contact with others, and reassure self-worth, which are all areas that should be addressed in treatment of the elderly. Dr. Leo Bustad, an international authority on the use of animals as a treatment tool in working with the elderly (population), discusses how animals can benefit the aging process in his text, *Animals, Aging, and Aged.* In it, Bustad (1980) presents evaluation tools to use for choosing appropriate pets and discusses how animal life-span studies have impacted a clearer understanding of the aging process by looking at changes in lifestyles. Because animals provide unconditional love and companionship they can be a critical element in the treatment of elderly patients.

Animals assist in facilitating social interaction between people, especially as a topic of interest as people enjoy telling favorite stories about pets. In a study done by Lapp (1991), "Nursing Students and the Elderly: Enhancing intergenerational Communication Through Human-Animal Interaction," she compared the participation of residents between a Pet Visitation session and the regularly scheduled session. The results indicated a higher attendance for the Pet Visitation program from 12 to 18 persons compared to the usual attendance of 8 to 10 persons. A cumulative evaluation data collected indicated that 81 percent of the participants held or played with one or more of the pets, and 90 percent verbally expressed thoughts related to pets they had in the past. In a study done by Fick (1993), "The Influence of an Animal on Social Interactions of Nursing Home Residents in a Group Setting," the purpose was to determine the effects on the presence and absence of a dog on the effects of the types and frequency of socialization among residents. The results indicated that the presence of the dog had a significant effect (p < .05 level) on increasing social interaction among residents thus improving the social climate for the residents and facilitating group process. Psychiatrists Corson and Corson (1980) researched pet-facilitated psychotherapy at Ohio State University. Fifty withdrawn patients were allowed to select a dog from the onsite kennels and interact with it each day. According to the Corsons, "the dog acted as a social catalyst, forging positive links between the subject and other patients and the staff on the wards."

A specialization that has emerged from Pet Facilitated Therapy is the use of Assistance Dogs, animals trained to assist owners with physical limitations. Assistance Dogs benefit persons with physical disabilities both in social and independent functions. There have been few studies to analyze the effects that assistance dogs have on the lives of individuals with disabilities. Two studies done by Lockwood (1983) and Messent (1984) indicated that the presence of an animal eliminated social barriers by enhancing how people are socially perceived and by promoting social interaction. Two other studies (Eddy, Hart, & Boltz, 1988; Mader, Hart, & Bergin, 1989) reported the effects of social acknowledgments of people in wheelchairs and the effects of service dogs. Both children and adults with physical disabilities using wheelchairs were studied in the research. All three studies support the hypothesis that service dogs facilitate social acknowledgment for both children and adults who are physically limited to the use of a wheelchair. A recent retrospective study of 300 assistance dog owners strongly indicated that the assistance dog helps and encourages individuals with disabilities to "go out more in public," "feel better about life," "feel happier," and "feel more independent."

Animal-Assisted Therapy as a Treatment Modality

Many health-care professionals today are implementing animal visitation and animal-assisted therapy programs in their facilities. Before developing a program, professionals need to have a clear understanding of the difference between animal visitation and animal-assisted therapy programs. The National Delta Society Standards & Guidelines for Animal-Assisted Activities and Animal-Assisted Therapy defines animal-assisted therapy (AAT) as a goal-directed intervention in which an animal meeting specific criteria is an integral part of the treatment process. AAT is delivered and/or directed by health/human service provider working within the scope of their profession. AAT is designed to promote improvement in human physical, emotional, social, and/or cognitive functioning. AAT is provided in a variety of settings and may be group or individual in nature. The process is documented and evaluated. Animal-assisted activities (AAA) is defined as opportunities for motivational, educational, and/or recreational benefits which enhance quality of life. AAA is delivered in a variety of environments by specially trained professionals, paraprofessionals, and/or volunteers in association with animals that meet specific criteria.

The AAT Team has three components; the professional/therapist, the animal handler, and the trained animal. According to the Delta Society National Standards and Guidelines, the professional who delivers and/or directs AAT is a health/human service provider with expertise in incorporating animals as a treatment modality, and is knowledgeable about animals. The AAT Specialist is licensed and/or recognized by a separate professional discipline. This individual complies with the legal and ethical requirements of his/her profession as well as local, state, and federal laws relating to this work. This may include, but is not limited to, the following professionals: Certified Therapeutic Recreation Specialist, Occupational Therapist, Speech Pathologists and Speech Therapists, Physical Therapists, Social Workers, Physicians, Psychiatrists, Psychologists, Pastoral Counselors, Licensed Professional Counselors, Registered Nurses, Special Education Counselors, School Counselors, and Vocational Rehabilitation Counselors.

The animal handler is defined as a specially trained person, either paid or volunteer, who accompanies an animal during the course of animal assisted therapy sessions. The animal handler's primary responsibility is to monitor and control the interaction between the client and the animal. The animal handler has been trained through an animal assisted therapy workshop and has a general understanding of the various settings and client populations that he/she may work with in the AAT program. The Delta Society offers a National Pet Partners Training Workshop for Animal-Assisted Activities and Animal-Assisted Therapy programs and Animal Screening Workshop (see reference list for address and phone number).

The animal is the third component of the AAT Team. According to the Delta Society, animal assistants can either be defined as activity animals or therapy animals based upon the animal skills. The social animal should be able to "meet and greet", brighten the day, be able to follow through with minimal skills (walk without pulling, sit, down, stay, and come). The animal should enjoy and welcome interaction with people and be confident and outgoing. The therapy animal is part of the treatment team. The animal and handler work together to assist in the treatment process. The animal performs advanced skills (including back up, move closer, wait, take it, hurry, slower) and also may respond to hand signals. Appropriate animal selection for the AAT program in any facility should be based on the following: controllability, predictability, trainability, zoonosis concerns, management concerns, and injury risk to both animal and human.

Program Development

Animal-Assisted Therapy can be utilized as a treatment modality for various populations ranging from children to the elderly. Before implementing an AAT treatment intervention or developing an AAT program, the health-care professional must conduct a needs analysis to identify if AAT would be appropriate and effective for the population identified. A needs analysis is a process of identifying and analyzing the gap between a current condition and a desired outcome. It provides goals and objectives, describes a desirable outcome, includes the content and methods, and uses assessment and evaluation to measure the program or treatment's effectiveness. A needs analysis will help the health-care professional identify the purpose of the program and the goals to be reached.

Once the needs analysis is complete and has identified a need for an AAT program, the health-care professional must develop the program mission, policies, and procedures and the short-term and long-term goals and objectives. Infection control policies and procedures must be addressed and implemented because of opportunity for zoonotic diseases. All animals need to be screened and temperament tested with proof of current shots and vaccinations to assure the animal's health and safety. If the program plans to use volunteers and their animals, the health-care professional must provide training of the facility, populations served, and the AAT program goals and objectives. The health-care professional is responsible for supervising the volunteers and should provide ongoing inservice training. Reassessment and evaluation of the program should be done periodically to measure the program's needs and effectiveness.

The AAT team can be an integral part of the interdisciplinary team in various healthcare and educational settings. The interdisciplinary team approach refers to each of the team members using his/her professional discipline in the treatment process but with overlapping disciplines creating a team approach. Each team member uses his or her disciplines to accomplish the same goals. The patient works on these common goals throughout the day giving the patient more opportunity to practice new skills. For example, the goal may be to increase range of motion in the right shoulder. The occupational therapist may work on this goal by performing range of motion exercises to the right shoulder. The recreation therapist may work on this goal by using animal-assisted therapy in which the patient combs a dog using the right arm to facilitate active range of motion.

Another treatment team approach is called the multidisciplinary team approach. This team approach uses each of the professional disciplines as a separate part to make up a "whole" treatment team. This approach has the patient in the middle with each treatment discipline completing its own piece of the treatment process. There are no overlapping disciplines in this approach. For example, the recreation therapist works on leisure skills and the occupational therapist works on life task skills.

A third type of treatment team approach is the consumer-centered approach. This approach has the patient in the middle and the therapy disciplines on the outside. The patient decides which therapy modality he/she wishes to utilize in his treatment. The consumer is responsible for setting his/her own treatment process and working with the various disciplines he/she chooses.

Animal-assisted therapy can be an effective therapeutic modality within the interdisciplinary team approach when used correctly. AAT can be employed to address patient needs or deficits in each of the four functional domains:

Physical Domain — Exercises that use range of motion in all extremities can be used and graded according to the patient's need for increased strength (brushing a dog to grooming a horse to shearing a sheep). Muscle facilitation and trunk stability can be used when riding a horse. Ambulation skills can be practiced when walking a dog, and wheelchair mobility and propulsion can also be used when exercising an animal. Fine motor coordination skill can be practiced by opening clasps to dog collars or horse bridals.

Social — Animals can facilitate interaction by acting as a bridge between a therapist or volunteer and the patient. Animals also can facilitate sessions between patients that may have a common interest in the animals. This provides opportunities for peer relationships.

Emotional — Animals motivate patients to set and achieve goals (walk after surgery with patient's pet dog). They offer opportunity to share one's feelings. Because animals provide unconditional love and are often less threatening than humans, children often share their problems with animals, offering opportunities for self-expression of feelings and fears. Animals encourage patients to exhibit nurturing behavior while caring for them. They also provide companionship and a sense of belonging.

Cognitive — Animals provide reality orientation to a patient and help keep the patient focused in the here and now. They provide opportunities for testing long-term and short-term memory by asking questions about the animal's name, breed, and remembering these events of the visit to share with the therapist.

The interdisciplinary team works together when incorporating a treatment plan based on the identified needs of the patient. AAT can be an integral component of the treatment plan in all disciplines in meeting patient goals. The animal is identified as the therapist's medium or tool to help the patient meet his/her goals. For example, the recreation therapist may use a leisure assessment as a tool to help the patient identify skills in social behavior adjustment which, in turn, will promote psychosocial interactions. A community outing is a tool that a recreation therapist may use to provide opportunity to practice the new skills learned in the hospital in order to facilitate community reintegration for the patient. When choosing a therapeutic activity for the patient, the therapist needs to do an activity analysis to assure that the activity and tool is an appropriate choice for the patient. Animal-assisted therapy can be used in all modalities of the treatment team to provide effective treatment.

The diagram in Figure 14 identifies how each therapeutic modality can use the animal in the AAT team as its tool or medium to facilitate the therapeutic activity and accomplish the patient's treatment goals. The diagram identifies the importance of integrating the medium across the disciplines to create a team approach toward treatment of the patient.

Figure 15 identifies the use of an interdisciplinary team approach in the treatment process for a patient on a burn unit. The team members consist of various healthcare professionals working together to create a team approach. The problem areas identifies the need areas of the patient in which the patient's goals will be based on. The goals are the

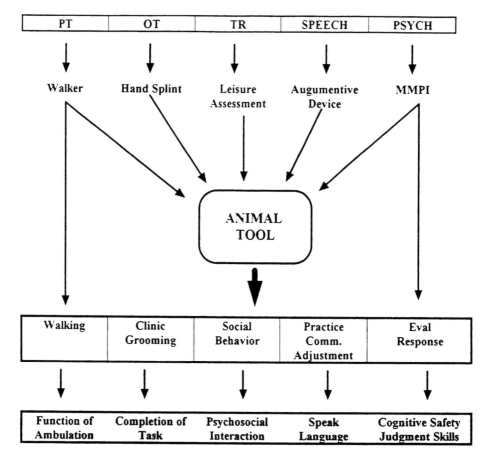

INTEGRATION OF AAT INTO AN INTERDISCIPLINARY TEAM APPROACH

Figure 14. Animal—animal handler—therapist animal-assisted therapy (K. Henderson, 1993).

foundation of the treatment plan. Each discipline will use the medium or tools to promote opportunities for the patient to meet these goals. An AAT program could assist in meeting several of these goals. For example, the animal could help facilitate the patient's upper extremity range of motion by combing the animal. The animal could assist in increasing ambulation as the patient walks the animal and the animal (large dog) could assist as a counterbalance in performing ambulation.

TEAM MEMBERS	PROBLEM AREA	GOALS
Physician	Medical Issues	1. Medical stabilization
Nurse	Safety	2. Monitor medication
OT	ADL's	3. UE ROM
		4. Hygiene Skills to I
PT	Physical Function	5. Functional mobility
CTRS	Leisure Planning	6. Leisure planning skills
		7. Social interactions
Speech	Communication	8. Demonstrate use of
		speech device I
Social Worker	Social	9. Community re-entry
Neurology	Cognition	10. Short-term memory
Psychologist	Adjustment/Community Re-Entry	11. Expression of feelings
Nutritionist	Diet	12. Maintain diet
Support Specialist		13. Demonstrate safety judgment
		14. Family education

Figure 15. K. Henderson, 1993.

AAT TREATMENT GOALS

Animal Assisted Therapy can be an effective approach in meeting several different patient goals. The following is a list of goals used in treatment in the four domains. The animal can be used as a tool in meeting these needs.

A. Physical Goals

1. *Increase trunk rotation.*

One method in increasing trunk rotation is to have the therapist and animal handler place the animal on the side of the patient's body (just out of reaching level) to help the patient rotate his/her body toward the animal in order to be able to play with the animal. Another method is placing grooming tools in a position that would facilitate trunk rotation when grooming a large animal such as a horse.

2. *Improve fine motor control skills.*

One method that can be used to increase fine motor skills is to have the patient put the collar on a dog or cat. The patient needs to use fine motor coordination in clasping the hook on the collar and in manipulating the collar. Another method is to have the patient hold a treat to give to the animal. This utilizes finger dexterity and pinch patterns using lateral or three point pinch.

3. *Improve ambulation.*

One method to assist in ambulation is to have the patient walking the dog. The dog also can act as a counterbalance to assist in maintaining balance when ambulating, especially if the patient has a hemiparesis to one side (a large dog would be appropriate for this activity). Ambulation can also be facilitated by having the patient walk to get items needed to care for the animal (i.e., going to the kitchen to get the animal's food and water).

4. *Improve wheelchair mobility.*

One method to assist in wheelchair mobility is to have the dog pull the wheelchair to facilitate wheelchair mobility. Again, a large dog would be preferable for this activity. Another method is to have the patient propel his/her wheelchair to get items needed for the animal's cares.

5. *Improve range of motion to upper extremity.*

One method to improve upper extremity range of motion is to hold the animal higher than the patient and encourage the patient reach to pet the animal (i.e., place the animal in front of the patient to use shoulder flexion when reaching, place the animal to the side of the patient to use shoulder abduction). Another method is to have the patient comb the animal.

6. *Increase finger flexion/extension and finger dexterity.*

One method to use finger flexion and extension is to have the patient put the collar on the animal. Another method is to have the patient give the animal a treat; the patient needs to grasp the treat, hold it, and release the treat.

B. Psycho-Social Goals

1. *Improve body awareness.*

One method to work on body awareness is to have the patient identify the body parts on the animal and on self. Another method is to use touch of the animal's fur to increase tactile stimulation and decrease hypersensitivity (i.e., use a chinchila or angora rabbit because their fur is very fine and smooth at first. Then incorporate other animals with thicker fur and skin texture).

2. ***Improve interaction styles/peer relationships.***

One method is to have the patient share about his/her animals or past experiences with animals in their life. Discuss the similarities and differences of these experiences. The animal is an "attention getter"; it often times attracts the attention of others.

3. ***Improve socialization through human animal bonding.***

One method is to use the animal to provide an opportunity for the patient to learn how to build a relationship with another by caring for the animal. This also provides an opportunity for human animal bonding.

4. ***Increase expression of feeling, experience joy.***

One method is to encourage the patient to express how he/she feels when interacting with the animal. Another method is for the patient to identify how the animal is feeling.

5. ***Decrease focus on pain (or injury).***

One method is to encourage the patient to interact with the animal when feeling in pain. To redirect his/her attention on something positive and decrease the focus around the pain. The patient can learn to transfer his/her focus onto other positive activities.

6. ***Increase self-esteem evidenced by stating positive affirmations of one's self.***

One method is to encourage the patient to identify one positive characteristic about the animal and then one positive characteristic about his/her self. Also to provide opportunities for positive success when interacting with the animal.

C. Cognitive Goals

1. ***Improve attention to task.***

One method is to have the patient teach the animal a trick or a command and encourage the patient to stay on task and follow through with the direction. Also increase the time or complexity of the task to increase the ability to stay focused onto the activity.

2. ***Improve development of sequencing.***

One method is to have the patient follow through with a two-step directive in the care of the animal. Then increase the directives to three and four steps once the patient has been successful. Another method is for the patient to learn and demonstrate the steps in grooming the animal.

3. *Improve awareness of left side (left side neglect).*

One method to improve awareness to the left side is to place the animal on the patient's left side and encourage the patient to reach to his/her left side. Another method is to teach the patient to locate the left and right side of the animal.

4. *Improve reality orientation.*

One method to increase reality orientation is to have the patient identify the name of the animal and what the animal is doing. Encourage the patient to focus on the animal's activity (to teach the patient to stay in the present moment).

5. *Improve sensory awareness.*

One method to increase sensory awareness is to have the patient pet the animals and identify the difference in each of the animal's fur/skin. Another method is to have the patient give the animal a bath and identify between hot and cold water and the texture of the liquid soap and lather of the soap.

6. *Improve awareness of environment.*

One method of improving awareness of the environment is to have the patient identify the different environments or habitats of animals. Bringing the animal into the facility also provides opportunity for environmental awareness to the patient (i.e., provides more of a natural setting, less sterile hospital focus).

CASE SCENARIOS

John was a 5-year-old boy admitted to the children's unit in a private psychiatric hospital for hyperactivity, fighting with kids at school, and not following through with rules at home. John had difficulty staying focused to task (he could only stay on task for about 1 minute) and was only able to follow through with one-step commands. John had difficulty with completing his grooming tasks and refused to take a shower or bath. John enjoyed animals and responded to positive reinforcement.

An animal-assisted therapy program was incorporated within the therapeutic recreation program. John participated in the AAT group. During the group, John was able to stay focused to the task (petting and grooming the animal), he was able to interact with his peers appropriately and follow through with group rules. John was able to successfully demonstrate an obedience command with the dog (teaching the dog to sit) and positively reinforce the dog. John also identified the importance of giving baths and grooming the animals and assisted in combing the dog. The therapist encouraged John to also follow through with grooming and used the animals as a transference model of teaching.

Joey was a 7-year-old male with postthermal burns over 50 percent of his upper body (trunk, head, and extremities). The injuries were a result of a house fire (playing with matches) occurring 11 months earlier. Joey had difficulty with flexion and abduction of upper extremities and limited fine motor skills. Joey's ferret did not survive the fire. Joey was hospitalized at a Burn Institute awaiting for subsequent surgeries. Joey had low self-esteem and self-worth, poor social interactions with peers, and depression. Prior to Joey's accident he was very outgoing and involved in Cub Scouts. His interests included camping, wildlife, and playing with his dog, Benji. An AAT program, offered through community therapy program, was incorporated into the treatment plan.

The AAT team addressed the following objectives during the therapy session:

1. Improve shoulder flexion by 10 percent.
2. Improve upper extremity abduction by 10 percent.
3. Improve fine motor skills through manipulation of two different collars/leashes independently within a single session.
4. Improve social relation through interaction with 1 peer for 5 minutes during AAT session.
5. Improve body awareness through recognition of body parts—name 3 parts of animal's body with one verbal cue.
6. Improve recognition of feelings by verbalizing 1 feeling per AAT session.

The AAT team used the following methods and techniques to meet Joey's treatment needs. The therapist had Joey sit in a chair and groom an animal placed on the table to encourage shoulder flexion and abduction. The therapist placed an animal on each side of Joey to encourage bilateral petting and grooming. Joey worked on finger dexterity and grasp by feeding small pieces of food to the animal. Joey also worked on hand manipulations through using various buckles and clasps on collars, leashes, and animal carriers. Joey also discussed the animal's body parts and related it to his own body and areas where he was injured. The therapist used role playing with Joey to identify his feelings and the animal's feelings. Joey also participated in the AAT group with other peers and was able to share his animal experiences with his peers.

SECTION 3: HORTICULTURAL THERAPY

Horticulture has been an effective modality for therapy and rehabilitation since ancient times, although it has only recently been recognized by practitioners. There is now a national organization, the American Horticultural Therapy Association (AHTA), which is comprised of professionals who use horticulture as an intervention technique in working with clients who are disabled. The AHTA is the certifying agency in the United States for horticultural therapists and serves as a facilitator in conducting research, disseminating information, and providing continuing education.

Sowing seeds, cultivating, harvesting, processing, and using plants in a variety of ways can be a valuable experience for a person of any age, but seems to be especially appealing to children. There are many horticultural activities to choose from that can be done indoors or out. Actual activities in which children can participate range from the simple planting of a seed to propagating plants asexually, building terrariums, planting gardens, arranging flowers, making herbarium sheets, eating fruits and vegetables they grow, to just visiting a beautiful garden and enjoying their surroundings.

In his well respected book, *Horticulture for the Disabled and Disadvantaged,* Olszowy (1978) discusses numerous benefits of horticultural therapy in relation to one's intellectual, emotional and physical development. Intellectually, one can learn about plants. Higher functioning youngsters can learn about plant anatomy, plant identification, food chains, ecology, etc. Lower functioning or very young clients can learn about touch, smell, taste, color, and other aesthetic qualities that plants possess. Patients who are terminally ill can be helped to understand death by discussing the life cycle that even plants must pass through: all living things come into being, live for a while, and must die. Some plants, of course, do this in the span of only one year, while others live thousands of years. Emotionally, children can attach themselves to the plant as well as to the activity. They learn to be patient in taking care of their crops, develop a greater sense of control over their environment and their own actions, and in group situations, they learn to interact with a team. Physically, horticultural activities promote physical exercise, manual dexterity, and if an outdoor activity, the opportunity to be in the fresh air.

Relf (1981) discusses the role that horticultural therapy plays in interaction, action, and reaction. Interaction refers to how people interact in settings that use horticulture. Action relates to how persons interact with plants, and finally, reaction pertains to the outcomes of this orientation. There are several critical elements within each of these areas. The most significant of the three is the action category. If a child is involved in a horticultural activity where plants are being grown and the child has been given the chore of watering them when needed, then a certain responsibility is undertaken. As the child interacts with the plants, he will see that if they are not watered, they will start to wilt and soon die. As the child assumes responsibility, he will take the appropriate action to water the plants.

Plants can bring immense pleasure to the person working with them or simply experiencing them in some way. In his biography of C.S. Lewis, English author A.N. Wilson tells of one of Lewis's early childhood memories. Lewis recalls a time when his older brother Warren brought into the nursery "the lid of a biscuit tin which he had covered with moss and garnished with twigs and flowers so as to make it a toy garden or toy forest—that was the first beauty I ever knew . . . As long as I live, my imagination of Paradise will retain something of my brother's toy garden" (Wilson, 1990).

Terrariums, of course, are easy to make and are a favorite of children to put together, take care of, and just look at. Almost any clear glass or plastic container can be used as a container; the wider the mouth, the easier the task. One should always remember to use lots of sphagnum moss to act as a buffer for over or underwatering. Little pockets of soil can be incorporated into the moss where the plants will be placed. In addition to the subject matter which can be incorporated into the terrarium building, certain motor skills must be developed to accomplish the tasks involved. The clients must also learn to focus on the job at hand and to exercise their creativity. The children should be allowed to choose from a selection of sizes, colors and shapes of young plants.

Sowing seeds is another interesting and useful horticultural activity for the disabled child. This teaches patience and also maintains the element of surprise. Is anything going to happen? What will happen? What kind of a plant will emerge? Am I responsible? Edible as well as ornamental plants can be easily started indoors with very little expense. The plants can either be maintained as indoor plants or can later be transplanted outside where they will get larger and flourish. A therapist can even turn this into a modest money maker by having the children start bedding plants which can be sold later.

Other methods of propagating plants can also be taught to and mastered by children with a variety of disabilities. Again, the activity can be done indoors or out with a minimum of materials and expertise. There are many house plants from which a cutting can be taken and rooted in any well drained medium. Some can even be rooted in water. Children seem to love seeing new plants made from the "mother" plants. Depending on the children's ability, the therapist can talk about cloning, the process occurring when plants are propagated plants asexually.

Throughout the country there are several programs focusing on the application of horticultural therapy. Several of these programs have developed comprehensive activity manuals that describe hundreds of horticultural activities. "Project Grow" is one such program that has received national attention for its impact in serving children. The core of "Project Grow" is a hydroponics greenhouse. In this garden facility located in northern California, children are responsible for cultivating and harvesting vegetable crops. They plant, fertilize and pollinate the growing plants. Additionally, the children are responsible for harvesting, packing and sorting the mature vegetables. "Project Grow" was established to mainstream children who are moderately retarded with students who are in the regular educational program. The curriculum manual was developed by the staff who administer the program and contains 14 essential skill areas based on approximately 150 horticultural activities that exercise the skill areas. The manual can be used for all grade levels and for children with various disabling conditions. The curriculum is multifaceted and deals with cognitive, affective, and vocational development. A resource handbook has also been established. The handbook contains the basic information necessary for a teacher to construct a greenhouse which can be adapted to many setting and up-to-date reference materials.

Gardening as Therapy for the Summer Season by Coxon and Tarrant (1979) is the second in a series of manuals designed to assist in developing a horticultural therapy program. The manual represents the input of several members of the University of British Columbia Botanical Garden staff. Twelve separate activities are described.

There are many other ways in which gardens and plants can prove to be useful tools in working with children. A children's play garden was created and developed at the Rusk Institute for Rehabilitation Medicine at the New York University Medical Center by landscape architects and the children's horticultural, rehabilitation, and teaching team at the hospital. The "PlayGarden" design was thought to be so innovative that it was awarded a grant by the New York Council on the Arts. The PlayGarden is capable of offering a wide range of activities to enhance the rehabilitative, educational, and social experience of the children at Rusk Institute. According to Chambers (1995), the design successfully integrates the needs of the children, the therapists, and the teachers and presents a model for other similar programs.

Another very interesting program was undertaken by horticultural therapists working at the Cleveland Botanical Garden (Kerrigan and Stevenson, 1995). An intergenerational horticulture program was initiated where children, age 9 to 11, from public and parochial schools, were paired with elderly volunteers from a neighborhood community center. The horticultural program was supervised by horticulture therapists at the Botanical Garden.

Most major botanical gardens have a sensory garden. These gardens attract a large number of visitors but are especially attractive to blind persons. Sensory gardens can easily be incorporated into an existing landscape and are usually established in raised planters. Pubescent (hairy) leaves, crinkley leaves, serrated edges, smooth or rough bark, fruits, and flowers are other morphological characteristics which can be felt by the sight impaired. And, of course, the many pungent odors that plants may emit range from very sweet, to just pleasant or very bad. All children can be captivated by employing senses other than sight to identify plants. Examples of plants that have particularly fragrant foliage are geranium, sumac, salvia and rosemary. Plants with interesting textures include lamb's ears, viburnum, holly, and salvia. All of these plants are easily propagated and grown.

Horticultural activities can easily be combined with other disciplines to create stimulating experiences for children. Chadwick (1995) initiated a project to introduce children to gardening and to create an awareness of the world and the value of recycling. More than 1000 children age 6 to 12 made biodegradable bird feeders from recycled containers to Moody Gardens to hang in trees. The project was so successful the first year that it has become an annual community event.

Using horticulture in working with children can produce long-term as well as short-term effects. Interests initiated in childhood can develop into avocations or lifelong hobbies. Since plants are easy to grow and have a multitude of uses, they can increase a child's self-esteem.

Within a therapeutic recreation program that one of the authors designed (Fine) while in Cincinnati, a staff member helped a group of students make terrariums that they were allowed to keep. One of the children showed particular interest in her terrarium and, because of her enthusiasm, the group leader decided to implement one of Coxon and Terrant's summer activities. The group leader was able to secure the use of a small garden, and the children planted an "easy-to-grow" garden consisting of lettuce, tomatoes, green peppers, and shallots. The commitment required of each of the children, the designation of different responsibilities and their rotation among the children, and finally the harvesting and eating of the vegetables at the end of the summer party were immeasurable benefits of this horticultural therapy program.

There are many good reasons to incorporate horticultural activities into the therapeutic setting, many of which have been discussed above. In addition to the positive effects horticultural therapy has been shown to produce, it is relatively easy to start a program. All one needs is a little growing area—outdoors or in—a few inexpensive tools, some horticultural knowledge, and a willingness to get one's hands dirty. Most kids love the getting dirty part of the horticultural experience. Horticultural activities could and should be a valuable part of a therapist's repertoire of intervention techniques. It is also good therapy for the therapist.

SUMMARY

The umbrella of play-facilitated approaches incorporates a wide array of techniques and applications; among the most eminent of them are play therapy, bibliotherapy, AAT, horticultural and art therapy, and each has been briefly introduced in this chapter. Play theorists have postulated that play is many things to many people; it serves many purposes. It can provide an observer with an opportunity to watch children alone or in a group setting while giving the child a sense of control and promoting creativity and responsibility. Various developmental areas in childhood, including intellectual, emotional, and physical development, are positively influenced by play. Through play, children develop ways to cope with their anxieties and stress, and they learn to work out their feelings and to vent frustrations. Most of all, children can gain a sense of satisfaction and joy as a consequence of their involvement in play. The implementation of various play therapy paradigms and intervention techniques within the repertoire of a therapeutic recreation professional expands the individual's abilities to apply viable strategies for promoting feelings of security and a sense of comfort in all children. While the usage of some of these techniques is strongly encouraged, it is also imperative that practitioners examine their level of competence in the techniques under scrutiny within this chapter. Conceivably, many may see it valuable to continue their training and develop the necessary skills to accurately apply some of the therapeutic play strategies in their own settings. In the long run, the initial investment should definitely pay off. We must admit that these interventive play strategies have generally not been investigated by most of our practitioners. Yet, the time seems ripe for a change. Thus, it is our duty, as a new generation of recreational professionals, to now begin expanding our horizons and truly taking advantage of all the advances and available alternatives that are offered to us for the betterment of human life and existence.

REFERENCES

Allan, J.A.B., Brandell, J.R., Fish, M.C., & George, M.H. (1988). Innovative interventions in child and adolescent therapy. *Child therapy and animals, pp. 401–413.* New York: Wiley-Interscience Publication.

Amster, F. (1943). Differential uses of play in treatment of young children. *American Journal of Orthopsychiatry, 13,* 62–68.

Arkow, P. (1982). *Pet therapy: A study of the use of companion animals in selected therapies, 3rd edition.* Colorado: The Humane Society of the Pikes Peak Region.

Axline, V. (1947). *Play therapy.* New York: Ballantine.

Beck, A. (1985). The therapeutic use of animals. *Veterinary Clinics of North America: Small Animal Practice, 15(2),* 365–375.

Beck, A. & Katcher, A. (1984). *Between Pets and People.* New York: Putman.

Baron, K.B. (1991). The use of play in child psychiatry: Reframing the therapeutic environment. *Occupational Therapy in Mental Health, 11(2–3),* 37–56.

Bettelheim, B. (1972). Play and education. *School review, 81,* 1–13.

Blackmon, W.D. (1994). Dungeons and Dragons: The use of a fantasy game in the psychotherapeutic treatment of a young adult. *American Journal of Psychotherapy. 48(4),* 624–632.

Bligh, S. (1977). *Theraplay: Opening the door for withdrawn and autistic children.* Paper presented to Illinois Speech and Hearing Association, Chicago, IL.

Bligh, S. (1977). Theraplay: Facilitating communication in language-delayed children. In J. Andrews and M. Burns (Eds.), *Selected papers in language and phonology, 2: Language remediation.* Evanston, IL: Institute for Continuing Education.

Bolig, R. (1990). Play in health care settings: A challenge for the 1990's. *Children's Health Care. 19(4),* 229–233.

Boone, D.R. & Hartman, B.H. (1972). The benevolent-over-reaction. *Clinical pediatrics, 11,* 268–271.

Brooks, H. & Oppenheim, C. (1973). Horticulture as a therapeutic aid. *Monograph Institute of Rehabilitation Medicine, New York University Medical Center 49.*

Burten, R. (1976). *Social Security.* Anaheim, CA: The Ungame Company.

Bustad, L.K. (1980). *Animal, Aging, and Aged.* Minnesota: Minnesota Press.

Carmichael, K.D. (1993). Play therapy and children with disabilities. *Issues in Comprehensive Pediatric Nursing, 16(3),* 165–173.

Chadwick, A.L. (1995). *A Christmas Tree for the Birds.* Proceedings from American Horticulture Therapy Association, 23rd Annual conference at Montreal, Canada, July 30–August 2, 1995, pp. 15–18.

Chambers, N.K. (1995). *The Children's Play Garden Project: At The Howard A. Rusk Institute of Rehabilitation Medicine New York University Medical Center.* Proceedings from American Horticulture Therapy Association, 23rd Annual conference at Montreal, Canada, July 30–August 2, 1995, pp. 19–21.

Cianciolo, P. (1965). Children's literature can affect coping behavior, *Personnel and Guidance Journal, 43,* 897–903.

Corbin, P. & Williams, E. (1981). Companion animals as bonding catalysts in geriatric institutions. In B. Fogle (Ed.), *Interrelations between people and pets.* Springfield, IL: Charles C Thomas.

Corson, S. & Corson, E. (1975). The child's relationship with household pets and domestic animals. pp. 19–36. *Pets Animals and Society* — Preceedings of the Symposium of the British Small Animals Veterinary Association on January 30–31, 1994. London: Bailliere Tindell.

Corson, S. & Corson, E. (1980). Pet animals as nonverbal communication mediators in psychotherapy in institutional settings. pp. 83–110. *Ethnology and nonverbal communications in mental health.* New York: Pergamon Press.

Coxon & Tarrant. (1979). Gardening as therapy for the summer season. Vancouver, B.C.: University of British Columbia Botanical Gardens.

Creative Health Services. (1983). *The self esteem game.* South Bend, IN.

Denny, J. (1975). Techniques for individual and group art therapy. In E. Ulman and P. Dachinger (Eds.), *Art therapy in theory and practice.* New York: Schocker.

Des Lauriers, A. (1962). *The experience of reality in childhood schizophrenia.* New York: International Universities Press.

Des Lauriers, A. (1967). The schizophrenic child. *Archives of General Psychiatry, 16,* 194–201.

Dinkmeyer, D. & Caldwell, E. (1970). *Developmental counseling and guidance.* New York: McGraw-Hill.

Eddy, J., Hart, L.A., & Boltz, R.P. (1988). The effects of assistance dogs on social acknowledgments of people in wheelchairs. *The Journal of Psychology, 122,* 39–45.

Elias, M.J., Tobias, S.E., & Friedlander, B.S. (1994). Enhancing skills for everyday problem solving, decision making, and conflict resolution in special needs students with the support of computer-based technology. *Special Services in the Schools. 8(2),* 33–52.

Elkind, J., Cohen, K., & Murray, C. (1993). Using computer-based readers to improve reading comprehension of students with dyslexia. *Annals of Dyslexia, 43,* 238–259.

Erikson, E.H. (1963). *Childhood and society* (2nd ed.). New York: Norton.

Fick, K.M. (1993). The influence of an animal on social interactions of nursing home residents in a group setting. *AJOT, 47(6), 529–534.*

Fine, A.H. & Fine, C. (1995). *Project PAL: A Celebration of intergenerational relationships, utilizing animals.* Paper presented at Animal's health and quality of life, 7th International Conference on Human Animal Interactions, Geneva, Switzerland, September 6–9, 1995.

Fine, A. & Siaw, S. (1987). *Therapeutic play for children with chronic illness in hospitals.* Manuscript submitted for publication.

Fine, A. (1985, May). *Secrets.* (Available from Aubrey H. Fine, Cal Poly University, 3801 W. Temple Ave., Pomona, California).

Fleshman, B. & Fryrear, J. (1981). *The arts in therapy.* Chicago: Nelson-Hall.

Friedmann, E., Katcher, A., & Meislich, D. (1983). When pet owners are hospitalized: Significance of companion animals during hospitalizations. pp. 58–72. A. Katcher, & A. Beck. (Eds.) *New Perspective of our life with companion animals.* Philadelphia, PA: University of Pennsylvania.

Gardner, R. (1971). *Therapeutic communication with children: The mutual storytelling technique.* New York: Aronson.

Gardner, R. (1973). *The talking, feeling, and doing game.* Cresskill, NJ: Creative Therapeutics.

Gardner, R. (1975). *Psychotherapeutic approaches to the resistant child.* New York: Aronson.

Gardner, R. (1975). In *Psychotherapeutic approaches to the resistant child.* New York: Aronson.

Gardner, R. (1983). The talking, feeling, and doing game. In C. Schafer and K. O'Conner (Eds.), *Handbook of play therapy,* 259–273. New York: Wiley.

Gardner, R. (1986). *The psychotherapeutic therapeutics of Richard Gardner.* Cresskill, NJ: Creative Therapeutics.

Gardner, R.A. (1988). *The Story Telling Card Game.* Cresskill, NJ: Creative Therapeutics.

Gardner, R.A. (1993). Mutual storytelling. In C.E. Schaefer & D.M. Cangelosi (Eds.), *Play therapy techniques,* 199–209. Northvale, NJ: Jason Aronson, Inc.

George, M.H. (1988). Child therapy and animals: A new way for an old relationship. pp. 400–418. C.E. Schaefer (Ed.), *Innovative interventions of child and adolescent therapy.* New York: John Wiley.

Ginnott, H. (1961). *Group psychotherapy with children.* New York: McGraw-Hill.

Golden, D. (1983). Play therapy for hospitalized children. In C. Schafer and K. O'Conner (Eds.), *Handbook of play therapy,* pp. 213–234. New York: Wiley.

Golick, M. (1973). *Deal me in! The use of playing cards in learning and teaching.* New York: Norton.

Guerney, L. (1983). Client-centered (nondirective) play therapy. In C. Schafer and K. O'Conner (Eds.), *Handbook of play therapy,* 21–64. New York: Wiley.

Guerney, L. (1983). Play therapy with learning disabled children. In C. Schafer and K. O'Conner (Eds.), *Handbook of play therapy*, 419–435. New York: Wiley.

Haley, J. (1973). *Uncommon therapy: The psychiatric techniques of Milton H. Erickson, M.D.* New York: Norton.

Haley, J. (1976). *Problem-solving therapy: New strategies for effective family therapy.* San Francisco: Jossey-Bass.

Hartley, R.E., Rank, L.K., & Goldenson, R.M. (1993). Water Play. In C.E. Schaefer & D.M. Cangelosi (Eds.), *Play therapy techniques*, 125–130. Northvale, NJ: Jason Aronson.

Hellendoorn, J. (1994). Play therapy with mentally retarded clients. In K.J. O'Connor & C.E. Schaefer (Eds.), *Handbook of play therapy, Vol. 2: Advances and innovations*, 349–369. New York: John Wiley & Sons.

Hopkins, M. (1991). The value of information technology for children with emotional and behavioral difficulties. *Maladjustment & Therapeutic Education, 9(3)*, 143–151.

Jenberg, A. (1979). *Theraplay: A new treatment for using structured play for problem children and their families.* San Francisco: Jossey-Bass.

Kale, M. (1992). How some kids gain success, self esteem with animals. *Interaction, 10(2)*, 13–17.

Kantrowitz, V. (1967). Bibliotherapy with retarded readers. *Journal of Reading, 11*, 205–212.

Katcher, A.H. & Friedmann, E. (1980). Potential health value of pet ownership. *The Compendium on Continuing Education, 2*, 117–122.

Katcher, A.H., Friedmann, E., Beck, A., & Lynch, J. (1978). *Talking, Looking, and Blood Pressure: Physiological consequences of interaction with the living environment.* Unpublished manuscript.

Katcher, A.H. & Wilkins, G.G. (1994). *The use of animal assisted therapy and education with attention-deficit hyperactive and conduct disorder.* 14th Annual Delta Society Conference, October 10–14, 1994 in New York City, NY.

Kerrigan, J. & Stevenson, N. (1995). *Behavioral Study of Youth and Elders in an Intergenerational Horticultural Program.* Proceedings from American Horticulture Therapy Association, 23rd Annual conference at Montreal, Canada, July 30–August 2, 1995, pp. 38–41.

Kidd, A.H. & Kidd, R.M. (1980). Personality characteristics and preferences in pet ownership. *Psychological Reports, 46*, 939–949.

Kidd, A.H. & Kidd, R.M. (1985). Animals: Good friends and good medicine. *Medical and Health Annual*, 909–1105. Chicago, Illinois: Encyclopedia Britannia.

Klein, M. (1932). *The psycho-analysis of children.* London: Hogarth.

Kramer, E. (1971). *Art as therapy with children.* New York: Schocken.

Landreth, G.L. (1993). Self-Expressive Communication. In C.E. Schaefer (Ed.), *The therapeutic powers of play*, 41–64. Northvale, NJ: Jason Aronson.

Lapp, C.A. (1991). Nursing students and the elderly: Enhancing intergenerational communication through human-animal interaction. *Holistic Nursing Practitioner, 5(2)*, 72–79.

Leitner, M. & Leitner, S. (1985). *Leisure in later life.* New York: Haworth.

Levinson, B.M. (1964). *Pet oriented child psychotherapy.* Springfield, IL: Charles C Thomas.

Levinson, B.M. (1969). Pets: A special technique in child psychotherapy. *Mental Hygiene, 48,* 243–248.

Levinson, B.M. (1969). Pets and old age. *Mental Hygiene, 53(3),* 695–698.

Levinson, B.M. (1970). Pets, child development, and mental illness. *The Journal of the American Veterinary Medical Association, 157(11),* 1759–1766.

Levinson, B.M. (1972). Pets and human development. Springfield, IL: Charles C Thomas.

Levy, D. (1939). Release therapy. *American Journal of Orthopsychiatry, 9,* 713–736.

Liebmann, M. (1986). *Art therapy for groups.* Cambridge, MA: Brookline.

Loomis, E. (1957). The use of checkers in handling certain resistances in child therapy and child analysis. *Journal of the American Psychoanalytical Association, 5,* 130–035.

Mader, B., Hart, L.A., & Bergin, B. (1989). Social acknowledgments for children with disabilities: Effects of service dogs. *Child Development, 60,* 1529–1534.

Malkiewicz, J. (1970). Stories can be springboards. *Instructor, 79,* 133–134.

Margalit, M. (1991). Promoting classroom adjustment and social skills for students with mental retardation within an experimental and control group design. *Exceptionality, 2(4),* 195–204.

Martinez, K.J. & Valdez, D.M. (1992). Cultural considerations in play therapy with Hispanic children. In L.A. Vargas & J.D. Koss-Chioino (Eds.), *Working with culture: Psychotherapeutic interventions with ethnic minority children and adolescents,* 85–102. San Francisco: Jossey-Bass.

Melamed, B.G. & Siegel, L. (1975). Reduction of anxiety in children facing hospitalization and surgery by use of filmed modeling. *Journal of Consulting and Clinical Psychology, 43,* 511–521.

Melson, G.F. & Schwarz, R. (1994). *Pets as social supports for families with young children.* 14th Annual Delta Society Conference, October 10–14, 1994 in New York City, NY.

Messent, P. (1985). Pets as social facilitators. *The Veterinary Clinics of North Americas and Small Animal Practice, 15(2),* 387–393.

McConkey, R. (1994). Families at Play: Interventions for Children with Developmental Handicaps. In J. Hellendoorn, R. van der Kooij, & B. Sutton-Smith (Eds.), *Play and Intervention,* 123–132. Albany, NY: State University of New York Press.

McCullock, M. (1983). Animal-facilitated therapy: Overview and future direction, 410–426. In A. Katcher & A. Beck (Eds.), *New perspectives on our lives with companion animals.* Philadelphia: University of Pennsylvania Press.

Mendell, A. (1983). Play therapy with children of divorced parents. In C. Schafer and K. O'Connor (Eds.), *Handbook of play therapy,* 320–354. New York: Wiley.

Millman, H. (1970). Minimal brain dysfunction in children. Evaluation and treatment. *Journal of Learning Disabilities, 3,* 89–99.

Muro, J. & Dinkmeyer, D. (1977). *Counseling in the elementary and middle schools.* Dubuque, IA: William C. Brown.

Nickerson, E. (1983). Art as a play therapeutic medium. In C. Schafer and K. O'Connor (Eds.), *Handbook of play therapy,* 234–250. New York: Wiley.

Olszowy, D. (1978). *Horticulture for the disabled and disadvantaged.* Springfield, IL: Charles C Thomas.

Peller, L. (1962). Daydreams and children's favorite books. In J. Posenblith and W. Allensmith (Eds.), *The causes of behavior.* Boston: Allyn & Bacon.

Peoples, C. (1983). Fair play therapy. In C. Schafer and K. O'Connor (Eds.), *Handbook of play therapy*, 76–89. New York: Wiley.

Phillips, W.R. (1991). Video-game therapy. *New England Journal of Medicine. 325(17)*, 1256–1257.

Pratt, S.R., Heintzelman, A.T., & Deming, S.E. (1993). The efficacy of using the IBM Speech Viewer Vowel Accuracy Module to treat young children with hearing impairment. *Journal of Speech & Hearing Research, 36(5)*, 1063–1074.

Relf, D. (1981). Dynamics of horticultural therapy. *Rehabilitation Literature, 42(5–6)*, 147–149.

Robbins, A. & Sibley, L. (1976). *Creative art therapy.* New York: Brunner/Mazel.

Rubin, P.B. & Tregay, J. (1989). *Play with them—Theraplay groups in the classroom: A technique for professionals who work with children.* Springfield, IL: Charles C Thomas.

Rubin, R. (1978). *Using bibliotherapy: A guide to theory and practice.* Phoenix, AZ: Oryx.

Schaefer, C.E. (1994). Play Therapy for Psychic Trauma in Children. In K.J. O'Connor & C.E. Schaefer (Eds.), *Handbook of play therapy, Vol. 2: Advances and innovations*, 297–318. New York: John Wiley & Sons.

Schafer, C. & O'Connor, K. (1983). *Handbook of play therapy.* New York: John Wiley & Sons.

Schafer, C. & Reed, S. (1986). *Game play.* New York: John Wiley & Sons.

Serpell, J. (1986). *In the company of animals.* New York: Basil Blackwell.

Singer, D.G. (1994). Play as healing. In J.H. Goldstein (Ed.), *Toys, play, and child development*, 147–165. New York, NY: Cambridge University Press.

Smith, E. (1982). Dolphins to elicit communication responses from autistic children. In Katcher, A., and Beck, A. (Eds.), *New perspectives on our lives with companion animals*, 460–466. Philadelphia: University of Pennsylvania Press.

Steelman, Jane D., Pierce, Patsy L., & Koppenhaver, David A. (1993). The role of computers in promoting literacy in children with severe speech and physical impairments (SSPI). *Topics in Language Disorders, 13(2)*, 76–88.

Sutton-Smith, B. (1971). Play, games, and controls. In J.P. Scott (Ed.), *Social control.* Chicago: University of Chicago Press.

Sutton-Smith, B. & Roberts, J. (1971). The cross-cultural and psychological study of games. *International Review of Sport Sociology, 6*, 78–87.

Wadeson, H. (1980). *Art Psychotherapy.* New York: John Wiley and Sons.

Watson, D., & Burlingame, A. (1960). *Therapy through horticulture.* New York: Macmillan.

Webb, N.B., Ed. (1991). *Play therapy with children in crisis: A casebook for practitioners.* New York: Guilford Press.

Whipple, G. (1969). Practical problems of school book selection for disadvantaged pupils. In J. Figurel (Ed.), *Reading and realism.* Delaware: International Reading Association.

Wilson, A.N. (1990). *C.S. Lewis: A Biography.* London: Harper Collins.

Wilson, J. (1964). *The mind.* New York: Life Science Library Series, Time.

Winnicott, D.W. (1971). *Therapeutic consultations in child psychiatry.* New York: Basic Books.

Zaccaria, J., Moses, H., & Hollowell, J. (1978). *Bibliotherapy in rehabilitation, educational, and mental health settings: Theory, research, and practice.* Champaign, IL: Stipes.

Zakick, R. (1975). *The ungame.* Anaheim, CA: Ungame.

Zakick, R. & Monroe, S. (1979). *Reunion.* Placentia, CA: Ungame.

Chapter 9

PARENTS—THEIR PERCEPTIONS AND INPUT: THE IMPORTANCE OF COLLABORATION

AUBREY H. FINE

Speak to us of Children. And he said . . .
Though they are with you yet they belong not to you . . .
You are the bows from which your children as living arrows
are set forth. . . .
Let your bending in the archer's hand be for gladness;
For even as He love the arrow that flies, so He loves also
the bow that is stable.

Kahil Gibran

One of the areas that is imperative to incorporate in this book is the value and the importance of collaborating and working closely with parents. I had the opportunity to be guided into this field by concerned and active parents who were committed to ensuring a better life for their child. After years of working with several families, I realized that they represented **the key** to a successful program. Since that time I have been motivated to teach those who serve any child so they could recognize and understand the value of parents' participation.

This chapter will present several issues that relate to parent participation and will discuss other important areas as they relate to providing services to the child and parents.

1. Parenting a child with a disability. What impact does the child have on the family?
2. Why is parental involvement important?
3. What is the rationale for enhancing parent-professional relationships?
4. How can parents and professionals relate to best serve the child?
5. What are parents searching for when asking recreational services for their child?

301

6. How is the least restrictive placement for the child explained to the parents?
7. How does one develop a parent component?
8. Why is recreation in the home important?

PARENTING A CHILD WITH A DISABILITY

All parents hope for the birth of a healthy, happy child. When parents are confronted with the birth of a child with a disability, some will have relatively no difficulty with acceptance. For others, the task will be arduous, perhaps impossible. On one hand, they want to love and care for the child, but on the other hand, they reject the young infant. The parents may feel dejected, confused, and insecure. These internalized feelings can persist because the problem can be envisioned as long-term. The adaptation to one's child is truly an individual phenomenon. Parental adjustment is depressed or enhanced by the sum total of the physical and the emotional resources that surface in coping with the environment.

Experiences of parenthood are frequently sprinkled with tremendous occasions filled with joy. Nevertheless, an honest portrayal of parenthood would not be complete without acknowledging the episodes of pain which may also be felt. Barbara Walters was once quoted as saying, "Being a parent is tough. If you just want a wonderful little creature to love, you can get a puppy."

Life is accepted as being full of mysteries and unanswered questions, questions which many of us would like to have had answered immediately. How tempting would it be to peak into the future and take a glimpse (even for a minute) into what life has in store for you and your significant loved ones? We usually come up empty-handed in predicting the future. Our challenge is to enjoy the present and do the best we can to prepare for a healthy future.

We are told that parenting any child is a tremendous opportunity as well as an enormous responsibility. Kogan once noted that "To be a parent, you have to put yourself second, to recognize that the child has feelings and needs separate from yours, and one must fulfill those needs without expecting anything in return." Nevertheless, to be the best, one must be able to be at peace with him/herself.

Many individuals see their children as an extension of themselves; others feel their children are a means to attain some degree of immortality. Having a child with any exceptionality may cause tremendous anguish, disappointment, and even anger. Dreams and hopes for the child's future may at times be shattered or tainted. Our misunderstanding of the child's inability to control impulses and attention may threaten parents' feelings of self-worth and dignity. The feelings of hopelessness may only be temporary or will possibly haunt families for the remainder of their lives.

The presence of a child with a disability need not create a family crisis. How the event is defined by the family determines whether or not a real predicament exists. This is not to say that there will not be any questions, and for that matter, frustration. However, to be accepting of a disability will dramatically influence the way the family responds to its ramifications. It is realistic for some to initially experience some pain and disappointment. However, these feelings of incompetence need to also be understood. So often parents feel that they must channel all their energies into their child. Unfortunately, this process leaves parents very vulnerable. If parents don't deal with their feelings appropriately, their lowered sense of efficacy may also obstruct the well-being of their child and the family.

For some parents the reaction to having a child with disability will vary greatly. All expectations of having the perfect child are shattered, leaving instead the feeling of despair and wondering, "What did I do to cause this? or "I don't deserve this!" Many emotions come into play once the diagnosis has been identified. Reactions may include denial (as a means of self-protection) against the painful realities, and blame (condemn oneself as a cause of the syndrome). Shock, the first reaction to hearing the news is quite common. Understandably, a parent usually experiences disbelief unless forewarned. A sense of numbness sometimes occurs as reported by some parents. Stewart (1986) quotes a group of parents who noted, "We were numb, we could scarcely walk about and do our normal day's work, or talk to other people" (p. 115).

Fear, anxiety, and guilt are usually other reactions which are quite common. Some parents may desperately search their memories for what they may have done wrong during the pregnancy or after the birth of the child. Another tendency some parents may demonstrate is blaming the disability on themselves or on their spouse. If this behavior occurs, it will only place the marital relationship in jeopardy at a time when mutual support is needed. Sometimes the feelings of anxiety can be alleviated by learning as much as possible about the disability. Knowledge and insight on the cause and treatment of the disability usually are helpful in coping with the disability. Parents should read as much as they can and possibly talk with other parents to get their perceptions.

A parent may unintentionally resent or be jealous of a friend with a normal child who progresses through life without a disability. Parents may feel they are missing out on their child's typical childhood, with all the new discoveries and usual landmarks in a child's life. At times, one may also feel alienated from friends if the child does not fit into the crowd or if others are uncomfortable being near a child with a disability.

For some, the initial battle of acceptance will end with these early internal conflicts. Parents will then begin to refocus their energy to secure a better understanding of the syndrome as well as the spectrum of methods which can be utilized to treat the syndrome. Acceptance usually leads to a more constructive approach in dealing with the child. For some families, this may mean doing everything that is universally possible to help a child cope and overcome.

The parental role of a child with a disability must be considered a monumental one. The parents of a child with a disability are not only the primary caregivers during childhood, but in most cases face a lifelong commitment. During different life periods, some of the previously noted feelings and reactions may resurface. It may take parents a shorter amount of time to resolve or they could find themselves in more significant positions.

Some parents may be side-tracked on the way and continue to search for an outcome which is not possible. These unrealistic desires, aligned with possible further disappointments in their child's progress, may influence the parents' well-being. These parents may experience a resurgence of hopelessness and want to give up. The anger may resurface and some parents will possibly revert back to their conflict with acceptance. This battle can be inferred both internally and externally. Internally suggests the dispute which is waged within the individual. Feelings of worthlessness, lowered level of efficacy, and confusion may be possible outcomes. Many of the physical ailments effecting the individual early in the process may continue to flourish. External conflicts may occur between the parent and any other member of a child's circle of life (e.g., professionals, relatives, peers, and friends of the child). It is also within this dimension that disharmony may be highlighted between the parents' expectations and those who provide remedial supports. Parents may develop a sense of resistance because the progress continues to be slow. They may also want to try and block out further disappointments in their child's growth or to try to avoid further ridicule from others. These conflicts may occur frequently or they may resurface at various highlighted developmental periods where possibly new issues may arise (entering junior high, etc.).

Nonetheless, as Kierkegaard points out, life can only be understood backwards, but it must be lived forward. To love a child with all one's heart a parent has to be at peace with him/herself. One does not have to like everything, but one should be accepting. If one cannot appreciate and enjoy what one has, it probably will never be appreciated. Children are like diamonds. At times, they will need to be polished so that their internal beauty can be savored.

To illustrate this point of view an example of going to an unexpected destination on a vacation will be given. One may have intentions of going to a specific attraction. When they arrive, to their surprise, they are told they were taken to a different site. Although the site isn't as luxurious as the previously selected attraction, it too has its merits and beauty. Unfortunately, if people cannot get over and accept the fact that they are not at their planned destination, they may never be able to appreciate the beauty of where they are. Wilde suggests that to regret one's own experiences is to arrest one's own development. It is only hoped that parents, will continue to mobilize with hope and not ruminate on the negatives.

Understanding the Implications of a Disability on the Sibling

Parents have to be conscious of their responsibilities to all of their children. Unfortunately, some mothers and fathers try to become superparents to compensate for their child with a disability.

Everyone experiences a number of feelings in his/her life, but siblings of children with special needs are highly affected by those feelings particular to them. The feelings and reactions noted that parents experience are similar with siblings. However, it seems that siblings are often afraid to discuss their emotions with their parents because they think that their parents have enough concerns already. A child may be bewildered by what is wrong with his/her new brother or sister and may be afraid that he/she is going to catch the disability. As irrational as this may seem, it is a fear children do report.

Meyer, Vadasy, and Fewell (1985) discuss the various feelings and experiences many siblings may encounter. They suggest that some of these feelings are hard to talk about with peers. Some of the children may benefit from a sibling support group. They note that the feelings of jealousy, a sense of neglect, worry, and embarrassment are some of the feelings that these children encounter.

Jealousy often arises because parents have to spend so much of their time, energy, and money on their child with special needs. The siblings may feel that they are being neglected. Sometimes parents have a hard time dividing their time equally between all of their children. This, however, does not mean that the parents do not care about all of their children, but simply that they have to devote more of their time to the child with a disability. Special medical care and self-help care require a great deal of time. A suggestion to siblings who feel as though they are being neglected is to discuss it with their parents.

Sometimes the siblings feel ignored by their parents. It may appear that their parents do not notice them unless they do something to get into trouble. Normal siblings may be burdened with excessively high parental aspirations to compensate for parental frustrations due to having a child with a disability. Furthermore, some children may be given excessive responsibility for taking care of their sibling who is disabled (Seligman, 1983).

It is important to reassure children that it is alright to get mad at their disabled sibling and express their feelings. Some children may feel their sibling with a disability is a major disruption in their life and resent the imposition. They may resent the time parents spend with their sibling and may express negative behaviors in order to gain attention. It is easy for the parents to mistakenly ignore the siblings of the child with a disability and assume that they do not need as much attention. It is typical for parents to forget that they have other children, especially if the demands of the child with a disability are enormous.

Explaining to the sibling what caused his brother's or sister's disorder, what is involved with the disorder now, and any changes which are possibly going to take place is a very helpful procedure. This information reassures the sibling that it was not his fault, and helps the sibling understand his brother's or sister's needs and prepares him for the future.

A sibling's understanding of his brother or sister's disorder alleviates any doubt about its cause and allows the sibling to feel more comfortable. This knowledge also allows the sibling to answer questions from friends and even prompts him to learn more on his own. Knowing more about a brother's or sister's disorder helps the sibling to understand his/her special needs and to know what to expect as the child develops.

When a sibling is allowed to contribute to a brother's or sister's care and to help in making decisions in future care, the sibling feels involved and appreciated, whereas a sibling who is uninvolved may only feel neglect, resentment, and jealousy. The feeling of importance created by active involvement increases the sibling's self-esteem and confidence.

The literature suggests that there are some positive aspects about having a sibling who is disabled. A number of studies point out that some siblings seem to be more tolerant and more aware of the consequences of prejudice. They also seem to be more sensitive to the needs of others. The strongest single factor affecting the healthy sibling's acceptance seem to be how parents react to the child, especially the mother (Seligman, 1983). Unfortunately, there is evidence that some siblings are hardened by the experience. Scholars suggest that these children may display bitter resentment to the family's situation, guilt about the rage, and anger they feel towards the parents and the sibling who is disabled, and the everlasting fear that they themselves might have a blemish (Seligman, 1983).

As can be seen, siblings do suffer from problems involved with their brother or sister. Emotions are strong and influential but can usually be controlled and understood with good communication. Behavioral problems in siblings can develop as a result of unresolved conflicts and extensive amount of stress. Despite all of the problems that these siblings experience, many lead healthy, happy lives with their parents, brothers, and sisters. The key is open communication and understanding. The world needs to realize that it is not only the parents and the child with a disability who need support and information, but the siblings as well. They have special needs just like everyone else. Once a sibling understands his own behavior and the behavior of his sibling who happens to have a disability, s/he can grow and adjust more effectively.

LEISURE WITHIN THE HOME: CONCLUDING REMARKS

Too much attention is always given to formal leisure participation outside the home. The reality is that most people learn to entertain themselves within the confinement of their own home. The home is the first school and recreation center; the parent is the first teacher and recreation leader. What goes on in the family is the foundation of learning. It includes guidance in play and recreation which, in turn, provides opportunities for growth. A home that provides options for wholesome leisure is preparing an individual for his/her adult years. When individuals recognize the wealth of options that can be selected and participation is considered more naturally, an individual is indirectly preparing himself/herself for the future.

Families are encouraged to look at the individual with a disability and try to remove the obstacles that prevent the prospect of family activities. In most cases, the drive to be constructive in utilizing leisure at home may not occur on its own. Families will have to make an effort (possibly at first) to expose and involve the individual (the child, or the adolescent) in diverse opportunities which can be participated in at home. After exposure, it is more realistic to expect that the individual will eventually become more inspired to make more reasonable choices. Adults who, as children, had a strong **positive** foundation of leisure within the home are more likely to continue this process as they age.

Recreation within the home may differ depending on the age of the individual as well as the individual's strengths, and preferences. It is imperative that attention be given at an early age to encourage families to learn about how they can help their child develop a routine at home which incorporates positive practice of leisure. Within the early years of a child's life, the professional community can share with families the position that to obtain optimal life satisfaction, families must also emphasize productive usage of free time. If the concept that developing well-rounded individuals is respected, and that an effective leisure lifestyle is a fundamental ingredient in life satisfaction, parents and other support individuals may become more motivated to exhaust energy in this direction. Their efforts may ensure that a home environment is established which encourages and offers diverse choices of activities to participate with others or by oneself. In doing so, we may be helping prepare the child for independent life as an adult (Fine, 1994). Practitioners need to emphasize this position with families so that they become more aware of their role in assisting maturation in applied leisure functioning.

THE IMPORTANCE OF PARENT INVOLVEMENT

Most parents of children with disabilities, like parents in general, come to know, respect, and love their children. While others may view a child as **handicapped** or **different,** these parents come to see within their child and recognize his/her individual strengths and limitations. Parents represent a rich and available resource not to merely advocate for their children but to help others understand who they are. Parents have seen their child conquer challenges, as well as fail, and have a wealth of information about their child. In regards to recreation, what parents want most of all for their child is for the child to be part of a group, to be wanted, and appreciated by others. One mother describes the feelings of isolation her son experiences. Groce (1985) tells her readers about the stares her son endures, as well as the superficial greetings he receives from many who pass him in the halls of school. What her son wants and needs is to be one of the crowd, for someone to know who he is.

Parents of a disabled child are often so anxious for their child to be rehabilitated that some often have unrealistic expectations for improvement from all of the services a child is involved in, including recreation programs (Kronick, 1973). Determining what types of programs disabled children would benefit most from in addition to when and where the programs should take place are typical questions that concern parents. Furthermore, these are questions that need to be addressed by the recreation therapists.

The insightful recreation therapist recognizes the important role that parents play in the total rehabilitation process of their child. Heward, Darding, and Rossett (1979) point out that parents need the support of professionals so that they can access relevant and understandable information about their child. Through collaborations, parents equip themselves with strategies for dealing with the everyday concerns of bringing up their disabled child and establishing long-term goals. Likewise, professionals need and benefit from the support and wisdom of parents.

The following examples illustrate the influences that parents can have on their child's rehabilitation. The first example portrays how important it is to work with parents. The situation that occurred fourteen years ago involved a seven-year-old named Barry who had a very poor self-concept. Barry was clumsy, had very poorly developed fine motor skills and, as a result, was very self-conscious about his abilities. He was involved in a social recreational program developed for children with learning disabilities. The staff was frustrated because they could not motivate Barry to participate in any of the art projects. After months of encouragement, Barry felt secure enough to complete a project. Although his project would not have been considered a masterpiece by many, he was proud of his work and that was all that really counted. When his father came to pick them up, Barry was seen exuberantly running out to show his father his completed work. To Barry's dismay, as well as to all those who observed, his father merely glanced at the piece of paper and said, "What is this garbage?" and then proceeded to crumple the paper and throw it on the ground. Barry was shattered emotionally and it would be a long time before he felt confident enough to try another art project.

With this awakening experience, it was discovered that designing programs which encourage parental involvement and commitment are of vital importance. These programs do vary in the demands placed on both parents and professionals. They range from simply making sure that appropriate channels are developed for open communication, to programs that have parent participation as a major component. Various programs will be elaborated later in this chapter.

Now let us examine a situation where parents facilitate positive outcomes for their child. For a year, Steven was enrolled in an individually prescribed recreation therapy program. Steve was diagnosed as autistic and displayed some of the severe ritualistic behaviors that are characteristic of autism (e.g., self-stimulation and rocking). He was also extremely manipulative and appeared to need a very structured program.

Steve's parents asked the recreation therapist for assistance to help Steve develop a few of recreational skills. His mother was very concerned that Steve had limited leisure abilities, which was evident each day after school when he had free time. This frustrated his mother, since Steven was difficult to manage and needed constant supervision. Because of Steven's age, the therapist felt that the primary emphasis of his training should be on developing functional play skills. A great deal of time was spent with his family to understand Steve's life-style and to determine what would be the most likely activities he could perform. After a period of collaboration, activities and goals were established.

Two students were trained as group leaders for Steve. They met twice a week for two hours. Since a child like Steven needed constant and consistent programming, progress would have been limited if the family did not work in close collaboration with the student therapists. Due to the parent-therapist interaction, Steve's parents worked on the same goals at home and kept the student therapists posted on Steven's progress. Furthermore, due to the complexity of the interventions applied in Steven's case, it was necessary for his parents to educate anyone serving their son about the program. This was done to ensure consistency in all interactions with Steven.

Over the next several months, progress with Steven was phenomenal. However, this was not totally due to professional involvement. Open communication was established between the therapists and Steve's parents. The role of his parents as adjunct therapists was clearly established. In this example, both parents seemed willing to be involved and contributed immensely to the ultimate success of the program.

THE RATIONALE FOR ENHANCING PARENT–PROFESSIONAL RELATIONSHIPS

Heward et al. (1979) provides a rationale for enhancing the parent-professional relationship. Foremost, parents can provide the professional community with a clearer understanding of the needs of their child as well as what they expect from the program. Several of the interviewing techniques as well as the developmental profiles discussed in Chapter 7 are viable avenues for gathering information from parents. Parents should be encouraged to be honest with professionals and to tell them as much as possible about their child. Unfortunately, parents are sometimes not given an opportunity to disclose all pertinent information. This is usually due to time constraints or staff limitations within a therapeutic recreation program. Professionals oftentimes neglect questioning the parents' intentions for enrolling a child in any given program. The rationale for enrolling a child and clarification of expectations need to be discussed.

When collaboration occurs, parents can represent a rich resource base. If parents know specifically what the professional is focusing on and are assisted in establishing a routine, children can practice similar play skills at home. The repetition would allow the newly established skills to become a more natural aspect of a child's play repertoire. For some children especially the severely disabled, limited structured recreation opportunities will not dramatically develop skills. They typically will be enhanced only if additional time is devoted outside the group to practice the skills. This is also true for children who are less disabled. It is imperative for the child to try out the new skills so that the child will eventually incorporate them into their daily life patterns. A major weakness in leisure skill instruction appears to be the lack of insight of professionals in training self-initiated play behaviors. It really does not matter in the long run if a child performs an activity only in the presence of an adult. For the behavior to have any long-lasting effect, it must occur spontaneously without the constant supervision of an adult.

It is noteworthy that the lack of self-initiated play behaviors is one of parents' most severe criticisms of recreation therapy programs. While they acknowledge that their child is enjoying the program, they cannot understand why the child does not use these trained skills at home.

Some of this pertains to perceived competence, while a portion can also be attributed to opportunity. Both of these variables will be discussed in detail in Chapter 10. However, by collaborating with parents, one can ensure that lack of opportunity and consultation are not considered as the source of the problem.

THE IMPORTANCE OF COLLABORATION
WHILE SERVING A CHILD

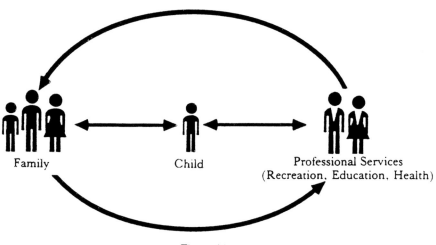

Figure 16.

Figure 16 portrays the collaborative relationship between parents and the professional community. The figure projects all sources commonly working with each other to strengthen the opportunity for a child's growth and learning. The cooperation between parents and professionals promotes greater consistency in a child's most important living environment. Emphasis in how school personnel can be helpful in this process is presented in Chapter 10. Note that unless a system that enhances the natural extension of skills taught in therapy is developed, there will always be a void in the provision process.

Parents cannot only encourage the practice of skills being taught, but they can also act as an informant to update the professional on their child's progress. Furthermore, parents should be approached to discuss their perceptions of programmatic goals. They may have extremely relevant ideas that may not have been incorporated into their child's program. Additionally, if parents are not consciously made aware of what a program entails, they may inadvertently discourage the acquisition and development of skills being generated. Therefore, uniformity of expectations must occur.

A situation occurred where program goals were not uniformly understood by a young boy's parents and his therapists. Within the leisure education and self-help aspects of the program, he began to develop an interest in cooking simple meals. However, this conflicted with his parents' expectations of him. When he attempted to employ his newly acquired skills at home, his family was not supportive. They were uncomfortable with the idea of their son utilizing the electric range and oven. After consultation with the therapists, the parents were willing to adapt their expectations and allow their son to cook at home.

Working with families provides increased opportunities for learning, and it also expands the likelihood for greater services to the child. Another factor that promotes quality interaction with parents pertains to consistency in methods of management. All too often there is a discrepancy between the approaches utilized in the home versus in outside programs. Expectations should be clarified to encourage more uniformity and consistency in approaches.

In 1975, Ed Sontag, then chief of the Division of Personnel Preparation for the Bureau of Education for the Handicapped, expressed his commitment to the parent-professional relationship. He stated that educational research indicated that when parents are involved in the educational process, their children are more likely to achieve on a higher level. When parents are involved, they tend to be more committed as well as cognizant of a program's goals.

Unfortunately, some professionals find it difficult to accept the position of working closely with parents. They believe in the myth that it is easier to facilitate programs for children if parents are kept out of the picture. Although parents have a right to be informed and involved in their child's treatment, the parents' involvement is often discouraged and considered meddlesome. For too long, this was the orientation chosen by most professionals. Kratoville (1973) suggests that parents hate to be stigmatized as meddlers, but sometimes their only alternative is to meddle.

Furthermore, parents must become more familiar with the resources that an agency can provide. Parents are often unfamiliar with or have misunderstandings about the field of therapeutic recreation. The need to define and clarify therapeutic recreation's role in rehabilitation is quite evident. Due to this lack of understanding, parents may have inaccurate expectations about what therapeutic recreation can offer. Many lay persons perceived the field as either exclusively recreation for the handicapped or to the opposite extreme: therapy. A parent who is expecting therapy when the purposes of the program are totally recreational can lead to frustration and misunderstanding. Nevertheless, this predicament has partially been resolved with the formation of the new philosophic definition adopted by the National Therapeutic Recreation Society. According to this new definition, the purpose of therapeutic recreation is the facilitation of the development of an optimal leisure life-style for individuals with a variety of disabling conditions. Three areas of professional services are incorporated in therapeutic recreation: (1) therapy, (2) leisure, and (3) recreation participation. While these three processes have unique contributions in relation to the clients' needs, conceptually (according to the definition) they are formulated employing similar processes. However, there is a lack of uniformity among professionals. There are simply too many programs that claim that they provide recreation therapy but provide services that are developed and executed poorly. Additionally, these programs are not based on the results of each participant's assessed needs but, rather, on a general program that attempts to cater to a multitude of different children. This issue is not to frustrate the reader but to inspire the individual to make an impact on the future. Professional leaders of today and those neophytes who are emerging as leaders must function as the change agents of the profession. These individuals need to assume responsibility for establishing and maintaining the profession's credibility and serve as advocates for helping others understand.

The program goals must be explained to parents. It is acceptable to tell parents that the sole purpose of the program is for fun (if that is the major goal). In fact, that is frequently what motivates the child to attend. The impact of therapeutic recreation originates with the participation in activities to promote changes that are desired. False expectations precipitate poor experiences that only frustrate families, which then questions the professional's credibility. Professionals, therefore, need to take the responsibility of clarifying to parents the type of entry information that would be helpful. It is crucial that all of those involved establish the ground rules at the beginning of the collaborative working relationship.

RECREATION WITHIN THE HOME

All of God's critter have a place in the choir.
Some sing low, some sing higher,
Some sing out loud on the telephone wires,
And some just clap their hands. . . .
                              Mantle (1985)

Children need to learn to identify as family members by actively joining the everyday routine in family responsibilities and actively sharing in the family recreation (Ferris, 1980). The home is the first school and recreation center; the parent is the first teacher and recreation leader. What goes on in the family is the foundation of learning. It includes guidance in play and recreation which, in turn, provides opportunities for growth (Brightbill and Mobley, 1977). Families who engage in enjoyable and rewarding activities together will enhance family interaction and maintain the involvement of the child in community functions. A child who knows how to play and has acquired leisure skills will be able to utilize his/her leisure time. Thus, the child will be less dependent on his/her parents and siblings for leisure activities. At times, families find themselves occupying every second of their child's time. This proves to be a great injustice to the child as well as to the family.

Parents are encouraged to look at the child and try to remove the obstacles that prevent family activities (Goodman, Grotsky, and Mann, 1979). Parents should take chances and try new activities. Some activities will spark interests and others may not. These activities can represent a special sharing time between child, parents and siblings. Sometimes, parents are so concerned about providing for the child's physical well-being that they neglect to join the child for fun. When parents and children enjoy a game or other activities, hostility is reduced and harmony can be enhanced. Play allows the child to see the child within the parent, not the authoritarian. The experiences allow the family to view the disabled child in another light. They may begin to recognize some of the child's assets and realize the disabled child's contribution to the family as a whole. The family can encourage social interaction and effectively teach interaction skills to other children. This becomes quality time which enhances all family members.

Some families incorporate a **family meeting** which is a special period of time set aside each week where the family comes together to talk and have fun. It may be quite a chore to get all family members together, but the end result is well worth the effort. Families can begin to see how enjoyable it is to be together. It is a must for all families. Dinkmeyer and McKay (1982) and Popkin (1987) are two excellent resources for the reader to learn how to initiate and organize these meetings.

Family recreation may differ depending on the level of functioning of the child. It may not be easy to involve the child, but it should not be impossible, either. If one looks for reasons why not to do things, one will find a million excuses for not attempting to do it. Parents need to look at the opportunities that are available. Most children like to have company, and being able to be part of the action is a wonderful learning experience. There are benefits to be gained both from participation and watching an activity. Nya Fine provides a personal point of view of her sister, who had a profound disability. "My sister enjoyed the company of people. My mother would have my sister in the room while she was performing homemaking tasks. If she was cooking, she would involve my sister in that activity. It may have been only to assist in the stirring, but what occurred? There was the contact, the experience of feeling the texture, smelling, and, best yet, the tasting. We quickly learned what she did like and what she did not. She did not have speech, but Lisa would definitely let the family know when things were not right."

It is important for families that have existing leisure interests to involve the child with the disability in those activities as much as possible. It is imperative to be realistic in the selection and the degree of participation. Parents are encouraged to look at the activity and see how the child can participate. What skills are required? What can be adapted? For example, within a family which enjoys camping, several aspects of the activity can be modified for almost any child's participation (e.g., assisting in setting up the tent, hiking and cooking).

SUMMARY

Parental involvement within the overall therapeutic recreation process is strongly recommended. Its benefits will be quickly evident and will far outweigh the initial hardships of developing such a program. Recreational personnel need to engage in a campaign to re-educate the community about how they can actively have an impact on a child and his/her family. When families recognize the quality program that has been established and how the parental component is an integral element, it is likely they will be more receptive to participate. In addition, parents must be encouraged to initiate positive family recreation. These experiences should be helpful in enhancing the family bond as well as promoting a more positive living environment.

REFERENCES

Bringtbill, C. & Mobley, T. (1977). *Educating for leisure-centered living.* New York: Wiley.

Dinkmeyer, D. & McKay, G. (1982). *Systematic training for effective parenting.* Circle Pines: American Guidance Service.

Featherstone, H. (1980). *A difference in the family: Life with a disabled child.* New York: Basic Books.

Fine, A.H. (1995). The Promise: With all my heart. *Living and Learning with Attention Deficit Hyperactivity Disorder, 3,* 1–2.

Fitts, W. (1971). *The self concept and self actualization.* Nashville: Counselor Recording and Tests.

Groce, N. (1985). *Everyone here spoke sign language.* Cambridge, MA: Harvard University Press.

Heward, W., Darding, J., & Rossett, A. (1979). *Working with parents of handicapped children.* Columbus: Charles E. Merrill.

Keat, D. (1976). Training as multimodel treatment for peers. *Elementary School Guidance and Counseling, 11,* 7–13.

Kratoville, B. (1973). Telling it like it is. In D. Kronick (Ed.), *A word or two about learning disabilities.* San Rafael, CA: Academic Therapy.

Kronick, D. (1973). *A word or two about learning disabilities.* San Rafael, CA: Academic Therapy.

Krouse, J., Gerber, M., & Kauffman, J. (1981). Peer tutoring: Procedures, promises and unresolved issues. *Exceptional Education Quarterly, 1,* 107–115.

Meyer, D., Vadasy, P., & Fewell, R. (1985). *Living with a brother or sister with special needs.* Seattle: University of Washington Press.

Powell, T. & Ogle, P. (1985). *Brothers and sisters: A special part of exceptional families.* Baltimore: Paul H. Brookes.

Popkin, M. (1987). *Active parenting: Teaching cooperation, courage and responsibility.* San Francisco: Harper and Row.

Seligman, M. (1983). *The family with a handicapped child.* New York: Grune and Stratton.

Silverstein, S. (1964). *The giving tree.* New York: Harper and Row.

Spaulding, B. & Morgan, S. (1986). Spina bifida children and their parents: A population prone to family dysfunction. *Journal of Pediatric Psychology, 11,* 359–373.

Stein, T. (1983). Recreation and persons with physical disabilities. In T. Stein and H. Sessoms (Eds.), *Recreation and special populations.* Boston: Allyn and Bacon.

Stewart, J.C. (1986). *Counseling parents of Exceptional Children, 2nd Edition.* Columbus: Charles E. Merrill.

Turnbull, A. & Turnbull, R. (1986). *Families, professional and exceptionality—A special partnership.* Columbus: Charles E. Merrill.

Wehman, P. (1979). *Recreational programming for the developmentally disabled persons.* Baltimore: University Park Press.

Chapter 10

THE GOAL OF LEISURE WITHIN THE SCHOOLS AND THE COMMUNITY

Aubrey H. Fine

All our dreams can come true
if we have the courage to pursue them.
Walt Disney

It has long been said that children are our most valuable resource. Today's youngsters will shape tomorrow's society. However, we are not presently harvesting our young people to meet the challenge of the future. The problem lies in the fact that while our patterns of work and leisure are changing, attitudes are not. Thus, archaic values become the legacy that is passed on to future generations. If filling gaps of free time is difficult under the present value system, it will necessarily become much harder in the future. It becomes imperative to teach children about the importance of leisure. Furthermore, we need to help children understand the relationship between work and play so they can gain an appreciation of both dimensions.

The nation's schools have been given the responsibility of educating children . . . more specifically, to educate them for work. Indeed, children have been indoctrinated to believe that success in school is necessarily tied to success at work. These same children will someday face the reality of fewer jobs and shorter working hours, and they will not be prepared for such a situation. Since the school system has been charged with educating our children, it appears that they need to recognize that there is more to preparation than just academic learning! Brightbill and Mobley (1977) stress that the ultimate test of our education system will pertain to its effectiveness in assisting students so they will have a well-balanced emotional and intellectual life that includes leisure participation.

Education within our schools must place far more emphasis on all aspects of preparation towards life rather than just education for work. Furthermore, education should prepare all of us for complete living (Brightbill and Mobley, 1977). The task of teachers should not be to cram knowledge into young minds but, rather, to cultivate potential and the thirst for the pursuit of knowledge.

There are many aspects of education, ranging from liberal, historical, scientific, physical, religious to vocational. All aspects of the education process are helpful in developing the complete person. Each element of learning is critical in building the well-rounded person. However, to this date, there is little evidence to suggest we are efficiently prepared (through education) to apply leisure in socially viable ways (Brightbill and Mobley, 1977).

When focusing specifically on exceptional children, there are several variables that must be incorporated. We believe that it is imperative to accept the position that leisure skill training should be incorporated within the special educational services. Bender, Brannan and Verhoven (1984) concur with the point of view that there is increased acceptance by educators that relevant education must extend beyond the contrived environment of the classroom. Many disabled persons are faced, when compared with others, with a disproportionately large amount of leisure time.

If children do not acquire the skills necessary to utilize leisure time, then the problem will be compounded as they become teenagers and then adults. One neglected area in the life of a teenager with a disability is recreation and socialization (Ayrault, 1974). My co-author (Nya) had the opportunity to work with two children with Down's syndrome at an early age. She had the unique privilege of watching these children grow up. As young children, there were many adults and older children who gave them a lot of attention. Many people played with them because they thought they were cute. However, as they aged, their child-like behaviors were not appreciated by many. As some would say, the sad part about the kitten is that one day it becomes a cat. Unfortunately, although the interactions began to cease, this did not eliminate the need for interaction and social recreational experiences.

This chapter is designed to orient the reader to the value of leisure instruction within the schools and how it can be incorporated. Barriers, both psychological and physical, will also be incorporated to give a global presentation of what may influence a child's leisure involvement.

Furthermore, attention will be given discussing the variables of leisure guidance (counseling and education) and how we must help the field of education recognize the importance of leisure time.

THE GOAL OF LEISURE
INSTRUCTION IN EDUCATION

The goal of leisure instruction, based on Gerson's leisure-educated adult, for exceptional children is to expose the student to a whole reservoir of different activities that are adaptable and pertinent to different situations and environments. The students should be encouraged to include some activity daily, to have at their disposal activities that can be conducted either alone or with others, and activities that involve active participation as well as being a spectator.

Each person in partnership with the student (parents, teachers, therapists) should respect the rights of a student to reject a particular activity and to respect the rights of others to indulge in activities they may not enjoy.

Through this process, the student should learn activities that will continue throughout a lifetime. When proper leisure guidance occurs, the inherent feelings of identity and self-worth carry over to the educational process and facilitate learning. Scholars stress that play and leisure involvement are an important part of the maturation process. In fact, some believe that the play act is a function of the ego, an attempt to bring into synchronization the bodily and social processes.

Leisure Instruction for the Severely Disabled

We recognize that there are curriculum differences between objectives formulated for the severely handicapped in comparison to students who happen to be more mildly disabled. Nevertheless, the importance of recreational skill acquisition is important for all.

In programs for the severely handicapped, less emphasis is typically placed on traditional academic skills and more attention is given to activities of daily living and functional development. Falvey (1986) has suggested that traditional curricula for students with severe handicaps have often included activities within the leisure domain. Recreation incorporates a set of activities that most nondisabled people engage in.

Consequently, providing children who happen to be disabled with the opportunities to develop a repertoire of skills is a normalizing experience.

However, it is equally as critical to recognize that individuals who are higher functioning would also benefit from training in areas that will assist in their adaptive living. Independent living (or the least restrictive alternative) and quality of life should be a prime concern in the total education of all children (Fine, Welch-Burke, Fondario, 1985). Developing self-satisfying recreational pursuits assists all children in avoiding dead time. In other words, recreation involvement can fill in free time and help an individual feel productive (Falvey, 1986).

Furthermore, it is important to recognize that all people have an enormous amount of time outside their obligations (work, school, etc.). Professionals must accept the responsibility of providing guidance so children can develop inventories of skills that will be utilized in their avocational pursuits. This appears to be of utmost concern. Too many exceptional children and adults do not utilize their free time effectively (Fine, 1982). Fine has noted that many children appear to lack the awareness, skills, and the internal drive to secure their desires. Many become passive recipients to whatever they are subjected. Unfortunately, for some, their homes become their asylums or jails, and their guardians their jailers. A couple of examples can illustrate this point of view.

I have worked with many parents who have felt trapped and frustrated. These parents were discouraged because they could not understand why their child did not appear willing to try and get involved in outside play pursuits. Although some of their children have developed partial skills and desired friendships, they appeared to lack the confidence and/or the drive to self-initiate the activity. This same dilemma appears to be evident in many sheltered activities for young adults who happen to be mentally retarded. Parents are overheard saying how dejected they were to observe their child sitting home idly, when activities were not planned for them. What has developed for many of these individuals is they tend to only get involved in activities when others structure the outcome. Although their involvement was enjoyable, we have not taught our children to make the necessary choices to self-select their leisure interests. As can be seen, the professional community should not only be investing energies in merely teaching or providing recreational programs but how and where individuals can utilize them. Within our schools, educators must spend time sensitizing individuals to the ultimate amount of resources that can be utilized.

RECREATION THERAPY WITHIN THE SCHOOLS

As previously stated, schools should have a great impact on encouraging recreational skill acquisition. Throughout the book, we have strongly advocated the development of leisure skills and the therapeutic application of recreational activities. The same premise holds true within the schools. Activities can be applied for their therapeutic benefits. Recreation can be considered as an intriguing, ubiquitous, and a developmentally significant phenomenon. Gottfried (1986) underlines this concept by indicating that play contributes to and reflects many aspects of psychological development. It should not be surprising that play should be taken advantage of for its inherent practical implications. It is an accepted fact that curricula in early childhood education has a strong emphasis on learning through play. This rationale needs to be considered within the elementary and secondary educational pursuits of children, including those persons who happen to be disabled.

Collaboration must occur between the community recreational therapist and the educational system. Previously, not enough co-active adventures have been initiated. It is imperative that those in leadership roles within special education are provided with the insight on how and why recreation should be incorporated within the schools. This should then be followed with an analysis on how this alternative of instruction will be funded, instructed, and incorporated. Although we would strongly advocate that recreational therapists be hired by the school districts to perform these duties, we believe that this will not occur in the immediate future. Consequently, energies need to be focused on helping educators develop the necessary skills to incorporate the application of recreation within the classrooms, or at least to hire recreation personnel as consultants. Realistically, community-based therapeutic recreators could have a significant role in this process. They could cooperate with schools to assist in educating for leisure (as well as how to apply recreational therapy principles in the classroom). Creative cost-sharing procedures could be developed at the local levels to assist in the funding of these programs.

RECREATION PROGRAMS FOR
THE SEVERELY HANDICAPPED

As indicated earlier, for children who are severely handicapped, recreational provisions should be incorporated for critical skill development. These activities, whenever possible, should be incorporated with the mainstream population. We have met many parents who are very frustrated with their child's segregated education program. Of primary concern is the lack of friendships the children have developed with neighborhood peers. This lack of peer interaction causes many of the children to become social outcasts. Recreational opportunities can be viewed as an avenue to promote friendships between children. If we were capable of providing leisure education within the schools, we would be helping children cope with the realities of excess time. Too many of our children today are dependent on external resources for their entertainment. In a recent report, Chance and Fischman (1987) surveyed children's involvement in the noted top ten activities listed for specific developmental age groups. On the whole, watching television was listed as the recreational activity in which the most time was spent (even more than informal play). Unfortunately, we have created television addicts. Qualitatively, it is only appropriate to suggest other recreational alternatives be taught to children so they do not get hooked on TV as their major source of avocation.

GUIDELINES AND CONCERNS FOR ENHANCING COMMUNITY LEISURE PARTICIPATION

It is critical to recognize that for community participation to occur, plans need to be made to assist children in accessing their opportunities. The following section addresses many variables which Fine (1994, and in press) noted as critical dimensions that need to be addressed both by the professional community as well as parents.

Integration

Integrative options and activities conducted in the least restrictive environment are now more than ever the accepted direction in the field of developmental disabilities. The position of integrative experiences is also strongly supported in the field of leisure/recreation. Nevertheless, there still exists a tremendous gap between this theory and philosophy versus the actual practice. However, integrative leisure experiences conducted in the least restrictive environment are now more than ever the accepted direction. Fine (1994) suggested that the position of integrative experiences is also strongly supported in the field of leisure/recreation.

Leisure and recreational experiences need to be conducted in the most natural living environment. For too long, the professional community has debated how to prepare for integration. For some, this meant that the participant was involved in quasi-integrated activities, but in most cases the experiences left a lot to be desired. There has been a proliferation of writing documenting the importance of integrated leisure experiences (Howe-Murphy and Charboneau, 1987; Knapczyk and Yoppi, 1975; Datillio, 1991; and Huthinson and Lord, 1979). It is not the author's intent to add any more to the arguments but rather to suggest that attention be given to how we make the process of integration more natural and pleasant for all those involved. It is vital that practitioners promote within the community the vitality of integration so that citizens and others involved with providing opportunities will have a better understanding of why this is being done.

Networking and collaboration is now being conducted nationally as a best practice in encouraging cooperation between various service providers. Traditional venues of recreation activities are now taking advantage of so many other community resources to safeguard more optimal leisure opportunities for all citizens. In doing so, the availability of a wider variety of leisure and recreational options can be more of a reality. In addition, the means to support the training and practice of applying leisure lifestyles can be distributed to more concerned parties (e.g., educators, social workers, parents, and lay personnel). This logically should broaden the scope of services and make them more efficient (Fine, in press).

It is vital that practitioners promote within the community the vitality of integration so that citizens and others involved with providing opportunities will have a better understanding of why this must be done. Too often, many lay individuals are skeptical of integrated opportunities because some are uncomfortable with the unknown. As a consequence, some might avoid the experiences or make others uncomfortable with their attitudes. In response to these behaviors, we must make a strong effort to educate the community as a whole to decrease the insensitivity and bias in regards to citizens with disabilities.

Implementing a Circle of Support to Enhance Integration

Additionally, for integration to occur smoothly, emphasis must be given on developing augmented natural supports in the community. The concept of developing a functional Circle of Support makes remarkable sense when assisting children with developmental disabilities in applying their leisure lifestyle. For genuine opportunities to become a reality, energy must be invested to provide an easier course for transition. Utilizing leisure coaches as well as family members and friends requires stronger consideration. These individuals can act as a conduit to promote successful early experiences. If coaches are taught well, they will eventually create opportunities where the individual him/herself will fit in more naturally.

It should be understood that the concept of **Circle of Support** represents the combination of the verification of the support personnel and services needed, the identification of the function and purpose of the services as well as the intensities of supports necessary for the outcome to occur. The American Association on Mental Retardation (1992) presents a thorough explanation of this concept. It defines the **support resources** as the individuals (e.g., family and friends, nonpaid support individuals, generic and specialized services) who could be utilized to assist the person in accessing the desired community activities. The dimension classified as the **support function** identifies the area in which the support resources will be applied (e.g., befriending, in-home living assistance, behavioral assistance). Finally, the specific supports-outcome model also recognizes the fact that some individuals will be in need of various degrees of support (e.g., intermittent, limited, extensive, and pervasive) to access the desired lifestyle or opportunity. This dimension is known as the **intensities of supports.** Fine (1994) points out that the concept of developing a functional Circle of Support makes remarkable sense when assisting persons with disabilities in applying their leisure lifestyle. At times, just having a friend or a family member assist an individual in getting to an activity may be all that is needed. In other cases, the need for more extensive supports may be more necessary (e.g., leisure coaches). It behooves the professional community to not undervalue this important resource. For genuine opportunities to become a reality, energy must be invested to provide an easier course for transition. Moreover, the concept of circles of support must also be viewed developmentally. At different eras in an individual's life, these resources may have more important value.

Developing Age Appropriate Leisure Options

Fine (1991) emphasized the importance of instructing age appropriate leisure skills as a primary goal of instruction. In addition, Fine (1991) also suggested the teaching of recreational/leisure skills which are environmentally adaptable. In early development, concentration should not only be given to fundamental skill development but in addition helping the child form a repertoire of skills which are as consistent to his/her mainstream peers. As the child ages, if the gap stays consistently modest, it will be easier and more natural for the youngster to integrate within community activities. The writer also suggests that although individual determination and choices are critical, it is also very important to help the individual to develop skills in areas which can generalize easily into everyday living. Selecting activities which are ecologically sound, in the long run, will aid a participant in more simply applying his/her repertoire of skills more naturally. To illustrate this contention, a comparison will be made to financial investing. When investing in stocks and commodities, it is easier to sell stocks which are more mainstream. The profit margin may not be as large, but the lack of major risk may be compensated by the fact that the commodities are easier to convert. The same notion holds true with helping guide an individual to develop interests which are more socially acceptable. Dattillo and Schleien (1994) strongly encourage that practitioners should assist participants in understanding the implications of their choices. Whenever possible, one should try and help a consumer redefine skills which may be age inappropriate and attempt to develop similar interests in activities which are more sound but similar. Again, this will help in the quest for successful integrative experiences.

The Pursuit of Lifelong Friendships

Lastly, for true integration to become a reality, practitioners must continue to give attention to improving the likelihood that children with disabilities will have more long-lasting and realistic friendships. As indicated earlier, one of the greatest challenges for persons with disabilities in general is the emergence of possible isolation and loneliness. These two elements are easily explained but have tremendous human implications. Although being independent has its merits, a life spent alone is a dreadful human tragedy.

Amado (1993) points out that some individuals with disabilities have very limited social networks and very few friends. He goes on to explain that loneliness within people with disabilities might be contributing to their health problems, moods, and overall behavior. One of the greatest challenges for adults with disabilities is the emergence of possible isolation and loneliness. These two elements are easily explained but have tremendous human implications.

Aristotle was quoted as indicating that friendship is a thing most necessary to life, since without friends, no one would choose to live, though possessed of all other advantages. A human life is shallow without the friendships that can be shared and the joyful experiences which make it meaningful. A well-rounded lifestyle which includes active leisure participation will issue tremendous joy to daily living because one has something to look forward to. A major problem in adulthood is the probable decline of the various options within the social support system that were made more available in childhood. This natural decline is unfortunate and may not have to occur. Nevertheless, as a consequence, adults are sometimes at a loss, and their integrative experiences celebrated in childhood are more limited. Strong attention must be given so that this momentum doesn't discontinue.

The professional community must give credence to this position to ensure lifelong quality living. Too often, the friendships of childhood are merely associations. Not enough has been done to really help children with mental retardation to refine some of the inherent social behaviors which lead to developing and sustaining true friendships. As children age, there are new barriers that develop which possibly discriminate against their active acceptance. Energies must be ongoing to fight the widening of the discrepancy in social competence so that as children age they will not regress even further.

Amado (1993) highlights the fact that working on friendship must be a priority with citizens with disabilities. He suggests that supporting friendships and building on a sense of involvement can realign and enhance the lives of many individuals. The professional community must give credence to this position to ensure lifelong quality living. Too often the friendships of childhood are merely associations. Not enough has been done to really help children to refine some of the inherent social behaviors which lead to developing and sustaining true friendships. As children age, there are new barriers which develop. These restraints possibly discriminate against their active acceptance.

The area of social behavior and social competence goes implicitly with adjustment in cooperative leisure adventures. By cultivating more prosocial skills and competence in leisure abilities, persons with disabilities will potentially fit in easier and more comfortably. Novak-Amado (1993) suggests many alternatives that can be utilized in assisting individuals in securing community connections. Attention was also given to four main categories of approaches which were identified in a report prepared by the Allan Roeher Institute in Toronto in 1990. The categories consisted of many ideas including using social networks and "Circles" to build friends, as well as encouraging one to one matching to get people started in becoming more comfortable with the community as a whole.

Self-Initiated Leisure Choices

Fine (1994) strongly argued that for leisure to be practiced more naturally, the behaviors must be self-initiated. A problem that is frequently discussed in regards to children and adults is that they often have the time but do not seem to have the drive to initiate the opportunities. What has developed for many of these individuals is they tend to get involved in activities when others structure the outcome. Although their involvement was enjoyable, emphasis on teaching how to make the necessary choices to self-select their leisure interests has been given little attention. It must be understood that the professional community should not only be investing energies in merely teaching or providing recreational programs but in addition spending the necessary time to teach and demonstrate where and how individuals can utilize them independently (Fine, 1994).

Practitioners must give attention to programming which not only reflects an emphasis on activity involvement, but in addition also attempts to enhance the individual's perceived competence toward a leisure lifestyle. Practitioners must also focus on educating these individuals on how to apply leisure in their lives.

The goal of leisure instruction should be to expose the individual to a whole reservoir of different activities that are adaptable and pertinent to different situations and environments. Iso-ahola (1980) strenuously points out that one must educate and train persons with disabilities on how to apply their leisure and recognize and appreciate its benefits.

Gerson, Ibrahim, deVries, Eisen, and Lollar (1992) utilize the term "leisure educated adult" as an expression to explain an individual who has a well balanced leisure lifestyle. Gerson et al. suggest that a leisure educated individual needs to have diversified interests and should be able to participate in leisure activities both individually as well as with others. Gerson and his fellow authors go on to explain that the process of developing a positive leisure lifestyle is the development of a frame of mind that recognizes leisure as distinctly different than just free time. This frame of mind develops chronologically and is impacted by many factors, such as the living environment, the individual's age, interests, physical ability, social maturity, and intellectual capacity.

A lifestyle enriched individual should be capable of engaging in activities which allow for active participation as well as observation. In this manner, an individual can participate in diverse options. Furthermore, an individual's interests should be expanded to include both interests in active as well as passive activities. It is also important to point out that knowledge of a full range of activities to meet one's needs in distinct situations and unique environments is extremely essential. This point suggests that an individual should be able to engage in activities that are individually enjoyable and that can be shared with a variety of people from the individual's circle of family and friends.

The philosophy of preparing for a life which includes leisure should be no different for persons with disabilities. What definitely needs to occur is an overt recognition that the ability and desire to engage in satisfying leisure activities is critical for all individuals. Furthermore, the position also acknowledges the importance of early preparation for independent leisure functioning. It recognizes that if we anticipate that adults will be able to optimally function independently, emphasis must be given to assist children to developmentally master this process. When this position is recognized and accepted by the individuals, their family and other members of their circle of support, the momentum of integrating leisure experiences evenly within the individuals' daily life will occur even more naturally. A life that is empty of quality social experiences may be safe but will be extremely limited.

It is imperative that attention be given by researchers in the future to investigate how perceived competence and freedom in leisure contributes to overall quality in life. Furthermore, researchers should make a serious effort to study the value and benefits of establishing **circle of supports** and their overall contribution to optimal leisure lifestyles. This futuristic conviction of leisure will most definitely value leisure and recreation experiences for their own merit. The primary research trends of the 1980s (while addressing leisure and citizens with disabilities) focused strongly on the therapeutic by-products which leisure/recreation activities contributed. Nevertheless, it is the opinion of this author that there has been a tremendous shift in viewing the value of leisure experiences. A major element in the shift change has been the global acceptance of the importance of securing rich and quality lifestyles for all citizens. It is definitely apparent that researchers and clinicians from diverse academic orientations are sincerely recognizing that recreation and leisure experiences fill a significant void in the lives of many individuals.

BARRIERS TO RECREATIONAL INVOLVEMENT

Psychological Barriers

While in London, England, I had the most extraordinary experience. I had a chance to see a play about a legendary train race in which the fastest trains from around the globe competed in this most prestigious event. There is Electra (the most technically advanced), Diesel (strong and powerful) and even Rusty the Steam Engine. When the rest of the competitors heard of Rusty's registration, they all were amused. They laughed and encouraged Rusty to reconsider. Rusty, however, informed them of his full intention to participate. He believed he was going to be successful because the Starlight Express was going to help him.

Within this imaginary world of trains, the Starlight Express is like a fairy train-mother. If you call to her loud enough, she may grant you your wishes. Rusty, over the entire year, had called upon Starlight to give him strength to compete. Unfortunately, he did not have confidence in his own abilities and was basing his probability for success on the help of others.

Rusty entered the first heat against many competitors, hoping that Starlight Express would grant him his wishes. Inauspiciously, several of the other competitors responded very angrily to his participation and indicated their displeasure with him. Others found his enrollment amusing and just laughed. They told him how outdated he was and how he did not have a chance against the more advanced trains. However, he did not let their kidding bother him. He lined up with the rest of the pack and the race began.

Nevertheless, Rusty could not live up to his pre-race enthusiasm. He could not compete with the internal strength that he needed to win. As a consequence, Rusty had a miserable experience. Immediately after he crossed the finish line, he was greeted by his disenchanted Dad. Rusty explained to his father that he was outdated and without Starlight's assistance, he could not win. His Dad seemed a little puzzled by this remark and told his son he would show him that steam was still good.

The next morning, his Dad entered the final preliminary race. To the surprise of everybody, he was a good competitor and won. However, since he did not **train** for the event, he physically was not prepared for the abuse his body had accepted. As a result, he did not feel that he could get ready for the final, which would be held on the next day. He asked his son to take his place. Rusty reluctantly accepted, but doubted his ability to succeed. This angered his Dad, who immediately snapped and told his son that the Starlight Express was really a figment of his imagination, a folklore. He went on to explain to his son that it was critical that he thought well enough about himself to succeed. He also attempted to instill within Rusty the courage he needed to be a competitor, an individual who was driven. Rusty respectfully listened to his father, and although he respected his input, he still had self-doubt about his skills.

That evening, in a dream, he heard the voice of the Starlight Express. She told him many things, but one statement seemed to have the greatest impact. I quote:

> . . . Only you have the power within you. Just believe in yourself, the sea will part before you. Stop the rain, turn the tide. If only you use the power within you, you needn't beg the world to turn around and help you. If you draw on what you have within you somewhere deep inside. . . . You are the starlight.

That next morning Rusty competed and won; a perfect ending for a fairy tale.

The synopsis you have just read is from the play, entitled **Starlight Express,** produced by Andrew Lloyd Weber. The play is now being presented in both London and Broadway. As I became enthralled with the production, I began to see beyond all of the interesting props. In fact, all I saw were children, similar to those who I had served who perceived themselves as being inadequate. These were the outcasts of our society, who unfortunately did not value themselves for their assets. As a consequence of their disabilities, society has made some of them feel different and incompetent. This is one of the most devastating tragedies that can influence a person. A famous quote by Goethe captures the significance of this outcome: "The greatest evil that can befall man is that he should come to think evil of himself."

Learned Helplessness

One of the most intriguing and important concepts developed in the field of social psychology is the syndrome of learned helplessness. This syndrome was classified by Seligman (1975) and his associates. Helplessness results when a person expects that the important events in his/her life are independent of his/her own responding. In essence, when the things that matter to a person are felt to be (or truly are) beyond that person's control, then she/he becomes a victim of learned helplessness.

It is easy to recognize how children with disabilities develop this sense of incompetence, which afterwards causes them to live more sheltered lives and become passive recipients of whatever their environment provides. Many scholars have suggested that individuals who have low estimates of their own ability to influence the outcomes of their performance are likely to perform incompetently.

Such feelings may or precipitate further problems, especially in response to daily failure experiences. Table 19 illustrates some of the potential hardships that children may encounter when they experience personal failure. What learned helplessness may indirectly cause is an increased probability of avoiding situations where there is a high possibility of failure. Children eventually attribute their failures to what they perceive as their own inadequacies.

Table 19. Implications of Learned Helplessness and Perceived Competence.

Able to cope	*Unable to cope*
Adapt	Adapt
↓	↓
Adjust	Adjust
↓	↓
Produces Maturity	Produces persistent anger
↓	↓
Increased probability of achievement behavior	Development of severe frustration
↓	↓
Augmented pride and enhancement of self-esteem	Higher probability of failure
↓	
Higher probability of success	

Acknowledgment is given to Doctor C. Papazian for allowing the author to adapt his unpublished model to include in this manuscript.

The first studies by Seligman were conducted with dogs. The animals were given unavoidable shock. The end result was that the animals became passive recipients of the aversive stimulation. They did not even try to avoid the shock, because they did not feel they had the power. In essence, the animals learned they had no control! This pilot research has generated significant insight into understanding individuals who feel they are inadequate. Individuals with any degree of learned helplessness lower their expectations for future success and attempt avoidance. This avoidance is initiated to offset future encounters with failure. In essence, it is clear that failure at a task eventually induces deficits in subsequent encounters. The sense of helplessness develops from an awareness of an inability to succeed in spite of trying and expecting to succeed.

It is probable that individuals take the most pride in those accomplishments that they attribute to be within their own abilities and efforts. Gottfried (1986) suggests that children play to experience control over their environment. Bandura (1978) found that most children were successful when they measured their behavior against personal standards of what constitutes a worthy performance. One of the key issues in developing a sense of helplessness pertains to the degree of locus of control.

Locus of Control

The theory of locus of control was developed by social learning theorists. Locus of control can be understood as a child's perception of who or what is responsible for one's success or failure in a particular area. Internal versus external locus of control pertains to the degree to which an individual feels that his/her outcomes are contingent upon his/her actions. Children who are oriented towards internal locus of control are those who perceive themselves as primarily responsible for their successes and failures. These are children who feel they are in control of their reinforcements. The opposite is true for children who feel their outcomes to be independent of their responses. This is classified as external locus of control. According to Weiner (1985), locus of control refers to a belief that a response will or will not influence the acquisition of a reinforcement. Locus of control, in essence, is a problem-solving expectancy that addresses whether behaviors are perceived as instrumental in obtaining the desired behavioral goal. Deci and Ryan (1985) state that locus of control refers to whether outcomes are believed to be contingent on one's behavior. They contrast this theory with locus of causality by suggesting that the locus of causality is concerned with why a person behaves as she or he does.

Weiner (1972) applies different terminology to explain causality. Attribution theorists investigate persons' perceptions of causes. Usually, the allocation of responsibility influences subsequent behaviors. In his recent writings, Weiner (1985) suggests that causes are identified on the basis of several factors, including such variables as specific informational cues (i.e. history of past successes or failures, patterns of performance), causal preferences, reinforcement history, and feedback from others. For example, a person who attributes playing a game to his/her performing inadequately will be a person who will probably not be motivated to play in future similar activities. Many who have investigated this process recognize the positive correlation between learning and performance. Dixon (1979) prepared an excellent document synthesizing the implications of this theory and participation in recreational therapy. The major impetus of the paper suggested that a better understanding of attribution theory (and the other theories noted within this section) would assist professionals in developing more efficient intervention techniques.

The literature suggests a positive correlation between internal locus of control and achievement in most areas. Those who believe that they are in control of their outcomes have a greater chance of being successful. Specifically in regards to the disabled population, there have been many researchers who have suggested that persons with disabilities have a higher expectancy of failure than those who are able-bodied. Studies by MacMillian (1969) and MacMillian and Knopf (1971) have tested situations where children were prevented from completing several tasks. Ironically, most of these children blamed themselves for not completing the tasks. Results of many studies suggest that many children who are disabled are external only in relation to success ("It was a fluke," or "They let me do well because they felt sorry for me"). Unfortunately, these same children consistently accept responsibility for failure but not for success. Many are likely to ascribe their success to whims of luck (Gibson, 1980). Weisz (1982) points out that in regards to mental retardation, the child's life may be something of a macrocosm of helplessness, in that it involves repeated exposure to failure. In many cases, persons with disabilities appear unlikely to accuse controllable factors for insufficient effort. Instead, they appear to see their failure as resulting from the stable uncontrollable factor of low ability. Finally, it is important to note how labels, such as learning disabilities, physical disabilities, mental retardation, and special education, affect the functioning of an individual. There is some evidence that such labels may encourage many to expect failure or below-standard achievement. The label may also lower expectations for the child's potential.

Locus of Causality Orientation

Deci (1980) was the first to introduce the concept of causality orientation. He applied the terminology developed in the word of Heider (1958) and DejCharms (1968) and developed three orientations. This work was eventually updated by Deci and Ryan (1985) to incorporate three areas of causality: autonomy, control and impersonal orientation.

Central to the autonomy orientation is the degree of choice that individual has made. Deci and Ryan (1985) state the autonomy orientation involves the tendency to select or interpret initiating and regulatory events as informational and to be associated with intrinsically motivated behaviors and extrinsically motivated behaviors. On the other hand, the control orientation focuses its attention on what controls. One's functioning is primarily based on controls in the environment or internal characteristics. The central element of this orientation is the struggle of being the controller or controlled. Behaviorally, most children and adults seek controlling situations. Furthermore, most individuals seek to conceptualize and understand predisposing controlling factors.

Finally, the impersonal orientation is based on areas where an individual feels incompetent to deal with the challenges of life. To its worst degree, a person may experience a severe degree of learned helplessness.

Being a Risk Taker

An individual's feelings of incompetence and sufficient effort to improve may impede the child's acquisition of developing appropriate functional skills. It appears that many children who feel incompetent lack being risk takers. This seems to occur because society has indirectly taught them that they are inadequate and, for that matter, helpless.

It is apparent that the most successful and independent people are those who are willing to take chances and be risk takers. They are usually people who experience positive responses to their curiosity and are gamblers because the outcomes seem to be worthwhile.

Canfield (1987) suggests that the only way to grow is to take risks and get involved. People have to value themselves as well as see themselves as worthwhile. In essence, a major element to securing and developing a positive self-esteem is the willingness of the individual to take chances.

One way of viewing success in risk-taking people is to recognize that most "risk takers make a habit out of doing uncomfortable things losers will not do" (J. Canfield, personal communication, May 23, 1987).

People who are risk takers gamble by trying to produce a unique outcome to their behaviors. In most cases, people complain about the outcomes in their life. However, we need to realize that we are capable of changes, if we so desire.

Canfield (1986) suggests that we spend too much time on what we have rather than what we do or contribute. He identifies three elements:

1. BE (Context)
2. DO (Process)
3. HAVE (Content)

He suggests that risk takers spend less time addressing the content of their behaviors but invest energies on their context (who you are rather than what you have).

Risk taking represents the feasibility of experiencing failure as well as adverse feelings. However, if one is not willing to embark on new adventures, he/she may never optimally grow. This appears to be a major obstacle facing many children we serve. They are not willing to take chances, because their fear of failure hinders their efforts. In fact, it reduces their drive to seek knowledge. I feel very strongly that all children, disabled and non-disabled, thirst for knowledge, except some may need some assistance to get to the fountain. What we need to do is to help children want to reach out and risk growing up. For example, a young man was being instructed on how to serve in tennis. At one point during the lesson, the instructor told his student to move his racquet back higher when he was to serve. The student immediately snapped and told his teacher he thought he had the racquet high enough. His teacher responded by asking, "How high is high enough?" This is a question we could formulate for most life experiences. We as individuals need to aspire to be the best we can while always appreciating the fact of who we are at a specific time.

There are many variables that influence a person on taking a chance to learn and experience. Figure 17, which was inspired with a conversation with Jack Canfield, graphically represents the basic influence of wanting to take chances (Fine, 1987).

For example, let us use a liking scenario. It appears only logical that an experienced hiker would regulate his/her water intake. Part of the decision would be based upon availability. Consequently, a hiker who had a larger reservoir of water would drink more liberally on the excursion. The figure basically describes this position. Risk takers tend to be people who have a larger reservoir of successful experiences. They are individuals who are willing to take chances, because they can afford failure (i.e., more water to drink). Those who repeatedly experience failure appear to become passive and conservative in taking chances (their glasses are empty in regards to obtaining success).

The Difficulty of being a Risk Taker

The   vs.   The
Empty   Full
Glass   Glass

Figure 17.

The following poem portrays the dilemma that we have tried to formulate in this section. The dilemma represents an overshadowing problem that many children with disabilities face: the willingness to take risks.

RISKS

To laugh is—to risk appearing the fool.
To weep is—to risk appearing sentimental.
To reach out for another is—to risk involvement.
To expose feelings is—to risk exposing your true self.
To place your ideas, your dreams before the crowd is—to risk their loss.
To love is—to risk not being loved in return.
To live is—to risk dying.
To hope is—to risk despair.

To try is—to risk failure.
But risks must be taken, because the greatest hazard in life is to risk nothing. The person who risks nothing, does nothing, has nothing, and is nothing. He may avoid suffering and sorrow, but he simply cannot learn, feel, change, grow, love—live. Chained by his certitudes, he is a slave, he had forfeited freedom. Only a person who risks is free. (Author unknown)

Implications

In regards to leisure education, we need to help children recognize their competencies so they will be willing to take a chance. Merely exposing children to activities and encouraging their involvement will not be enough to stimulate self-initiation. Children must feel a sense of competency if they are willing to risk failure. Parents and teachers must help children develop a more realistic acceptance of abilities and develop a more positive internal locus of control. This can initially be accomplished by selecting activities that will allow for success. When programming, one should take advantage of children's abilities and develop activities that highlight their strengths rather than their limitations. This will eventually give these children the internal confidence to take risks while engaging in activities which they are less adequate at. We should also teach and motivate children to have greater control over self-generated effort, so they can begin to believe that their own effort influences their ability to perform in other contexts.

Whenever possible and the conditions are appropriate, we should attempt to encourage intrinsic motivation as the primary driving force. Research reported by Deci and Ryan (1985) suggests that when the conditions are right, student's learning, particularly conceptual learning and creative thinking, are more dramatically increased when facilitated by intrinsic motivation rather than being fostered by extrinsically rewarded learning. Holt (1964), an outspoken critic of education and how we fail children, condemns the usage of extrinsic rewards to encourage growth. He states: "We destroy the love of learning in children by encouraging and compelling them to work for petty and contemptible rewards; gold stars, or papers marked 100 on the walls . . . " (p. 168). These perceptions are also espoused by other noted educators such as Montessori (1967) and Neil (1960). Montessori suggested that rewards are not necessary and are at times even harmful. The writer would concur with her position but points out that with some children, one may have to initially incorporate the application of reinforcers. As discussed in Appendix II on behavior management, it is critical to select the appropriate strategies that are least restrictive in nature. The ultimate goal for any child is to have them **self-actualize,** a term suggesting internal controls. However, we realize that this will never be possible with all children.

We also should be focusing some of our energies to help children overcome their dysfunctional reaction to failure. We should help children interpret failure as feedback, an indication that more information is needed. We also must assist individuals on focusing attention on effort rather than blaming it on personal ability.

Seligman (1975) suggests that behavioral immunization ought to be started in childhood, so children can develop feelings of personal control. The child can learn to establish realistic personal goals and expectations. This should not be misunderstood as placing ceilings on attributions. Rather, the effort is made to help children realistically understand their strengths and limitations. Not all people will be able to climb to the tops of mountains, but attempts are just as important. Bob Weiland, a disabled athlete, has recently been the subject of an enormous amount of press for completing the New York and Los Angeles Marathons by walking the entire race on his hands. At a recent lecture at the California State Polytechnic University, he stated, "Success is never based on where you start, but where you finish." We must help individuals aspire but be careful and not support the cultivation of unrealistic goals. Although the example of Rusty is beautiful, not all people will win the race. It is, however, equally important to appreciate the endeavors. We have to help children recognize their efforts and improvements. Too often we focus on the final accomplishment. By doing so, we ignore all of the ingredients and efforts put into the process. We have to give children reasonable control over their lives and help them experience success. Finally, many children do not know how to react to their failure. Consequently, we should take the time and model to individuals how to react realistically to failure. By taking advantage of modeling, we will begin to assist children to use feedback as information. We should teach children to take advantage and observe those who accept their failures logically. These individuals may become helpful in demonstrating that inadequacies are not always generated because of personal incompetency.

It is imperative to understand that if needed energies are not placed on changing attributions, involvement in independent leisure pursuits will probably not occur. We have to help children see their adequacies, so they will be willing to take chances. Providing recreational experiences within any environment must focus on this issue. Without changing attributions, I definitely do not feel that significant long-lasting effects will be generated. Dixon (1979) and Niles, Ellis, and Witt (1981) suggest some other alternatives that can be utilized in recreation programming to decrease perceived incompetence. The author encourages the readers to review these documents to learn about some other prominent points of view. Furthermore, Weiner (1986) devotes part of a chapter dealing with a review of various procedures that can be utilized to influence dysfunctional attributions. In the document, several primary research studies are identified with the solutions obtained. The reader should find this chapter rich with theoretical information which is combined with useful practical suggestions.

Other Related Environmental Barriers to Leisure Acquisition

There are a variety of other obstacles that naturally influence leisure involvement. Many of the elements pertain to ecological constraints such as accessibility to recreational environments (transportation, proximity of activities, environmental accessibility), financial support, and leisure awareness.

Environmental Barriers

Is there really a conceivable barrier-free environment? What constitutes an accessible environment for one population could possibly make the surroundings inaccessible for another. For example, the modifications made to areas allowing people in wheelchairs free mobility may be oppositional to the needs of persons who utilize walkers or who are visually impaired. Most often, persons with disabilities are forced to take it upon themselves to find resources that allow them full access. However, as we can all appreciate, many venues have not been developed with the disabled community in mind. In most cases, access to the disabled person is given as an afterthought. Psychologically, inaccessible environments send the disabled community an unconscious message to stay out.

Adults with disabilities (especially physical disorders) usually have to develop what is called **environmental cognition.** Since many have experienced segregation due to inaccessibility, they have learned to develop internal maps to help them think through the gaps. Also, unlike most citizens, many persons with disabilities develop lists of resources of areas within their neighborhood that allow them free access. However, the outcome can represent a significant hardship when a surrounding area does not have enough resources providing optimal leisure involvement.

Although buildings are more accessible today to wheelchair users, playgrounds are just beginning to be modified. Parks are designed primarily with only able-bodied children in mind. The equipment is usually surrounded with landscape, which prohibits mobility in a wheelchair. Stairs are usually the only means to gain access to the top of the slide. Simple modifications can be incorporated to alleviate these existing problems.

Natural barriers also place significant hardships on the leisure pursuits of persons with disabilities. Forest trails, beaches, and campsites are often too narrow or have rough terrain. As can be easily seen, although progress is being made, change is slow. Consequently, many children with disabilities will still be impeded by the environment for many years to come. In fact, in the mid-1970s, the Architectural and Transportation Barriers Compliance Board determined that one of the major problems facing the disabled community in regards to recreation was the inaccessability of facilities and transportation (Vellman, 1979). Furthermore, Vellman (1979) reports that one of the reasons we are not seeing the outcomes of progress reached as early as we would like is the failure on behalf of politicians to commit themselves fully to follow through and legislate the change.

Transportation and Financial Restrictions

Transportation to the various sites as well as financial restrictions can also cause barriers to leisure involvement, especially in families with limited funds. Due to some of the special needs a person with a disability may have, families may encounter a greater expense in bringing up their disabled child. Recreation provisions usually are not considered as a priority. As a consequence, if there are not many moderately priced activities (or the child or parents are not aware of these), children may not be enrolled in or taken to a wide range of experiences. Furthermore, some of the accessible or perhaps specialized activities may be a greater distance to the child's home. Therefore, transportation becomes a factor.

Family and Peer Support

All children need to have the opportunity to interact positively with others. Some children with disabilities lead restrictive lives. A major void appears to be in the area of social contemporaries. Furthermore, if a child is in a special school, away from his/her neighborhood, he/she may lack the opportunities to develop local friendships. This lack of exposure may be devastating. Efforts must be initiated to ensure that provisions are established that the child receives sufficient social stimulation. As was discussed earlier in the chapter, the parents' attitude about the child, and their willingness to strive forward, are very important ingredients to encourage independent leisure involvement. Families who are supportive are usually more instrumental in rearing a more independent child.

THE CONTROVERSY OF LEISURE INSTRUCTION

Several terms are often confused by school personnel, parents, and others that delay the integration of leisure guidance within the school. This confusion is especially apparent in dealing with the child with disabilities.

The term **leisure-facilitated instruction** represents a systematic teaching process that will culminate in the students becoming aware of the role of leisure in their life and how leisure contributes to their ability to adapt to their environment. A knowledge of leisure allows a daily, liberal inclusion of leisure into the life-style of the leisure-educated person.

Within the field of therapeutic recreation, there exists a problem in defining the scope of leisure education and leisure counseling. In fact, this controversy appears to have stagnated the growth of this area and has caused some undue stress.

McDowell (1976) reviewed the existing literature and identified three areas that he assumed were under the rubric entitled **leisure counseling.** The first category he classified as **leisure counseling as a leisure resource guidance service.** It is within this category that one assists an individual in matching proposed interests with possible alternatives. McDowell (1976) points out that within this component, no efforts are made to treat the elements that cause unproductive usage of free time. For example, this form of leisure guidance would be helpful if an individual moved to a new geographic area. Potentially, under this domain, a person would be assisted in identifying prospective interests without any attention given to possible underlying barriers.

Leisure counseling as a therapeutic remedial service pertains to an individual's lack of skills relating to leisure involvement. This lack of skills could be due to absence of knowledge or limitations in performing desired leisure activities. Finally, **leisure counseling as a life-style developmental-educational service** focuses on the barriers individually developed that discourage leisure involvement. The problems faced by a workaholic would be best treated by this orientation.

The Leisure Education Component

On the other hand, Mundy and Odum (1979) defined leisure education as a total developmental process through which individuals create an understanding of self, leisure and the relationship of leisure to their own life-styles and the fabric of society. Friedrich Froebel understood that in small children, play was life itself. Joseph Lee, like Maria Montessori, believed play to be a serious educational tool and a part of nature's law of growth. He pointed out that play is purposeful and rooted in a person's desire to produce results. Play at its best is the challenge to creative skills, ingenuity and enthusiastic application to a task and to accomplishment.

Mundy and Odum (1979) identified five integral components in an inclusive leisure education program. Therapeutically, emphasis on these areas depends on the population served and the individual needs. The five components are listed in Table 20.

Applications of Leisure Education Components and Exceptional Children

Mundy and Odum's leisure education process has numerous universal benefits. Although I agree with the elements incorporated, I feel that when working with children who have many limitations and barriers to face, the process of changing their involvement is not a simple procedure of education. Too often, we tend to focus on superficial areas which influence the acquisition of leisure behaviors. As a consequence, our efforts ineffectively influence the prevailing problems.

Secondly, there are some individuals who have difficulty selecting areas of emphasis when developing programs. The two easiest areas to introduce in a curriculum are those that focus on leisure awareness and leisure skill development. I do suggest that these two components are initially focused upon in any leisure education program. Social skills should be an emphasis in any educational pursuit; therefore, aspects of this dimension should always be incorporated.

The areas of self-awareness and decision making appear to be the hardest to develop within children, especially elementary school age. In addition, I strongly suggest waiting to focus on these areas until the child is over the age of nine or ten. Furthermore, when one is working with children who have cognitive impairments, these programmatic domains will be more difficult to focus upon. Even children with mild disabilities (i.e. learning disabilities) may have difficulty focusing specifically on this area. There may have to be other alternatives incorporated to assist children in developing the necessary prerequisite skills. For example, there are social problem-solving programs (i.e. Shure and Spivak, 1976) that attempt to assist children in developing social competence. There are also self-instructional training programs (i.e. Bash and Camp, 1985) that attempt to teach children appropriate strategies to mediate their behavior. Some of these approaches would be valuable additions in providing leisure guidance.

Table 20. Leisure Education Components.

Leisure Awareness. Emphasis within this area is given to assisting the individual in taking information one has about leisure and relating the findings to his/her life situation. It is within this component where an individual is assisted in learning about the vast amount of opportunities available to him/her.

Self-Awareness. Within this component, emphasis is given on encouraging individual understanding, and relating how leisure participation fits a need in one's life.

Decision Making. Within this component, attention is given to developing appropriate problem-solving skills. These skills are promoted to assist in exploring and selecting potential leisure opportunities.

Social Interaction. Within this area, focus is given to the development of appropriate social skills. Well-chosen social behaviors are correlated positively with productive leisure experiences. Consequently, direct and indirect instruction of this area are incorporated within the gestalt of leisure education.

Leisure Skills. Within this final aspect of the continuum, attention is given to assist an individual in identifying and developing the skills necessary to engage in leisure activities. An analysis is conducted assuring compatibility with one's awareness of self and leisure.

The Dilemma

Over the past two decades several have argued about the true nature of leisure consultation (Reynolds and O'Morrow, 1985). A great deal of time has been invested debating the process as well as the terminology applied (leisure counseling or leisure education). Tinsley (1984) suggests that recreators, as a whole, are ill equipped and prepared to deal with the total ramifications of poorly developed leisure behaviors. He cautions that many recreators appear to superficially address leisure problems and attempt to merely treat the apparent, overt leisure dysfunction. All of us can appreciate the complexity of developing leisure behaviors. There are many psychological, financial, environmental as well as health factors that come into play that influence our possible involvement in leisure time. Tinsley (1984) cautions that recreators (in general) might be inadequately prepared to deal with these overwhelming problems. He also strongly argues that one should not call him/herself a counselor if he/she has limited training in counseling. I concur with this point of view and strongly advocate performing within the guidelines of our training.

Furthermore, Edwards (1981), a strong critic of recreators, states:

> [R]ecreators are neither philosophically, socially, or professionally attuned to the requirements of counseling. They must use psychology in their work with others, of course. But they use it to spur others to action rather than self-examination. They are basically action people while counselors are basically contemplative people who emphasize self-awareness (p. 42).

Consequently, there has been a move by some in higher education to develop a specialty area within the field of parks and recreation. Within this area of special concentration, those who are interested can take the added training and academic courses to develop the skills to perform effectively and reliably. Furthermore, there are some professionals such as Hayes (1977) and Fine (1985) who strongly argue that recreators should not feel they are the only professionals competent in treating leisure-developed problems. Therefore, consultation must be done with other disciplines such as psychology, counseling, and education to develop course work within this area.

Fine (1986) has argued that professionally we have expelled too much energy on semantics. We need to become more clear on the scope of our teachings. What matters is that we are capable of articulating what we are competent in performing, and that we are well versed in various strategies. For this reason, I have classified both of these two interventions under the rubric of **leisure guidance.** At times, it may be necessary to utilize verbal facilitation strategies (counseling) to assist an individual in understanding barriers to leisure involvement. On the other hand, we also may want to incorporate some instruction (education) to enhance an understanding as well as the application of activity involvement. These can be initiated in small groups or individually. Furthermore, one can provide services prior to a problem's initiation (prevention) or when it has already been manifested. It should be evident, as indicated in these writings, that it would be preferable for leisure guidance to be initiated prior to the onset of any problems. The literature strongly points out that it is likely that some persons with disabilities will encounter leisure barriers. If these barriers are not removed, it is very probable that some of the individuals will experience significant problems. For this reason, the position for preventive maintenance is highly suggested.

Guidelines for Implementing Leisure Guidance Within the Schools

The inclusion of the leisure guidance within the schools should be carefully administered. The following represents a brief outline of the various elements that need to be focused upon to successfully develop a viable instruction plan.

The recreational therapist or leisure educator should be a member of the school guidance team and provide input through the aforementioned process. The leisure guidance facilitator will provide:

1. An identification of the handicap as it relates to leisure guidance. An evaluation must be conducted, articulating both the child's strengths and limitations. Additionally, a realistic account must be incorporated addressing the accessibility to leisure pursuits.
2. An overview of the student's current level of performance in basic areas that influence recreational participation. Furthermore, an analysis should be incorporated of realistic opportunities where leisure skills can be naturally enhanced within the academic environment.
3. The development of realistic student goals based on current level of performance. The genesis of goals must be defined, with appropriate attention given to a clear plan of action.
4. Instructional objectives should be prepared based on the broader goals. In addition, an evaluation plan must be expatiated so an identification of what is to occur will be established.
5. Attention must be given to the availability of community resources outside of the school setting. Collaboration must be initiated with

the family and community recreators to assure realistic application. Furthermore, an inventory of potential recreational sites and resources should be established to assure appropriate follow-up.

7. The role and function of the primary recreation programmer will have to be examined. Furthermore, a realistic overview of how other educators will apply leisure instruction within the class will also have to be reviewed. At times, the instruction by the leisure guidance specialist will be exclusive. Nevertheless, my initial reaction and perception is that leisure guidance and recreational programming should become an integral component of the educational process. For this reason, I do not feel it should be given special individual attention. If leisure is to be given equal consideration, then it should be just that: a critical domain in the educational training of our students.

SUMMARY

Within this chapter, an overview has been presented addressing some of the variables of incorporating leisure instruction in the education of our children. Perhaps, the change in the proposed new focus pertains to the awareness of educators that they are charged with the responsibility of educating the whole child. Too often, many confuse the purpose of education as being merely preparation for employment. While this may be partially true, the education process is initiated to prepare our young (disabled and able-bodied) for the realities of their life (both at the present time or in the future). This also definitely includes leisure time. We are seeing too many children becoming dependent on others (including television) to provide them with the appropriate sources to secure pleasure. It is unfortunate that many children with disabilities fail to achieve optimal leisure involvement. Some may blame some of the many variables discussed earlier in the chapter. I, too, would concur partially to this assumption. However, I also see the problem being generated by apathy and lack of willingness to accept responsibility. For too long, we have been misled that academy preparation does not incorporate the social domain. We are now becoming more conscious of the fact that this lack of attention can no longer be tolerated. As concerned parents, students and professionals serving children with disabilities, we must become advocates and help inform the educational community in regards to the importance of the leisure domain and the need for educational attention in this area. With appropriate consultation between the fields of recreational therapy and education, we may be able to diminish this present void in our children's education. Consequently, we can help enhance the likelihood of more productive leisure involvement for our youth with disabilities.

Endnote

The author is indebted to the input provided for this chapter by Doctor Gus Gerson, Professor, California State Polytechnic University. Specifically, Doctor Gerson was very helpful with editorial comments. He also prepared some of the information included within the section entitled leisure guidance in the schools.

REFERENCES

Amado, R. (1993). Loneliness: Effects and Implications. In A. Novak-Amado (Ed.), *Friendships and community connections between people with and without developmental disabilities,* 67–84. Baltimore: Paul H. Brookes.

American Association on Mental Retardation. (1992). *Mental retardation: Definition, classification and systems of support.* Washington, DC: American Association on Mental Retardation.

Ayrault, E.W. (1974). *Helping the handicapped teenager mature.* New York: Association Press.

Bandura, A. (1977). *Social learning theory.* Englewood Cliffs, NJ: Prentice-Hall.

Bender, M., Brannan, S., & Verhoven, P. (1984). *Leisure education for the handicapped.* San Diego, CA: College Hill.

Brightbill, C., & Mobley, T. (1977). *Educating for leisure-centered living.* New York: Wiley.

Camp, B., & Bash, M. (1985). *The think aloud.* Champaign, IL: Research Press.

Canfield, J. (1986). *Self-esteem in the classroom.* Pacific Palisades, CA: Self-Esteem Seminars.

Carlson, B., & Ginglend, D. (1968). *Recreation for retarded teenagers and young adults.* New York: Abingdon.

Chance, P., & Fischman, J. (1987). The magic of childhood. *Psychology Today, May,* 48–58.

Datillo, J. & Schleien, S. (1994). Understanding leisure services for individuals with mental retardation. *Mental Retardation, 32,* 53–59.

Datillo, J. (1991). Mental retardation. In D.R. Austin & M.E. Crawford (Eds.), *Therapeutic recreation: An introduction,* 163–188. Englewood Cliffs, NJ: Prentice-Hall.

Deci, E.L. (1980). *The psychology of self-determination.* Lexington, MA: D.C. Health (Lexington Books).

DejCharms, R. (1968). *Personal causation: The internal affective determinants of behavior.* New York: Plenum.

Dixon, J. (1979). The implications of attribution theory for therapeutic recreation service. *Therapeutic Recreation Journal, 8,* 3–11.

Edwards, P.B. (1981). Leisure counseling: Recreators, keep out. *Parks and Recreation Magazine, 16(1),* 106.

Falvey, M. (1986). *Community based curriculum, instructional strategies for students with severe handicaps.* Baltimore: Paul H. Brookes.

Fine, A. (1982). Therapeutic recreation: An aspect of rehabilitation for exceptional children. *The Lively Arts, 4.*

Fine, A. (1985). *Leisure counseling: Implications for individuals with learning disabilities.* Paper presented at the 63rd annual convention of the council for Exceptional Children, Anaheim, CA.

Fine, A., Welch-Burke, C., & Fondario, L.J. (1985). A developmental model for the integration of leisure programming in the education in individuals with mental retardation. *Mental Retardation, 23(6),* 289–296.

Fine, A. (1986). *Children and leisure: Leisure guidance counseling in the schools.* Paper presented at the 38th Annual California and Pacific Southwest Recreation and Parks Conference, Fresno, CA.

Fine, A.H. (1991). *Recreation: Community integration and quality of life.* Paper presented at the 114th Annual Meeting of the American Association on Mental Retardation, Atlanta, Georgia, May 27–31.

Fine, A. (1994). Life, Liberty and Choices: A commentary of leisure's values in life. *Journal on Developmental Disabilities, 3,* 16–28.

Fine, A.H. (in press). Leisure, Living, and Quality of Life. In Rebecca Renwick, Ivan Brown, & Mark Nagler (Eds.), *Quality of life Health Promotion and Rehabilitation: Conceptual Approaches, Issues and Applications.* Beverly Hills, CA: Sage.

Gerson, G., Ibrahim, H., deVries, J., Eisen, G., & Lollar, S. (1992). *Understanding leisure: An interdisciplinary approach.* Dubuque, IA: Kendall-Hunt.

Gibson, B.J. (1980). *An attributional analysis of performance outcomes and the alleviation of learned helplessness on motor performance tasks: A comparative study of educable mentally retarded and nonretarded boys.* Unpublished doctoral dissertation, University of Alberta, Calgary.

Gottfried, A. (1986). *Introduction.* In A. Gottfried and C. Brown (Eds.), *Play interaction: The contribution of play materials and parental involvement to children's development.* Cambridge, MA: Lexington.

Hayes, G.A. (1977). Professional preparation and leisure counseling. *Leisure Today, April,* 14.

Heider, F. (1958). *The psychology of interpersonal relations.* New York: Wiley.

Holt, J. (1964). *How children fail.* New York: Doll.

Howard, W., Darding, J., & Rossett, A. (1979). *Working with the parents of handicapped children.* Columbus, OH: Charles E. Merrill.

Howe-Murphy, R., & Charboneau, B.G. (1987). *Therapeutic recreation intervention: An ecological perspective.* Englewood Cliffs, NJ: Prentice-Hall.

Hutchinson, P., & Lord, J. (1979). *Recreation integration: Issues and alternatives in leisure services and community involvement.* Ottawa, Ontario: Leisurability.

Iso-Ahola, S. (1980). *The psychology of leisure and recreation.* Dubuque, IA: William C. Brown.

Knapczyk, D.R., & Yoppi, J.O. (1975). Development of cooperative and competitive play responses in developmentally disabled children. *American Journal of Mental Deficiency, 80(3),* 245–255.

MacMillian, D.L. (1969). Motivational differences: Cultural-familial retardates versus normal subjects on expectancy for failure. *American Journal of Mental Deficiency, 76,* 185–189.

MacMillian, D.L. & Knopf, E.D. (1971). Effect of instructional set on perceptions of event outcomes by EMR and nonretarded children. *American Journal of Mental Deficiency, 76,* 185–189.

McDowell, C.F. (1976). *Leisure counseling: Selected lifestyle processes.* Eugene, Oregon: University of Oregon, Center of Leisure Studies.

Montessori, M. (1986). *Spontaneous activity in education.* New York: Schocken.

Musselwhite, C.R. (1986). *Adaptive play for special needs for children: Strategies to enhance communication and learning.* San Diego, CA: College Hill.

Neil, A.S. (1960). *Summerhill: A radical approach to child rearing.* New York: Hart.

Niles, S., Ellis, G., & Witt, P. (1982). Attribution scales: Control, competence, intrinsic motivation. In G. Ellis and P. Witt (Eds.), *The leisure diagnostic battery: Background conceptualization and structure.* Texas: North Texas State University.

Novak-Amado, A. (1993). Steps for supporting community connections. In A. Novak-Amado (Ed.), *Friendships and community connections between people with and without developmental disabilities.* (pp. 299–326). Baltimore, MD: Paul H. Brookes.

Reynolds, R., & O'Morrow, G.S. (1985). *Problems, issues and concepts in therapeutic recreation.* Englewood Cliffs, NJ: Prentice-Hall.

Spivak, G., Platt, J.J., & Shure, M. (1976). *The problem-solving approach to adjustment.* San Francisco: Jossey-Bass.

Vellman, R. (1979). Serving physically disabled people. New York: R.R. Bowker.

Wehman, P. (1977). *Helping the mentally retarded acquire play skills.* Springfield, IL: Charles C Thomas.

Wehman, P. (1979). *Recreation programming for developmentally disabled persons.* Baltimore: University Park Press.

Weiner, B. (1972). Attribution theory achievement motivation and the educational process. *Review of Educational Research, 42,* 203–215.

Weiner, B. (1985). *Human motivation.* New York: Springer.

Weiner, B. (1986). *The attributional theory of motivation and emotion.* New York: Springer.

Weisz, J.R. (1982). Learned helplessness and the retarded child. In E. Zigler and D. Balla (Eds.), *Mental retardation: The developmental difference controversy* (pp. 27–39). Newark, NJ: Lawrence Erlbaum.

Chapter 11

FUTURE TRENDS AND CONCLUDING REMARKS

AUBREY H. FINE

Children are the world's most valuable resource and its hope for the future.
John F. Kennedy

One of my favorite and recently acquired hobbies is magic. I became interested solely for professional purposes. As a mental health provider, magic provided me an avenue for enhancing rapport with children. Curiosity is aroused and, in most cases, inhibition is lowered and a comfortable environment is created. Magic is a tremendously creative pursuit (Tarr, 1976). Magicians are always conjuring new ways to do things. They dream up their tricks and write their own script to accompany the act and thus ensure each illusion's success.

Why this introduction to the chapter? My response is simple. If I were a sorcerer, I would be able to tell what the future would be like. My simple illusions, while they have an entertainment value, cannot shed any light on years to come. However, I believe that we can all make educated assumptions of what may occur. We will never know how accurate our predictions will be until time passes. So let us enter the future and peer into what may transpire.

Peering into the immediate future, one may not see marked improvements, partially because we may not see the forest from the trees. Developments are ongoing, incremental, and cumulative. Service provisions for children with disabilities have changed significantly over the past decades. Today, there are more programs more readily available than ever before, and their content is becoming increasingly sophisticated.

Toeffler (1980) noted that in today's fast-paced world, we are presently experiencing overwhelming and rapid changes in our society. How does one respond to and prepare for change? Archaeologists are constantly unearthing the remains of ancient societies that once existed but ultimately vanished because they could not cope with the upheaval of change. What makes a social system, whether it be an entire society or just one component, willing to adapt to the demands of the future? It appears that the most effective systems are flexible, fluid, and willing to take risks. They are also cognizant of the personality of their constituents and strive to recognize what needs must be met to ensure continued viability.

Just like infants and children, productive systems are usually open, curious, and receptive to trying new things. Being prepared for the future entails incorporating a framework where continuous innovation, renewal, and rebirth can occur (Gardner, 1981). How does recreation and the disabled fit into the system? Flexibility to accommodate change means that service providers must be sensitive to the current needs of special populations. So let us begin by first discussing the importance of services being rendered.

IMPORTANCE

Over the past few decades, providing structured-play opportunities for exceptional children has undergone a metamorphosis. While more children are being served in a more efficient manner, services may be limited and inadequate in certain geographic regions. However, progress has been made. Benefits should not only be measured by the quantity of growth but also by the quality of the experiences gained by the children. Children play for the pleasure attained from it. They are not concerned about or even aware of the therapeutic value of their experiences but rather of the quality of their interaction.

PUBLIC AND COMMUNITY EDUCATION

Children with disabilities have long been denied the right to participate in recreation activities. This was partially due to societies' difficulty in understanding and accepting persons with disabilities. The nondisabled have gradually learned to recognize that there are more similarities between them and those with disabilities than there are differences. Nevertheless, while progress has been made, I do not feel that the barriers of handicappism have been totally eliminated. Although studies have been conducted concerning integration, I sometimes wonder if we are promoting more tolerance by society rather than acceptance.

A girl with a birth defect told her dad how frustrated she felt being made to feel so different. At one point in her conversation, she looked helplessly at her father and, with tears in her eyes, she said: "You know, life is not a fairy tale, Dad." Although his daughter had made significant progress, she was still viewed as different and this bothered him very much.

Kenneth Kriegel (1969) discussed his frustrations on the social implications of disability. He recounts a situation in which he engaged in an argument with another boy in his neighborhood. After great verbal abuse, Kriegel finally challenged the boy to a fight. The boy agreed reluctantly. "Fighting a cripple" would not reflect credibly in the neighborhood. True to the obligations of adolescence, he knew that to not accept would be a sign of weakness and sentiment. So the fight began and Kriegel lost. Immediately after the confrontation, he forgot momentarily about his disability. He was able for the shortest time to meet with an individual as an equal. However, his feelings of being ordinary were shattered when he overheard the other boy's mother instructing him to never fight with a "cripple." Kriegel was experiencing discrimination or, in this case, handicappism.

The first step in preparing for the future is to educate today's population to this important segment of society. The population as a whole must be educated to understanding that persons with disabilities are entitled to the same provision of services and rights of access as the rest of us.

Biklen (1985) suggests several principles which logically impact the integration of disabled persons. He proposes that as long as we view integration as an experiment, the process is truly tenuous. Rights must be viewed as constitutionally guaranteed. Pity, compassion, and benevolence foster discrimination.

In our conscious society, it is amazing how few people understand why recreational provisions are just as important for the disabled person. Those involved in the community sector often do not recognize the value of recreational therapy. Some have a limited awareness of the meaning of recreational therapy and are ignorant of the types of services that can be made available. Consequently, these people need to be educated not only in understanding the disabled but, additionally, in becoming familiar with the applications of therapeutic recreation. Recreation therapy is not merely the process of conducting recreational experiences for the disabled; rather, it is the integration of specific content and the application of various processes that cause change to occur.

A poignant story of Eli Wiesel, the 1986 Nobel Peace Prize recipient, comes to mind. Wiesel was the keynote speaker at an annual dinner of 600 survivors of the holocaust in January 1987. At the reception, he shared his insightful perceptions on the struggles of humanity to provide equal access to all its citizens. The audience was moved by an anecdote which captured his feelings. When Wiesel was a student, he once came across a man carrying a bird in a cage. The man was bringing a friend a birthday gift. "Does your friend like birds?" Wiesel asked. "I do not know," replied the man, "but come with me and see what happens." As the man was about to give his friend the gift, the friend asked him to open the cage and set the bird free. The wish was granted, and the man immediately beamed with internal joy. That was his gift. Wiesel went on to explain that there is no greater joy, no greater reward, or act of faith, than setting another creature free or at least promoting its salvation or welfare.

In the introductory chapters of this book, examples illustrated the frustration that some children have encountered in attempting to access their leisure time. For some of these children, their feelings of captivity are similar to the bird in the cage. These are feelings that we hope will be eliminated in the future. The goal is to have a society with an increased knowledge and commitment to change, as well as a spirit to promote equal access so all children will have the freedom to engage in constructive-play opportunities.

DIRECT BENEFITS

It has been suggested from the writings of Crawford and Mendell (1987) that therapeutic recreation can have lifelong benefits to the person with a disability. The experiences can assist in removing road-blocks that prohibit the person's environmental freedom. Probably the most noteworthy accomplishment is therapeutic recreation's ability to facilitate and enhance the quality of life of children with exceptionalities.

Structured free time has allowed children to feel a sense of belonging, in addition to recognizing their accomplishments. Furthermore, with recreation opportunities as an option, children and their families can explore several viable and productive options for the child to engage in. This is extremely important, because it allows the child the freedom of getting involved. It is not uncommon for children to bond with certain programs and stay involved for a long time. In most situations, these programs become an important element of a child's life.

Unfortunately, if many of the previous suggestions are not initiated, especially the assurance of availability of services, the diversity of opportunity may never come into existence. Responsively, we need to investigate how we can make the opportunities available. Logically, community-sponsored activities should be our first choice; however, there are several religious and private organizations who would be willing to expand their services but lack the education of where and how to proceed. To accomplish this goal, we must be forceful in our campaign to educate and advocate. If we do not demonstrate our advocacy roles, we will significantly diminish the opportunity for success. An example will be used to illustrate this point.

I recall Terry Fox, a Canadian, who became an amputee due to cancer. In the early eighties, Terry was one of the first persons with a disability to try and run across a nation. He called his mission "The Marathon of Hope." Others considered his mission as a run of courage to dispel perceptions about the disabled. He ran to raise money for cancer research, but what he actually accomplished was a heightened level of curiosity and possible acceptance towards persons with disabilities. We, too, must enlighten those responsible for creating new opportunities. With their assistance, we then can proceed and develop a multitude of structured recreational alternatives. Advocacy should take place not only at national and state levels but in local cities. Education begins at home. It is here that the actual services are rendered. We must help community members recognize the necessity for developing recreational programs so that all children may have an opportunity.

For too long we have ineffectively utilized our efforts. As rehabilitative professionals, we need to expand our energies in educating our fellow citizens about the disabled person. For too long this area has been neglected. Consequently, although we have placed an enormous amount of energy on the habilitation/rehabilitation process of our clients, our efforts will never be reached unless the rights of persons with disabilities are guaranteed. We must demand that human services be considered a right, not a privilege. Morally, as well as ethically, we should be responsible for promoting this change.

Robert Carkhuff (1982), a noted humanistic psychologist, expresses his dismay and frustration with our civilization with its inability to meet the needs of the children of our universe. Millions of children die each year due to starvation and neglect. Many of us become so engaged with our own hardships that we face that we cannot appreciate the warmth shared through the sounds made by children. He wrote:

> Whatever personal struggles we have, whatever obstacles we must overcome, our concerns are dwarfed by these final consequences of our neglect. Each civilization will be judged by how it treats those of its members who are most vulnerable. We cannot yet call ourselves a civilization. Perhaps we simply cannot hear the music. . . . We only hear the noise. (P. 1.)

Certainly the same joys and sounds of life are elicited by all children, including those who are disabled. We cannot discount their needs simply because they may differ from ours.

Therefore, to assure a barrier-free life-style for exceptional children, we must continue our concentrated advocacy roles. Unfortunately, formalized recreational experiences represent only one facet of growth. Our efforts must also be directed toward ensuring informal experiences at home, within the parks, and on the streets. Within our range of services, we should take it upon ourselves to educate parents on how they can develop a climate within their home that encourages individual and family play experiences. Some parents may feel inadequate in providing these opportunities. Some may not feel they have the time. I suggest that for the time being, we do not worry about how many will carry out these suggestions, but rather concern ourselves with improving the quality of life for those who wish to make the concentrated effort.

CONCLUDING REMARKS

What more can be said? We have provided the reader with our perspectives and ideas for providing recreational and play opportunities for exceptional children. We have provided an overview of the rationale for providing specialized services for the disabled as well as some insight to how this monumental task can be accomplished. We have drawn from personal experiences encountered by both children and their families whom we have worked with. We have attempted to present a balanced picture of both positive and negative situations and outcomes. Some children have been able to receive optimal services, while others have been significantly deprived or underserved. Unfortunately, some of the children who are underserved may reach a ceiling on how much they could gain from existing programs. The intent of this writing was to lift the ceilings and to orchestrate more positive opportunities. Children and their families have been led astray for too long by our unwillingness to assume some responsibility for these consequences. Human beings deserve opportunities to enhance their quality of life. For this reason, we were inspired to write this document.

Of course, good intentions do not always lead to positive results. The growing interest in pediatric recreational therapy will hopefully inspire professionals to develop the unique skills necessary to provide more dynamic and viable services to young persons of special populations. With this comes a stronger need for us to master the strategies and content necessary to intervene and cause change. There are significant differences between working with children versus adults. Furthermore, there are a multitude of subgroups within the classification of exceptional. Therefore, we must become sensitive to each population's specific needs and treatment objectives.

Most of all, we have to remember why all of this is important. All children have the right to be active and contributing members of our society. By assisting children, we will begin to unlock many doors and become a contributing factor to their well-being. We must not continue to look at differences between others and ourselves and to point out the multitude of reasons for their distinctions. Rather, we must try and become bridge builders and open up as many avenues as possible for their growth. By doing so, we remove barriers and promote access.

What does this access represent? Access is an element of freedom, the right to participate in meaningful experiences including those in free time. Social growth was not a priority in the past. Parents were forced to expend much of their energies on areas related to the physical well-being of a child. However, as time changes, so do human values and conditions. Today, we recognize the merits of social experiences. As the climate for rehabilitation has become accepted in Western society, we have developed an appreciation that all persons must find a purpose in their life.

Recreation and leisure fill a significant need in the lives of many children. Channa is a 12-year-old girl who lives in Israel. Although she has been blind since birth, she is a creative musician who has shared her talents with many. I heard a piece of music she had written describing her impressions from a recent trip to a cave. She was able to visualize what she felt through her music. She has used music as a mode of expression and a method to overcome her visual impairment.

Then there is Peter, a young lad with a mild developmental disorder. I met Peter in Europe as he was about to embark on a sixteen-day guided tour of Europe. There were eighteen other members in his group, mixed only in gender and abilities but not in enthusiasm. Twenty years ago, a trip such as this was unheard of. But today, the dreams of people like Peter are coming true and are provided an opportunity to explore the world like the rest of us.

Finally, there is Loretta. When she was in high school, she was not allowed to run on the track team. Ability was not the problem, she noted, attitude was. Loretta, now a grown woman, was in special education and diagnosed as mentally retarded. She was told that because she was in special education, she could not be on the team. Loretta had a difficult time understanding why she was being judged before anyone knew her abilities. In 1983, Loretta showed them all. She won a gold medal in the International Special Olympics in the mile run, setting a record of 5 minutes, 42 seconds. She also won the standing long jump event. These milestones were extremely memorable for Loretta and her family.

Peter, Channa, and Loretta are just a few of the human examples that demonstrate the impact of recreational experiences. There are still many unlike these three who have not experienced the inner joy that play promotes. For these children, we must continue our efforts to move forward and unlock more doors. If this book will assist some of our readers in fulfilling this milestone, then we have accomplished our goal.

Hopefully, in the near future, none of us will go to the gates of a park and silently hear children calling, "Let me in!"

REFERENCES

Biklen, D. (1985). Integration in school and society. In D. Biklen (Ed.), *Achieving the complete school.* New York: Teachers College, Columbia University.

Carkuff, R. (1982). *The noise.* McLean, Virginia: Bernice Carkuff.

Crawford, M., and Mendell, R. (1987). *Therapeutic recreation and adapted physical activities for mentally retarded individuals.* Englewood Cliffs, NJ: Prentice-Hall.

Fine, A., Welch-Burke, C., and Fondario, L. (1985). A developmental model for the integration of leisure programming in the education of individuals with mental retardation. *Mental Retardation, 23*(6), 289–296.

Gardner, J. (1981). *The individual and the innovative society.* New York: W.W. Norton.

Iso-Ahola, S. (1980). *The psychology of leisure and recreation.* Dubuque, IA: William C. Brown.

Kennedy, D., Austin, D., and Smith, R. (1987). *Special recreation: Opportunities for persons with disabilities.* Philadelphia: Saunders.

Kriegel, L. (1969). Uncle Tom and Tiny Tim: Some reflections on the cripple as negro. *The American Scholar, 38,* 412–430.

Lewdo, J., and Crandall, R. (1980). Research trends in leisure and special populations. *Journal of Leisure Research, 12*(1), 69–79.

Mundy, J., and Odum, C. (1979). *Leisure education: Theory and practice.* New York: Wiley.

Seligman, M. (1975). *Helplessness: On depression, development and death.* San Francisco: W.H. Freeman.

Sessoms, D. (1979). Organized camping and its effects on the self-concept of physically handicapped children. *Rehabilitation Literature, 13,* 39–43.

Tarr, B. (1976). *Now you see it, now you don't.* New York: Vintage.

Thacker, R. (1979). The effect of a two week camping experience on the self concept of physically handicapped children (Doctoral Dissertation, the University of North Carolina 1978). *Dissertation Abstracts International, 39*(7-A), 4113.

Toeffler, A. (1980). *The third wave.* New York: Bantam.

APPENDICES

Appendix I

OUTLINE OF THE ACTIVITY ANALYSIS PROCEDURE

Jesse T. Dixon

I. The Activity: Describe the objective or the nature of participation, e.g. group or individual, competitive or non-competitive.

II. Rationale: Indicate the intended benefits for programming the activity.

III. Equipment: Indicate any materials necessary for participation or teaching the activity.

IV. The Composite Learner: Briefly provide objective and subjective information about the child, e.g. prosthetic equipment, motivational preferences.

V. The Method of Participation: Briefly describe the way the activity is to be performed or demonstrated.

VI. Criterion: Indicate how the child will be evaluated and the level of independent participation necessary for terminating instruction.

VII. The Content of Participation: Briefly identify the steps or behaviors in the activity. Consider how each of the steps can be made informational rather than judgmental.

VIII. The Process: Planning the teaching interaction. Identify the motivating feedback from participation, consider teaching cues, and select an appropriate format for presenting information to the child.

IX. Conclusion: Summarize your insights into participation and consider alternative teaching cues and motivational preferences for the child.

X. Data Sheet: List the steps of the activity content and indicate whether the child has:
   - failed to meet criterion
   - met the criterion with strong teaching cues
   - met the criterion with light teaching cues
   - met the criterion identified for terminating instruction (a level of independence) for each of the steps.

Appendix II

AN OVERVIEW OF BEHAVIORAL MANAGEMENT STRATEGIES

Aubrey H. Fine

Specialists devising activities must incorporate strategies that will enhance outcomes as well as productivity. This appendix will present an overview of applied management and appropriate strategies for specific special populations.

UNDERSTANDING BEHAVIOR; DREIKURS'S PRACTICAL EXPLANATION OF HUMAN DRIVES

Dreikurs in his writings (Dreikurs and Soltz, 1964; Dreikurs, Grunwald and Pepper, 1971) points out that there is a force behind every human behavior. He also stresses that most human behavior is goal oriented. This is a perspective that was first espoused by Alfred Adler, a pioneer in the field of psychology. Followers of Adlerian psychology contend that a child's behavior will reflect an attempt to achieve constructive goals first. Children will usually progress to the more destructive aspects of behavior when they are not achieving the desired goal (Dreikurs et al., 1971).

Table 21 lists four categories that describe purposes of behavior (both positive and negative). The goals were formulated by Dreikurs in his quest to explain the rationale for most overt-elicited behaviors. These behavioral goals appear to be germane to most age periods in life, although they do not provide an adequate explanation for severe pathological disorder.

Attention-getting behavior can be positive or negative. The negative behavior that is directed at attention getting is generally some type of inappropriate behavior or misbehavior.

A second goal for misbehavior is power. Power-seeking children believe they are only significant when they are in control (Dinkmeyer and McKay, 1982).

This brings us to the third goal of behavior, which is revenge. The goal of revenge is extremely complex. Children who pursue revenge usually feel rejected. They believe they are not accepted and feel the need to be spiteful and get even with others (Dreikurs et al., 1971). Finally, the fourth goal of behavior is applied to children who misbehave due to a sense of inadequacy. Some children misbehave to protect their sense of self. These problems could be circumvented by planning activities for the children where they experience success.

367

Table 21. Four Goals of Behavior.

Goal	*Purpose*
Attention	Recognition and Acknowledgment
Power	To display control
Revenge	To get even
Inadequacy	A call for help

Suggested Disciplinary Alternatives

Dreikurs et al. (1971) stress that the teaching of discipline should be considered an ongoing process, not something to resort to only in times of stress or misbehavior. Discipline should not be confused with punishment. Children learn self-discipline through the setting of clear-cut limits, as well as obtaining approval or disapproval from significant others. For children who do not have severe cognitive or emotional disabilities, discipline may be interpreted as teaching children a set of inner controls that will allow them to become productive members of society.

Dreikurs et al. (1971) in their text **Maintaining Sanity in the Classroom** list 27 effective disciplinary procedures. A synthesis of these 27 procedures will be presented in Table 22 rather than each individual one.

DEFINITIONS OF VARIOUS PRINCIPLES OF APPLIED BEHAVIOR MANAGEMENT

What Is Behavior Management?

Behavior management represents a process in which some overt behavior is changed by the systematic application of techniques which are based on learning theory (O'Leary and O'Leary, 1977; O'Leary, 1972; O'Leary, 1978).

The A.B.C.'s of Behavior Management

The tenets of behavior management pertain to the relationship between behavior and environmental events. Another way of explaining this relates to the antecedents and consequences that influence the occurrence of a behavior.

It has only been recently that attention has been given to enhance the antecedents preceding the occurrence of behavior. The word **antecedent** relates to the multiple factors that constitute the situation preceding the occurrence of a behavior. Relevant antecedents may be critical in understanding the roots of a behavior problem. On the other hand, consequences are usually responsible for determining how frequently as well as how long a behavior will occur. Consequences refer to the multiple factors that constitute the situation that follows a behavior. There are three major principles that

Table 22. Disciplinary Procedures Following Dreikur's Approach.

1. A leader must always try first to recognize the purpose of behavior. As discussed earlier, attention must be given to why a child is misbehaving prior to determining a more reliable solution for the dilemma.
2. Do not emphasize past behaviors of children. Be more concerned in regards to the future.
3. Give children the opportunity to either discontinue their behavior or else potentially face a specific consequence. The consequence should relate to the behavior at hand. Two general forms of consequences can be applied: natural or logical. Dreikurs and Gray (1970) define natural consequences as representing the natural flow of events without the interference of an adult. For example, the child who refuses to go to sleep usually will be tired the next morning. This represents the natural consequence. On the other hand, a logical consequence is correlated directly to the act. For instance, the child who continually does not clean up after a snack may lose his/her privileges. In this way, the consequence is directly related to the act.
4. Always give a child a choice to either cooperate or else to leave the environment.
5. All children have their strengths and limitations. Attempt to accentuate the strengths.
6. Consistency is of critical importance. Too often our inconsistency in managing children confuses them. We need to show children that we do not change our disciplinary actions arbitrarily. We must respond consistently so children clearly understand our expectations.
7. Allow children the opportunity to be involved in planning future goals, as well as solving their own problems. Too often, it is for our own convenience that we provide solutions for problems. By involving a child in the problem-solving process, s/he may become more committed in carrying out the solutions. Problem ownership is essential in getting a child committed to following through applying the selected alternatives. Furthermore, children may learn from these situations and become more cognizant of how they can internally solve and cope with problems.
8. We must allow children the opportunity to take greater responsibility for their actions. To learn to take responsibility does not occur unless avenues for growth are provided.
9. Children need direction and guidance. We need to recognize however that our major goal is to assist a child in becoming as self-sufficient as possible.
10. Finally, children see adults as role models. They watch and learn from us. When we are wrong, we need to admit this to children. They will usually respect us more for honesty and realize that we are only human.

may be applied as contingencies to alter behavior: (a) reinforcement, (b) punishment, and (c) extinction. A brief description of each will follow.

Reinforcement. A reinforcer is a contingency that increases the frequency of a behavior. Basically, it can be defined as a consequence that increases the likelihood that a specific behavior will recur. There are several different types of positive reinforcers that can be applied.

Three of the most common categories of positive reinforcers are tangible rewards, activity rewards and social rewards. Tangible rewards represent such items as food, stickers, small trinkets, check marks, and certificates. On the other hand, favorite games and activities represent a sound alternative for increasing behavior. The final form of reinforcer is social rewards. Social reinforcers are sometimes the most effective rewards for increasing behavior. Social rewards can be communicated in a variety of ways, ranging from a simple hug or a pat on the back to an actual statement of recognition (e.g., "Good job!" "Excellent work!"). Social reinforcers are usually the most preferred reward, since they occur more naturally in the living environment (Foxx, 1982a).

Negative Reinforcement. Negative reinforcement is the removal of an aversive stimuli in an effort to increase the frequency of a desired behavior.

Punishment. Punishment is usually understood as a procedure that causes a decrease in the future probability of a behavior occurrence. Ayllon and Azrin (1968) point out that in everyday terms, punishment is understood as being applied for performing a specific act or at least for retribution. Punishment's main purpose is to decrease the frequency of a specific act.

There are two types of punishments (aversive and removal). The most common form is when one applies an aversive event following an unacceptable behavior. On the other extreme is the form of punishment that involves withdrawing positive reinforcers following an unacceptable behavior.

Time-out and social disapproval are both examples of this form of punishment (removal). Time-out represents the temporary withdrawal from a rewarding situation following the occurrence of an undesirable behavior. The term **time-out** means time away from the event that seems to be reinforcing the behavior.

Extinction. Extinction is the technical term for the procedure in which a reinforcer that has been applied to sustain an undesirable behavior is withheld. Technically, extinction is a behavioral weakening procedure that involves the consistent failure to deliver a reinforcer following a behavior that had previously produced that reinforcer. Most commonly, this procedure is the most applied of all behavioral processes which attempt to weaken a behavior. Extinction typically involves the removal of attention that appears to be maintaining the behavior under focus. It seems logical that if one ignores a behavior, the behavior will eventually subside.

METHODS TO INCREASE POSITIVE BEHAVIOR

Premack Principle. This is a procedure in which the behavior that a child frequently performs is used to reinforce a behavior that is seldom displayed (Premack, 1965).

Shaping. Shaping is the process of gradually altering the quality of a behavior. Becker (1969) suggests a simple response is required initially, and the criteria for reinforcement is gradually made more stringent so as to produce more complex or refined behavioral responses. Martin and Pear (1983) stress that it is impossible to increase the frequency of nonexistent behavior by waiting until it occurs and then reinforcing it.

Shaping is frequently referred to as a method of applying successive approximations. New behaviors can be shaped by the successive reinforcement of closer approximations. Successive approximations are accepted for reinforcement because they resemble the terminal behavior that is being molded and shaped. In essence, the instructor continually modifies his/her expectations.

Chaining. To apply the principles of shaping, a determination must occur of the sequence of skills necessary to perform the act. This sequence is defined as a chain. Chaining is the process in which simple behaviors already in the repertoire of an individual are reinforced in a particular fashion so they eventually form a more complex behavior. There are two feasible chaining methods. Forward chaining is where the first response in a behavior chain is taught first and the last response is taught at the end. However, when the child does not possess any of the prerequisite skills necessary to complete the desired response, teaching using forward chaining may not be effective. It therefore has been argued that when working with individuals who do not possess the prerequisite skills, it may be helpful for the facilitator to instruct the chain backwards. In essence, the components that comprise the task are taught in reverse order. This means that instruction begins with the last behavioral component in the chain. The logic behind the decision to apply this procedure is simple. The final step in the chain continuum is the most powerful, because it is always associated with the immediate delivery of the terminal reinforcer. Most children appear more excited when they are rewarded for the completion of an entire task rather than its elements. Ironically, the first response in a chain is the weakest of all.

Task Analysis. To initiate either forward or backward chaining, a list must be formulated representing the sequence of steps necessary to accomplish the behavior. This determination is known as task analysis. Task analysis has been defined by Howell, Kaplan, and O'Connell (1979) as any set of behaviors that a learner must engage in to demonstrate the acquisition of the skills. The theoretical origin of the task analysis originates from the research of several applied behavioral analysts and educational theorists (Bijou, 1970; Bloom, 1978; Gold, 1976; Skinner, 1968; Gagne, 1974).

The primary element of the analysis is a complete and detailed description of every behavioral element within the desired behavior. The underlying aspect of this approach is the analysis of the behavior in terms of the skills necessary to accomplish the entire chain. The investigation incorporates the breaking down of the identified behavior into small specific steps. The splintered tasks which will be instructed represent all of the elements of the behavioral chain. Utilizing a task-analysis format theoretically provides the best instructional sequence in which to teach a task (Scanlon and Almond, 1981).

Once the actual task analysis has been formulated, time must be designated to develop instructional strategies. Ironically, some may blame the ineffectiveness of the process on the task analysis rather than recognizing that the deficiency may exist at the instructional level. Initially, physical guidance may be necessary to help the individual perform the subskill appropriately.

Fading. Fading is the term applied to the gradual removal of a prompt. Fading is utilized to encourage independence. This is done by reducing the control of the instructor by altering the locus of authority to the learner. Fading is incorporated to eliminate the control of the instructor in a gradual fashion. Table 23 lists several strategies that directly relate to the process of fading.

Behavioral Contracting. A behavioral contract is a written agreement between two or more individuals. The final document specifies both the behavior that is required of an individual in addition to the consequence(s) that will be implemented contingent on the performance of those designated required behaviors.

Contracting is based on good behavioristic and humanistic principles of learning. As

Table 23. Procedures Which Can Be Utilized in Fading.

1.   Verbal cueing.
1.1 Instructional cue hierarchy—Verbal cueing that is utilized with other techniques (Wehman and Marchant, 1978).
1.2 Prompter—A cue utilized after other instructional techniques have been faded out (Paloutzian, Hasafi, Streifel, and Edgar, 1971).
1.3 Indirect verbal cues—Cues which indicated a response was necessary without directly indicating the response to be performed.
1.4 Direct verbal cueing—Cues that are directly utilized to indicate the desired response (Nietupski and Svoboda, 1982).
2.   Physical prompting—Represents a technique (manual guidance) that is usually applied when modeling and demonstrating are ineffective. In essence, prompting is other-directed and requires little or no input from the participant. Prompting can be naturally (totally) faded so that through the shaping process, less manual guidance will be needed.

Source: Fine, Welch-Burke and Fondario, 1985; Hooper and Wambold, 1978.

a procedure, it works well with elementary school-age and older children. Furthermore, this procedure is efficient with those who are capable of taking an active role in collaborating. A contract is simply a clear articulation of what is expected of an individual and how s/he will be reinforced.

Contracts should encourage and recognize successive approximations of the final outcome. In this way, the child will experience success and be motivated to work on the behavior. Furthermore, the most effective contracts are those that are generated collaboratively. It has always been understood that the more involved people are in the process, the more involved they are in generating solutions.

The classic text on how to prepare effective contracts was written by Homme, Csanyi, Gonzales and Rechs in 1969. They suggest ten basic rules. A synthesis of these basic rules and a sample contract are displayed in Table 24.

Token Economies. A token economy can be considered as a motivational system in which tokens are earned for the performance of previously defined appropriate behaviors and subsequently exchanged for previously defined rewards (known as backup reinforcers). The notion of an economy pertains to the fact that tokens are utilized in the same fashion as money in an ordinary economy. In fact, many of the basic principles of economics are directly incorporated in this behavioral technique (e.g., earnings, savings, banking systems). Kazdin (1980, 1978) defines token economy as a reinforcement system where tokens are earned for a variety of behaviors and can be used to purchase items. Within token systems, the tokens themselves have no specific value. However, their power lies within the ability to be exchanged for backup rewards such as tangibles, selecting favorite activities, and privileges.

METHODS OF DECREASING BEHAVIOR

Time-Out. Time-out involves the temporary removal of an individual from a rewarding situation following the occurrence of the undesirable behavior. Time-out is a process where a child is removed from an environment that is reinforcing to a setting that is presumably nonreinforcing. Time-out represents time away from the reinforcement. It is the least restrictive form of punishment and usually works extremely well with a variety of children. Table 25 represents a simplified listing of how one can apply the time-out procedure.

Satiation. Repp (1983) defines satiation as a temporary decrease in the elicitation performance of a behavior due solely to the repeated presentation of the reinforcer. Satiation can also be understood as the elimination of an unacceptable behavior due to its increased reinforcement.

Differential Reinforcement of Other Behavior (DRO). DRO is a schedule through which reinforcement is delivered at the end of a period of time during which no instances of the target behavior occurred. In essence, one is reinforcing the omission of the negative behavior, for that is what is required for reinforcement to be delivered.

DRO is understood as reinforcing a child for not eliciting the undesirable behavior. Unlike the application of other behavioral paradigms, this approach is an instructional technique that should be administered only at specific times. Prior to initiating the process, baseline data needs to be collected (Foxx, 1982b).

Differential Reinforcement of Appropriate (DRA) or Incompatible (DRI) Behaviors. Both of these two approaches are considered to be more effective than DRO. However, they are formulated primarily on the same principles. DRA is an approach where attention is given to develop alternative appropriate behaviors. The advantage of this approach is in the development of a newly learned skill. However, attention is not directly given to how the misbehavior will be diminished (a major criticism). On the other hand, DRI offers the specialist with the greatest reinforcement control over the inappropriate behavior (Foxx, 1983). Within DRI, a reinforcer is presented following the performance of a behavior which makes the negative behavior virtually impossible. This can occur because the designated requested task makes it impossible for the child to engage in a negative pattern.

SUMMARY

An understanding of behavior and its consequences is a must for persons engaged in working with others. Therefore, the initiation of effective behavior management interventions requires thorough training. It is hoped that this overview has provided the reader with a basic awareness of effective techniques used in behavior management. Throughout this appendix, I have integrated a number of procedures with considerations for their implementation, in an effort to facilitate humane, ethical and the responsible use of the techniques discussed.

The original meaning of the word **discipline** (from the Oxford definition) suggests that it is an instruction to be imparted to "disciples," two words that stem from the Latin root, which means **a learner.** The idea of imparting discipline must then be understood, not only as the management of others, but rather through the combination of teaching, mutual respect and care, an attempt to instill into our charges desirable values and the importance of self-discipline (Bettelheim, 1987). If this flavor is incorporated in our interactions with children, we will become better models and teachers.

Table 24. Guidelines for Successful Behavioral Contracting.

1. The contract should reward performance immediately.
2. As noted previously, contracts should be organized to develop gradually the desired behavior. It seems ridiculous to quickly expect dramatic growth, even with this procedure.
3. Contracts should provide frequent rewards in small increments as well encourage reward accomplishment rather than mere obedience. This helps the child eventually develop the behavior into his/her life-style and enhances the transfer maintenance. If we can help children recognize that they are changing for their own good, they appear more likely to comply.
4. Rewards should only be presented contingent upon the elicitation of the contracted behavior.
5. A contract should always be written in the positive and has to be clearly understood by all parties involved.
6. A contract should be developed fairly for both the child and the facilitator. It would be unfortunate if those responsible for developing the contract were not being honest with the other party. Furthermore, although it is expected that the contract's major purpose is to motivate a child externally, one should genuinely respect the integrity of the child.
7. Contracts should be negotiated, as well as agreed to by all parties involved.
8. The contract must clearly define the rewards, as well as build in a time for evaluation and renegotiation.

SAMPLE CONTRACT

Child's name _____

Instructor's name _____

Date of Agreement. Contract begins on _____ and ends on _____
                                                  (Date)   (Date)

(should also have a space on the contract which identifies when the contract will be reviewed). If (clearly identifies the expected behaviors, criteria for acceptance, as well as and where they are to occur) _____

_____

_____

By (identifies when the behavior is to be accomplished) _____

_____

Then (what is the instructor's part of the agreement in addition to the rewards) _____

_____

Child's signature _____

Instructor's signature _____

Table 25. Guidelines for the Application of Time-Out

1. Time-out must be applied immediately following every occurrence of the target behavior.
2. The area that one utilizes for the time-out should not be reinforcing or rewarding to the individual.
3. There should be a prescribed limit set in advance for the duration of the time-out punishment.
4. A procedure should be formulated, articulating what behaviors must occur for the child to reenter the learning environment.
5. A procedure should be formulated describing what will occur if the undesirable behavior is reintroduced.

REFERENCES

Ayllon, T., and Azrin, N. (1968). *The token economy: A motivational system for therapy and rehabilitation.* New York: Appleton-Century-Crofts.

Becker, W. (1969). In L. Homme et al. (Eds.), *How to use contingency contacting in the classroom.* Champaign, IL: Research.

Bettelheim, B. (1987). *A good enough parent.* New York: Alfred A. Knopf.

Bijou, S. (1970). What psychology has to offer education—Now. *Journal of Applied Behavior Analysis, 3,* 65–71.

Bloom, B. (1978). New views of the learner: Implications for instruction and curriculum. *Educational Leadership, 35,* 563–575.

Dinkmeyer, D., and McKay, G. (1982). *The parent's handbook: Systematic training for effective parenting.* Circle Pines: American Guidance Service.

Dreikurs, R., and Soltz, V. (1964). *Children: The challenge.* New York: Hawthorn/Dutton.

Dreikurs, R., and Grey, L. (1970). *A parent's guide to child discipline.* New York: Hawthorn/Dutton.

Dreikurs, R., Grunwald, B., and Pepper, F. (1971). *Maintaining sanity in the classroom: Illustrated teaching techniques.* New York: Harper and Row.

Fine, A., Welch-Burke, C., and Fondario, L. (1985). A developmental model for the integration of leisure programming in the education of individuals with mental retardation. *Mental Retardation, 23,* 289–297.

Foxx, R. (1982a). *Increasing behaviors of severely retarded and autistic persons.* Champaign, IL: Research.

Foxx, R. (1982b). *Decreasing behaviors of severely retarded and autistic persons.* Champaign, IL: Research.

Gagne, R. (1974). Task analysis—Its relation to content analysis. *Educational Psychologist, 11,* 11–18.

Gold, M. (1975). *Try another way.* The California Project.

Homme, L., Csanyi, A., Gonzales, M., and Rechs, J. (1969). *How to use contingency contracting in the classroom.* Champaign, IL: Research.

Hooper, C., and Wambold, C. (1978). Improving the independent play of severely mentally retarded children. *Education and Training of the Mentally Retarded, 13,* 42–46.

Howell, K., Kaplan, J., and O'Connell, C. (1979). *Evaluating exceptional children: A task analysis approach.* Columbus: Charles E. Merrill.

Kazdin, A. (1980). *Behavior modification in applied settings.* Homewood: Dorsey.

Kazdin, A. (1977). *The token economy: A review and evaluation.* New York: Plenum.

Martin, G., and Pear, J. (1983). *Behavior modification: What it is and how to do it.* Englewood Cliffs, NJ: Prentice-Hall.

Nietupski, J., and Svoboda, R. (1982). Teaching a cooperative leisure skill to severely handicapped adults. *Education and Training of the Mentally Retarded, 17,* 38–43.

O'Leary, K.D., and O'Leary, S. (1977). *Classroom management: The successful use of behavior modification.* New York: Pergamon.

O'Leary, K.D. (1972). Behavior modification in the classroom: A rejoinder to Winett and Winkler. *Journal of Applied Behavior Analysis: 5,* 505–510.

O'Leary, K.D. (1978). The operant and social psychology of token systems. In A.C. Catina and T.A. Brigham (Eds.), *Handbook of applied behavior analysis: Social and instructional processes.* New York: Irvington.

Paloutzian, R., Hasazi, J., Streifel, J., and Edgar, D. (1971). Promotion of positive social interaction in severely retarded young children. *American Journal of Mental Deficiency, 75,* 519–524.

Premack, D. (1965). Reinforcement theory. In D. Levine (Ed.), *Nebraska symposium on motivation.* Lincoln: University of Nebraska Press.

Repp, A. (1983). *Teaching the mentally retarded.* Englewood Cliffs, NJ: Prentice-Hall.

Scanlon, C., and Almond, P. (1981). *Task analysis and data collection.* Portland: ASIEP Education Co.

Skinner, B.F. (1968). *The technology of teaching.* New York: Appleton-Century-Crofts.

Wehman, P., and Merchant, J. (1978). Improving free play skills of severely retarded children. *The American Journal of Occupational Therapy, 32,* 100–104.

AUTHOR INDEX

A

Abidin, Richard, 231
Adkins, C., 236, 240
Adler, Alfred, 367
Allan, J.A.B., 294
Allen, A.S., 76, 81
Allensmith, W., 299
Almond, P., 371, 376
Alpern, G.D., 217, 238
Amado, R., 327, 328, 349
Amster, F., 245, 294
Anastasi, A., 190, 238
Andel, G., 80
Andrews, F.R., 84, 92
Andrews, J., 294
Arcus, D.M., 57, 60
Aristotle, 328
Arkow, P., 294
Arnheim, D., 151, 176
Austin, D.R., 12, 30, 64, 73, 75, 80, 125, 176,
    349, 361
Auxter, D., 151, 176
Avedon, E., 135, 176
Axline, Virginia, 246, 294
Ayllon, T., 370, 375
Ayrault, E.W., 320, 349
Azarnoff, P., 51, 58
Azrin, N., 370, 375

B

Baker, E.L., 87, 92
Balla, D., 351
Bandura, A., 43, 59, 334, 340
Barnett, L., 41, 58
Barnett-Morris, 50, 51
Baron, K.B., 248, 294
Bar-Tal, D., 143, 176

Bash, M., 345, 349
Beach, F.A., 35, 58
Beck, A., 294, 296, 297, 298, 299
Becker, W., 370, 375
Bee, H., 40, 58, 85, 86, 92
Belsky, J., 56, 58, 200, 238
Bender, M., 320, 349
Bergin, B., 277, 298
Berlyne, D.E., 53, 58, 181
Berndt, Joyce, 119
Berryman, D.L., 237, 238
Bettelheim, Bruno, 49, 58, 259, 294, 373, 375
Beyer, G., 67, 80
Bijou, M., 245
Bijou, S., 371, 375
Biklen, D., 6, 10, 30, 355, 360
Blackmon, W.D., 260, 294
Blatt, B., 127, 128, 178
Bligh, S., 294
Block, J., 59
Bloom, B., 371, 375
Bogden, R., 6, 30
Boggiano, A., 54, 60
Bolig, R., 247, 295
Boll, T.J., 217, 238
Boltz, R.P., 277, 295
Boone, D.R., 51, 59, 248, 249, 268, 295
Bradke, L., 145, 176
Bradley, 145
Braley, W., 150, 176
Brandell, J.R., 294
Brannan, S., 320, 349
Branston, M., 239
Brigance, A., 220, 239
Brigham, T.A., 376
Brightbill, C., 315, 317, 319, 320, 349
Brightman, A., 7, 30
Bronfenbrenner, U., 56, 58
Brooks, C., 189, 239

SUBJECT INDEX